Theodore Noethen

A Compendium of the History of the Catholic Church

Theodore Noethen

A Compendium of the History of the Catholic Church

ISBN/EAN: 9783742856692

Manufactured in Europe, USA, Canada, Australia, Japa

Cover: Foto ©Lupo / pixelio.de

Manufactured and distributed by brebook publishing software (www.brebook.com)

Theodore Noethen

A Compendium of the History of the Catholic Church

A COMPENDIUM

OF THE HISTORY OF THE

CATHOLIC CHURCH,

From the Commencement of the Christian Era,

To the Ecumenical Council of the Vatican,

In which are Narrated her Combats, and her Victories in Times of Persecution, Heresy, and Scandal, and wherein is shown that her Preservation is a Divine Work.

Compiled and Translated from the Best Authors.

BY REV. THEODORE NOETHEN.

Second Revised Edition.

BALTIMORE:
PUBLISHED BY JOHN MURPHY & CO.
182 BALTIMORE STREET.
1870.

Entered according to Act of Congress, in the year 1870, by
JOHN MURPHY,
in the Office of the Librarian of Congress, at Washington.

PREFACE.

A GENERAL knowledge of what is termed "Profane History," or the record of the principal facts and events of all the nations and peoples who have lived and flourished from the Creation to the present time, is deemed a necessary portion of a thorough education, and every effort is used to store our minds with this important and interesting information.

While there are numerous and excellent works of profane history published, a reliable and authentic history of the Catholic Church has been an acknowledged want, particularly at the present time, when the Ecumenical Council of the Vatican, now in session, is awakening an interest in all the nations of the world, Catholic and Protestant, in regard to the Future of that Church, which, from her very foundation, was the means of the wonderful spread of the Gospel among all nations.

In our own country, Catholic Missionaries have been the zealous and successful pioneers, not only in civilizing the Aborigines, but in discovering and developing the sources of our greatest treasures, and consequently of diffusing civilization and refinement wherever their salutary and enlightening influence has been extended.

In order to supply this want, the present work has been compiled and translated from the ablest and most reliable authors. Every important event connected with the History of the Church, her trials and her progress; her victories over persecutions, heresies, and even scandals, are briefly and impartially stated.

As some are frequently deterred from reading books of this nature, by their length, and not less by the high prices they command, this volume has been prepared with the view of placing it within the reach of all, and in such language, as will prove interesting to the most casual and hasty reader.

It is confidently hoped, that this work will inspire all with a new love and reverence for our Holy Mother, the Church; while the touching examples of the martyrs' constancy in persecution and torments, and the edifying lives of the saints who have adorned every century, will animate and encourage the practice of piety and virtue.

THE TRANSLATOR.

ALBANY, *May*, 1870.

INTRODUCTION.

The Church is that society which Jesus Christ established in order to give a spiritual birth to the children of God, and to form in virtue and holiness, those who are destined one day to become the citizens of heaven. As the execution of this design embraces all ages, it is necessary that the Church should exist without interruption until the end of the world; she must be always visible, and always pure in faith and morals; she must always possess saints, and charity must always abide with her. "The race of Christians," says St. Bernard, "shall never fail, neither shall faith among men, nor charity in the Church, because Jesus Christ has sanctified all ages."

Nevertheless it has been predicted that the Church shall be persecuted by the powers of this world; that she shall be torn by heresies and schisms; that scandals shall spring up in her midst, and that tares shall grow up with the wheat. It is therefore evident, that, attacked on all sides, she could not have existed, much less have established herself, unless she had been sustained by an All-powerful hand. Her Divine Author has also promised to be with her until the end of time; that is to say, He will always assist her with His invisible protection.

Her birth was miraculous, and she has been sustained by a continual miracle; it was necessary that God should enable her to triumph over every obstacle that men have never ceased to place in her way. Without His protection she would have perished under the sword of persecutors, who endeavored for three centuries to strangle her in her cradle; but persecution, instead of destroying, has only served to extend and multiply her. God has inspired a multitude of heroes with supernatural courage and patience, and the admiration which their virtues excited converted the executioners themselves.

The Church would have perished owing to the efforts of numerous heretics who have successively attacked the dogmas of faith; but their efforts, although often supported by the power of emperors and kings, instead of changing the faith has only served to place it in a brighter light and exhibit it to greater advantage.

God has raised up a vast army of holy Doctors to refute each error as soon as it appeared. He has facilitated the holding of councils where all novelties in faith have been solemnly condemned, and where the truth has been declared authoritatively in terms which admit of no equivocation or subterfuge.

The Church would have perished owing to the laxity of morals, which at certain times prevailed among her children, and even among her priests; but, notwithstanding the vices and disorders which have sometimes reigned in her midst, the pastoral authority has always been recognized, her discipline has ever remained holy, and her teachings irreprehensible. She has never ceased to oppose to indifferentism and sin, the holy maxims of the gospel; she has never ceased to form perfect christians, whose eminent sanctity has loudly condemned the prevailing vices, and she has held up to the gaze of the Universe, models of every virtue. This abiding victory which the Church has obtained over tyrants, over heresies and over sin, is a striking miracle of the power of God; the waters have sought to engulf her, the winds have howled and raged against her, but she has never fallen, because she is founded upon the rock which is Jesus Christ and upon his inviolable promises. How beautiful, how worthy of veneration, is this Church, which, in its duration as well as in its origin, gives evidence of its divine character.

There is nothing more admirable than a society of men, who alone remain unchangeable in the constant vicissitudes of human events, who, although every thing else crumbles around them, stand firm and immovable, like a rock in the midst of the sea, always *One*, always Holy, always Catholic, always Apostolic; that is to say, the Church has preserved without interruption all her marks and prerogatives, although assailed by violent tempests. It is the visible accomplishment of the words of her divine Author: "All power is given to me; go teach all nations; and behold I am with you always, even to the consummation of the world." Nothing less than an omnipotent power could preserve the Church from that instability which belongs to the things of this earth; nothing less than a divine hand could build an immortal edifice which neither violence nor storm could shake or destroy, and which, instead of being weakened, is strengthened and fortified by the very means used by its enemies to overthrow it.

"No," exclaims the illustrious Bossuet, "there is nothing greater, nothing more divine in the character of Jesus Christ than for Him to have predicted on the one side that the Church would always be attacked, either by persecutions, by heresies and schisms which would spring up daily, or by the coldness of charity which would result from relaxation of discipline, and on the other hand to have promised, that, despite all obstacles, nothing should prevent this Church from preserving her vitality, from always having pastors who would transmit from one to the other, from hand to hand, the authority of Jesus Christ and with it the holy doctrines and sacraments. No other founder of a new sect has ever dared to say what would either become of him or of the society he established. Jesus Christ is the only one who has explained in clear and precise terms, not alone the circumstances of His passion and death, but also the combats and victories of His Church. "I have established you," said He to the Apostles, "that you shall go, that you shall bear fruit, and that your fruit shall remain." And how shall it remain? He does not hesitate to declare, and He announces in emphatic language a duration without interruption and without any other end than that of the Universe itself.

These are the promises which He has made in return for the labors of twelve fishermen, and behold the manifest seal of the truth of His words. We are confirmed in our belief of past events, by remarking the distinctness with which He saw into the future.

Two things strengthen us in our faith—the miracles worked by Jesus Christ in the presence of the Apostles and the people, and the visible accomplishment of his predictions and promises.

The Apostles saw but the first of these two things, and we see but the second, nevertheless it is as impossible to refuse to believe in one who worked such prodigies and to deny the truth of His predictions, as it is to deny that He was capable of performing such wonders. "Therefore," says St. Augustine, "our faith is confirmed on two sides, neither the Apostles nor we can doubt, that which they saw in the beginning assured them of what would follow— that which has already happened assures us of that which they saw and admired in the beginning."

Bossuet again says: "Beside the advantage which the Church of Jesus Christ possesses of being founded upon divine and miraculous facts which were recorded with due solemnity and without fear of contradiction at the very time of their occurrence, there is another in favor of those who did not live at that time, a perpetual miracle, which confirms the truth of all the others, and that is the continuance of a religion always victorious over the efforts made to destroy it."

What a consolation for the children of God, what a convincing argument of the truth of their faith when they are enabled to trace it back in uninterrupted succession from Pius IX, who now fills the pontifical chair, to St. Peter, who was made the Prince of the Apostles by Jesus Christ Himself. And from thence ascending to the pontiffs of the old law, they trace it back to Aaron and Moses, and then to the patriarchs—and from them to the very beginning of the world.

What a succession! what a tradition! what a mar

velous chain of events! If our mind, naturally unstable, has become by reason of its uncertainty the sport of its judgment, and therefore requires, when questions arise which concern our eternal salvation, a fixed and absolute authority—what greater authority is necessary than that of the Catholic Church which unites in itself all the authority of past ages, all the ancient traditions of the human race to its very origin, which justifies itself by its succession, and which carries in its eternal duration the plain impress of the hand of God.

HISTORY OF THE CHURCH.

PART FIRST.

PREACHING OF THE APOSTLES.

When Jesus Christ had ascended into heaven, the Apostles returned to Jerusalem, and, according to the command they had received, retired to the Cenacle, in order to prepare themselves by seclusion and prayer for the reception of the Holy Ghost who had been promised them. On the tenth day, which was that of Pentecost, the Holy Spirit descended visibly upon them, and they were made new men. Endowed with a celestial strength, inflamed with a divine fire, the Apostles began to speak different languages and to proclaim the greatness of God. The people who had repaired in crowds to Jerusalem in order to celebrate the feast, ran with eagerness to hear them.

They had come this year from all parts of the world, and in a greater number than usual, because they were convinced throughout all the east, that the Messiah was about to appear. This vast concourse, a mixture of so many nations, were amazed to hear the Apostles speak the languages of different countries. St. Peter took occasion from it to say to them: "The wonder which astonishes you is the evident fulfilment of the prophecy of Joel, expressed in these words—'And it shall come to pass after this that I will pour out my spirit upon all flesh. And I will show wonders in heaven and on earth, and your sons and your daughters shall prophecy.'" He then announced to them the divinity of Jesus Christ whom they had crucified, declaring to them that He was truly the Messiah expected by their fathers from the beginning of the world. He exhorted them to be baptized in His name, in order to receive the remission of their sins, and the gift of the Holy Ghost. In fine, three thousand were converted and added to the number of the disciples. They persevered in the doctrine of the Apostles, listening diligently to their instructions.

God confirmed this doctrine by a great number of miracles, which filled the people with a holy fear. St. Peter and St. John, having gone up to the temple at the hour of sacrifice, found at the door a man forty years of age, who had been lame from his birth. This man asked alms of them according to his custom. St. Peter said to him: "Silver and gold I have none; but what I have, I give thee: In the name of Jesus Christ of Nazareth, arise, and walk." The lame man was cured on the spot, began to walk, and entered the temple transported with joy, and praising God. The people hastened to the temple when they heard the news of this miracle, and St. Peter delivered a second discourse, which converted five thousand more.

The high priests, and the officers of the temple, enraged at the wonderful success of the preaching of the Apostles, arrested them, and threw them into prison. The next day the Sanhedrim, which was the supreme council of the nation, was assembled, and having had the Apostles brought before them, they asked them by what authority they acted. Then St. Peter, full of the Holy Ghost, replied with boldness: "It is in the name of Jesus Christ, whom you have crucified." All those who composed the council were struck with astonishment at seeing the firmness of the Apostles, whom they knew to be only men of the people. They contented themselves with forbidding them to teach in the name of Jesus. The Apostles answered them, with a holy intrepidity: "If it be just in the sight of God to obey you, rather than God, judge ye. For we cannot but speak the things which we have seen and heard, when God commands us to make them known." Thereupon they let them go.

The Apostles summoned the faithful together, to relate to them that which had passed; all then returned thanks to God, and asked of Him the courage to announce His word without fear of the prohibition or of the threats of men, which should be counted as nothing, when it was their duty to accomplish the law of God.

The faithful assembled in the temple to pray, in the gallery of Solomon. The people did not dare to join them, for fear of being disturbed by the public authority; but nothing could prevent them from honoring and praising them, at the sight of the wonders which they wrought every day. They exposed the sick on their beds along the streets, so that the shadow of St. Peter might fall on them when he passed by. Many were even brought from neighboring cities, and all returned to their homes cured.

The high priest, filled with rage, had the Apostles thrown a second time into prison; but an Angel delivered them, and commanded them to go to the temple, and fearlessly preach the word of God. The council sent an order for the Apostles to appear before them; but although the prison had been securely locked, no one was found there. Some person came at the same time to give notice that the prisoners were in the temple, teaching the people. Then the captain of the guards of the temple repaired to it with some officers, and carried away the Apostles, but without using force, because he feared the people.

When they were presented to the council, he who presided said to them: "Have we not expressly forbidden you to preach in the name of Jesus? Why, therefore, have you filled Jerusalem with your doctrine, and why do you charge us with the blood of this man?" Peter and the Apostles replied, "We ought to obey God rather than man." When the human law is found to be in opposition to that of God, there should be no doubt as to the choice; we should always give preference to the divine law. Generous reply! which all the martyrs, inspired by the example of the Apostles, have repeated in the presence of tyrants, who forbade them to do that which God commands, or commanded them to do that which God forbids.

The members of the supreme council, transported with rage, considered how they should put the Apostles to death, but one among them, named Gamaliel, counselled moderation. "If this undertaking comes from man, it will disappear very soon of itself; but if it comes from God, you cannot prevent it from succeeding." His advice was followed; nevertheless they had the Apostles beaten with rods before they were dismissed, and renewed the prohibition for them not to speak again in the name of Jesus. The Apostles went away full of joy, because they had been judged worthy to suffer this affront for the name of their Master; they continued to preach Jesus Christ in the temple, and to teach the faithful daily in their own houses.

WONDERFUL PROGRESS OF THE GOSPEL.

The disciples of Jesus Christ increased from day to day; the number of the faithful belonging to the Church of Jerusalem was already large when St. Luke wrote the Acts of the Apostles. We read that it was composed of persons of each sex, and of every condition; but it was not only at Jerusalem that the faith made conquests. The Apostles, having been obliged to separate, on account of the persecution which broke out in that city, scattered everywhere the seed of the Divine word, and established, in the places where they sought refuge, other Churches, composed of Jews and Gentiles.

St. Peter travelled through many provinces and founded many churches. He at first established his chair at Antioch, and went afterward to Rome, which was at that time the centre of idolatry, in order to oppose it, even in the place where it ruled with the greatest sway. He had also preached to the Jews, settled in Pontus, in Galatia, Cappadocia, Asia and Bithynia, and to them he addressed his first letter. He sent some of his disciples to found churches in the west.

St. Paul also preached Jesus Christ to the Gentiles with the same success; he then went, first to Seleucia, to Salamina, to Paphos, and there converted the proconsul Sergius Paulus, who was governor, and the greater part of the island received the Gospel. He travelled over Pisidia, Pamphylia, Lycaonia, Phrygia, Galatia, Mysia, and Macedonia. His preaching was always followed by the conversion of the people, and he established at Philippi a church which remained inviolably attached to the doctrine, and to the person of the holy Apostle.

After having reaped an ample harvest on his way, he stopped at Thessalonica, the capital of Macedonia, and there founded a church, the zeal of whose members served as a model to all other churches. Thence he passed into Achaia and preached in Athens, where he delivered in the Areopagus a celebrated discourse, which was followed by the conversion of St. Denis and of many others. He repaired to Rome and remained there two whole years, announcing the kingdom of God, even in the palace of the Emperor Nero, where he converted several persons.

The other Apostles scattered themselves also through the different provinces of the Roman Empire, in order to carry there the good and admirable tidings of salvation. The conversions were so frequent in the commencement of the church, and the light of the gospel was diffused in so many places, that at the end of the first century, Christians were found throughout the greater part of the Roman Empire. It was thus in the face of all nations, of Jews and of Gentiles, of Greeks and of Barbarians, of the wise and of the ignorant, of the people and of princes, that the Apostles bore testimony to the miracles of the Son of God, and especially to that of His resurrection,—miracles which they had seen with their eyes, heard with their ears, and touched with their hands. They continued to give this testimony without any profit to themselves, contrary to all the dictates of human prudence, even to their last breath, and they finally sealed it with their blood.

The unheard-of rapidity with which the Christian religion established itself everywhere proves clearly that it is divine, and that it is the work of God. It is a manifest prodigy which incredulity would not deny, if it did not close its eyes to the truth. Jesus Christ had prophesied that the Gospel would be preached over all the earth; this wonder was to happen immediately after His death; He had said that when He should be raised from the earth—that is to say, when He would be fastened to the cross—He would draw all things to Himself.

The Apostles had not yet finished their course when St. Paul announced to the Romans that the faith was proclaimed to all the world; he wrote to the Colossians that the gospel was heard by every creature, that it was preached, that it would bear fruit, and that it would increase throughout the whole world. In short, tradition teaches us that St. Thomas carried the gospel to the Indies, St. John to Asia Minor, St. Andrew among the Scythians, St. Philip to Asia, St. Bartholomew to Great Armenia, St. Matthew to Persia, St. Simon to Mesopotamia, St. Luke to Arabia, and St. Matthias to Ethiopia. But there is no need of histories in order to confirm this truth, the result speaks for itself. The numerous churches established at the end of this century were not formed of themselves, but they show with how much reason St. Paul applies to the Apostles this passage of the Psalmist: "Their voice is heard over all the earth, and their word has been carried even to the extremities of the world."

VIRTUES OF THE FIRST CHRISTIANS.

Nothing is more beautiful, nor more touching, than the picture of the infant Church; it has been described by St. Luke in the Acts of the Apostles: "All the multitude of those who believed had but one heart and one soul, and not one of them appropriated to himself that which he possessed; but they had all things in common. There were no poor among them, because all those who had lands or houses sold them, and brought back the price; they placed it at the feet of the Apostles, and they distributed it to each one according to his need. The faithful persevered in the doctrine of the Saviour, in prayer, and in the breaking of the bread, that is to say in the participation of the Divine

Eucharist." And in another place: "They were all united together, and all that which they had was in common; their possessions and their goods they sold, and divided them among all, according as every one had need. And continuing daily with one accord in the temple, and breaking bread from house to house, they took their meat with gladness and simplicity of heart, praising God, and having favor with all the people."

"A great many miracles and wonders were worked by the hands of the Apostles, and they were all animated by the same spirit. Not one of the others dared to unite themselves with them in the temple; but the people bestowed great praises upon them; and the number of those who believed in the Lord, increasing more and more, the Church established herself thus, walking in the fear of the Lord, and she was filled with the consolation of the Holy Ghost."

The sacred historian speaks of the Church of Jerusalem. Although the other churches, composed principally of Gentiles, had not arrived at this perfection, we cannot but think they were prodigies of virtue and sanctity, if we consider the state in which the Gentiles were found before their conversion. When they had once received baptism they were no longer like the same persons; they commenced to lead a new and truly spiritual life, and they found that easy which had formerly appeared impossible to them. Those who had been slaves to voluptuousness became suddenly chaste and temperate; the ambitious saw no real greatness but in the cross; the passions were conquered, and virtue practiced; they renounced all that was sweet and agreeable in life; labor and retirement, fasting and silence, had now only attraction for them.

The first and principal of their occupations was prayer, which is also that which St. Paul recommends in the first place; and as he exhorts them to pray without ceasing, according to the precept of Jesus Christ, they employed all kinds of means in order to interrupt as little as was possible the application of their mind to God and to celestial things. They prayed in common as often as they could, persuaded that the greater the number that met together to ask of God the same graces, the more certainly would their petitions be granted, for the Saviour says: "If two among you unite together on earth to pray, all that which they ask will be given them by my Father who is in Heaven; for where two or three persons assemble in my name I am found in their midst." In order to keep their thoughts fixed upon God, they said special prayers before commencing and after finishing their work; they studied the law of God, repeating in their houses that which they had heard spoken in the place of assembly, and they fixed in their memory the explanations of the pastor by conversing with one another on the subject. Fathers, especially, exhibited great care in the religious training of their children.

Thus the life of a Christian was a continual course of prayer, reading and labor, one duty succeeded the other without other interruption than that which the necessities of life demanded. This conduct was the

more admirable in a number of men, who, until
their conversion, had given themselves up to all the
disorders of idolatry. Whence came so sudden and
wonderful a change? They must have been very
sensibly impressed by the miracles and the virtues of
those who announced this new religion. The spirit
of God must have acted very powerfully in their
souls to have made them chaste and mortified men,
detached from riches, and only desirous of obtaining invisible and eternal good. Such a change was
clearly the work of that power which has created
the world out of nothing, and which is still more
glorious when it triumphs over hearts without
impairing their liberty. On one side God acts as
Master and finds no opposition; on the other,
although He exacts implicit obedience from man,
He nevertheless leaves him the power to resist.

COUNCIL OF JERUSALEM.

Some of the lately converted Jews still remained
attached to the law of Moses, and they wished the
Gentiles who had become Christians to be subject to
it. This opinion spread as far as Antioch, where
St. Paul and St. Barnabas were residing at that time,
and it caused great trouble among those Gentiles
who had been converted to the faith, when they were
told that they could not be saved without submitting to the law of circumcision and other practices
commanded by Moses. St. Paul and St. Barnabas
opposed it, affirming that Jesus Christ had come to
free men from this subjection, and that His grace

would avail nothing to those who regarded circumcision as necessary.

It was therefore determined that they should go to Jerusalem to consult the Apostles on this question. On their arrival they were received by all the Church. St. Paul had been divinely inspired to undertake this journey. He conferred with the Apostles who were at Jerusalem, that is to say with St. Peter, St. James, and St. John, who were looked upon as the pillars of the church. He compared their doctrine with that which he preached to the Gentiles, and which he had not learned from any man, but by the revelation of Jesus Christ, and his teachings were conformable to theirs.

The five Apostles and the priests then assembled together in order to examine and determine the question which had arisen, and after a long discussion, St. Peter rose and said: "Men, brethren, you know that in former days God made choice among us, that by my mouth the Gentiles should hear the word of God and believe, and God who knoweth the hearts gave testimony, giving unto them the Holy Ghost as well as to us (he spoke of the conversion of Cornelius). Now, therefore, why tempt you God to put a yoke upon the necks of the disciples, which neither our fathers nor we have been able to bear? But by the grace of the Lord Jesus Christ we believe to be saved in like manner as they also."

St. Peter having thus spoken, all the assembly kept silence, and they listened to the wonders that St. Paul and St. Barnabas related, which God had wrought among the Gentiles through them. St. James then continued the discourse, and confirmed the counsel of St. Peter by the testimony of the prophets respecting the vocation of the Gentiles. "For which cause, said he, I judge that they who from among the Gentiles are converted to God are not to be disquieted. But we write unto them that they refrain from the pollutions of idols, and from fornication, and from things strangled and from blood." The Apostles warned the Gentiles to avoid fornication because the atrocity of the crime was not acknowledged in paganism, and as for the prohibition to eat strangled things and blood, it was a condescension of the Apostles, who wished to preserve for a time, at least, this one lawful observance, in order the more easily to reunite the Gentiles with the Jews.

When the question had been decided, the Apostles, the priests, and all the Church, resolved to choose some one from among themselves and to send him to Antioch with Paul and Barnabas. And they intrusted him with a letter which contained the decision of the Council, expressed in these words: "It hath seemed good to the Holy Ghost and to us, to lay no further burden upon you than to abstain from things sacrificed to idols, and from blood, and from things strangled, and from fornication."

The Apostles in this first Council have given the example which the Church has since followed in all her general councils; that is to say, all questions of faith and whatever relates to the salvation of souls as well as to discipline, is decided by a sovereign authority without any reference to the secular power

It was the occasion of a dispute among the faithful; they therefore sent to consult the church of Jerusalem, where the preaching of the gospel had begun, and where St. Peter then was.

The Apostles met together; St. Peter presided over the assembly. He proposed the question, and was the first to give his opinion; but he was not the only judge. St. James also gave his decision; the decision was founded on the Holy Scriptures and formed by the common consent of the clergy; they committed it to writing, not as a human judgment, but as a decree of the Holy Ghost, and they said with confidence: "It hath seemed good to the Holy Ghost and to us." They sent this decision to their particular churches, not to be questioned, but to be received and executed with entire submission. The Holy Ghost therefore makes Himself heard through the voice of the Church.

St. Paul and Silas also, who carried to the faithful this first decree of the Apostles, far from permitting a new discussion on that which they had decided, went through the cities teaching them to keep the laws of the Apostles. It is thus that the children of God comply with the decrees of the Church, convinced that they hear through her mouth the voice of the Holy Ghost. It is for this reason, that after having said in the creed: "I believe in the Holy Ghost," we add immediately, "and in the Holy Catholic Church," by which we oblige ourselves to acknowledge an infallible and perpetual truth in the universal Church, since this same Church that we believe in, during all time, would cease to be the Church, if she ceased to teach the truth revealed by God.

This belief is founded on the solemn promise which Jesus Christ has made in these words: "All power is given to me, in Heaven and on earth; going therefore, teach ye all nations, teaching them to observe all things whatsoever I have commanded you, and behold, I am with you all days, even to the consummation of the world." Jesus Christ has given His almighty power for the foundation of this promise. "With this all-powerful help, teach all truth, combat all errors; nothing shall be able to overthrow you, and this aid will never fail you; all days I will be with you, and I will be with you until the end of the world."

DEATH OF ST. JAMES THE LESSER.
Year of Our Lord 52.

St. James, surnamed the Lesser in order to distinguish him from the other Apostle of the same name, had been appointed Bishop of Jerusalem. It was he, who in the first council spoke after St. Peter. He was beloved by all the faithful, and respected even by the Jews on account of his eminent sanctity. His life was austere: his hair and beard were never cut, and he drank no wine.

It is added that he wore no shoes, and that he had only one tunic and a simple cloak of coarse stuff. He had a habit of going to the temple at an hour when no one was there, and, prostrating himself before God, he prayed for the sins of the people.

He remained for so long a time upon his knees that they became hardened like the skin of a camel. It was this diligence in prayer and his ardent charity that caused him to be called the Just.

After the death of Festus, governor of Judea, and before the arrival of his successor, the high priest Ananus wished to profit by this interval to arrest the progress of the gospel. He assembled a great council before which St. James was brought. Ananus pretended at first to consult him on the subject of Jesus Christ. "The people take Jesus Christ for the Messiah," said he to him; "it is for you to dissipate this error, since every one is ready to believe that which you will say."

Then he was made to ascend the steps of the temple in order that he could be heard by all the multitude. When he appeared on this elevated place the scribes and the pharisees cried out to him, "O just man whom we ought all to believe, since the people go astray in following Jesus crucified; tell us what we should think of it." Then St. James replied in a loud voice: "Jesus, the son of man, of whom you speak, is now seated at the right hand of the Sovereign Majesty, as the Son of God, and He is to come on the clouds of Heaven to judge all the world." Such clear testimony rendered to the divinity of Jesus Christ served greatly to confirm the new Christians in the faith which they had first embraced. They all cried out with one voice, "Glory to the son of David! honor and glory to Jesus!" But on the other side the pharisees, seeing themselves foiled in their attempt, said one to the other: "What have we done? why have we excited this testimony in favor of Jesus? We must overthrow this man." They therefore began to cry: "What? is the Just also in error?" Then, animated by a blind fury, they ascended to the pinnacle of the temple and hurled the holy Apostle from it. Nevertheless, St. James was not killed immediately, but had still enough strength to kneel down and address God in this prayer: "Lord, forgive them, for they know not what they do!"

The cruel men now said: "We must stone him!" and they immediately threw on him a shower of stones. One alone among them, touched by some feeling of humanity, said to the others: "What are you doing? stop; the Just prays for you, and you put him to death." These words could not subdue their rage; a fuller, who was present, took his rod and aimed a heavy blow at the head of the Saint and completed his martyrdom.

The holy Apostle had such a great reputation for sanctity among the people, that they attributed to his death the ruin of Jerusalem, which shortly after followed. He was buried near the temple on the same spot where he was martyred, and there they erected a monument to him.

St. James wrote an epistle, which is to be found in the New Testament, and one of the seven which are called Catholic; that is to say, addressed to the universal Church. He endeavors in this epistle to prove the necessity of good works in order to be saved, because he had heard that some persons pretended that faith was sufficient without works.

The holy Apostle, on the contrary, teaches that justice, when it is true, is willing to observe the commandments, and that the servants of God are always faithful in good works, which he shows by the example of all the saints, who are in all times distinguished for their virtuous actions.

FIRST PERSECUTION UNDER THE EMPEROR NERO.

Year 54.

The Church had already suffered greatly on the part of the Jews and Pagans, but these persecutions were not general. The Emperor Nero was the first who employed his sovereign power against the Christians.

This cruel prince, enraged because several persons in his palace had abandoned the worship of idols, published an edict forbidding any one to embrace the Christian religion. It was on the occasion of the great fire which consumed nearly the whole city of Rome. Many believed that Nero himself had set fire to the city in order to rebuild it afterwards with more magnificence.

With the view of pacifying the angry rumors which were being circulated against him, and to give an object to the public hatred, he accused the Christians of being the incendiaries, and commenced to persecute them in the most barbarous manner. A great number of them were put to death, say the Pagan authors themselves, not because they were convicted of the crime of incendiarism, but because

FIRST PERSECUTION UNDER NERO.

they were odious to mankind on account of the religion which they professed.

Nero did not content himself in their regard with even the customary torments; some of them were wrapped in the skins of wild beasts and exposed to the dogs to be devoured by them; others, after having been dressed in tunics soaked in pitch, were fastened to posts, they were then set on fire, and thus served for torches to give light during the night. The emperor made a spectacle of them in his gardens, where he himself drove his chariot by the glare of these horrible torches. The Roman people, who otherwise hated the Christians, nevertheless felt compassion for them, and saw with sorrow that they were sacrificed to the cruelty of the tyrant.

It was during this persecution that St. Peter and St. Paul ended their lives by martyrdom. It is said that these holy Apostles were kept nine months in a prison which was at the foot of the capitol; that two of their guards, astonished at the miracles which they saw them work, were converted, and that St. Peter baptized them with forty-seven other persons who were at that time in the prison.

The faithful who were at Rome conveyed to St. Peter the means of escape, and urged him to make use of them in order to preserve his life, so precious to the Church. The holy Apostle yielded at length to their entreaties, but when he had arrived at the gate of the city, Jesus Christ appeared to him, and told him that He was going to Rome to be there crucified over again. St. Peter penetrated the meaning of these words, and understood that it was in the person of His Vicar, that the Saviour was to be a second time crucified. He returned to the prison and was condemned to the torment of the cross; but he asked to be fastened to it with his head downwards, judging himself unworthy to die in the same manner as his Divine Master.

St. Paul, being a Roman citizen, was beheaded. It is related that on his way to execution he converted three soldiers, who suffered martyrdom shortly afterwards.

Such was the origin of the first persecution which the Church suffered from the Roman emperors, and it is glorious for her to have had for persecutor a prince who was an enemy to every virtue. The most wicked of men was worthy to be the first of persecutors.

TERRIBLE PROPHECY CONCERNING THE CITY OF JERUSALEM.

The time drew near when the prophecy of Jesus Christ should be accomplished against the city and the temple of Jerusalem. The generation was not to pass away before the misfortunes which were foretold should happen. It is a perpetual tradition, certified to in the Talmud of the Jews and confirmed by all the rabbi's, that forty years before the ruin of Jerusalem, which goes back to the time of the death of Jesus Christ, they did not cease seeing strange things in the temple. Every day there appeared new wonders, so that a famous rabbi cried out one day: "O temple! O temple! what causeth thy commotion, and why art thou terrified for thyself?"

What could be more dreadful than the frightful noise which was heard in the sanctuary on the day of Pentecost, or more fearful than the voice which resounded all through the sacred place: "DEPART HENCE! DEPART HENCE!" The holy angels, protectors of the temple, declared loudly that they abandoned it, because God, who had chosen it as His dwelling place for so many centuries, had condemned it.

At length, forty years before the war in which Jerusalem was destroyed, the Jews received a terrible warning, which appeared before the eyes of all the people. Josephus, the Jewish historian, thus relates it:

"One, named Jesus, son of Ananus, having come from the country to the feast of the Tabernacles, when the city was still in a profound peace, began suddenly to cry out: 'Woe to the city! woe to the temple! voice of the east, voice of the west, voice of the four winds; woe to the temple! woe to Jerusalem!' He never ceased, day or night, traversing the city, repeating continually the same threat. The magistrates in order to stop him caused him to be severely punished. He did not say a word to clear himself nor did he make a complaint, but he continued to cry out as before: 'Woe to the temple! woe to Jerusalem!' Then they took him to the Roman governor, who had him beaten with rods. The pain did not make him ask for mercy, nor did it cause him to shed a single tear; at every blow that they gave him, he repeated in a still more mournful voice: 'Woe! woe to Jerusalem!' He redoubled his cries on feast days; and when they asked him who he was, from whence he came, and what he meant by his cries, he replied to none of these questions, but continued in the same manner and with the same vehemence, so that they dismissed him as a madman. It was remarked that his voice, although incessantly and violently exercised, never became at all weakened.

"At the last siege of Jerusalem he shut himself up in the city; and walking indefatigably round and round the ramparts, he cried out with all his strength, 'Woe to the temple! woe to Jerusalem. woe to the people!' At the end he added, 'Woe to myself!' and immediately afterwards he was killed by a stone thrown from a machine."

Is it not manifest that this man was but an instrument in the hands of God, and that he only existed in order to announce these judgments? He was not only the prophet and the witness, but the victim, for the manner of his death only made the threats of God more conspicuous. This prophet of the misfortunes of Jerusalem called himself Jesus. It seemed that the name of Jesus, the name of salvation and of peace, was destined to become an omen of calamity to the Jews, who despised it in the person of our Lord; and that because this ungrateful people rejected one Jesus, who announced to them pardon, mercy and life, God sent them another Jesus to foretell irremediable evils, and the inevitable decree of their approaching ruin.

THE DESTRUCTION OF JERUSALEM.

The Jews, who had always detested the yoke of the Romans, revolted against them, and this revolt caused their ruin. The wisest among them left Jerusalem, foreseeing the misfortunes which were about to befall her. It was then that the Christians who were in the city retired to the little city of Pella, situated in the midst of the mountains of Syria, thus following the advice given by our Lord to His disciples, when He predicted to them the destruction of the temple.

The Roman army at first suffered a slight defeat, which emboldened the rebels; but the command of the army having been given to Vespasian, that general very soon regained the advantage over them. Then commenced divisions and dissensions among the Jews, and different parties were formed in the city, all of whom committed the greatest excesses. This unhappy city was attacked on both sides — by cruel factions within and by the Romans without. Vespasian, informed of what was taking place in Jerusalem, suffered the Jews to destroy themselves, in order that he might the more easily gain his own ends.

Being at that time the recognized emperor, he entrusted Titus, his son, with the continuation of the siege. This young prince encamped three miles from Jerusalem and closed all the entrances to the city. As it was near the feast of the Passover, a great number of Jews were shut up in the city, and they consumed in a short time all the food that was there. Famine was most terribly felt. The factions rushed into the houses to search them; they illtreated those who had hidden any food, and compelled them by cruel torments to give up all that they possessed. The greater part of the citizens were obliged to eat any thing they could find; they even snatched the food from one another, and they would take away from the children the bread which they held in their hands. The seditious were not at all affected by these evils, and they were only more enraged and more determined to continue the war. Nevertheless, Titus, having taken the fortress called Antonia, advanced his works, went as far as the temple, and made himself master of the two exterior galleries.

It was then that the famine became horrible; the people searched in the gutters for something to eat, and they devoured food that was even tainted. A woman, overcome by hunger and reduced to despair, took her child still at the breast, and looking at it with frenzied eyes, exclaimed: "Unhappy wretch, for what do I reserve thee? To die of hunger or to become a slave of the Romans?" She cut its throat immediately, roasted it, ate a part of it, and hid the rest.

The rioters, attracted by the odor, entered the house and threatened to kill the woman if she did not show them what she had concealed. She laid before them that which remained of her child, and seeing them transfixed with horror, she said to them: "You can certainly eat of it, if I have done so; it is my child; it is I who have killed it; you are neither more delicate than a woman, nor more tender hearted than a mother." They left the house trembling with fear.

Titus now attacked the second enclosure of the temple and set fire to the gates, commanding them, however, to preserve the body of the edifice; but a Roman soldier, impelled, says Josephus the historian, by a divine inspiration, took a firebrand, and causing himself to be raised up by his companions, he threw it into one of the rooms which the temple contained. The fire instantly caught, penetrated into the interior of the temple, and entirely consumed it, notwithstanding the efforts which Titus made to arrest the flames.

The Romans massacred all whom they found in the city, and destroyed every thing by fire and by the sword: thus was accomplished the prophecy of Jesus Christ. Titus himself declared that this success was not his work, and that he had only been the instrument of divine vengeance. There perished in this siege eleven hundred thousand inhabitants. The remainder of this unhappy nation were widely scattered over the empire.

Who does not see in this terrible disaster the just punishment of the impious rage which the Jews had exercised against the Messiah? Other cities have had to endure the horrors of a siege or of a famine; but it has never happened that the citizens of a besieged city have carried on the war with so much fury, or that they ever practiced against one another a more atrocious cruelty than that which they suffered from the hands of the enemy itself.

This is a solitary example, and will always be so; but this one example was necessary to verify the prediction of Jesus Christ, and to render the punishment of Jerusalem proportionate to the crime which she had committed in crucifying her God; a crime which stands alone, and which has never had an example in the past nor will have in the future.

SECOND PERSECUTION UNDER DOMITIAN.

The wars in which the emperors who succeeded Nero were engaged, and the pacific character of Vespasian and of Titus, gave the Christians some respite, until the time when Domitian commenced the second general persecution.

This emperor, who had all the vices of Nero, imitated him also in his hatred of Christians. He published an edict intended to overthrow, if it had been possible, the Church of God, already firmly established in a great number of places. God had warned His servants of this tribulation before it came to pass, in order that they might prepare for it by a renewal of zeal.

We can judge of the violence of this persecution by the manner in which the emperor treated the most distinguished persons, and even his nearest relatives. He put to death the consul, Flavius Clemens, his first cousin, and banished Domitilla, the wife of the consul, because they became Christians. Two of their slaves, Nereus and Achilleus, who were also converted to the faith, suffered many torments, and were at last beheaded.

There were a great many others who were put to death, or deprived of their possessions; but that which rendered the persecution of Domitian most famous is the martyrdom of St. John. The holy Apostle was brought to Rome, where he was thrown into a vessel of boiling oil, but without receiving any injury. Jesus Christ, who had specially favored him among all the Apostles, granted him, like the others, the glory of martyrdom; but He did not wish to leave to men the power of shortening so precious a life. Thus was accomplished that which our Lord had prophesied, that this Apostle would drink the chalice of His passion. This miracle happened near the Latin gate, according to the tradition which is yet preserved in Rome, and there is still to be seen an illustrious and most ancient memorial of it. It is a church that the Christians erected on the spot, and it bears his name, in order to perpetuate the remembrance of this event.

St. John, having escaped death by so evident a miracle, was exiled by Domitian to the Island of Patmos, which is one of the islands of the Egean sea. It was in this place that he wrote his Apocalypse; far from the intercourse of men he had prophetic revelations, which he addressed to the seven principal Churches of Asia, more particularly committed to his care. In this divine book, after giving to his Churches such advice as was expedient for each of them, he, enlightened by the Spirit of God, predicts under the most sublime images the destruction of idolatry and the triumph of the Church.

When, after the death of the tyrant, the senate had annulled all his decrees, St. John returned to Ephesus, and there passed the remainder of his life, watching over the interests of the Churches of Asia. He was then ninety years old, but his great age did not prevent him from sometimes going into the neighboring provinces to ordain bishops, or to form and establish new Churches.

He wrote his Gospel at the solicitation of the Bishops of Asia, who entreated him to give in writing an authentic testimony of the divinity of Jesus Christ, which some heretics had attacked; he wrote it after proclaiming a fast and public prayers. His epistles date from about the same time; they breathe throughout the most tender charity, and it can be easily seen from them that his heart was filled with that divine fire which he had drawn from the bosom of the Saviour, on which he reposed at the last supper. The first is addressed to the Parthians, and the two others to particular persons; he does not take there the title of Apostle, but that of the Ancient, which they commonly gave him.

THE LAST ACTION OF ST. JOHN.

There is related of St. John a very touching event, and which forcibly portrays the ardor of his charity. In one of his journeys, after having delivered an exhortation to the faithful of a city of Asia, he observed in the assembly a young man of attractive appearance, to whom he became attached, and addressing himself to the bishop, he said to him before all the people: "Take care of this youth; I recommend him to you in the presence of the Church and of Jesus Christ," and then St. John departed for Ephesus. The bishop instructed the young man, and prepared him to receive baptism.

After having admitted him to the sacrament of confirmation, and the Holy Eucharist, and believing him worthy of Christ, he ceased to watch over him, and gave him more liberty. The young man abused the confidence placed in him, and became intimate with some libertines of his own age, who persuaded him to indulge with them in all kinds of vice; and he even went to greater extremes than his disorderly companions, for he finally became chief of a band of robbers.

Some years afterwards St. John returned to this same city, and demanded of the bishop an account of the trust he had confided to him. The bishop was at first surprised, thinking that he had reference to some money, "It is the youth whom I have intrusted to you," said the Apostle, "it is the soul of your brother." "He is dead," answered the bishop, concealing his eyes. "Dead?" asked the Saint, "of what did he die?" "He is dead to God," replied the bishop; "he has become a wicked man and a robber, and has taken possession of a mountain, where he dwells with a band of wretches like himself."

At this intelligence, the holy Apostle groaned aloud. "Give me a horse and a guide," said he. He left the Church, and repaired to the place where the robbers were to be found. Their sentinels arrested him and took him before their captain, who waited to receive him. The young man, having recognized St. John, was seized with shame, and fled. Then the holy Apostle, forgetting his great age, pursued him and cried out to him: "My son, why do you fly from me; why do you fly from your father, an old man, without weapons? My son, have pity on me; do not fear; there is still hope of your salvation. I will answer for you to Jesus Christ. I would willingly give my life for you, as Jesus Christ has given His for us; stop, believe me, it is Jesus Christ who has sent me to you." At these words, the robber stopped, let fall his arms, and burst into tears. The holy old man embraced him with tenderness, reassured him, and promising him, on the part of the Lord, the forgiveness of his sins, he took him back to the Church; prayed for him, fasted with him, conversed with him on the most edifying subjects, and did not leave him until he had reconciled him with God.

St. John lived until he was one hundred years old. His advanced age did not impair his usefulness; he wished the people to take innocent recreations, and himself set the example. One day when amusing himself by petting a tame pigeon, he was met by a sportsman, who appeared astonished to see so great a man indulge in such a pastime. "What have you in your hand?" said St. John to him. "A bow," replied the sportsman. "Why do you not always keep it bent?" "It would lose its strength," said the sportsman. "Well," responded the holy Apostle, "it is for the same reason that I give some recreation to my mind."

THE DIVISION IN THE CHURCH OF CORINTH.

After the death of St. Peter, the Church of Rome was governed by St. Linus, and then by St. Cletus, who was succeeded by St. Clement, who is spoken of in the Epistle to the Philippians.

A great trouble occurred in the Church of Corinth during his life-time. Some of the laity, excited by a spirit of faction, rose against the priests, and caused several of them to be unjustly deposed. Pope Clement wrote them a most affecting and instructive letter on this subject. After the Holy Scripture, it is one of the most beautiful monuments of ecclesiastical antiquity. It begins thus: "The Church of God which is at Rome, to the Church of God which is at Corinth, elect, sanctified, by the will of God, through Jesus Christ our Lord: grace and peace from the Almighty God, by Jesus Christ, be multiplied unto you."

After inspiring them with horror at the division which was agitating the Church of Corinth, he describes the excellence of their lives as Christians. "For who that has ever been among you has not experienced the firmness of your faith and its fruitfulness in all good works; and admired the temper and moderation of your religion in Christ. For you did all things without respect to persons, and walked according to the laws of God; being subject to those who had authority over you, and giving the honor that was due to such as were aged among you. You commanded the young men to think those things that were modest and grave. The women you exhorted to do all things with an upright and pure conscience; loving their own husbands, as was fitting; and that, keeping themselves within the bounds of a lawful obedience, they should order their houses gravely with all discretion. You were all of you humble minded, not boasting of any thing; desiring rather to be subject than to govern; to give than to receive; being content with the portion God had dispensed to you; and, hearkening diligently to His word, you were confirmed in your charity, having His sufferings always before your eyes.

"Thus a firm, and blessed and profitable peace was given unto you; and an insatiable desire to do good; and a plentiful effusion of the Holy Ghost was upon all of you. And being full of good designs, you did, with great readiness of mind, and with a religious confidence, stretch forth your hands to God Almighty; beseeching Him to be merciful unto you, if in anything you had unwillingly sinned against Him. You contended day and night for the whole brotherhood; that with compassion, and a good conscience, the number of His elect might be saved.

You were sincere, and without offense towards each other; not remembering injuries; all sedition and schism were an abomination unto you. You bewailed every one his neighbor's sins, esteeming their defects your own. You were kind one to another without grudging; always ready to perform every good work. And being gifted with a conversation altogether virtuous and religious, you did all things in the fear of God, whose commandments were written upon the tables of your heart."

The Holy Pope then pictures the evils occasioned by discord. "From thence came emulation, and envy, and strife, and sedition, persecution and disorder, war and captivity." He produces proofs from the Old Testament in order to show the bad effects of jealousy; he exhorts the Corinthians to repentance, charity and humility by the example of the saints, the consideration of the goodness of God, and finally by the sacred ties which unite all Christians.

"Wherefore are there strifes, and anger, and divisions, and schisms, and wars, among us?" he exclaims. "Have we not all one God, and one Christ? Is not one spirit of grace poured out upon us all? Have we not one calling in Christ? Why then do we rend and tear in pieces the members of Christ, and raise seditions against our own body, and are come to such a height of madness, as to forget that we are members one of another? Your schism has perverted many, has discouraged many; it has caused diffidence in many, and grief in us all. Let us therefore with all haste put an end to this sedition; and let us fall down before the Lord and beseech Him with tears that He would be favorably reconciled to us, and restore us again to a seemly and holy course of brotherly love."

This letter produced the effect the holy Pope desired, and he had the consolation of suppressing this schism which distracted the Church of Corinth.

THIRD PERSECUTION UNDER TRAJAN.
(Year 106.)

The third persecution commenced during the pontificate of St. Evaristus, who had succeeded St. Clement. Although less violent than the two first, it lasted a long time, and made a very great number of martyrs. The emperor Trajan, whom history otherwise praises for his wisdom and clemency, encouraged the barbarities which were practiced against the Christians. Although he had not issued new edicts against them, he nevertheless wished the cruel laws to be executed which had been made by his predecessors throughout the different provinces of the empire.

A remarkable memorial of this fact has been handed down to us in the reply of this prince to Pliny the Younger, governor of Bithynia. Pliny wrote to Trajan, in order to consult him as to the course of conduct he should pursue with regard to the Christians; he declared that he finds them innocent of any crime. "All their error, he says, consists in this one thing, that on a certain day they assemble before sun-rise and with two choirs sing hymns in honor of Christ, whom they look upon as a God. They also pledge themselves by oath not to commit such crimes as robbery and adultery, to be faithful to their word, and to confess the truth. I have not discovered any superstitious practices in their worship, and for this reason I have suspended all the laws against them until further orders from you. The affair has appeared to me

THIRD PERSECUTION UNDER TRAJAN.

worthy of your consideration, on account of the vast number of those who are implicated in this accusation; for there are a great many of every age, of each sex, and of all conditions; this contagious evil has not only infected the cities, it has extended to the villages and country places. On my arrival in Bithynia, I found the temples of our gods deserted, the feasts abolished, and it was difficult to find any one to bury the victims."

This letter of a Pagan governor shows how much the Church had progressed at the end of the first century, and the great purity of the faith professed by the Christians. This testimony rendered to their innocence by a persecutor is a glorious tribute paid to the religion of Christ. Trajan replied to him that it was not necessary to institute inquiries about the Christians; but that if they, when denounced, acknowledged themselves Christians, they should be punished with death; an absurd and extraordinary answer on the part of an otherwise estimable prince. If the Christians are guilty, why forbid any inquiries about them? If, on the contrary, they are innocent, why punish them as soon as an accusation is made against them? How limited is the knowledge of men when they are not enlightened by the torch of faith! How imperfect and defective is even their justice!

This prince put to death several Christians. One of the first who suffered martyrdom was St. Simeon, a near relative of Our Lord. He was Bishop of Jerusalem, and one hundred and twenty years of age when he was denounced as a Christian and as being of the race of David. For this double crime they made him undergo many torments, which he endured with an admirable constancy. The spectators were amazed to see so much courage and strength in a man of such advanced age. At length he was condemned to be crucified, and he had the glory of giving his life for Jesus Christ, and of dying by the same punishment as his Divine Master.

TRAJAN INTERROGATES ST. IGNATIUS AND CONDEMNS HIM TO DEATH.

The emperor Trajan not only instigated the magistrates against the Christians, but took part himself in the persecution. In passing through Antioch on his way to make war on the Persians, he ordered Ignatius, surnamed Theophorus, Bishop of Antioch, to be brought before him.

"Is it thou," said Trajan, "who like a wicked demon dares to violate my commands, and seekest by thy example to induce others to ruin themselves?" Ignatius replied, " Prince, none other than thyself has ever called Theophorus a wicked demon (he alluded to the signification of the Greek word Theophorus, which means, one who carries God in his heart); far from the servants of God being evil spirits, know that the demons tremble before them, and take flight at the sound of their voice."

"And who is Theophorus?" asked the emperor. "It is I," replied Ignatius, "and whosoever like me carries Jesus Christ in his heart." "Dost thou then believe," asked Trajan, "that we also carry in our hearts the gods who combat for us?" "They are not Gods, they are devils," replied Ignatius, "there is but one God, who has made heaven and earth, and there is but one Jesus Christ, the only son of God, in the kingdom to which I aspire." "Speakest thou," asked Trajan, "of that Jesus whom Pilate had fastened to a cross?" "Say rather," answered the holy bishop, "that Jesus fastened to the cross sin and its author, and that He then gave to those who carry Him in their hearts the authority to confound hell and its powers." "Thou carriest then Christ within thee?" said the emperor. "Yes, undoubtedly," replied Ignatius, "for it is written: 'I will dwell within them, and I will accompany all their steps.'"

Trajan, annoyed by the ready and apt replies of St. Ignatius, pronounced sentence against him. "We command that Ignatius, who glories in carrying within him the Crucified, shall be placed in irons, and conducted under a strong guard to Rome, to be there exposed to wild beasts, and to serve as a spectacle to the people." Upon hearing this decree, the Saint cried out in a transport of joy: "I return thee thanks, O Lord, for having given me a perfect love for thee, and for honoring me with the same fetters with which thou didst formerly honor the great Paul, thy Apostle." While uttering these words he fastened the chains upon himself, and with tears recommended the Church to God. He then placed himself in the hands of a band of cruel and inhuman soldiers, who were to conduct him to Rome, to serve as food for the lions, and amusement for the people.

In his impatience to shed his blood for Jesus Christ, he joyfully left Antioch in order to repair to Seleucia, where he was to embark. After a long and dangerous voyage, he landed at Smyrna. As soon as he reached the shore, he went to see St. Polycarp, who was the bishop of that city, and who had been, like himself, a disciple of St. John. St. Ignatius expressed the joy he felt at being in chains for Jesus Christ. At Smyrna he found deputies from all the neighboring churches, who had come to salute him, and who were eager to have some share in the spiritual grace with which he was filled. The holy bishop entreated them all, and particularly St. Polycarp, to unite their prayers to his, in order to obtain for him the grace to die for Jesus Christ.

From Smyrna he wrote to the Churches of Asia letters full of the apostolic spirit. Then, addressing himself to the deputies who had come to visit him, he implored them not to retard him in his journey, but to suffer him to go quickly to Jesus Christ, by means of the teeth of the wild beasts who waited to devour him. As he feared that the Christians who were at Rome would put obstacles in the way of his ardent desire to die for Christ, he sent them an admirable letter by the Ephesians, who were to precede him, imploring them not to prevent him from suffering the torments to which he was condemned.

LETTER OF ST. IGNATIUS TO THE FAITHFUL AT ROME.

St. Ignatius, in the letter he wrote the faithful at Rome, commences by expressing the joy he experienced in the hope of seeing them soon again. He entreats them in the most ardent and affectionate language not to deprive him of the fulfilment of his desires by preventing, through their influence, his being immolated to Jesus Christ by martyrdom.

He writes, "I fear your love, lest it do me an injury. For it is easy for you to do what you please; but it will be hard for me to attain unto God, if you spare me. But I would not that ye should please men, but God, whom also ye do please. Neither shall I ever have such an opportunity of going unto God; nor will you, if ye shall now be silent, ever be entitled to a better work. For if you shall be silent in my behalf, I shall be made partaker of God. But if you shall love my body, I shall have my course again to run.

"Wherefore ye cannot do me a greater kindness than to suffer me to be sacrificed unto God, now that the altar is already prepared. Only pray for me, that God would give me both inward and outward strength, that I may not only say, but will; nor be only called a Christian, but be found one. For if I shall be found a Christian, I may then deservedly be called one; and be thought faithful, when I shall no longer appear to the world. Nothing is good that is seen.

"A Christian is not a work of opinion; but of greatness of mind, especially when he is hated by the world. I will write to the Churches and signify to them all, that I am willing to die for God, unless you hinder me. I beseech you that you show not an unseasonable good will towards me. Suffer me to be food for the wild beasts; by which I shall attain unto God. For I am the wheat of God; and I shall be ground by the teeth of the wild beasts, that I may be found the pure bread of Christ. May I enjoy the wild beasts that are prepared for me; which also I wish may exercise all their fierceness upon me. And for that end I will encourage them, that they may be sure to devour me, and not serve me as they have done some, whom out of fear they have not touched. But, if they will not do it willingly, I will provoke them to it. Pardon me in this matter; I know what is profitable for me.

"Now I begin to be a disciple; nor shall any thing move me, whether visible or invisible, that I may attain to Jesus Christ. Let fire, and the cross; let the companies of wild beasts; let breakings of bone, and tearing of members; let the scattering in pieces of the whole body, and all the wicked torments of the devil come upon me; only let me enjoy Jesus Christ. All the ends of the world, and the kingdoms of it, will profit me nothing. I would rather die for Jesus Christ than rule to the utmost ends of the earth. Him I seek who died for us; Him I desire, that rose again for us. This is the gain that is laid up for me.

"Permit me to imitate the passion of my God. If any one has Him within himself let him consider what I desire; and let him have compassion on me, knowing how I am straitened. For though I am alive at the writing of this, yet my desire is to die. My love is crucified; and the fire that is within me does not desire any water; but being alive, and springing within me, says, 'Come to the Father.' I take no pleasure in the food of corruption, nor in the pleasures of this life. I desire the bread of God, which is the flesh of Jesus Christ, of the seed of David; and the drink that I long for is his blood, which is incorruptible love. I have no desire to live any longer after the manner of men.

"Remember in your prayers the Church of Antioch, which now enjoys God for its shepherd instead of me; let Jesus Christ only oversee it, and your charity." It is unnecessary to remark that the spirit of God speaks in this letter; it is evident it is not the language of man.

MARTYRDOM OF ST. IGNATIUS.
Year 107.

After remaining for a while at Smyrna, St. Ignatius continued his journey; being eager to arrive at Rome, as the time appointed for the games was near. Anchoring at Troas, they crossed through Macedonia, and, finding a ship ready to sail on the coast of Epirus, they embarked on the Adriatic Sea, and soon reached the Bay of Tuscany. The wind favored the eagerness of the holy martyr, and the vessel was anchored at the mouth of the Tiber.

At the news of his arrival, the faithful of Rome went to meet him. They were greatly rejoiced to see and converse with him; but their joy was mingled with sadness when they remembered that he was soon to be put to death. As the people were sometimes moved to compassion, several of the faithful proposed that they should try and persuade the emperor to spare the life of the venerable old man; but the holy bishop spoke to them with so much eloquence and force, imploring so earnestly not to be deprived of the happiness of going quickly to God, that they yielded to his prayers. Falling upon their knees, the Saint elevated his voice in the midst of them, and asked of Jesus Christ to put an end to the persecution, to give peace to the Church, and to maintain in the hearts of all the faithful a tender and mutual charity. The prayer finished, he was led by the soldiers into the amphitheatre.

It was one of those days which Pagan superstition had consecrated to the worship of Saturn. The whole city was present; on entering the arena the holy martyr heard the roaring of the lions, but neither his firmness nor ardor was abated at the sight of his tormentors; his face and deportment on the contrary announced a great joy and perfect peace. He had not long to wait for death; in one moment two lions tore him to pieces, and in a short time nothing remained of his body save a few bones, which were collected with respect by the faithful, and conveyed to Antioch as a treasure of inestimable value.

Wherever these holy relics were carried, they were received with reverence by the Christians, and were finally placed in a casket and deposited in a cemetery near the gate of the city.

Those who have written the history of this martyr terminate it thus: "We were eye-witnesses to this glorious death, which caused us to shed a torrent of tears, and we passed the night in vigils and prayers, supplicating on our knees Our Lord to sustain our weakness. The holy martyr Ignatius appeared to us in the form of an athlete who comes out of a painful and glorious combat; he was standing before the Lord, surrounded by an ineffable glory. Filled with joy at this vision, we returned thanks to the Author of all good, and blessed Him for the happiness He had accorded His servant. We marked the day of his death, that we may be able to meet together every year to honor his martyrdom at the time he suffered, in the hope of participating in the victory of this generous athlete of the Church, who has despised the demon through the help of Our Lord Jesus Christ, by whom and with whom, glory and power be to the Father, with the Holy Ghost, in all ages. Amen."

APOLOGY OF ST. JUSTIN.
Year 150.

While the holy martyrs, by the effusion of their blood, rendered a bright testimony to the truth of the Christian religion, the holy Doctors defended the faith by learned apologies. The first of these which have come down to us is the Apology of St. Justin; he had the courage to commence it with his name, and addressed it to Antoninus, and his two sons, Marcus Aurelius and Commodus.

St. Justin was born in paganism, and did not embrace the Christian religion until the age of thirty, after a serious examination and deep reflection, based upon the most solid reasons. The constancy of the martyrs filled him with admiration and confirmed his judgment. The study which he made of the Holy Scriptures, especially of the prophets, convinced him of the truth of the Christian religion.

In his apology, he begins by entreating the Emperor to judge by their actions, and not simply by their name, those who would be brought to him as Christians; not to condemn them solely because they are Christians. "We pray you," said he, "listen neither to passion nor false reports in pronouncing decrees, which will injure you alone, for they could not harm us, should they even deprive us of liberty or of life. That strict inquiries may be made into the crimes imputed to us; if proved, that we be punished; but, if not found guilty of any offense, justice demands the exoneration of the innocent. How can we be treated as impious men, we, who adore the true God, the Father Eternal, Creator of all things; His Son, Jesus Christ, who was crucified under Pontius Pilate, and the Holy Ghost, who has spoken by the prophets?"

In order to show that this crucified Jesus is truly God, he says that Jesus Christ is the Sovereign Truth, which changes the hearts of those who follow his doctrines. "We were formerly slaves of pleasure, and now we lead a pure and chaste life; we were fond of riches, and now we place our goods in common, so as to share with each other; we hated our enemies, and now we love them and pray for them."

He then quotes some of the precepts of the law of Jesus Christ. "If you will deign," adds he, "to examine our principles and our conduct, you will be convinced that you have not more submissive subjects, none more disposed to maintain peace and the public tranquillity. Neither your laws nor your punishments restrain the wicked; they know they can conceal from you the commission of crime; as for us, we are certain that nothing is hidden from the eyes of God; that He is to judge us one day, and punish or reward us according to our works. We worship God alone, but we cheerfully obey you in every thing else, acknowledge you as our Emperor and as master of the world. Our most fervent supplications ascend daily to the throne of God in your behalf, that you may unite to the sovereign power an upright mind and prudent counsel."

Then the holy Doctor proves the truth of the religion by the prophecies, which have been collected and preserved according to the order of time in which they were written. He dwells upon those that relate to the destruction of Jerusalem, the dispersion of the Jews, and the calling of the Gentiles. After showing how the then recent accomplishment of so remarkable a prophecy is a decisive proof of the truth of the Christian religion, he concludes from thence that the other prophecies, and particularly those which refer to the second coming of Jesus Christ, the resurrection, and the last judgment, will also be fulfilled.

Finally, in order to reply to the calumnies concerning the Christian assemblages, he explains in detail all their ceremonies, and we see with satisfaction a perfect conformity between those spoken of by St. Justin, and those practiced among us at the present day. He concludes with these words: "If this doctrine appears reasonable to you, estimate it as it deserves; on the contrary, if it does not please you, do not embrace it; you should not condemn to death, however, those whose only fault is its profession." St. Justin had, afterwards, the happiness to seal with his blood this public defense of the Christian religion.

FOURTH PERSECUTION UNDER MARCUS AURELIUS.

Year 166.

At this time the still growing Church was spread over all the world; it extended not only through the East, where it had commenced, that is to say, in Palestine, Syria, Egypt, Asia Minor and Greece, but also in the West, through Italy, the different nations of the Gauls, all the provinces of Spain, Africa, Germany and Great Britain. It extended to places hitherto impenetrable to the Roman arms, and beyond the limits of the empire; into Armenia, Persia and the Indies; among the most barbarous people, such as the Sarmatians, Dacians and Scythians, and even in the most obscure islands Christians were to be found.

The blood of its martyrs rendered the Church fruitful. The emperor Marcus Aurelius, unfortunately prejudiced by the calumnies alleged against Christianity, manifested great severity towards those who professed the faith. From the great number of those who then suffered martyrdom, the persecution appears to have been very violent. It began in Asia, and the first cruelties were practiced at Smyrna. Several Christians were brought from the neighborhood and conducted to the tribunal of the governor of Asia, who resided in this city.

After generously confessing Jesus Christ, they were made to endure all kinds of tortures, the details of which are related in the beautiful letter the faithful of Smyrna wrote to the other Churches on this occasion. "These holy martyrs," says this letter, "were so torn with lashes that the veins, arteries and even their entrails could be seen. In the midst of this cruel torture, they remained firm and unshaken; and, whilst even the spectators were moved to tears at the dreadful sight, these generous soldiers of Jesus Christ did not utter the least cry nor the faintest groan.

"They saw, without flinching, their blood flowing from a thousand wounds; beheld with calmness their palpitating entrails; they advanced joyously to execution, suffered in silence, and their mouths, closed to complaint, opened but to bless the Lord. It seemed as if their souls had already left their bodies and were listening to the voice of Jesus Christ speaking within them; the joy of His presence caused them to despise every torture, and they were happy to escape eternal punishment by the endurance of a momentary pain, the flames that consumed them appearing as nothing in comparison to those everlasting fires which are never extinguished.

"Their thoughts were fixed on the ineffable happiness God reserves for those who persevere to the end; happiness which the eye hath not seen, nor the ear heard, nor hath it entered into the heart of man to conceive, but which God disclosed to them, because they were no longer men, but angels.

"Those who were condemned to the wild beasts bore the weariness of a long imprisonment until the arrival of the day destined for the attainment of their glorious crown. Others were stretched naked and bleeding on beds of shells and pointed stones; a thousand species of torture were used to weaken their courage and to induce them to renounce Jesus Christ, for there is no invention hell has not employed against them, but through the grace of God they were not overcome by the most dreadful sufferings.

A young man, named Germanicus, strengthened the others by his example. Before he was exposed to the wild beasts, the proconsul, through a feeling of humanity, exhorted him to save his life by denying his faith; but the holy martyr boldly replied, "that he preferred losing his life a thousand times, rather than preserve it at the price of his innocence." Then, fearlessly advancing towards a lion that approached him, he was immediately devoured by the infuriated animal; thus hastening to quit the bloody tabernacle of his body and a world full of impiety and crime. This heroic action so exasperated the people, that a thousand enraged voices made the amphitheatre resound with these cries: "May the impious be punished, let the bishop Polycarp be brought forth!"

ST. POLYCARP, BISHOP OF SMYRNA, IS SEIZED AND BROUGHT BEFORE THE PROCONSUL.

Search was everywhere made for St. Polycarp in order to put him to death, as the people, irritated by the admirable constancy of the martyrs, loudly demanded that he should be given up to their rage. The holy bishop experienced no fear, and wished to remain in the city, but he yielded to the entreaties of the faithful and retired to a house not far distant.

Some days after, the search being still continued, he sought refuge in a house in the country; when leaving this last asylum, his pursuers entered it. Not finding him they seized two young men, one of whom, overcome by the torture, revealed the new retreat of the holy bishop. The archers arrived there one night armed as if to apprehend a robber. St. Polycarp was asleep in an upper chamber, and had he wished, could easily have escaped, but he said: "The will of God be done." He therefore descended and spoke to the archers, who, seeing his great age and wonderful courage, could not refrain from saying: "Was it necessary to hasten so much in order to seize this good old man?" They were angry at having been sent on so odious an errand, but would have been still more enraged had they lost the reward these arrests insured.

St. Polycarp had a supper prepared for them, and being permitted a short time for his devotions, prayed for the whole Church with so much fervor that those present, even his enemies, were filled with admiration.

On their journey homeward, the holy bishop was mounted on an ass, and upon arriving in the city was immediately conducted to the amphitheatre, where the people were assembled. He was taken before the proconsul, who exhorted him to obey the commands of the emperor in order to preserve his life. "Have pity on thy gray hairs," said the magistrate; "dost thou believe thyself able to endure tortures, the sight alone of which causes the bravest youth to tremble?" But the holy bishop was as little moved by the false compassion exhibited for him, as by their threats and menaces.

The proconsul urged him, saying: "Blaspheme Christ, and I will let thee go!" Polycarp replied, "For eighty-six years have I served Him, and He has never injured me, how then can I blaspheme my King who is my salvation?" The proconsul continued: "Swear by the wealth of the Ceasars." "Thou givest thyself useless trouble," answered the Saint, "as thou art not perhaps aware what faith I profess. I declare it boldly; I am a Christian. If thou dost wish to hear what is the doctrine of the Christians, I will make it known to thee."

Then the proconsul threatened to expose him to the wild beasts. "It is profitable for me," said the holy bishop, "to attain by sufferings to perfect justice!" "Since thou dost not fear the wild beasts," added the proconsul, "I will have thee burned alive!" Polycarp replied: "Thou dost threaten me with a fire which is extinguished in a moment, because thou dost not know of the eternal fire reserved for the impious. What delays thee? Do with me as thou pleasest!"

While thus speaking, he appeared full of confidence and joy, and his sublime faith made his countenance so radiant that the proconsul gazed at him with astonishment. Then the enraged people cried out: "Deliver him up to the wild beasts; he is the father of the Christians, the enemy of our gods!" But as the time for the games was ended, the proconsul condemned the holy bishop to be burned alive.

MARTYRDOM OF ST. POLYCARP.
Year 166.

As soon as the sentence was pronounced, the people ran in crowds to look for wood in order to construct the pyre. The holy martyr then took off his girdle, divested himself of his garments, and, like a victim chosen from the flock, ascended the pyre as if it were an altar, to be there sacrificed for his Lord.

They prepared to fasten him, according to the custom, with iron chains; but he said to his executioners: "Leave me thus. He who will give me strength to endure the flames will cause me to remain firm on the pile without being bound by your chains." His hands were therefore only tied behind him, and they laid him down. Then raising his venerable eyes to Heaven, the holy martyr said the following prayer:

"Almighty God, Father of Jesus Christ, thy Only Son, through whom we have received the grace to know thee, I thank thee, for what it hath pleased thee to grant me this happy day, when I shall enter into the company of thy martyrs, and participate in the chalice of thy Son, that I may attain unto eternal life, and be soon admitted into thy presence as an acceptable sacrifice. I praise thee, I glorify thee, I bless thee, with the eternal Pontiff Jesus Christ, thy Son, through whom, glory be given to thee and the Holy Ghost, now and forever. Amen."

When his prayer was concluded, the wood was kindled, and a great flame immediately arose from it, which, by a wonderful miracle, did not touch the body of the Saint, but surrounded him in the form of an arch. He lay in the midst of the fire, like gold in the crucible; and he emitted an odor as agreeable as that of the most delightful perfumes.

The Pagans, seeing that his body was not consumed, caused him to be pierced with the point of a sword, and the blood gushed forth so profusely as to entirely extinguish the fire. This touching history of the martyrdom of St. Polycarp was written by those who witnessed it. They add that the Pagans did not allow them to remove the body, but had it burned, fearing lest the Christians should forsake the Crucified and adore this man. To which groundless apprehension the writers of this history reply: "Do they not know that we can never forsake Jesus Christ, who has suffered for the salvation of us all, nor honor in the same manner any other? For we adore Him, because He is the Son of God; we only consider the martyrs as His disciples, and His imitators, and we justly revere them on account of their fidelity to their King and Master."

The narrative concludes thus: "We gathered his bones, more precious than jewels, from the smouldering ashes, and placed them in a secure spot, where we hope to meet together every year to joyfully celebrate the feast of the holy martyr, to the end that the faithful hereafter may be inspired by his glorious example to prepare for the combat."

We see by these words that the Catholic Church honored the Saints from the earliest ages, as being the servants and friends of God; and that she has at all times regarded with religious veneration their relics or their remains, as having been sacrifices to God, by martyrdom or by penance, and the living members of Jesus Christ and temples of the Holy Ghost. This holy practice is therefore authorized by the traditions of all ages, and consequently rests on the same foundation as religion itself.

THE THUNDERING LEGION.
Year 174.

The emperor Marcus Aurelius put an end to this persecution on occasion of a signal favor received from Heaven through the mediation of the Christian soldiers serving in his army; for the camps, as well as the cities and country places, were filled with the followers of Christ. God made use of the Roman soldiers as missionaries, to carry the faith into the most distant countries, whither they were ordered in the service of the state, and He wrought miracles from time to time in their behalf. The miracle granted to the prayers of the Thundering Legion was very extraordinary.

The emperor was at war with the Sarmatians and

other German tribes; at a certain time the Roman army found itself in the arid mountains of Bohemia, surrounded by these barbarians, who were their superiors in regard to numbers. It was in the middle of summer, during an excessive heat, and there was no water to be had in the place. The Romans were in danger of perishing from thirst. In this extremity, the Christian soldiers fell on their knees and addressed fervent prayers to God, that He would grant them relief.

Their enemies, beholding this, scoffed at and ridiculed them. Suddenly the heavens were covered with clouds, and an abundant rain fell on the side of the Romans, who raised their drooping heads to receive the water in their mouths, so excessive was their thirst. They then filled their helmets, drinking plentifully themselves, offering it also to their suffering horses. The barbarians, conceiving this a favorable moment for an attack, whilst they were engaged in allaying their burning thirst, prepared to fall upon them. But the elements, at the command of God, warred against the scoffers, and a frightful hail storm, accompanied by thunderbolts, crushed their battalions, whilst the troops of Marcus Aurelius were refreshed by a soft and abundant rain.

This astonishing miracle insured the victory to the Romans, for the barbarians, throwing down their arms, sought refuge among their enemies from the thunderbolts which carried destruction into their camp. This event was universally considered as miraculous; and the Christian troops, who had obtained this favor from Heaven by their prayers, were called the "Thundering Legion."

The emperor himself wrote to the Senate on the subject. The historian Eusebius relates, that Marcus Aurelius asserts in that letter that the army, nearly lost, had been saved by the prayers of the Christians. This victory of the Roman arms disposed the emperor more favorably towards the Christians; he ordered that their treatment should be less severe, and prohibited their being persecuted on account of their religion.

In order to perpetuate the remembrance of this miracle, a monument was erected in Rome, and there can be seen in that city at the present day, as a representation of this event, a bas-relief on the Column of Antoninus, raised at that time. The Romans appear armed against the barbarians, who lie stretched on the earth beside their horses, whilst a rain, accompanied by lightning and thunderbolts, descends upon them.

It was on this occasion that the army gave the title of Imperator to Marcus Aurelius for the seventh time, although the right of bestowing it belonged exclusively to the Senate. The emperor accepted this title of dignity as being decreed by Heaven.

PERSECUTION IN GAUL.
Year 177.

Three years after the miracle of the Thundering Legion the persecution again broke out under the name and authority of Marcus Aurelius. Whether he had been afterwards persuaded that he was indebted to his gods for this prodigy, or whether it was through the blind fury of the people, and the hatred of the Roman officers, who caused the old edicts to be revived whenever they pleased, is not known.

This new storm raged especially in Lyons. It is believed that the faith had been carried there by the disciples of the Apostles, and that St. Trophimus, first bishop of Arles, was sent to this city by St. Peter. From thence the gift of faith was communicated to the neighboring provinces.

The rapid progress of the gospel in this country excited the rage of the idolaters, who commenced the persecution by rendering the Christian name odious, and by imputing to them the most enormous crimes; refusing them at the same time admission to the markets and public places. These oppressions were accompanied by all kinds of outrages; the Christians were insulted wherever they appeared, beaten, stoned, and finally taken before the magistrates.

An account of this persecution is found in an interesting letter, written by the faithful of Lyons to their brethren of Asia: "Those among us," they write, "who were questioned as to their faith, confessed it with courage, and were immediately placed in bonds, until the arrival of the president." Some days after this official had returned, they were ordered before his tribunal, and treated with so much harshness that a young man named Epagathus, who was present, could not refrain from testifying his indignation. He was a Christian, inflamed with an ardent love for God, and perfect charity for his fellow-men. His morals were pure, his life austere, although still at an age when the passions are strong; but he walked in the way of the Lord and fulfilled His precepts, always ready to serve God and assist his neighbor, ever animated with zeal for the glory of his Master, and filled with fervor for the salvation of his brethren. He therefore asked permission to say a word in defense of the Christians, showing that the accusation of impiety and irreligion was a mere calumny; but a thousand voices instantly arose against him.

The judge, irritated at his request to speak in favor of the accused, asked him if he was a Christian. Epagathus boldly confessed himself a follower of the Crucified, and was immediately placed in the ranks of the martyrs. Out of derision the angry judge bestowed on him the glorious title of "Defender of the Christians," thus unwittingly pronouncing his eulogy by a single word. This heroic example encouraged the other Christians, who, with glowing countenances and joyful voices, declared their eternal allegiance to Jesus Christ.

In the mean time orders had been given to seize

the blessed Pothinus, bishop of Lyons, who to a weak body united the qualities of a young and vigorous soul; his great infirmities rendered assistance necessary, and he was borne in the arms of soldiers, who placed him at the foot of the tribunal; the people, following in crowds, loaded him with opprobrious epithets. The holy patriarch then rendered a glorious testimony to the divinity of his King and Master, for, the president having asked him who was the God of the Christians, the bishop replied: "Thou shalt know Him, if thou art worthy."

He was instantly seized, dragged with violence, and overwhelmed with blows; those who were near the Saint struck him with their feet and hands; others more distant threw at his defenseless form whatever missile they could find, without the least regard for his advanced age. All the rabble would have believed that they had committed a great act of impiety, had they failed to insult the enemy of their gods. He was taken half dead from the hands of the infuriated populace, and cast into a prison, where he expired a few days afterwards.

TORMENTS OF THE HOLY MARTYRS.

The rage of the magistrates and the people then pursued Sanctus, deacon of the Church of Lyons; Maturus, who was still a neophyte; Attalus and a young girl named Blandina, who was a slave. The extreme delicacy of Blandina caused her companions to fear that she had not the courage to confess the faith; but this generous maiden astonished them all by her heroic answers, and tired out the executioners who successively tortured her from morning until night. After exhausting on her tender frame all the torments cruelty could suggest, they were compelled to desist, and acknowledge themselves conquered by a young girl. That she still breathed was a miracle, as a single one of the tortures she had endured was more than sufficient to cause her death; but this youthful martyr gained new strength with every additional suffering. The testimony she so generously rendered Jesus Christ seemed to infuse new life into her, and her only solace consisted in uttering these words: "I am a Christian; no crime is committed among us."

The deacon Sanctus also endured incredible torments. The Pagans hoped to make him use some expression unworthy of the faith he professed, but he had sufficient firmness neither to reveal his name, country nor condition. His only reply to all the questions addressed to him was: "I am a Christian." This resolution irritated the president and the executioners; after the customary tortures, they heated plates of copper and applied them to the most tender parts of his body. The holy martyr felt his flesh burning without evincing the least emotion or allowing the slightest sign of pain to escape him. The executioners only desisted when his body was one great wound, scarcely a vestige of the human form remaining; his contracted and mutilated limbs were no longer in their natural position; and his quivering, bleeding flesh was a dreadful sight to behold.

All disfigured as he was, he now became an object of admiration, as he was animated by Jesus Christ, who wrought in his poor, mortal frame, wonders worthy of Omnipotence; causing these shapeless remains to confound the tyrant, vanquish the demon and destroy the power of hell. Thus it is evident that the perfect and ardent love of God dispels fear and deadens all sensation of pain. The blood-thirsty Pagans again seized the holy martyr in order to torture him anew, and flattered themselves that they could weaken his constancy by re-opening his still inflamed wounds, and applying once more the red-hot irons, while he was in such a state as scarcely to bear the slightest touch; but these impious men were frustrated in their diabolical attempt by an evident proof of the Divine power. The new torture served as a remedy to the wounds made by the first, and after this second application the body of the martyr was found entirely healed.

All these different torments proving useless, the holy martyrs were cast into a frightful dungeon, and their feet placed in the stocks, a wooden machine which held the limbs of the victims firmly compressed. In this condition, the most horrible that can be imagined, the executioners, enraged at being foiled so often by these intrepid saints, practiced upon them all the cruelties their wicked hearts could devise. These last torments were so terrible that several died under them; God thus permitting some to perish for His greater honor and glory; others, however, He preserved through all this suffering, restoring health to their bodies and strengthening their souls for new combats. Although deprived of all human aid, they were so supernaturally fortified that they consoled and encouraged the faithful who were among the spectators.

HUMILITY OF THE HOLY MARTYRS.

The profound humility of the holy martyrs strengthened their other virtues, and rendered them still greater objects of admiration. Although they had repeatedly confessed Jesus Christ, and endured the most horrible torments with wonderful constancy, bearing on their bodies the glorious marks of their victories over the demon, they did not consider themselves, even then, worthy of the name of martyr, and would not permit the title to be given to them. "Whenever," say the writers of this affecting account, " we called them thus, in our conversations, or when they received letters bearing this inscription, they were much grieved, and could not refrain from giving us mild but earnest reproofs for thus designating them. 'This great name,' they would say, 'belongs only to those who have run their race, and to whom Jesus Christ opened the gates of Heaven at the moment of their confession, and not to vile creatures like ourselves.' Then, clasping our hands and bathing them with tears, they implored us to obtain through our prayers a happy termination to their labors.

"They possessed all the virtues of martyrs, their mildness, patience and glorious courage raised them above all fear, and made them worthy of the heroic title their meekness and humility refused to accept. Divine charity reigned in their hearts and souls, and their greatest desire was to endeavor to imitate the example of Jesus Christ, who so loved ungrateful man as to suffer the ignominious death of the cross for his salvation. Like this merciful Saviour they forgave their enemies, and addressed fervent prayers to the throne of God in behalf of their persecutors.

"They censured no one, were forbearing to all, and especially to repentant sinners. Some, through dread of the torture, succumbed at the first question, but were, nevertheless, placed in the same prison with the holy martyrs, who did not, however, treat them with severity, but like a tender and compassionate mother, led them gently back to the feet of the loving Jesus, whom they had denied through human weakness, and, by the torrent of tears they shed in the presence of the Lord, obtained from His infinite goodness the reconciliation of their erring brethren.

"In fine, those who had fallen, acknowledged their fault, and afterwards repaired it by a generous confession of the faith. Their return was not less glorious to Jesus Christ than amazing to the Pagans; for in the second examination they underwent separately, and only for sake of form, as they were to be immediately sent back to prison, the judge was astonished to hear them recant their former errors and proclaim themselves followers of the Crucified. They were greatly encouraged by a zealous Christian, named Alexander, a physician by profession, who approached the tribunal, and by animated signs exhorted them to remain firm in the faith. The people observed him, and, furious at seeing those who had renounced Christianity return to their allegiance, and boldly confess their Lord, directed their rage against Alexander, and denounced him to the president. The magistrate asked him who he was. Alexander replied: "I am a Christian." At this answer he was placed in the ranks of the martyrs, and, having been condemned to the wild beasts, received the bright crown promised to those who persevere to the end."

LAST COMBAT OF THE MARTYRS.

After the holy martyrs had been in prison some days they were led out, once more, in order to have the sentence executed which condemned them to different kinds of death. Maturus, Sanctus, Blandina and Attalus were destined for the amphitheatre, and a day was appointed when they were to afford a spectacle to the people. After again enduring the torture, which served as a prelude to the execution, they were exposed to the wild beasts, who, not being as ravenous as usual, did them no harm.

The people then demanded that Maturus and Sanctus should be seated in iron chairs heated red hot, but as, notwithstanding their dreadful sufferings, they still breathed, the executioners were obliged to end their torments by the stroke of a sword. Blandina had been fastened to a stake with her arms extended, and the sight of this youthful Saint, thus representing our Saviour on the cross, sustained the courage of her companions.

As the wild beasts had not approached her, she was reserved for another day, but the enraged populace demanded Attalus, who was well known to them. He was made to walk round the amphitheatre bearing on his breast a placard inscribed with these words: "Attalus the Christian." The people uttered the most abusive cries against him, clamoring loudly for his death; but the president, learning that he was a Roman citizen, remanded him to prison with the other martyrs, there to await the reply of the Emperor, to whom he wrote on the subject. This prince announced that it was necessary for the safety of the empire to put to death all those who persisted in confessing Jesus Christ, but to release those who would renounce Him. The president being seated in his tribunal, the prisoners were again summoned to his presence and questioned as before, but as they all reiterated their first confession, sentence was immediately pronounced against them.

The next day the physician Alexander was conducted into the amphitheatre accompanied by Attalus, whom the judge, in order to please the people, had condemned to the same punishment, notwithstanding his having the rank of a Roman citizen. After enduring all the customary tortures, these generous martyrs perished by the sword. Finally, on the last day of the public games, Blandina and a Christian youth named Ponticus, fifteen years of age, were brought forth and subjected to all kinds of tortures without consideration either for the age of the one, or for the sex of the other. They remained steadfast in their faith, and joyfully met their death.

Ponticus was the first to consummate his sacrifice, and Blandina remained alone in the arena. She was confined in a net, and exposed to a furious bull, which tossed her and trampled on her for a long while, but the blessed hope of eternal bliss and her ardent love for God rendered her insensible to its rage. At length, like a pure and obedient lamb, she presented her delicate throat to the knife which immolated this acceptable victim to the God of Virgins.

On the admission of the Pagans themselves, a woman had never before suffered such cruel and multiplied torments. Their hatred was not yet satiated, but vented itself on the mangled remains of the victims, and, losing all sense of humanity, they cast the bodies of the holy martyrs to the dogs. Then, collecting all the scattered bones, they burned them, and threw the ashes into the Rhone. All these human precautions availed nothing against the power of the Lord, as the place where their ashes reposed was afterward revealed, and they were ultimately secured and placed under the altar of the Church erected in honor of these holy martyrs, and which is now called St. Nizier.

These holy martyrs were forty-eight in number, and their names have been preserved.

MARTYRDOM OF ST. EPIPODIUS AND OF ST. ALEXANDER.

The blood of so many martyrs had not extinguished the fire of persecution. A great number of others suffered at that time in Gaul, and the city of Lyons had again the glory of giving to the Church two of her sons, called Epipodius and Alexander. These young men were of distinguished birth, and united by a tender friendship, sanctified by their pious lives. Having been denounced by the president, they left the city and took refuge in the hut of a poor widow, remaining there for some time in safety. But as a strict search was instituted, they were soon discovered and cast into prison; in a few days they were brought before the tribunal.

The judge asked their names and the religion they professed, to which questions they replied, boldly declaring themselves to be Christians. The clamorous voices of the people instantly arose against them, and the judge, in a passion, cried out, "What, dare they again violate the edicts of the emperor? What have availed the torments we have caused the martyrs to endure?" To prevent their encouraging one another, they were immediately separated. Alexander, the eldest, was sent back to prison, and the torture applied to Epipodius, who appeared to be the weaker of the two.

Before applying the torture, the judge, hoping to

win him by flattering speeches, thus addressed him: "Thou must not perish through obstinacy; we adore the immortal gods, whom the emperor and the whole world worship, and we honor them by joyful festivals and public games. Thou adorest a crucified man whom thou canst not please without renouncing all pleasures. Deny Christ, and enjoy the good things of this life which especially belong to thy age!" Epipodius replied, "Thy false compassion does not affect me. Thou knowest not that Jesus Christ, after being crucified, arose, and, being, at the same time, by a wonderful mystery, God and man, he opened to his faithful servants the portals of the heavenly Jerusalem. But, to speak of things more comprehensible to thee, art thou ignorant of the fact that man is composed of two parts, the soul and the body? The pleasures to which thou yieldest flatter indeed the senses, but kill the soul. We make war against the body in order to enfranchise the soul, and to preserve the sway of the spiritual over the material. After yielding like the beasts of the field to the gratification of your appetites, a sad and hopeless death awaits thee; whereas, when we die, we enter into eternal life."

The judge, provoked at this bold answer, ordered one of the attendants to strike him across the mouth with his clenched fists. He was then extended on a wooden horse, and two executioners on either side tore his limbs with iron claws; but this cruel sentence was too lenient for the enraged multitude, who demanded with loud cries that he should be given up to them, that they might tear him to pieces.

The president, fearing to lose the respect due his position, would not accede to their wishes, and ordered him to be beheaded. After an interval of a day, this wicked tyrant, desiring to gratify his rage as well as that of the people, by the torments reserved for Alexander, caused him to appear before his tribunal, and said to him: "Thou canst yet profit by the example of the others; we have sustained so long a war against the Christians that thou art now the only one remaining among us." Alexander answered: "I return thanks to God that, in recalling to me the triumphs of the martyrs, thou dost animate me by their heroic example; for the rest thou art mistaken, the name of Christian cannot perish. I am a Christian; and with the grace of God will always be one."

The judge then ordered him to be stretched on a wooden horse, and beaten by two executioners, who relieved each other at intervals. During this torture, the holy martyr ardently invoked the aid of Heaven, and he received from the Lord so much strength that the executioners were more wearied with striking him, than he was tired of suffering. Finally, seeing that he was immovable, they condemned him to be crucified.

MARTYRDOM OF ST. SYMPHORIAN.

During this persecution the city of Autun presented a most edifying spectacle in the person of St. Symphorian, a young man of distinguished birth. One day, when the feast of Cybele, a pagan goddess, was being celebrated with much pomp and splendor, Symphorian publicly avowed the horror he felt at the impious worship. He was seized and taken before the governor, who was then in Autun for the purpose of persecuting the Christians.

This man said to him: "How hast thou hitherto escaped my vigilance, for I believed that I had purged this city of all the followers of the Crucified. Tell me, why thou dost refuse to worship the 'great Cybele.'" Symphorian replied: "I am a Christian, and adore but one God, who reigns in Heaven; as for the statue of thy goddess, I not only refuse to adore it, but would joyfully destroy it." "Thy birth apparently inspires thee with this impious presumption," said the judge; "but dost thou know the decrees of the Emperor?" Then the edict was read, which ordered the immediate execution of all those who should refuse to sacrifice to the gods. "What hast thou to reply," added the magistrate, "can we violate the commands of the prince?" "This idol," answered Symphorian, "is an invention of the devil, who makes use of it, in order to ruin men; a Christian who abandons himself to crime will fall into the eternal abyss, as God punishes sin and rewards virtue. I will never reach the haven of a blessed eternity but by steadfastly persevering in the confession of His holy name."

At this response, the judge had him beaten with rods and sent to prison, causing him to be brought out some days after, and offering him a gift from the public treasury, and a commission in the army if he would adore the statue. "A judge," said Symphorian, "should not waste his time in useless discourses, nor lay snares for innocence. I do not fear death; we should return our life to Him who is the author of it; why should we not offer as a voluntary gift, that which we are obliged to pay Him one day as a debt? Thy favors are but venomous poisons, hidden under the guise of a treacherous bribe; time, like a rapid torrent, carries away your possessions; God alone can bestow everlasting and unutterable happiness on His faithful servants. The remotest antiquity saw not the beginning of His glory, and future ages will not behold its end!" "I cannot have patience with thee," angrily said the judge; "if, therefore, thou dost not instantly sacrifice to Cybele, I will condemn thee to death this day, after having made thee suffer the most terrible torments human ingenuity can devise." Symphorian answered: "I only fear the God who has created me, and serve Him alone; my body is in thy power, but not my soul."

Then the enraged magistrate pronounced the sentence in these words: "Let the sacrilegious Symphorian die by the sword, and thus avenge the gods and the laws." As he was being led to execution, his mother ran up to him, not to move him by her tears, but to strengthen and encourage him by her exhortations. She cried out to him: "My son Symphorian, my dear son, think of the living God and show thy courage; we should not fear a death which surely leads to everlasting life. Do not regret leaving the earth, but raise thy eyes to Heaven, and despise torments which only last a few moments, and if thou art constant will soon be changed into eternal felicity." The sublime faith which made this noble mother victorious over the tenderness nature inspires, is not less admirable than the heroic courage which enabled her son to triumph over the horrors of death.

APOLOGY OF TERTULLIAN.

Knowledge as well as sufferings contributed towards the progress of Christianity; and the Church was no less avenged by the solid writings of her defenders, than honored by the invincible courage of her martyrs. Tertullian, a priest of Carthage, published at this period a work in behalf of the Christian religion, entitled "The Apology," which struck a mortal blow at paganism.

He commences by complaining that the Christians are condemned without allowing them any defense: "The Christians alone," he writes, "are deprived of the privilege of defending themselves before their judges, and of producing testimony which, if received, would prove their innocence." He shows that the laws condemning the Christian religion were manifestly unjust, as they were made by wicked princes, whose memory and actions are detested by the pagans themselves. He replies to the reproach of not adoring the gods of the empire, and after exposing the origin of the pagan divinities, the absurdity of their worship, and the indecencies of their ceremonies, draws the conclusion, that these idols are unworthy of adoration, and are only devils who deceive men. "Bring forth," said he, "some one of the statues believed to be divinely inspired, having the power to deliver oracles; the first word of a Christian, commanding him to speak, will force him to avow that he is in reality a wicked demon. If he does not instantly acknowledge the power of the Holy Name of Jesus, I consent that the Christian who questions him shall be put to death."

The gift of casting out devils must have been very common in the Church, to justify the boldness of Tertullian in making so public a challenge. He then exonerates the Christians from the accusation of impiety, by explaining the true object of their worship. "The God of the Christians," he writes, "is the Creator of the Universe, who has made the world out of nothing by His power, arranged it by His wisdom, and directs the whole by His providence. The magnificent spectacle of nature renders the most glorious homage to this Supreme Being, and the pagans themselves, blinded as they are by their passions, and the prejudices of education, acknowledge Him, when in the midst of danger they cry out: 'Great God! Good God!' thus giving proof of the soul being naturally Christian. This great Lord has made Himself known during all ages by oral traditions, and the writings of the prophets, whom He has raised up and filled with His spirit. These writings cannot be doubted, as they are in the hands of our enemies the Jews, who read them publicly in their synagogues; and their antiquity is incontestible, it being certain that the first of these authors lived before there was question of either Greeks or Romans, and those prophets who appeared at a later day, were cotemporary with your first historians and lawgivers. The accomplishment of these predictions clearly proves their divine origin, and affirms the truth of those yet to be fulfilled.

"The Scriptures announced the destruction of the Jewish nation, which prophecy we see literally verified at the present day. God had loaded this ungrateful people with favors on account of the piety of their fathers, and He continued His protection until they proved themselves unworthy. His avenging hand cannot be mistaken when we behold the unhappy state to which they are reduced; exiles from their native land, wanderers over the whole earth, without laws, magistrates or country. The same prophecies which foretold their misfortunes, also declare that God will choose faithful worshipers from all nations, to whom He will communicate His grace through the saving merits of His Crucified Son."

Tertullian then speaks of Jesus Christ, and of the mystery of the Incarnation; establishes the Divinity of Our Lord by the prophecies, by His miracles, and by His resurrection; and says that the circumstances of His death on the Cross appeared so extraordinary to the pagans themselves, that Pilate advised the Emperor Tiberius to have an account of them deposited in the public archives of Rome, and further adds, that this Emperor would have believed in Jesus Christ, if he could have been a Cæsar and a Christian at the same time.

CONTINUATION OF THE APOLOGY OF TERTULLIAN.

After establishing the truth of Christianity, Tertullian energetically refutes the calumnies alleged against the Christians: "We are accused of not honoring the Emperor by sacrifices: it is true we do not offer victims, but we pray to the one true God, for the salvation of our princes; we respect them, but we cannot perjure our souls by calling them gods. Our perfect fidelity to our Lord and Master cannot be doubted, for our patience in enduring the most cruel sufferings for His sake proves it. We are frequently stoned by the enraged populace, our houses are burned, and in the wild frenzy of the bacchanals even the sacred dead are not spared, but are dragged from their silent tombs and torn to pieces. How have we revenged ourselves for all these wrongs? If we desired to make war against you have we not hosts of Christian soldiers? We are comparatively but of yesterday, and already we fill your villages, castles, boroughs and fields; we are found in the Senate and the public places; nothing remains to you but your temples. Could we not even war with unequaled forces, we who fear not the most excruciating torments, it being one of our precepts to suffer death rather than inflict it. We might be avenged by withdrawing entirely from the empire, and you would then be astonished at the immensity of your loss."

In order to show that the assemblies of the Christians were not seditious, Tertullian thus describes their proceedings: "We form but one body, because we have the same religion, the same doctrines, the same hopes; and we meet together to render our prayers more importunate and powerful, this violence being agreeable to God. Those who preside at our assemblies are old men of tried virtue, who have attained this honor, not through bribery, but by reason of their good lives and holy examples; for in the Church of God money is powerless."

"If we possess a treasury, it reflects not on our religion, for every one contributes toward it according to his means, all donations being entirely voluntary. This sum is a sacred deposit, which is not spent in useless festivities, but serves to maintain orphans, and comfort the poor and afflicted. It is strange that this charity should be a subject of censure. 'Behold!' they say, 'how Christians love one another; behold! how ready they are to die for each other!'

"Our union astonishes the pagans, because they indulge in cruel hatreds among themselves. As we possess but one soul and one mind, it is not difficult for us to share our goods in common, and it is not surprising that so disinterested a friendship should cause strange reports. Our public meals are called Agapes, signifying charity; and the poor as well as the rich are admitted to them, everything being conducted with modesty and decency. Before sitting down at table, a prayer is said, invoking the blessing of God; the conversation is always most edifying and instructive, ever remembering the presence of God. The repast finishes in the same manner as it commenced — that is to say, by thanksgiving and prayer." Such were the assemblies of the Christians, so much decried by unbelievers.

"How can they say," adds Tertullian, "that we are helpless in the ordinary affairs of life? We live with you, eat the same food, wear the same apparel, and use the same furniture, and reject nothing God has created. We only use all His gifts with moderation, returning thanks to Him who is their author. We navigate the seas, till the ground, bear arms, and trade with you. Why, therefore, do we deserve death? Is a Christian ever found among the criminals brought before your tribunals? I refer to your records for the truth of my assertion. If a Christian is condemned, it is only on account of his name; if any other cause is alleged, he is not a Christian. Innocence of life is a necessity with us; we follow the example of Our Divine Saviour, who is Holiness itself, and we endeavor to keep our consciences pure and unsullied as commanded by this great Judge, 'Who cannot deceive nor be deceived.'" Such was the life of the Christians in the third age of the Church.

FIFTH PERSECUTION UNDER THE EMPEROR SEVERUS.

A. D. 202.

After the death of Marcus Aurelius the Church enjoyed an interval of peace; the Emperor Severus was at first noted for his clemency, and it was even believed that he was inclined towards Christianity;

but his future course proved that he had only permitted the numbers of Christians to increase in order to immolate more victims to his rage. In the tenth year of his reign he published bloody edicts against them, which were enforced with so much rigor that the faithful believed the time of Anti-Christ had arrived.

The persecution commenced in Egypt, and was very violent. Among the martyrs who then shed their blood for the faith, a young slave, named Potamiena, signalized herself. The master to whom she belonged attempted several times to corrupt her, but she firmly resisted his solicitations. Enraged at his repulse, he determined to destroy this holy maiden, and accordingly denounced her as a Christian to the governor of Alexandria; at the same time he engaged the governor to assist him in his designs by promising him a large sum of money if he could induce Potamiena to yield to his desires. It was agreed that she was not to be condemned to death except in the event of her persisting in her refusal. She was therefore conducted before the tribunal of the governor, who employed every imaginable art to tempt her. The noble maiden remained firm and did not allow herself to be moved, either by the false kindness of the iniquitous judge, or by fear of the torments with which he threatened her.

This constancy so incensed the governor that he condemned her to be thrown into a cauldron of burning pitch. As they proceeded to disrobe her, she implored the executioners not to divest her of her garments; in exchange for this favor which modesty obtained, she consented to be lowered slowly into the cauldron; the continuance of her sufferings was a proof of the power of Jesus Christ in strengthening and sustaining those who devote themselves to Him. The executioners granted her request, and proceeded so slowly that her tortures lasted three hours. They were then convinced that the grace of Jesus Christ sustained His servants through the longest and most painful trials. One of the guards named Basilides, who assisted at her execution, manifested compassion towards the saint, and prevented the populace from insulting her; when, regarding him with gratitude, she promised to intercede with God for his conversion.

Some time afterward, Basilides, inspired by God, declared himself a Christian. At first it was thought that he did so in order to mock and ridicule Christianity; but persisting in the confession of his faith, he was taken before the judge, who sent him to prison. Faithful Christians visited him, and baptism was administered to him. The next day he was beheaded, after having gloriously confessed Jesus Christ. It is only the one true religion which has power to sustain its followers through prolonged and cruel torments.

MARTYRDOM OF ST. IRENEUS, BISHOP OF LYONS.

This persecution extended even into Gaul, and there is every reason to believe that during its continuance St. Ireneus, Bishop of Lyons, obtained the crown of martyrdom. He had been the disciple of St. Polycarp, and while attending his school imbibed a knowledge of the religion which rendered him one of the lights of the church. St. Polycarp trained both his mind and heart by his holy teachings and pious example; the disciple, filled with veneration for the eminent virtues of his master, carefully watched his deportment and actions, so that he might acquire also the spirit which inspired him. "I listened," he says, "carefully to his instructions, and engraved them, not on tablets, but in the depths of my heart. I still vividly remember the dignity of his movements, the majesty of his countenance, the purity of his life, the holy exhortations with which he nourished his people. It seems to me that I hear him now describing his conversations with St. John and others who had seen Jesus Christ; the words which he had heard from their mouths; all the particulars they had learned of the miracles and of the doctrine of the divine Saviour; and all that he related of it was in conformity with Holy Scripture."

St. Irencus was chosen to succeed St. Pothinus in the Episcopal See of Lyons; he had all the requisite qualities to confirm and console the church in those troubled times: knowledge, an ardent zeal, profound erudition and a tried sanctity. These characteristics were needed to repair the losses the Church had sustained, and to form a new army of martyrs who would soon renew her triumphs. It is asserted, that the Emperor Severus, learning the increasing numbers of the faithful in Lyons, under the labors of this holy prelate, adopted a resolution worthy of his cruel heart. He ordered his soldiers to surround the city, and to put to the sword all those who declared themselves Christians. The massacre was almost general. St. Ireneus was conducted before the tyrant, who condemned him to death, exulting at having thus destroyed the pastor and the flock.

These events we learn from the acts of St. Ireneus, and from other memorials confirming them. St. Ado, in his chronicle, relates that St. Ireneus suffered martyrdom at the same time with an innumerable multitude of Christians, and an ancient inscription, which is still to be seen in Lyons, shows that without counting the women and children, the number of martyrs amounted to nineteen thousand. This can easily be believed, if we consider the cruelty of the Emperor Severus, and the constancy of the faithful.

It is this fact, without doubt, which induced St. Eucherius to say, that Lyons had given birth to a race of martyrs. The great St. Gregory said: "There was so vast a multitude of Christians slain for the faith, that their blood flowed like a stream through the public places." The holy fathers have bestowed magnificent eulogies on this great bishop. One holy priest, named Zacharias, who escaped the slaughter, took care of his tomb, and was, it is believed, his successor; God having preserved him like a spark, in order to rekindle in the Church the same fire which had purified so many victims.

MARTYRDOM OF ST. PERPETUA AND ST. FELICITAS.

A. D. 205.

The persecution was not less violent at Carthage. Four young men were arrested in that city, Saturnin, Revocatus, Secundillus and Satur, and with them two young women, Perpetua and Felicitas. The first, who was of noble condition, and sister of Satur, had an infant still at the breast. Felicitas was pregnant. Nothing is more interesting than the history of their combat, written by Perpetua herself. She expresses herself in these words: "When we were apprehended, they guarded us for some time before throwing us into prison. My father, the only member of the family who was not a Christian, hastened to us, and endeavored to make me change my resolution. As he implored me most earnestly not to declare myself a Christian, I showed him a vessel, and said: 'Father, can there be any other name given to this vessel than the one which belongs to it?' 'No,' he replied. 'Well, I cannot call myself that which I am not.' At these words he rushed at me as if he would tear out my eyes. He then withdrew, ashamed at his outburst of passion, and did not return for some days, thereby giving me a little rest. In this interval we were baptized, and the Holy Ghost then inspired me not to ask for any thing but constancy during my torments.

"A short time afterwards we were led to prison. I was shocked on entering it, for I had never before been near such places. What painful days of intense heat; it was suffocating; we were so much crowded; and, added to this discomfort, was the brutality of the soldiers who guarded us. But the greatest distress I suffered was separation from my infant. At length they restored it to me, and two deacons, Festus and Pomponius, obtained, through a bribe, permission to have us removed for a few hours every day to a more comfortable place. Each one thought of that which affected him most: for me, I had nothing more urgent than to nurse my infant, who was dying of hunger. I earnestly solicited my mother, when she visited me, to protect it. I was deeply grieved at seeing my family so afflicted on my account, and this sorrow continued for many days, but it left me after a while; the prison even became to me an agreeable abode.

"One day my brother said to me, 'You can obtain much from our Lord, pray to Him to make known to you if you shall suffer death, or if you will be dismissed.' As I had already experienced the goodness of God, I promised my brother to inform him of the result the next day. In fine, after my prayer, I beheld a golden ladder which reached heaven, but so narrow, that but one person could ascend it at a time; the sides of the ladder were bordered with swords, daggers and lances, in such a manner that without great care, and without looking up, you could not escape being wounded in all parts of the body. At the foot of the ladder was a terrible dragon, ready to rush upon those who went up. Satur, my brother, had ascended, and from the top of the ladder said to me, 'Perpetua, I wait for you!

but take care of the dragon!' I replied, 'It will do me no harm, I trust in our Lord Almighty.' In short, I approached, and the dragon gradually lowered its head as if afraid of me; I put my foot on its head, which served me for the first round of the ladder.

"On gaining the top I beheld an immense garden, and in the middle of it a venerable man, under the appearance of a shepherd, surrounded by a vast multitude of people robed in white. This venerable personage said to me, 'Welcome, my daughter,' and he put in my mouth a delicious food, which I received with folded hands. All the immense crowd responded 'Amen,' which awakened me, and I perceived that I was still eating something of a wonderful sweetness. The next day I related this dream to my brother, and we concluded that we would very soon suffer martyrdom. We commenced to detach ourselves entirely from all earthly things, and to turn our thoughts towards Eternity."

EXAMINATION AND CONDEMNATION OF THE HOLY MARTYRS.

St. Perpetua thus continues the account of her martyrdom: "Some days after, it was noised abroad that we were to be examined. My father came again to the prison, and, overwhelmed with grief, said to me: 'My daughter, have pity on my white hairs, have pity on your father. If I have reared you with tender care, if I have cherished you more than any other of my children, do not now cover my old age with reproach. Have consideration for your mother; think of your infant who cannot live without you, and cease this obstinacy which will ruin us all!' In speaking thus, he took me by the hands, kissed them, and bathed them with his tears. His entreaties pierced me to the heart, and I lamented that he only, of all my family, grieved at my approaching martyrdom. Nevertheless, without allowing myself to be affected, I said to him, 'The result of this examination will be as God pleases, for we are not in our own power, but in His.'

"The next day, while we were at dinner, the guards entered, and commanded us to proceed to the tribunal; the greatest excitement prevailed, and we found the place crowded with people. We were made to ascend the scaffold; my companions were first interrogated, and courageously confessed Jesus Christ. I was next questioned. My father, with my child in his arms, forced his way through the crowd, attempted to drag me from my place, and implored me more vehemently than ever to change my resolution. The judge added his entreaties to my father's. 'Have compassion on the old age of your father, and on the infancy of your son — sacrifice to the prosperity of the Emperor!' 'I will not sacrifice,' I replied. 'You are then a Christian?' 'I am one.' As my father tried to pull me from the scaffold, the judge ordered that he should be removed himself, and they went so far as to strike him, in order to enforce obedience. I felt the blow they gave him as keenly as if I had received it myself, and my heart ached at witnessing this ill-treatment of my father in his venerable age.

"Then the judge pronounced our sentence: we were all condemned to the wild beasts. We returned filled with joy to our prison, but our joy was troubled by the condition of Felicitas who was in the eighth month of her pregnancy, and from this fact she feared greatly that her martyrdom would be deferred. We all united in fervent prayer that Felicitas might be delivered before the day appointed for the combat. Scarcely had we ended our prayers, when Felicitas felt the pangs of child-birth, and, as her full time had not arrived the pains were very severe, so much so, that from time to time she cried out in her agony. One of the guards said to her: 'If you complain now, what will you do when you are being torn to pieces by the wild beasts?' To which this noble woman replied, 'Now it is I who suffer, but then there will be another within me who will suffer for me, because I will suffer for Him.' Felicitas gave birth to a daughter, whom a Christian woman received and promised to care for as her own child.

"In the mean time the jailer of the prison, named Pudens, perceiving that God had granted us signal favors, had great consideration for us, and allowed a free entrance to all who desired to visit us. A few days previous to that appointed for our death, I saw my father enter the prison. He had come to make a last appeal; he was inexpressibly dejected. He tore his beard, he threw himself on the ground and remained there on his face, uttering the most lamentable sighs and groans, and cursing his old age. His anguish overwhelmed me with grief, but God sustained me against the violence of this last effort to change my resolution." Here ends the narrative of the saint; the continuation has been written by an eye-witness.

EXECUTION OF THE MARTYRS.

When the day of the spectacle had arrived, the holy martyrs were led to the amphitheatre. Joy was painted on their countenances, it sparkled in their eyes, it animated their gestures, it resounded in their words. Perpetua walked the last—the tranquillity of her soul was evinced in her manner and in her gait; she kept her eyes cast down in order to hide their brilliancy from the spectators. Felicitas' satisfaction at being sufficiently recovered to proceed with the others was equally manifest. Saturnin and Satur threatened the idolatrous people who surrounded them with the anger of God, and when they approached the judge who had condemned them, they said to him, "You condemn us to-day, but soon God will condemn you."

The people, irritated at these reproaches, demanded that they should be scourged. Overjoyed at gaining this new feature of resemblance to the Saviour, the holy martyrs only manifested the greatest contentment. God accorded them the kind of death each one had desired, for, when conversing together regarding the different punishments usually inflicted, Saturnin expressed his wish to combat against all the beasts of the amphitheatre.

In truth, after having been assailed, in company with Revocatus, by a furious leopard, they were then both mangled by a bear. Satur, on the contrary, feared nothing so much as a bear, and wished that a leopard would kill him at the first attack. Nevertheless, he was at first exposed to a wild boar, but the animal turned against the keeper who led him, and wounded him mortally. They then exposed him to a bear, but the animal would not leave its den; thus Satur did not receive a single wound.

The two Saints, Perpetua and Felicitas, were exposed in a net to a mad bull. The animal first attacked Perpetua, tossed her in the air, letting her fall with great violence to the ground. Perpetua raised herself up, re-adjusted her hair, and perceiving Felicitas, whom the bull had also assaulted, and who was stretched on the ground all bruised from her wounds, she gave her her hand and assisted her to rise. During this time she was not conscious of what had occurred, but asked, "When will they expose us to the bull?" In order to convince her that she had already suffered, they pointed to her torn garments and the wounds she had received. Then, having recognized a Catechumen named Rusticus, she begged him to call her brother Satur, and when they approached her she exhorted them to remain firm in the faith.

Satur, having withdrawn under one of the porticos of the amphitheatre, said to the jailer, Pudens, who was there stationed: "Did I not tell you that the beasts to which we would first be exposed would not injure me, but that it would be the tooth of a leopard which would cause my death?" When brought forward for the third time a leopard rushed upon him, and in an instant wounded him so severely that he was covered with blood. The delighted spectators cried out: "Behold, he is baptized a second time!" Then Satur, turning his eyes on Pudens, said: "Farewell, dear friend, bear testimony to my faith, and imitate it." He then asked the jailer for the ring he wore on his finger, dipped it in his blood, and returning it said: "Keep this as a testimony of my faith and a pledge of my friendship," and immediately expired.

Thus Satur died first, in accordance with the vision of St. Perpetua. Towards the close of the spectacle, the people demanded that the martyrs should be brought back to the center of the amphitheatre to receive the death blow. They came forward, and of their own accord submitted their throats to the knife without manifesting the slightest agitation. Perpetua fell into the hands of a clumsy gladiator, who tortured without killing her; until at last, fainting and exhausted, she was obliged to guide his hand to her throat, thus indicating the place where the blow should fall. Such heroism in delicate women is so contrary to nature, that it is evident, nature alone could not sustain them, and that we must therefore ascribe it to grace.

BEAUTIFUL CHARACTERISTICS OF ORIGEN.

During this period, Origen, from his earliest youth, had become famous throughout the whole Church. He was the son of St. Leonidas, who suffered for the faith in the persecution of Alexandria, under the Emperor Severus. The holy martyr had educated him with the greatest care in the liberal arts and belles-lettres, he had also instructed him in the Holy Scriptures, causing him every day to commit some portion to memory. The young Origen applied himself to study with incredible ardor, but his father admired in him the virtues with which grace had endowed him, more than the acquisitions gained by his natural talents. Often, while Origen slept, his father would enter his room, reverently uncover his breast, and kiss it with respect, as being the temple of the Holy Ghost.

During the persecution, Origen conceived so lively a desire to undergo martyrdom that he would have presented himself for it, had not the tears and prayers of his mother prevented him. When his father was arrested, his eagerness was redoubled, and they were obliged to hide his clothes in order to prevent him from leaving the house. Not being able to join his father, he wrote him a most touching letter, in which he exhorted him to endure martyrdom: "Have no anxiety about your children," he wrote, "God will take care of us." Leonidas was beheaded. His property having been confiscated, his family were reduced to actual poverty.

For some time Origen found an asylum in the

house of a wealthy lady; he soon opened a grammar school in order to support himself; and finally he was appointed the head of the school of Alexandria, which had become very celebrated. Origen sold all his profane books, in order to apply himself wholly to the study of the Scriptures, and at the same time to provide a subsistence for himself—the lessons of the school being gratuitous. He took from this scanty sum but six cents a day, and this pittance sufficed for the self-denying life he led.

Notwithstanding this austerity, the sweetness and gentleness of his manners charmed every one, and the amenity of his disposition as much as the brilliancy of his talents, attracted a prodigious crowd of scholars not alone from among the youths, but from among philosophers, whether Christian or Pagan. He made a great number of conversions, and several of his disciples became illustrious saints; some of them even obtained the crown of martyrdom. It was above all in regard to those who were arrested for the faith, that he fulfilled with zeal the functions of a Christian master. He visited them in prison, when lying there, bound in fetters; he accompanied them to the examination, and even to the place of execution, where he encouraged them by signs and the most animated exhortations.

He exposed his life fearlessly in this zealous exercise of charity, and was frequently in danger of being stoned and otherwise ill-treated. He was eventually arrested, loaded with chains and cast into a dungeon. That they did not immediately put him to death, was owing to the hope his persecutors indulged of tiring out his patience, and of thus perverting numbers of Christians by the example of so illustrious a man. They caused him to endure hunger, thirst, nakedness and imprisonment, without disturbing in the least degree either his patience or courage. The austere habits of his life had strengthened him against all trials; he fasted almost continually; he passed the greater part of the night in prayer and meditation on the Holy Scriptures; and, during the slight repose he was obliged to yield to nature, the bare earth sufficed for his bed.

His wonderful genius was universally admired; there was no kind of learning in which he was not proficient, and with him this diversity of knowledge did not in the least weaken the solidity of his judgment. His manner of expressing himself was so clear, that he made the most difficult subjects easy of comprehension, and he spoke with a grace which inspired love for the truths he taught.

WORKS OF ORIGEN.

The most celebrated writing of Origen is the one he published against Celsus, in order to refute the calumnies this pagan philosopher had circulated against Christians. This work is regarded as the most complete apology of the Christian religion which has been handed down to us from antiquity. This is the substance of the document: "It would, perhaps, have been more appropriate," says Origen, "to imitate Jesus Christ, who kept a profound silence before his judges, and who opposed to the slanders of his enemies, the sanctity of his life, and the luster of his miracles: thus, it might be considered useless to refute, by argument, the falsehoods which the malice of men ceases not to circulate against Him, because he defends himself only by the solid virtues of His disciples, whose holiness confounds the cunning of their accusers. I do not, therefore, write for the faithful; for them an apology is superfluous; but I write for the infidel, to whom this instruction may be useful."

After proving the falsity of the particular objections brought forward by Celsus, he victoriously establishes the truth of the Christian religion by incontrovertible facts, by the prophecies which foretold Jesus Christ, by His miracles, and by the holy lives of His disciples. "As to the prophecies, is it not just," he asks, "to put faith in the Jewish books? their antiquity cannot be doubted, if we consider the proofs given by Josephus and Tatian, whose authority is of great weight." Origen quotes the prophecies which distinctly predicted the birth, the passion, the death and all the circumstances attending the coming of Jesus Christ. He remarks, that since the coming of Jesus Christ the Jews have neither prophecies nor miracles, nor any other mark of the divine protection, as manifested among Christians.

With regard to miracles, Celsus does not deny that Jesus Christ performed them, but he attributes them to magic. Origen replies, that "there are some means by which the illusions of the devil can be discerned from the real miracles which have God for their author. These means consist in examining the morals of those who perform them, their doctrine, and the effects which these miracles produce. Moses and the prophets have taught nothing which is not most worthy of God, entirely conformable to reason, and every way useful to the good morals of civilized society. They have first practiced that which they taught, and the effect has been great and lasting. Moses established an entire nation governed by holy laws. Jesus Christ has united all nations in the knowledge of the true God, and in the practice of all virtues. Charlatans and impostors do not seek to reform mankind, and their delusions are of short duration. The resurrection of Jesus Christ, which is a great miracle and the foundation of Christianity, cannot be suspected of any artifice. After being buried, after remaining three days in a tomb sealed by his enemies, the Jews, and guarded by Roman soldiers, He appeared again during forty days; first to Peter and the twelve apostles, then to five hundred disciples at one time. If they had not seen Him risen, if they had not been convinced of His divinity, they would never have exposed themselves to suffering and to death, in order (in obedience to His commands) to announce to all nations the religion they had received from Him.

"His ignominious death on the Cross would have shaken their faith; they would have considered themselves deceived, and they would have been the first to condemn Him. It is evident they must have witnessed something very extraordinary to induce them to embrace His precepts, and to cause others to embrace them at the expense of their peace, their liberty and their life. How could coarse and illiterate men, if they had not felt themselves sustained by supernatural grace, undertake to reform the world? How would the people under the influence of their preaching have forsaken their ancient customs to follow a contrary doctrine, if they had not been changed by an extraordinary power and convinced by wonderful facts?

CONTINUATION OF THE APOLOGY OF ORIGEN.

Origen proves the divinity of the Christian religion by the astonishing change it produces in those who embrace it. "The great end of the preaching of the gospel," he says, "is the reformation of morals. If some one had eradicated from a number of persons the vice of impurity, it would be difficult to believe that he had nothing supernatural about him; what, then, should be thought of the doctrines of Christianity influencing so vast a multitude, who have become other men since they received these truths, and whose members extend throughout the whole empire?

"The morals of the Christians place them very far above those who have not the faith; a Christian overcomes his most violent passions with the view of pleasing God, whereas, the pagans abandon themselves to the most shameful voluptuousness without a blush, and while in the indulgence of their vices they pretend still to retain the character of pure and honest men. The simplest Christian is infinitely more enlightened upon the excellence and merit of chastity than the philosophers, the vestals and the priests, who are supposed to lead the most regular lives among the pagans. None among us are sullied by these excesses, or, if one is found guilty of them, he is not of the number of those who assist at our assemblies, for he is no longer a Christian. In truth, they who fall into any sin, above all, that of impurity, are expelled from the Church, they are mourned over as being dead to God, and when they return by repentance and penance, they are subjected to longer probation than those preparing for baptism, neither are they permitted to exercise any public function in the Church.

"The fidelity of Christians to the laws is well tested; they are so averse to exciting the slightest disturbance, that, in obedience to the commands received from their lawgiver, they employ no other weapon than patience against their enemies. Jesus Christ has commanded that they should allow themselves to be slaughtered like sheep rather than oppose the least violence; God takes charge of their interests and their defense, and they gain more by this mildness than they would by resenting injuries. So far from the pagans being able to exterminate the Christians, the death of the martyrs has tended only to augment the number.

"The severities practiced towards the Christians could not diminish their zeal for the conversion of infidels; among them were some whose only occupation was to travel through cities, burroughs and villages, in order to announce the Gospel; and, lest they should be suspected of interested motives, they refused all recompense and every delicacy, accepting only the plainest food for the sustenance of nature. Now," adds Origen, "if among those who are converted there are found the rich, persons of established rank, and women of distinguished position, it may be said perhaps that there is some glory in making known our doctrine to such as these; but this suspicion could never have arisen in the beginning. At the present time the honor received from some does not equal the contempt and insults we endure from the Pagans."

Origen shows that the Christians, notwithstanding the ardent zeal which animated them, in order to attract infidels to the faith, did not hesitate to test as much as possible those who wished to embrace it. They were instructed in private before being received into the assembly, and when it was evident that they really had a sincere determination to lead a new life, they were allowed admission, being still divided into two ranks, the one of the beginners, and the other of those who were more advanced.

Persons were employed to watch over these neophytes, to separate them from those whose lives were not conformable with the sanctity of Christianity, and to direct them in the practices of piety. Such was still the virtue of Christians a long time after the age of the Apostles, which ancient apologists, witnesses of these facts, have cited, to prove the divinity of the Christian religion, to confute the injustice of their persecutors, and to reproach the excesses of the pagans.

SIXTH PERSECUTION UNDER THE EMPEROR MAXIMIN.

Year 235.

During the space of twenty-four years the Christians were left in peace; the Emperor who succeeded Severus did not persecute them. Alexander was even favorable towards them, he honored Jesus Christ as one of his own gods, and placed his statue in his domestic temple; he conceived the design of having it solemnly placed among the divinities by the Senate. This prince approved particularly of this precept which he had learned from the Christians: "Do unto others, what you would wish others to do to you!" He had it engraved on the walls of his palace, and when he had condemned some malefactors to punishment, he caused it to be cried through the streets by a herald.

Alexander's kind disposition towards the Christians, was a sufficient reason for Maximin to persecute them. This prince, who was naturally cruel, published new edicts against them. It is believed that a Christian soldier, by a singular act which caused a great sensation at the time, was the innocent cause of this persecution. When Maximin was proclaimed Emperor, he made, according to custom, presents to the troops. Every soldier was obliged on such occasions to present himself before the Emperor with a crown of laurel on his head. There appeared one among them whose head was bare, and who carried his crown in his hand; he had already passed the Tribune without attracting notice, when the murmurs of his companions caused him to be observed. This officer asked the soldier why he did not, like his companions, wear his crown on his head. "It is because I am a Christian," he replied, "and my religion does not permit me to wear your crowns!" It appears the wearing the crown was an idolatrous custom. The soldier was immediately divested of his uniform and imprisoned.

This affair created so great an excitement that a general persecution was the result; nevertheless, the Emperor did not issue sentence of death indiscriminately, but only against those who taught others, and those who governed churches, being persuaded that the people, deprived of the support of their pastors, would be easily conquered. Besides, he was afraid of depopulating the empire, should severe measures be extended to the multitudes of the faithful; for the cities and the country, the armies and the courts of justice, were filled with Christians. The rigors of the persecution fell, therefore, on the bishops and priests; the tribunals condemned to the greatest torments all those whom they arrested. The Pope Pontian was one of the first who then suffered for the faith. St. Antherius, who succeeded him, occupied the chair but for six weeks, and it is believed that he also received the crown of martyrdom.

The reign of Maximin was but a continuation of cruelties, but the details have not been handed down to us; it is only remarked that he caused the churches to be burned, which shows conclusively that the Christians had public places wherein to hold their assemblies. This persecution continued only three years, because Maximin, by his cruelties, had rendered himself so extremely odious that he was killed by one of his own soldiers.

SEVENTH PERSECUTION UNDER THE EMPEROR DECIUS.

A. D. 249.

The Emperor Decius was the instigator of the seventh persecution. At the commencement of his reign he published a bloody edict against the Christians, which was sent to all the governors of the provinces. This edict was executed with such extreme rigor that the only occupation of the magistrates was to search for Christians, and to invent every variety of punishment with which to torment them. Prisons, whips, fire, wild beasts, boiling pitch, melted wax, sharp stakes and red hot pincers, were all put in use; but the Church had the consolation to see her children remain firm, and suffer the longest and most cruel tortures with an admirable constancy.

The Pope, St. Fabian, set them an example, and was one of the first victims immolated in this persecution. St. Alexander, bishop of Jerusalem, a venerable old man, was presented before the tribunal of the governor of Palestine, and generously confessed the name of Jesus Christ for the second time, for he had already rendered testimony under the Emperor Severus, about forty years before. He was cast into prison and died in his chains. St. Babylas, bishop of Antioch, also received the crown of martyrdom at the same time with three young children whom he had instructed. The number of those who at this time suffered for the faith was so great, according to the historian Nicephorus, that it was impossible to count them. After having employed in vain the most violent punishments, the persecutors, in order to wear out their patience, inflicted slow and agonizing tortures, varied by all the allurements of pleasure, in vain efforts to corrupt them. We will give two examples of the refinement of cruelty to which they had recourse.

A Christian had already endured the torture of the iron claws and of red-hot plates; his whole body was covered with wounds; honey was then spread over him, his hands were tied behind his back, and he was laid down in the burning sun to be stung to death by bees and other insects. Another Christian who was still very young, was, by order of the judge, led into a delightful garden, adorned with lilies and roses, and all other exquisite and fragrant flowers, and through which flowed a gentle rivulet. The attendants laid him on a soft bed, to which they bound him with silken cords. He was then left alone. A young and beautiful courtesan whom the judge selected on account of her singular and varied fascinations, and whom he had commanded to use all her arts and allurements for the ensnarement of the youth, then approached him. So violent was this temptation, and so great his danger, that, for want of other means of defense, this heroic youth bit off his tongue and spat it in the face of the

114 HISTORY OF THE CHURCH.

wretched woman, who retired from the contest utterly confounded at his invincible virtue.

A great many Christians, in order to escape from this persecution, in which sometimes violence and sometimes seductions were employed, fled into the deserts. Of this number was St. Paul, born in Thebais, a province of Egypt. When very young he retired into a solitude, and led there an evangelical life, in an entire separation from the world and in close union with God.

MARTYRDOM OF ST. PIONIUS.

Among the generous champions who suffered death for Jesus Christ, during the persecution of the Emperor Decius, there was none more illustrious than St. Pionius, a priest of Smyrna. One day, while at prayer in the church, it was revealed to him that on the following day he would be arrested. He immediately placed a chain around his neck, so that his persecutors might know he was prepared to suffer; and, in the event of his being taken to the temples of the false gods, that the spectators might perceive it was against his will. Pionius was arrested the next day, and when the officer asked him if he was aware of the commands of the Emperor, he replied: "We are not ignorant of the fact that there is one Supreme command; it is that which obliges us to adore one God alone." "Proceed to the square," said the officer, "and you will see the edict of the Emperor which orders every one to sacrifice to the gods."

A multitude of Jews and pagans followed in the procession. St. Pionius delivered a long discourse to the people, who listened with attention, and when at the conclusion he declared that he would not adore their gods nor their images, they entreated him to change his resolution. "Allow yourself to be persuaded," they said to him; "a man of your merit is worthy to live and enjoy the pleasures of life." "Without doubt," answered the holy priest, "life is a blessing, and a Christian does not despise it, but we aspire to a higher life, which is in every way preferable. I thank you for your sympathy, but I suspect the artifice; open malice is less dangerous than deceitful caresses." Then, turning towards the judge, he said: "If your office is to convert me or to punish me, punish me, for you will never persuade me."

The judge then commenced the examination in legal form, in order that all things should be in readiness for the arrival of the proconsul, who was expected in a few days. This magistrate, having arrived at Smyrna, commanded St. Pionius to be brought before him. "Do you persist in your determination, or will you change while there is yet time?" "I will never change," replied the holy martyr. The proconsul reiterated his persuasions, granting a still longer time for consideration. "The delay is useless," said St. Pionius; "I shall remain firm." The judge then pronounced the sentence; it was written on a tablet in these words: "We command that the sacrilegious Pionius, who has avowed himself a Christian, shall be burned alive, in order to avenge the gods and give warning to men." The martyr walked with a firm step and cheerful countenance to the place of execution. He disrobed, stretched himself on the stake, and was nailed to it. When all was ready, the executioner said to him: "Forsake your error, there is still time; promise to do that which is asked of you and we will remove the nails." "No," answered the martyr; "I hasten to die, in order that I may live again." They then raised him, fastened to the stake, and turned his face towards the east, heaping around him a great quantity of wood, which they' set on fire.

Closing his eyes, the people thought him dead, but he was only absorbed in prayer. The prayer ended, he opened his eyes as the flames arose around him, and, looking at the fire with a joyous air, he said: "Amen; Lord receive my soul!" Immediately after, with a gentle sigh, he expired. When the fire was extinguished, the faithful, who were present, found his body entirely perfect and apparently in full health; the hair unsinged, the beard beautiful, and the whole countenance bright and glorious. The Christians retired from the scene confirmed in their faith, but the pagans with perplexed minds and troubled consciences.

EIGHTH PERSECUTION UNDER THE EMPEROR VALERIAN.

Year 257.

The persecution, which had abated a little, commenced with renewed violence under the Emperor Valerian. This prince was excited against the Christians by one of his ministers who hated them, and who persuaded him that, in order to succeed in a war in which he was engaged, he should abolish Christianity. With this view, he published edicts which procured the crown of martyrdom for many Christians.

The most illustrious among these martyrs was St. Laurence, the first deacon in the Roman church. When the Pope St. Sixtus, who had elevated him to the deaconship, was being led to execution, St. Laurence followed him weeping, and said to him: "Where are you going my father, without your son? Holy Pontiff, where are you going without your minister?" St. Sixtus replied to him: "My son, a still greater combat is reserved for you. In three days you will follow me." Laurence, consoled by these words, prepared himself for martyrdom, and hastened to distribute to the poor all the money deposited with him, for it was the duty of the deacons to distribute the alms of the church. The prefect of Rome, having been informed that the Church possessed a large treasure, desired to obtain it, and he said to St. Laurence: "You complain to other Christians that you are treated with severity, but here no torture is to be used. I ask you simply for that which you can give me. I know that you have vases of gold and silver for your sacrifices; deliver them to me; the Emperor has need of them in order to maintain his troops!" St. Laurence answered: "I acknowledge that our Church is rich, and that the Emperor possesses no treasures so precious; I will show you a good portion of them; grant me but a little time to put all things in order." The prefect, not understanding what riches he spoke of, accorded three days' delay.

In this interval the holy deacon went over the whole city, in order to assemble all the poor whom the church maintained; he then reported to the prefect that all was ready. The prefect followed him, and seeing a crowd of blind, deformed and wretched creatures, instead of the precious vases he expected, cast on the holy deacon a threatening look. "What you behold, disappoints and enrages you," said St. Laurence to him; "gold is a base metal, the cause of many evils; the true gold is the divine knowledge which enlightens these poor people; these are the riches which I have promised you!" "Is it thus you mock me?" exclaimed the prefect in a rage; "I know that Christians pretend to despise death, so do not hope to die quickly; your tortures shall be so prolonged that you shall die by degrees." Accordingly they commenced by tearing his body with lashes; they then placed him on an iron gridiron over lighted coals, and fastened the holy martyr to it in such a manner that his flesh was very slowly penetrated by the heat.

The fire of charity which inflamed his heart was

stronger than that which consumed his body, and rendered him insensible to the torture. His only thought was the law of the Lord, and his torment became to him a real refreshment. After enduring for a long time this horrible suffering, he said calmly to the judge: "My body is sufficiently burned on this side, have it turned on the other;" and some moments after he added: "My flesh is now roasted enough; you can eat it." Then, raising his eyes to Heaven, he prayed to God for the preservation of Rome, and expired. What courage, what calmness in the midst of the most acute sufferings! in vain would we seek for the motive elsewhere than in the all powerful strength of the divine aid.

ST. CYPRIAN IS ARRESTED AND SENT INTO EXILE.

It was in the same persecution that St. Cyprian, bishop of Carthage, suffered martyrdom. He was born in Africa of a distinguished family, and previous to his conversion had acquired a great reputation by teaching Rhetoric. It was only when he had reached a mature age, and after profound reflection, that he embraced Christianity, for he hesitated a long time before renouncing the errors of paganism. He found it difficult to uproot old prejudices, to lead a new life, and to become a new man. "How can we," he asks, "destroy inveterate habits, which have become a second nature; how practice frugality, when we are accustomed to an abundant and luxurious table?" This is what he wrote to one of his friends. "But," he adds, "when the water of regeneration had washed away the stains of my past life, and my purified heart had received the celestial light, all my difficulties vanished. I found that easy which had appeared impossible."

He made such great progress in virtue, that he was considered a proper candidate for the priesthood, a short time after his baptism. In the course of time, the bishop of Carthage having died, the faithful of that city entreated that he should be made their pastor. On receiving this intelligence, the holy priest secreted himself, desiring to yield to his elders an honor of which he believed himself unworthy. The place of his concealment being discovered, he was obliged to submit. His virtues shone with redoubled lustre in this distinguished position. His charity for the poor knew no bounds. He at once applied himself with indefatigable zeal to strengthen discipline, and to instruct his flock. He escaped the persecution of the Emperor Decius, by withdrawing for some time from the city, because it was he whom the pagans especially sought to put to death, and several times the amphitheatre had resounded with the cry: "Cyprian to the lions! Cyprian to the lions!" He was not idle in his retreat, but toiled unceasingly for the good of his people, either by letters or by the ministry of those to whom he had confided them. On returning to Carthage he extended his vigilance into the interior of Africa. Nothing escaped his pastoral care. A schism had sprung up in Rome. Novatian had been then ordained bishop in the life-time of St. Cornelius, the legitimate Pontiff.

When this news reached St. Cyprian his zeal was enkindled, and he commenced writing against the intruder. "It is in this way," said he, "that all schisms arise, when by impious rashness some persons depose the bishop, of whom there can be but one in a see, and reject him whom God has appointed. There is but one God, but one Jesus Christ, but one Episcopal see, originally founded by St. Peter, on the authority of our Lord. No other altar can be erected, nor any other priesthood established. It is erecting another altar to raise a new bishop in the place of him whom the church has appointed. All that which men undertake, contrary to divine institutions, is false, profane and sacrilegious. The church of Jesus Christ is essentially one, it cannot be divided; Jesus Christ tells us there is but one fold. In order to make this unity more evident, the Lord has built His Church on one alone — on St. Peter, to whom He has given the power of the keys.

"Cornelius has been appointed, according to the holy canons, to the pontifical chair; therefore, he who claims to be bishop of Rome breaks the unity. His ordination cannot be legitimate. As there cannot be two bishops in the same see, he who is created bishop after the first, is not the second; he is nothing — he has neither the power nor the rank of bishop. He is not a pastor, but a profaner, a stranger, an apostate; he succeeds no one, he begins with himself. He endeavors to establish a new church, a purely human church, in the place of the Church of God; this is what Novatian has done. He has been elected, against all the laws of discipline, by the deserters who have abandoned their true pastor. When a bishop has been once established, there is no way of appointing another in the same place. It is a monstrous crime to attempt to elect a second; it is so great a sin, that martyrdom even could not expiate it. There is no real martyrdom out of the church. Schismatics can be put to death, but they cannot be crowned. Whoever divides the flock of the Lord becomes corrupt, a stranger, and an enemy. They cannot have God for a father, when they have not the Church for a mother."

MARTYRDOM OF ST. CYPRIAN.

St. Cyprian zealously engaged in the discharge of his holy functions, when the persecution of Valerian broke out. Paternus, proconsul of Africa, had him brought before his tribunal: "The Emperor commands me," said he, "to force all his subjects to embrace the same religion which he himself professes; who are you?" "I am a Christian and a bishop," answered Cyprian; "I know but one true God, who has made heaven and earth. It is this God whom we serve, and to whom we pray in a special manner for the prosperity of the Emperors." "I wish to know," inquired the proconsul, "who are the priests attached to your church?" "I cannot reveal them," replied Cyprian; "your own laws condemn informers." After more questions, and as firm replies, the proconsul ordered him to be exiled to Carube, a little city situated on the coast, not very far distant from Carthage.

Several other African bishops and a great number of priests were banished at the same time, and dispersed through uncivilized places, where they had every kind of privation and inconvenience to undergo. St. Cyprian comforted them by a letter, which cannot be read without our feeling some degree of the divine warmth with which his heart was filled, and which made his happiness consist in suffering for Jesus Christ. He remained a year in exile; he was then recalled to Carthage, to be there judged by the new proconsul who had succeeded Paternus. The persecution was commenced with redoubled violence, and the edict of the Emperor Valerian ordered, that the bishops, priests and deacons should be immediately put to death. St. Cyprian was confided to the captain of the guards who resided in a suburb of Carthage; his friends were permitted to visit him, and his faithful people flocked around him. The Christians, fearing he would be put to death during the night, passed the whole night at the door of the house where he was guarded.

The proconsul was residing at his country house, and thither the holy bishop was conducted, the weather being intensely warm. The soldiers, seeing him overcome by profuse perspiration, offered him a change of garments. "For what purpose" said the Saint, "would you endeavor to mitigate sufferings which will soon end?" When they had reached the end of their journey the proconsul asked the bishop if he was called Cyprian. "That is my name," he replied. "The Emperor commands you to sacrifice to the gods," said the proconsul. "I will not do it," replied Cyprian. "Think of the danger in which you stand," said the judge. St. Cyprian answered, "In so just a cause there is no deliberation." The proconsul, after consulting with his council, spoke thus to the holy bishop: "For a long time you have made a profession of impiety, and our Emperor has not been able to bring you back to better sentiments. Since you are the head of this pernicious sect, you shall serve for an example to those whom you have led into disobedience; the discipline of the laws shall be strengthened by your blood." He then read from the tablet, on which it was written, the sentence of condemnation. It was expressed in these words: "It is commanded that Cyprian shall be punished by the sword." The holy bishop responded, "I return thanks to God." The faithful, who were very numerous in the assembly, cried out, "May we also be beheaded." They had appointed for the place of execution a square bordered with large trees, at some distance from the city. Although the place was very spacious it was too small for the vast multitude who assembled there.

The holy bishop gave proofs, even to the end, of his solicitude for his flock, for, knowing that in the crowd there were many helpless women, he directed that care should be taken to protect them from all dangers. Arrived at the place of execution, he prostrated himself on the ground in fervent prayer to God. When it was concluded, he removed his garments, giving them to his deacons; he then took the bandage in order to cover his eyes, but, as he had some difficulty in tying it, a priest and deacon performed this last office for him. The executioner then appeared, to whom the holy martyr presented twenty-five gold pieces; then, kneeling down, he crossed his hands over his heart and waited for the stroke which was to change for him, time into a glorious eternity. The faithful collected his blood on the linen cloths which they had spread around him before he was beheaded, and preserved with religious respect these sacred relics.

CONTINUATION OF THE PERSECUTION IN AFRICA.

The persecution did not end with the death of St. Cyprian, for, a few months afterwards, a multitude of martyrs attained the crown. The account of their martyrdom, written by themselves while in prison, is still extant, and was completed by an eyewitness. It says: "When we were arrested we learned that the governor had decided that we should be burned alive, and that the execution would take place the next day; but God, who holds in His hand the hearts of Judges, did not permit them to torture us in this manner. The governor altered his determination and we were remanded to prison. This place was not terrible to us; its darkness was changed to a celestial brightness, a ray from the Holy Ghost penetrated this gloomy dwelling and dispersed all fear. The next day, towards evening, we were conducted by the guard to the palace to undergo our examination. Oh, happy day! oh, how light appeared the chains with which they loaded us. The governor put several questions to us, intermingled with threats and promises. Our replies were modest but firm, generous and christian-like, and we went forth from our interrogation, victorious over the demon. We were sent back to prison, and there prepared ourselves for a new combat.

"The most painful trial we had to endure was hunger and thirst; for, after compelling us to work all day, they denied us every thing, even a little water. God, himself, comforted us, by making known to us in a vision that we had but a few days more to suffer, and that He would never forsake us. Through the instrumentality of two Christians, provisions were conveyed to us. This assistance relieved us a little; our sick recovered; we soon forgot our troubles, and we blessed the divine mercy which had deigned to alleviate our sufferings. The intimate union which exists among us contributes greatly towards sustaining and consoling us; we are but of one mind, and pray and converse continually together. Nothing is sweeter than this fraternal charity, which is so agreeable to God, and by which we obtain from Him all that we ask, according to the consoling promise of Jesus Christ: 'If two persons unite on earth in asking something of my Father, they will certainly obtain it.'"

Finally the governor again summoned them before

his tribunal. All boldly avowed their firm adherence to their first confession of faith. Then the governor read the sentence condemning them to be beheaded; and they were led to the place of execution where they found a great concourse of people; the faithful and the gentiles both hastening to the spot. The countenances of the holy martyrs were illumined by a heavenly joy at the blissful hope of soon being admitted to the presence of the Lamb; they courageously exhorted the eager spectators: the faithful to remain firm in their faith, and carefully guard this precious gift of a loving Father; the idolaters to acknowledge and adore the one true God. "Every man," said the martyrs to the pagans, "who sacrifices to the false gods shall be exterminated; it is a horrible impiety to abandon the true God and worship demons." The executioners then advanced and with their cruel weapons released these impatient souls from the bondage of this life.

ADMIRABLE CONSTANCY OF A CHILD.

Almighty God, in His infinite power, can endow the tongues of children with eloquence when He desires to add to His glory, and He also causes them to be the means of triumph to the faith by generously confessing it. At Cesarea, in Cappadocia, a child, named Cyril, displayed an extraordinary courage, which filled the faithful with joy and admiration. The sacred name of Jesus Christ was incessantly on his lips, and he derived so much strength in pronouncing it as to become insensible to the threats and promises addressed to him by his inhuman judges. His father, who was an idolater, could not induce him to invoke the false gods, and after shamefully ill-treating him drove him from his house.

The judge of the city, hearing of what had happened, sent soldiers to arrest the youthful Cyril, and conduct him before his tribunal. "My child," gently said the magistrate, "I am most anxious to pardon your offense in consideration of your tender age; you can regain your father's favor and return to your home if you will be docile and obedient. Comply, therefore, with our wishes, and renounce Christianity." The holy child replied: "I am rejoiced at being enabled to suffer reproaches for my conduct. God will receive me, and I shall find Him a tender, loving parent. Most happy am I in being driven from the paternal roof, as I shall dwell in a mansion a thousand times more spacious and beautiful. I willingly renounce temporal goods, in order to gain heavenly treasures; death has no terrors for me, because it is the entrance to eternal life." He uttered these words with a marvelous courage, showing that he was animated by the divine spirit. Then the judge, assuming a severe tone with the intention of terrifying the holy child, threatened him with death, ordered him to be bound as if to be carried to execution, and commanded a pile of wood to be prepared and ignited. But this admirable child, far from manifesting the slightest fear, only appeared firmer and more confident, and did not shed a single tear at the sight of the horrible death that awaited him. The executioners led him to the fire and threatened to throw him into the flames, but Cyril lost none of his sublime fortitude, and remained unmoved.

The judge had privately given orders only to frighten him, and when they saw that the sight of the punishment made no impression on him, he was once more conducted before the tribunal. The magistrate thus addressed him: "You have seen the fire and sword prepared for you, and I trust will show yourself obedient and submissive to my will and that of your father. Are you not desirous of regaining his affection and of returning home?" Cyril answered: "You have deprived me of celestial happiness by recalling me to your presence; I fear neither the fire nor the sword, but languish for my heavenly home, and sigh for imperishable riches, exceeding all the wealth of my father. Jesus Christ our Lord will receive me into the home of the blessed, and reward me with a crown of everlasting glory; hasten, then, and put me to death, so that I may go to Him the sooner."

The assistants wept at hearing him speak thus, but he said to them: "Do not mourn for me, but rejoice at the happy fate which awaits me; seek not to weaken me by your tears, but rather encourage me to suffer every thing for God. You know not the glorious destiny I shall obtain, nor the bright hope of a blissful immortality by which I am animated and sustained. I am eager to terminate my mortal life, and ready to endure the most excruciating torments. Come, then, and open for my eager soul the golden portals of the heavenly Jerusalem." In these holy dispositions he was led to execution; but the kind of death he suffered is not mentioned in the account of his martyrdom. It is thus that the power of religion, of which we have seen such evident proofs, in a weak and delicate sex, is also manifested at an age when timidity and inconstancy are so natural.

PUNISHMENT OF THE PERSECUTORS—CHARITY OF THE CHRISTIANS.

Divine vengeance overtook Valerian, who was one of the most inhuman persecutors of Christianity. This prince, after experiencing a defeat, imprudently engaged in a conference with Sapor, King of Persia, by whom he was seized, confined as a prisoner, and treated with the greatest indignity. When Sapor wished to mount his horse he made the Emperor bend before him, and placing his foot on his neck leaped into the saddle. Finally, the unhappy Valerian was flayed alive; and his skin, after being dyed red, was suspended in a Persian temple as a monument of the ignominious defeat of the Roman arms. The pagans were horror stricken at the dreadful fate of the Emperor, but the Christians recognized the avenging hand of God in the punishment of a prince who had cruelly persecuted His children.

The empire was, at that period, plunged into the most unhappy condition by the barbarians, who ruthlessly invaded all its provinces. The Goths overran Thrace and Macedonia, and devastated Greece; the Germans crossed the Alps and advanced into Italy as far as Ravenna; other tribes entered Gaul and passed into Spain; the Sarmatians ravaged Pannonia, and the Parthians penetrated as far as Syria. Civil wars raged throughout the empire, and as many as thirty tyrants sprang up, who called themselves Roman Emperors. Earthquakes were of frequent occurrence, and the sea overflowed, completely inundating several cities. The plague succeeded all these evils, and was so violent in Rome as to carry off several thousand victims in one day.

This dreadful scourge made no less havoc in Alexandria. "Universal mourning prevailed," says St. Denis, bishop of this great city; "cries of lamentation issued from every house, and the deserted streets resounded with the groans and shrieks of the dying." The holy bishop adds, "that this disease was, for the pagans, the greatest of all calamities, and, for the Christians, an occasion to practice the most heroic charity; as they alone nursed the sick and buried the dead." "The Christians," he writes, "have acted nobly, visiting the sick, consoling the bereaved, and, heedless of the contagion, have frequently fallen victims to the pestilence, while serving others. A number of priests, deacons and the laity have thus sacrificed their lives, but those who remain replace them, and continue to labor in the cause of charity. The pagans, on the contrary, fly from the scourge; abandon those who are dearest to them; cast the bodies of their relatives into the street before life is extinct, leaving their remains without burial, to become the food of dogs, so great is their dread of contracting the fatal disease, which nevertheless they cannot avoid." This extraordinary difference of conduct created much remark, and the pagans themselves openly declared that the Christians alone exercised true piety. The Church still honors those martyrs who, at the time of this plague, fell victims to divine charity.

NINTH PERSECUTION UNDER THE EMPEROR AURELIAN.
A. D. 274.

The Emperor Aurelian, who, in the first years of his reign, had not shown himself adverse to the Christians, suddenly changed his conduct in their regard, as he thought to win the affection of the senate and the people by persecuting the enemies of their gods. He was prevented from signing a terrible edict against them by a thunderbolt falling at his feet, which so overpowered him with terror, as to cause him to abandon his design; but his determination was not altered, and the persecution was only deferred. "Soon after, being given up to the corruption of his heart," says Lactantius, who lived at a nearly cotemporary period, "Aurelian published bloody edicts against us; but it was happily at the end of his reign, which was very short, so that the laws had not yet been enforced in the more distant provinces at the time of his death." Thus our divine Lord shows, that He has not confided unlimited power to the hands of earthly rulers, but governs the world by His justice and providence. Nevertheless, as the known wishes of Emperors are not less effective than their commands, the hatred of the Christian name, manifested by Aurelian before his death, did not fail to make a great many martyrs.

One of the most illustrious was St. Conon, who suffered in Lyconia. When the judge derided his austere and mortified life, the holy martyr boldly replied: "The cross constitutes all my delight; do not, therefore, think to intimidate me by the preparation of tortures. I am sensible of their value, and know how much they contribute to true happiness; the longest and most painful sufferings are the objects of my ardent desire." In order to shake his resolution, the judge asked him if he had any children. "I have one son," he answered, "and I most earnestly wish he could participate in my joyful fate.' The child was immediately summoned, and condemned to the same punishment as his father. Their hands were severed from the wrist by a wooden saw, and the martyrs then placed on a bed of red hot coals, and finally cast into a caldron of boiling oil, where they gave up the ghost, while praising the goodness of God.

The martyrdom of St. Denis, first bishop of Paris, is also said to have occurred during this persecution This holy prelate, after establishing a flourishing church in Paris, labored, through the ministry of his disciples, to extend the faith into the neighboring provinces, with a zeal which merited for him the title of the apostle of Gaul. The detailed account of the lives of these apostolic men is not extant; but that they cultivated most successfully this barren field is shown by their heroic deaths, not hesitating to shed their blood to render it more fertile and productive of abundant fruit. God crowned the labors of their noble leader by a glorious martyrdom, of which, however, there is no record; it is only known, that, during a persecution which suddenly broke out, St. Denis, a priest named Rusticus, and the deacon Eleutherius, were seized by order of the president Fescennine, and, after generously confessing the faith, were scourged, tortured, and finally beheaded.

An old tradition, supported by the testimony of ancient monuments, relates that it was on a mountain near Paris that these servants of God were executed, called for this reason the Mount of Martyrs, or as it is styled at the present day — "Montmartre." The place where St. Denis was imprisoned is still shown in Paris, as also the spot where he was tortured; and two churches were subsequently erected in his honor. The president had commanded that the bodies of the martyrs should be thrown into the Seine; but a pagan lady, who was favorably disposed towards Christianity, bribed the men intrusted with this commission, and had the holy relics secretly buried.

TENTH AND LAST PERSECUTION UNDER DIOCLESIAN.

A. D. 303.

The Roman empire, which had for three centuries directed almost continual attacks against Christianity, made a last effort to destroy it; which, however, instead of overthrowing, served more completely to establish the religion of Jesus Christ. Dioclesian reigned at this period in the East, and Maximian in the West. The former published an edict in Nicomedia, in the year 303, ordering the churches to be destroyed, and the Holy Scriptures to be burned. This was only a prelude to the cruel laws which followed, and which caused rivers of blood to flow in all the provinces of the empire; for Maximian, his colleague, readily imitated an example so consonant with his ferocious disposition. He practiced the most unheard of cruelties towards the Christians, and employed tortures hitherto unknown.

In Mesopotamia, some of the faithful were suspended with the head downwards, and suffocated by a slow fire; in Syria they were roasted on gridirons; in the province of Pontus, sharp reeds were driven under their nails, and melted lead poured over their bodies; in Egypt, after being torn and lacerated with red hot pincers, they were flayed alive with pieces of broken iron; in Phrygia, a Christian city was surrounded by soldiers and destroyed by fire. Men, women and children perished in the flames, while fervently invoking the assistance of Jesus Christ. The historian Eusebius, an eye-witness of some of these barbarous scenes, says that the cruelties practiced against the servants of God during this horrible persecution surpassed all belief. "The whole earth," says Lactantius, "streamed with blood, from the East to the West."

The Church, however, was visibly sustained during

this terrible trial, and God bestowed His divine aid when every thing was looked upon as lost. The persecution commenced in the imperial palace. Several of the highest officers were Christians, and were commanded to sacrifice to the gods; but they preferred to lose the favor of the prince, be divested of their rank and endure the cruelest tortures, rather than fail in their fidelity to God.

One among them, named Peter, suffered, with an invincible constancy, the most excruciating torments, the recital of which would make us shudder. After stripping him of his garments, the executioners fastened him to a machine, which suddenly elevated him to a great height and then let him fall again on the pavement. Although his body was all crushed and mangled by this fall, they struck him with a heavy club, thus breaking all his bones; salt and vinegar were then poured into the deep, gaping wounds; but the agonizing pain which ensued did not for a moment shake his courage. He was then placed on a gridiron over a hot fire, and slowly roasted; in order to prolong this frightful torment, the fire was allowed to go out at intervals and was then rekindled. All this refinement of cruelty was in vain; the heroic martyr, who conquered physical pain and his inhuman enemies at the same time, expired on this dreadful bed without allowing the faintest sigh to escape his parched lips. What wonderful strength! What sublime constancy! Weak human nature could not display such supernatural fortitude, if not assisted by divine grace and miraculously sustained in the midst of a fiery furnace.

MARTYRDOM OF ST. QUINTIN.

Rictius Varus had been appointed prefect in Gaul by Maximian. Imitating the cruelty of his master, this man hurried from city to city, creating fear and terror wherever he went, and shedding Christian blood in all the places through which he passed. He proceeded to Amiens, where the holy teachings of the Gospel were proclaimed with zeal and success by St. Quintin. The holy apostle was arrested and summoned before the tribunal. On being asked his name, the Saint replied: "I am a Christian and am called Quintin." "Who are your parents?" said the prefect. "I am a Roman citizen, and son of the senator Zeno," answered the holy man. "How is it," asked the prefect, "that, being the son of so noble a parent, you have allowed yourself to become attached to such foolish superstitions?" "The most exalted nobility," said Quintin. "consists in knowing God, and in keeping His commandments. The Christian religion cannot be superstitious, since it is through its means that we obtain eternal happiness, and learn to know the one true God and His Son, Jesus Christ, the Creator of all things, and who in all things is equal to His Father." "If you do not sacrifice instantly," angrily exclaimed the prefect, "I swear by our gods, that I will condemn you to the most frightful tortures, and the most agonizing death." "And I," said the intrepid Saint, "swear by the Lord, my God, that I will not obey your impious commands. I no more fear your threats, than I dread the anger of your false gods."

He was immediately seized and cruelly scourged, then manacled and thrown into a narrow prison. An Angel visited him in his loathsome cell, and ordered him to go and instruct the people. Miraculously released from his fetters, the Saint left the dungeon without meeting the slightest obstacle, and hastened to the public square, where he began to preach to the populace. This wonderful miracle, and the sufferings he had endured for Jesus Christ, lent such power and unction to his words, that he converted nearly six hundred persons. Even his guards, eye witnesses to his supernatural deliverance, were convinced of the truth, and believed in Jesus Christ, who thus visibly protected His servant. St. Quintin was summoned a second time before the prefect, who endeavored to win him over by flattering promises, which proving as useless as his threats, the tyrant had recourse to new tortures, in order to overcome the constancy of the holy martyr. His body was stretched in so violent a manner, by means of pulleys, that all his limbs were dislocated, and his flesh torn with blows from a heavy iron chain. Boiling oil, pitch and melted grease were poured into the quivering wounds, and finally burning torches applied to the bleeding mass.

The cruelty of men has never been exercised with so much cunning and ingenuity as against the martyrs of Jesus Christ. The inhuman Varus, finding, that, notwithstanding these excruciating torments, Quintin did not cease praising the Lord, caused his mouth to be filled with lime and vinegar; then had him loaded with chains and led into the hospital of Vermandois. Providence, however, had destined the holy martyr to be the patron of this city which now bears his name. Varus here made a last effort to destroy this noble soul, but in vain. Perceiving that the Saint appeared to derive new strength from his torments, he openly vented his rage, by ordering him to be pierced with two rods of iron from the neck to the thighs. Sharp irons were then driven under his finger nails, and, as after this last torture the Saint still breathed, he was condemned to be beheaded.

Having been carried to the place of execution, Quintin requested a few moments of time for prayer. On finishing his petition to the throne of grace, he turned towards his executioners and said: "I am now ready; perform your duty." He was immediately beheaded, and his head and body thrown into the river Somme, but God did not allow the blessed remains of so illustrious a martyr to be lost to the Church; a Christian lady, named Eusebia, found the body and interred it with respect. This account of the martyrdom of St. Quintin was written by an eye witness.

MARTYRDOM OF THE THEBAN LEGION.

Maximian proceeded to Gaul, in order to repress a faction which had sprung up in that portion of the Roman Empire. As he thought it was necessary to re-enforce his army, the Theban legion was summoned from the East. This legion was entirely composed of Christians, whose faith inspired them with the most ardent and daring courage. These generous soldiers were commanded by an officer named Maurice, and the next in authority were Exuperus and Candidus. Before crossing the Alps they joined the body of the army and sojourned for a short time at Octodurum, called at the present day Martigny in Valois.

Maximian, who was more bent on exterminating the Christians than crushing the enemies of the State, commanded the Theban legion to persecute the faithful, or as other accounts relate, wished to compel them to participate in the solemn sacrifices he offered to his gods on entering Gaul. These brave soldiers replied, that they had come to oppose the enemies of the State, and not to dip their hands in their brothers' blood or sully them by a false worship. Maximian was so enraged at this response, that he immediately ordered every tenth soldier of the legion to be punished by death. Those on whom the lot fell, suffered their throats to be cut without offering the slightest resistance. This horrible slaughter did not terrify their comrades, but only augmented their desire to share the same glorious fate, and caused them to loudly proclaim their utter detestation of the pagan divinities. On being informed of this noble declaration, Maximian commanded the legion to draw lots a second time; when urged to obey the orders of the tyrant, these fervent champions of Jesus Christ presented the following address:

"We are your soldiers, O, powerful prince, but we are also the servants of God; we owe you our services on the field of battle, but must render homage to God, by the innocence and purity of our lives; we receive pay from you, but He has created and preserved us; we cannot obey you, our earthly monarch, by renouncing our Omnipotent Lord and Master; we are willing to execute your commands in every thing that does not offend Jesus Christ; but, if we are forced to choose between disobeying God or man, we prefer to obey God. Lead us to battle; we are ready to combat the enemy, but cannot shed the blood of our innocent brethren. We pledged ourselves to God, before swearing allegiance to you; how then could you rely on our fidelity, if we fail in our inviolable promise to the God of truth. If you seek to destroy Christians, put us to death; we believe in one God — Creator of the Universe, and in Jesus Christ, His Son; we are prepared to suffer the same punishment as our companions, whose fate we envy. Do not fear a revolt; Christians know how to die but not to rebel; we have arms, but we will not use them against our prince, desiring rather to suffer an innocent death, than to live a guilty life."

So noble and prudent a remonstrance only inflamed the rage of the tyrant, and in despair of overcoming Christian heroism, he resolved to massacre the entire legion. The gallant band was surrounded by the whole army, and its generous members condemned to pass successively under the blade of the sword; these courageous warriors threw down their weapons, cast off their breast-plates, and presented their bare necks to the executioners.

Neither groans nor lamentations were heard, but they exhorted and encouraged each other to suffer for Jesus Christ. In a short time the ground was strewn with the mangled bodies, and dyed with the sacred blood of more than six thousand victims.

What a beautiful spectacle is presented to our contemplation, in beholding a whole legion of armed soldiers animated by such a holy, sublime, and extraordinary spirit, which led them to execution with unfaltering steps, and obtained for them the glorious title of soldiers of the Cross! Does not a religion which is capable of forming such perfect men, bear on her brow the evident marks of a divine origin? The grace of God can alone inspire such heroism, and such great prudence, which knew how to perform every duty; to remain faithful to God, and, at the same time, not to oppose their earthly ruler, even when he proved himself a most unjust and cruel prince.

MARTYRDOM OF ST. VICTOR OF MARSEILLES.

A short time after the massacre of the Theban legion, St. Victor of Marseilles, rendered a most glorious testimony to Jesus Christ. He was in the army, and belonged to a distinguished family; he was noted also for his gallantry and bravery, and especially for his steadfastness in the faith. The Emperor Maximian had directed his march towards Marseilles, and the rumor of his approach caused the persecution to rage with ten-fold violence. Victor endeavored to encourage and re-assure the faithful; he visited the soldiers constantly, exhorting them to behave on this occasion like true warriors of Jesus Christ, and to despise the pains of a death which conducted their souls to the eternal joys of Paradise. He was arrested while thus laboring for the salvation of his brethren, and carried before the tribunal of prefects; but as he was of noble rank, it was thought advisable to refer the judgment of his case to the Emperor.

On the arrival of Maximian, Victor was summoned before him; promises and threats were vainly tried, to induce him to sacrifice to the gods; but the holy martyr confounded the tyrant and his officers, by demonstrating to them the divinity of Jesus Christ, and the folly of worshipping idols. Then the Emperor, thinking that a soldier would be more susceptible to disgrace than to pain, condemned him to be dragged through the streets, bound hand and foot. After this first punishment, the holy martyr was conducted, all covered with blood, to the tribunal of prefects. These men, supposing him vanquished by all that he had endured, urged him to sacrifice to the gods of the empire, but he replied with a noble courage, that he had not been guilty of any offense against the State or the Emperor, and would never consent to adore the pagan deities, whose abominations he openly proclaimed. He was then fastened to a wooden horse, and most cruelly tortured for a long time; while undergoing this dreadful agony, the Saint raised his eyes to Heaven, and supplicated Almighty God for patience, constancy and fortitude.

Jesus Christ appeared to him holding His Cross, and said to him: "Peace be with thee, I am the Jesus who suffers in the persons of my Saints; take courage, my son, I will sustain thee in the combat, and will reward thee with a bright crown of everlasting glory after thou hast achieved a victory over the powers of the world, the flesh, and the devil." These consoling words reanimated Victor, and rendered him insensible to physical pain. As nothing was gained by torturing him, he was reconducted to prison. God visited his servant in his gloomy dungeon, and during the night his cell was filled with a shining light; three of his guards, on beholding this celestial radiance, cast themselves at the feet of the Saint and entreated him to baptize them.

On learning of the conversion of his soldiers, Maximian ordered them to be put to death, if they did not abjure the faith; all, however, courageously confessed Jesus Christ, and were beheaded. The Emperor then commanded Victor to appear before him; and after applying new tortures exhorted him to offer incense before an altar which had been erected, promising to restore him his liberty and rank if he would obey. Victor approached, as if about to sacrifice, and kicked the altar over with one of his feet; the infuriated tyrant ordered the foot to be immediately cut off, and sentenced the Saint to be crushed under the grindstone of a mill; this cruel order was executed at once, but Victor still breathed when the machine broke and released its victim. He was finally beheaded, and a voice from Heaven was heard saying: "Thou hast conquered; Victor, thou hast conquered." Maximian commanded the bodies of the martyrs to be cast into the sea, but the waves threw the sacred remains on the shore and they were buried by some of the faithful in a cave, where God wrought a great number of miracles.

MARTYRDOM OF ST. VINCENT OF SARAGOSSA.

A. D. 304.

During this same persecution, Spain also testified her adherence to the faith, and produced a great many martyrs; the most illustrious of whom was St. Vincent, of Saragossa, a deacon of the Church. Dacian, at that time the governor, was the most inhuman enemy of Christianity. He caused Vincent to be arrested, and thrown into a dark prison, where he was left almost entirely without food of any kind, in order to diminish his courage, and weaken his body by the pangs of hunger. Finding that he remained immovable, Dacian summoned him once more to his presence, and tempted him with the fairest promises; but failing to make the slightest impression on the saint, he threatened him with excruciating tortures if he refused to worship the idols. The holy deacon, however, remained indifferent either to smiles or frowns, declaring that he was a Christian, and ready to suffer everything for the one true God. He was then fastened to a wooden horse, which was stretched with so much violence as to dislocate his bones, and almost tear limb from limb. While in this horrible state, his sides were lacerated with iron claws, in such a manner, that the entrails were visible.

In the midst of these agonizing sufferings, the holy martyr testified the greatest joy. His unalterable patience and serene countenance enraged the judge, who ordered the executioners themselves to be seized and beaten, in order to make them redouble their cruel efforts. They commenced anew, therefore, to torture the holy martyr, and expended so much strength on their victim, as to be forced to desist through weariness. The magistrate himself, seeing that the blood flowing from every part, and the frightful condition of the martyr, made no change in the constancy of Vincent, was overcome with astonishment, and secretly acknowledged himself conquered by this true and invincible soldier of Jesus Christ. He then essayed other means to accomplish his designs. "Have pity on yourself," he said mildly to the holy deacon; "sacrifice to the gods, or at least, deliver the writings of the Christians to me!" Vincent replied that he dreaded tortures infinitely less than a false compassion.

Dacian, more furious than ever, had the martyr stretched on a bed of iron, the bars of which were furnished with sharp points, and then placed on a red hot furnace; heated plates were applied to all portions of the body that did not touch this painful couch; salt was thrown into the agonizing wounds, the particles of which penetrated into the quivering flesh. During this horrible punishment, Vincent remained immovable, his eyes raised towards Heaven, as if already beholding the glorious reward that awaited him in the abode of the blessed. Dacian, wholly disconcerted, was at a loss what course to pursue, and sent him back to prison, with orders to lay him on pieces of broken earthenware, and to place his feet in the stocks, and distend his aching limbs with the utmost violence. But God did not desert His servant, bright angels descended from Heaven and comforted this heroic soul, and the holy martyrs united their voices with his in praising the goodness and mercy of a God, who had sustained them through similar combats.

The jailer heard the celestial music, and was immediately converted, while Dacian wept with rage when informed of what had happened, and in order to deprive the holy martyr of the glory of dying during the torture, he commanded him to be placed on a soft bed. Then this generous champion, whom the iron claws and fiery furnace had been unable to conquer, was much distressed at this alleviation of his sufferings, which retarded his eternal happiness, and, earnestly entreating the Lord to bestow upon him the crown promised to those who persevere to the end, he yielded up the ghost.

Never had the triumph of Jesus Christ over the demon been more manifest; every species of torture was vainly exhausted on this admirable martyr, but God inspired His servant with a courage far exceeding the most frightful sufferings, and forced the inhuman tyrant to confess himself vanquished by an humble Christian. No effort of man or Satan can oppose the almighty power of the Lord Jesus Christ.

REFLECTIONS ON THE PERSECUTIONS.

In order to demonstrate the divine origin of the Church, God has ordained that she should establish herself, notwithstanding the opposition of the world, the flesh, and the devil; and that the blood of her martyrs should fertilize her soil. He had, Himself, predicted to His disciples, that they would be persecuted, dragged before kings and magistrates, maltreated and put to death for His sake, but He at the same time promised to overthrow all the efforts of their enemies. "Be not afraid of those who kill the body; not a hair of your head can fall without the permission of your Heavenly Father. By patience you will possess your soul in peace, and I will be your helper; I will give you courage and strength to overcome your enemies; I have overcome the world, and so shall you likewise."

In truth, since the foundation of Christianity, all the powers of the earth have risen up against it; the senses, the passions, human interest were in favor of idolatry; pleasure, amusements, games, spectacles, and licentiousness composed the pagan religion, and were a part of the divine worship; their feasts were scenes of debauchery, and all the laws of virtue and decency were violated in their ceremonies and mysteries. The Christian faith, chaste and severe, the enemy of the senses, and only attached to invisible gods, could not please the corrupt minds of the pagans; and the followers of the God-man, who refused to participate in their abominable festivities, naturally incurred the hatred of their base natures.

To the motives above mentioned were united the interests of the State, as the Roman government considered its gods as the powerful protectors of the public good, and, consequently, feared the slightest innovation in their form of worship.

Rome boasted of being a holy city from her very foundation, consecrated from the beginning under divine auspices, and dedicated by her founder to the god of war. She believed herself indebted to her religion for her victories, and through its means she imagined she had conquered nations and extended her empire over nearly the whole of the known world. Not to acknowledge her gods was to attack the very basis of the empire, and despise the virtue and power of the Roman arms. Thus the Christians, enemies of her gods, were regarded at the same time as enemies of the republic; and the Emperors were more earnestly bent on their extermination than on subduing the Parthians, Sarmatians and Dacians.

From the reign of Nero, the Christians were continually persecuted by the good as well as bad Emperors. These persecutions were sometimes commenced by the command of an Emperor, or by the private hatred of the magistrates; sometimes the decree of the senate, or the rage of the populace, which was excited by the calumnies proclaimed against the servants of Jesus Christ. Occasionally the persecutions were abated for a short time, but the public hatred soon prevailed, the fury of the pagans was redoubled, and the whole empire streamed with the innocent blood of thousands of Christians of every age and sex. When sanctioned by the authorities the persecution became more violent and general; and church historians count ten frightful persecutions under the approbation of as many Emperors. The martyrs were innumerable, and are computed at several millions. The idolatrous princes hoped to annihilate by this wholesale carnage a religion which they hated; but the Church of God received additional strength, and augmented the number of its followers in the midst of consuming flames and excruciating tortures. The most dreadful torments were employed in vain; claws of iron, wheels armed with sharp blades, red-hot gridirons, the stake, wild beasts, and a thousand other cruelties were daily suffered by the Christians with admirable courage.

The more violent the persecutions, the more victims presented themselves; the blood of the martyrs proving a prolific seed, which produced most abundant fruit, and continually supplied the persecutors with new objects, on which to vent their diabolical rage. The meek followers of the Lamb, only opposed patience to the fury of the tyrants, and according to the promise of their divine Master, this patience enabled them to triumph over all the efforts of their enemies. They never offered the slightest resistance, and during centuries of persecution the Church has never wavered for a moment, nor has one of her children proved himself unworthy of the glorious title of soldier of the Cross. We see the church as submissive under Dioclesian, when she was spread over the whole world, as under Nero, when she was struggling into existence. "Suffer every thing for the truth," was the motto of the faithful, and they hastened to the place of execution with more eagerness, than did the pagans to their bacchanals. Infirm old men, delicate virgins, and weak children, braved the tortures, joyously ascended the scaffold, allowed themselves to be bound to the stake, and fearlessly confessed Jesus Christ, enduring without a groan the most frightful torments.

The sword often fell from the hand of the executioners, who, suddenly converted by such heroic examples, presented themselves in their turn to the judges, and were condemned to the same punishment they had inflicted on others. The vanquished tyrant was often obliged to abate the persecution, for fear of depopulating the empire. How manifest is the hand of God! The pagans themselves, astonished at the constancy and miraculous endurance of the martyrs, acknowledged them to be sustained by a divine power, and frequently the crowded theatre resounded with the cries of the people: "The God of the Christians is great! how mighty is the God of the Christians!"

Surely we cannot contemplate the continuance, extent, and cruelty of the carnage which laid waste the infant church, without recognizing the extraordinary virtue, indomitable courage, and supernatural endurance of the martyrs as the work of God. If there are a few examples of fanatical men, who have sacrificed their lives in defense of error, it should be remembered that it was merely for the sake of an opinion, and not through a divine motive; whereas, the martyrs shed their blood in testimony of well substantiated and immutable facts. The appearance of truth sometimes deceives; but falsehood rarely prevails for any great period of time; men are not willing to be put to death, in order to support doubtful facts. The martyrs suffered cheerfully for a cause which visibly bore the impress of truth itself. We must, therefore, conclude, that the many vain attempts of the whole Roman empire to exterminate the Christians, that is to say, men who were ready to suffer and die for their religion, demonstrates that this religion is the work of God, and that men could not have established what men could not destroy.

The Catholic Church exists, then, not only without support, but even in spite of the opposition of the powers of the world. She remains immovable; never changing her hierarchy, her laws, or her spiritual authority, but maintaining the same doctrine, pure and uncorrupted as she received it from her divine Founder. This extraordinary perpetuity and wonderful courage in the midst of violent assaults could only be the work of God. According to the promise of Jesus Christ, the Church, His Spouse, will exist until the consummation of time; unshaken by the tempest of persecution; uninjured by the waves of time, and unsullied by the designs of men. She stands like a lily in the midst of thorns, pure and immaculate; always One, Holy and Apostolic, and visibly sustained by the all powerful hand of God.

CONSTANTIUS CHLORUS PROTECTS THE CHRISTIANS.

A. D. 305.

At the height of the most violent and wide-spread persecution to which the Church had yet been exposed, God, whose command stills the fury of the tempest, put a stop also to the authority of the two tyrants Dioclesian and Maximian, who were compelled to abdicate the imperial throne in favor of Constantius Chlorus and Galerius, who were next in rank and bore the title of Cæsars. Galerius was of obscure and poor parentage, and his inclinations and tastes were of the lowest order; he continued the persecution in the East. Constantius Chlorus, on the contrary, merited equally the eulogies of the Christians and pagans; full of goodness and clemency, his glory consisted in rendering his subjects happy and gaining their love and affection; he esteemed and protected the Christians because he loved virtue.

A remarkable fact is related, which is no less honorable to him than to religion. When he filled the office of Cæsar there were a great number of Christians in his palace and among the officers attached to his person. After the edict of Dioclesian against the Christians was published, Constantius Chlorus assembled all the Christian officers, notified them of the commands of the Emperor, and ordered them to sacrifice to the idols or resign their positions in the imperial household. This command, on the part of a prince who had always been favorably inclined towards religion, excited the utmost consternation among the Christians; but the greater number protested that they preferred sacrificing their fortunes and their lives rather than dishonor the faith. A few, however, who, like true courtiers, were completely swayed by the will of their sovereign, consented to offer incense to the pagan divinities, in order to retain the royal favor and their positions in the palace. Then Constantius declared his true sentiments, loudly praising the courageous firmness of the former, and severely censuring the criminal sycophancy of the latter. "How," said he to the latter, "will you be faithful to the Emperor when you are treacherous and perfidious to your God?" and they were dismissed from the palace as unworthy of remaining in his service. Those, however, who had so generously preferred to renounce wealth and dignities, rather than deny their Lord and Master, were regarded as true and faithful servants. They retained their offices and enjoyed the affection and confidence of Constantius, who declared that subjects with such principles were the most precious treasures of the empire.

So noble a prince could not persecute the Christians, and religion was protected during the whole of his reign as Emperor. The faithful in Gaul, who were under his dominion, soon repaired the losses they had suffered under the cruel Maximian. When peace was once more restored to the church, the Gospel spread rapidly throughout all the provinces, and the harvest was most abundant, in a field which had been rendered fruitful by the sacred blood of innumerable martyrs. The ranks of the priesthood, which had been decimated by the sword of the persecutors, were soon filled with zealous pastors, but this was only the glimmering of the dawn of peace, which was to shine upon the afflicted Church; it was, however, reserved for the son of Constantius Chlorus to become the champion of the faith, and he it was who caused it to triumph over the pride of the Cæsars. Although favorably disposed towards Christianity, Constantius had not the courage to become a Christian; and God, in establishing the power of his family, rewarded him on earth for his moral virtues, but which, without faith, are worthless in the sight of Heaven.

CONVERSION OF CONSTANTINE.
A. D. 312.

When God had plainly manifested His protecting hand in the establishment of His Church, and shown that all the powers of earth could not destroy the sacred fabric, He at length admitted Emperors into His fold; and the great Constantine became the declared protector of religion. That prince was the son of Constantius Chlorus, and united in his person the most eminent qualities; a brilliant intellect, tempered by a rare wisdom, was still more enhanced by a splendid form and noble countenance. The Emperor Galerius, who hated him, endeavored on several occasions to destroy him; but God, who had special designs in his regard, always delivered him from the snares of his enemy.

After the death of his father, Constantine was declared Emperor, at the age of thirty-one. His right to this dignity was disputed by Maxentius, son of the Emperor Maximian; they had several encounters in which Maxentius gained the advantage, and, finally, Constantine resolved to have a decisive battle. With this intention he led his army into Italy, and advanced towards Rome. As the troops of Maxentius far exceeded his forces in number, Constantine felt that he had need of extraordinary succor, and he determined to solicit the protection of the God of the Christians. He prayed most earnestly that God would make Himself known to him, and his petition was immediately answered. About the hour of noon, on a calm, serene day, when marching at the head of his men, he perceived in the heavens a brilliant cross, on which were traced in luminous characters these words: "By this sign thou shalt conquer." The entire army beheld this prodigy, but no one was more sensibly struck by it than the prince, and he spent the remainder of the day in trying to decipher the signification of this wonder.

The following night during his sleep, Jesus Christ appeared to him, bearing the same sign, and commanded him to have a banner made according to this model, to be carried in battle as a safeguard against his enemies. In the morning the Emperor sent for workmen, and drew the design of the standard he desired them to make. It was a species of pike, plated with gold, with extended poles in the form of a cross, from which hung a veil of golden tissue. The cross was surmounted by a crown, enriched with jewels. The letters "J. C.," incrusted with precious stones, forming the center, and beneath the veil appeared the portraits of the Emperor and his children. This banner was called the "Labarum," and Constantine chose fifty of the bravest and most pious of his guards to carry it in succession. Encouraged by this celestial vision, he no longer hesitated to commence the combat. A bloody battle ensued, in which Maxentius was conquered, and, while endeavoring to escape, his whole army was driven into the Tiber. Rome immediately threw open her gates to the victorious Constantine, who entered the city in triumph, and, soon after his arrival, he was instructed at his own request in the truths of Christianity, and made a public profession of faith.

No historical fact is more clearly attested than this miraculous event, related by the historian Eusebius of Cesarea, and confirmed by a vast number of writers, and monuments erected in commemoration of the extraordinary occurrence. "If the great Constantine had not himself related the fact," says the historian Eusebius, "we might doubt its truth; but, having heard the account from his own lips, which account he affirmed by oath, there can be no question as to its truth, especially as the result justified the promise." These are the words of a writer who was a cotemporary of Constantine, and whose narration, if false, could have been contradicted by the many eye witnesses of the miracle.

TRIUMPH OF CHRISTIANITY.

Constantine, after the defeat of Maxentius, returned thanks to Jesus Christ, the God of battles, for having crowned his arms with victory; and he used every means to establish the true faith, throughout the whole extent of his empire. As he understood the spirit of Christianity, which only employs instruction and persuasion in order to gain disciples, he was careful not to excite opposition by any severe measures.

Although hating idolatry, he, nevertheless, allowed his subjects entire liberty in religious matters; a sudden suppression of paganism, which had been the only form of worship for so many centuries, would have caused a general revolution throughout the empire; and he believed it sufficient to protect Christianity, and place the Church in a position to overthrow her adversaries by the wisdom of her dogmas, and the purity of her morals. Mild and temperate means were, therefore, used to win the pagans to a renunciation of their false gods, and this moderation converted a great number. He commenced by repairing all the evils that had been perpetrated by the preceding Emperors; recalling those in exile, and restoring to the Christians all their places of worship which had been seized by the persecutors; full of zeal for the glory of God, he enriched the churches with precious vases and magnificent ornaments, and caused the religious services to be celebrated with great splendor and pomp.

This truly Christian prince paid every honor to the priests and prelates, and conferred many privileges upon the ministry. The bishop of Rome, who had been persecuted in a special manner, attracted the attention of Constantine; he presented him with the Lateran palace, and an adjacent palace he converted into a basilica, under the name of Constantine, known now as the Church of St. John of Lateran, and this was the first patrimony of the popes. The Christians rejoiced in being delivered from the persecutions they had endured during three centuries; and beheld with astonishment and thankfulness the miracles wrought in their behalf. A Christian prince on the throne of the Cæsars, the worship of the true God honored and reverenced, the exiles recalled to their native land, and churches rebuilt and decorated with magnificence. A change so little anticipated inspired sentiments of the purest joy, and excited the sweetest hopes for the future.

The Christian religion was venerated by even pagans when they beheld the great Constantine publicly practicing all its duties. In the imperial palace an oratory had been arranged, where the Emperor was accustomed to repair at certain hours for prayer, meditation, and for the reading of the holy Scriptures. This pious example converted a number of idolaters to Christianity. The true faith penetrated even into the Roman senate, which was considered the strongest bulwark of paganism. Anicius, an illustrious senator, was the first who embraced Christianity, and in a short time the most distinguished men in Rome humbly bowed their proud heads to the yoke of the Gospel. Constantine experienced the greatest joy at these conversions, and was more gratified at winning one single soul to the fold of Jesus Christ than at hearing of the conquest of a province. His zeal extended beyond the limits of the Roman empire; and he sent missionaries among the barbarous nations who were not under his dominion, as he was desirous that the saving light of the Gospel should awaken these heathen people from the dark slumber of idolatry into which they were plunged.

At his entrance into Rome he desired that the Cross, which had been the token of his victory, should also be the most conspicuous ornament of his triumph; and the statue, which was erected in his honor, represented him as holding in his hand this blessed sign of redemption. Thus the Cross, which had been an object of ignominy and the punishment of slaves, became a glorious sign of salvation to the Cæsars, who adorned their imperial diadems with this symbol and placed it on the dome of the capitol, as if to announce to the whole world the triumph of a Crucified God over paganism.

FINDING OF THE HOLY CROSS.

The most striking proof Constantine gave of his respect for Christianity was his veneration for the sacred places consecrated by the visible presence of Jesus Christ. He proposed building a magnificent church in Jerusalem, and St. Helena, his mother, entertaining, like her son, a great devotion for the Holy Land, went to Palestine, although then in her eightieth year. On arriving in Jerusalem she felt animated with an ardent desire to discover the Cross upon which our divine Saviour had suffered for mankind. This was a very difficult undertaking, as the pagans, wishing to abolish the memory of the resurrection of Jesus Christ, had raised a great mound of earth before the entrance of the sepulchre, which served as the foundation of a temple of Venus, which they had erected on this site, in order to prevent the Christians from visiting this sacred spot.

No human obstacle, however, could deter the pious princess, and she conferred with the patriarch of Jerusalem, who assured her if she could discover the holy sepulchre she would certainly find the instruments of the Passion; as it was customary among the Jews to inter with the body all the implements of torture used at the execution of a criminal.

The Empress immediately ordered the idolatrous temple to be razed to the ground and the earth cleared away; the workmen were soon amply rewarded for their labors, by discovering the entrance to the grotto of the Holy Sepulchre. Near the tomb were three crosses; and the inscription, I. N. R. I., was found at a little distance detached from the cross on which Jesus Christ had suffered death, and the cruel nails that had pierced His sacred flesh lay beside it. The identification of the true cross was now the only difficulty; but a lively faith can remove the most insurmountable obstacles. St. Helena, by the advice of

St. Macarius, bishop of Jerusalem, had the crosses carried to the house of a sick woman who had been afflicted for a long time with an incurable malady, and each of the crosses was applied to her, while fervent prayers were offered to Jesus Christ that He would make known the one which He had consecrated by the effusion of His sacred blood. The two first crosses effected nothing; but, when the third was brought, the sick woman rose from her bed, instantly and completely cured.

The historian Sozomen also asserts that, on its being applied to a corpse, the body was immediately resuscitated; and St. Paulinus relates a similar miracle. The pious princess was transported with joy at witnessing the proof of the sacred properties of the true cross, and at finding herself in possession of a treasure she valued more than all the wealth of the Roman empire. She reserved a piece of the true cross for her son, and, having inclosed the rest in a silver casket, placed it in the hands of the bishop of Jerusalem, to be deposited in the church which Constantine had commanded to be erected over the Holy Sepulchre. This edifice was constructed on a scale of magnificence worthy of the sanctity of its foundation, embracing the Holy Sepulchre in its inclosure, and extending as far as Mount Calvary.

St. Helena also built two other churches: one on the spot where our Saviour ascended into Heaven, and the other at Bethlehem, the place of His birth. Her piety was not confined to the erection of splendid temples in honor of the crucified Jesus, but was manifested, in all the cities through which she passed, by munificent acts of charity. She comforted widows, orphans and the poor, by distributing abundant alms among them; and having a particular affection for virgins consecrated to the service of God, she invited all those who were in Jerusalem to a banquet, at which she herself served the guests. She did not long survive her journey to Jerusalem, but terminated her virtuous and saintly career in the arms of Constantine. God had been pleased to call her son first to the knowledge of the true faith. His example induced St. Helena to embrace Christianity; and it was through her labors and zeal that the Church recovered the very wood upon which a God-man expired for the redemption of His ungrateful creatures.

ORIGIN OF THE HERMITS—ST. ANTHONY.
A. D. 306.

When the persecutions ceased, the Church presented to the world a new spectacle, as edifying as the one she exhibited in the sufferings of her martyrs. We behold at this period, arid and barren deserts inhabited by saintly hermits, who led the most angelic lives. In former ages there had been fervent Christians called Ascetics, who, renouncing the world, applied themselves exclusively to prayer and works of mortification, living in perfect solitude in the neighborhood of cities and towns. At the time of which we speak, however, all these holy solitaries met together and formed themselves into communities.

St. Anthony, the founder of this new institution,

was born in Egypt, of rich, noble and virtuous parents, who brought up their son in the most Christian manner, and carefully guarded him from the dangers that beset youth; but he was so unfortunate as to lose his estimable parents at an early age. Having heard one day during divine service these words of the Gospel, "If thou wilt be perfect, go sell what thou hast; and give it to the poor, and thou shalt have treasures in Heaven," he applied them to himself, and returning home, sold all his possessions and distributed the proceeds to the poor; then returning into his solitude, he was only occupied with the affairs of salvation. Being animated by a spirit of pious emulation, he went in search of the most fervent servants of God, in order to derive some spiritual benefit from their teachings and example.

Pursuing this exemplary mode of life, Anthony soon became an accomplished model of every virtue. The arch-enemy of mankind, enraged at foreseeing the glorious termination of so happy a beginning, had recourse to all kinds of temptations, with the design of overcoming the Saint. The young hermit, however, was victorious over all the assaults of Satan by means of prayer and mortification. His bed consisted of a straw mat, but he frequently slept on the bare ground; and after sunset took his only meal, composed of a little bread and salt; water was his only beverage, and he wore a garment made of sackcloth, a mantle of sheep-skin and a cowl over his head. As he was destined to be the founder of the hermits, he retired into the most complete solitude, crossing over the Nile and penetrating as far as Thebes.

After a long period of separation from all human intercourse, God, who wished to proclaim the virtues of His servant, bestowed upon Anthony the gift of miracles. The cures he effected soon attracted a crowd of disciples, who begged to remain under his holy guidance; and accordingly a great number of monasteries were built to receive them. Anthony instructed his followers both privately and publicly, and made rules for the regulation of their lives. "May the remembrance of eternity," said he to them, "never leave your minds; think every morning that perhaps you may not survive until evening, and each night that you may not see the morrow. Perform every action as though it were to be your last; be always on your guard against temptations, and courageously resist all assaults of the devil, who is very easily conquered when we know how to disarm him. He dreads fasting, prayer, humility, and all good works, the blessed sign of the cross will immediately dispel all his wicked suggestions and illusions. Yes, this sacred sign of the Saviour, who has deprived him of his dominion over the world, is sufficient to make him tremble in the very depths of hell."

Sanctified by his admirable example and holy precepts, the disciples of St. Anthony attained so high a degree of perfection as to become objects of admiration to the great St. Athanasius. "Their monasteries," he writes, "resemble so many temples, where they pass their lives in chanting psalms, reading, praying, fasting and watching; placing all their hopes in a life to come. United by perfect charity, they labor less for their own maintenance than for the benefit of the poor. Their communities are like a vast country, which is entirely separated from the rest of the world, and whose happy inhabitants are only solicitous about the affairs of heaven."

ST. HILARION ESTABLISHES MONASTERIES IN PALESTINE.

A. D. 327.

That which St. Anthony accomplished in Egypt was imitated by his disciple, St. Hilarion, in Palestine and Syria, he being the first who established monasteries and introduced the austere life of the hermits in these countries. The parents of Hilarion were idolaters, but as God had special designs with regard to their son, he embraced Christianity when only twelve years of age. He was sent from the town of Tabbath, his birthplace, to study in the celebrated schools of Alexandria, where, beside acquiring the natural sciences, he attained the priceless knowledge of God and His holy Church; and, in order to become more perfect, this fervent Christian went in search of St. Anthony, with whom he lived for some time, conforming to the ascetic life of the holy solitary by frequent prayer, profound humility, perseverance in daily toil, and in the practice of all kinds of austerities.

On leaving this excellent school of virtue, he, together with some monks, returned to his country, with the intention of continuing the same solitary and mortified life. His parents having died during his absence, he distributed all his possessions to the

ST. HILARION ESTABLISHES MONASTERIES. 167

poor, and retired with his companions into the desert, which, beginning at the city of Gaza, extended as far as the sea-shore. This wilderness was infested with robbers, who plundered unwary travelers, or despoiled shipwrecked mariners of what little they had saved from their vessels. Shortly after St. Hilarion had taken up his abode in this desolate region, several of these brigands entered his cell. He met them so calmly that the ruffians were completely abashed. "I see you do not fear us," said one of the band. "Why should I fear you?" answered Hilarion, "since I have no possessions?" "We can take your life, if we please," said the man. "When one is detached from all the things of earth," answered the youthful Hilarion, "he does not regret leaving a wicked world."

In truth, all that belonged to the hermit, was a sack and a tunic of sheep skin, given him by St. Anthony; his bed consisted merely of a rush mat, and his cell was so small he could hardly stand upright in it, which made it look much more like a sepulchre than the home of a human being. Six ounces of bread and a few dried herbs was his daily allowance, but notwithstanding his austere and mortified life, he attained the advanced age of eighty years. His occupation was tilling the ground and weaving rush baskets, and, while working, he meditated on the Holy Scriptures, which he had learned by heart. In order to manifest the sanctity of His servant, God bestowed upon him the gift of working miracles, and the wonderful cures he effected attracted such a number of disciples, that Palestine was soon filled with monasteries.

When Hilarion visited the hermits under his guidance, they assembled around their master to the number of three thousand. Several cities were reclaimed from idolatry and converted to Christianity through his labors and zeal; but as his solitude was disturbed by frequent visitors, and his humility wounded by the marks of respect paid to his many virtues, he complained of these distractions, saying: "Alas! I, who have renounced the world, am receiving my reward in this life." He was desirous of retiring into some remote region; but the news of his intended departure having spread abroad, all Palestine was filled with as much grief and consternation as if a national misfortune was about to befall the country. He was followed by crowds who reverenced him as being a man of God, who had the power of curing the sick, casting out devils, and obtaining the conversion of souls through his intercession.

When healing the sick he always added a pious exhortation, and endeavored to impress the afflicted person with the magnitude and danger of the maladies of the soul; showing how much more they were to be dreaded than the most painful corporeal diseases. Although his whole life had been a series of penances and mortifications, and adorned with every good work, the fear of the terrible judgment seized him at his last hour, and he strove to recover confidence in the mercy of God by uttering these words: "Arise, my soul, arise! Wherefore this uneasiness and dread? Thou hast had the happiness of serving Jesus Christ for eighty long years, and still thou fearest death!"

LIFE OF THE HERMITS.

The attainment of Christian perfection was the object of all the desires and actions of the holy solitaries, by the practice of the evangelical counsels of perpetual chastity and voluntary poverty. They employed four principal means to accomplish this end — solitude, labor, fasting, and prayer — and they renounced the world and retired into vast deserts. These deserts were not large forests, nor wildernesses which could be cultivated, but arid and uninhabitable plains, barren mountains, and frightful precipices. The hermits built their miserable huts of wood or reeds, near the few springs which were occasionally found in these desolate regions. In complete solitude, entirely separated from the world, these holy recluses strove to acquire that purity of heart which merits admission into the presence of God. They endeavored to avoid the least sin, and applied themselves to the zealous practice of every virtue, combatting avarice by poverty, and by the determination to possess every thing in common.

Indolence was conquered by perpetual labor, which did not however disturb their pious meditations on the great truths of religion. Their occupation of weaving mats and baskets of rushes, possessed the double advantage of enabling them to avoid idleness, and of securing for them a livelihood. As their expenses were few, they gave abundant alms, and always distributed to the poor a part of the proceeds of their daily labor. These holy solitaries fasted every day in the year except Sundays, and during the paschal season; their food consisting of bread, and water from the springs. The quantity of bread allowed was regulated by a Roman measure, and they made but two meals, one in the morning and the other after sunset; confining themselves to this small amount of nourishment, after finding by experience that it was sufficient to sustain life, and render them capable of a great deal of hard labor. In truth this austere and frugal diet prolonged their lives, and preserved their health, as they generally attained advanced ages and were seldom ill.

St. Anthony, the founder of the hermits, was over one hundred years old when he died. The hours for prayer were regulated with the same wisdom; they assembled together twice during the day; when they recited twelve psalms, intermixed with short prayers, and terminating with two lessons from the Bible. The brothers each chanted a psalm in succession, standing in the middle of the assembly, all the rest being seated in profound silence. The remainder of the day was passed in prayer and labor in the solitude of their own huts, where they meditated on the truths of religion, and on the precepts of the Gospel. Implicit obedience was the remedy they opposed to pride, which is so strong in the hearts of men, but so unworthy the character of a Christian; they were as submissive as little children to their superiors, although large communities were often under the sole guidance of one Abbot, for these monasteries soon became very numerous, and an austere and self-denying life was embraced by a great many of the faithful.

The deserts were filled with holy penitents, who mortified their bodies, and punished the wicked inclinations of human nature, by depriving themselves of whatever is agreeable to the senses. These sacred retreats became so crowded, that those who aimed at a very high degree of perfection were obliged to seek some more retired place, so attractive was a contemplative and solitary life to these fervent Christians. Such were the fruits of virtue produced by the teachings of the Gospel, the hitherto persecuted Church becoming rich in the sanctity of her saints, thus plainly demonstrating the holiness of her doctrines.

THE ARIAN HERESY.
A. D. 319.

"Hell," says St. Cyprian, "beholding its idols completely overthrown, invented a new means for destroying the peace of the Church, by exciting heresies and schisms, which strove to corrupt the faith and disturb its unity; but these new assaults of the demon only afforded her an opportunity for still greater triumphs. Heresies had already arisen, but none so widely spread and so disastrous as Arianism."

Arius, a priest of the Church of Alexandria, was an ambitious and violent man, who aspired to the bishopric of that great city; but being frustrated in his hopes by the election of St. Alexander to this dignity, he was filled with jealousy and revenge, and began to oppose the teachings of this holy prelate by introducing a new doctrine. A spirit of pride always originates heresies, hidden, however, under a guise of humility. Thus, an affected modesty and a mortified exterior, joined to an advanced age, enabled him to attract some followers. Arius dared to attack the divinity of Jesus Christ, and declared that the Son of God was not equal in all things to His Father. This new doctrine, entirely opposed to the teachings of the Church, was the cause of great scandal. The faithful immediately rejected it, and regarded this most wicked insult to our divine Lord with sentiments of horror and disgust. St. Alexander, at first, endeavored to reclaim Arius, by charitable warnings and mild remonstrances, but seeing that his moderation and paternal exhortations were without effect, and that the impious creed was beginning to spread, he boldly and fearlessly excommunicated the leader of the heresy, in a synod composed of all the suffragan bishops. He then wrote an explicit account of the whole affair to the Pope and bishops of the Church, warning them of the danger that menaced the faith, and asking their approbation of the course he had pursued.

This unexpected sentence astonished Arius, but did not in the least abash him, and retiring to Palestine, he made a few proselytes; from thence crossed into Nicomedia, where the Emperor usually resided, and succeeded in gaining the bishop Eusebius as a partisan and protector. Finding himself sustained by so powerful an adherent, he strove to promulgate his impious doctrine among the common people, and, in order to accomplish his designs, composed hymns in which he introduced the new creed. Through these artful means, the people sucked in the poison without perceiving their danger. The Emperor was much grieved at this division in the Church, and remonstrated with Eusebius, who told him that the evil was occasioned by the hatred of the bishop Alexander for Arius, and advised him to arrest the further progress of the scandal by imposing silence on them both. Constantine, thus deceived, believed it sufficient to write to Alexander and Arius, exhorting them to unity of sentiment.

With this object in view, he sent Osius, bishop of Cordova, in whom he reposed great confidence, to Alexandria. Osius was a venerable old man, had occupied the episcopal chair for thirty years, suffered in the persecution under Maximian, and was renowned for his sanctity throughout the whole Church. On arriving in Alexandria with the Emperor's letter, he called together a synod, used every means to conciliate all parties, but so much dissension prevailed, that he was obliged to return to Nicomedia without having accomplished any good. Arius and his partisans, with the usual obstinacy of heretics, refused to submit to the silence imposed on them by the Emperor; and, on the other side, Alexander and his clergy, feeling sure that they possessed the true faith, which God commanded them to preserve inviolate, and transmit to their successors, could not consent to remain passive. Osius reported the unsuccessful result of his visit to the Emperor, and convinced Constantine of the errors of the new doctrine, and showed the magnitude of the evil which threatened to fall upon the Church.

THE COUNCIL OF NICE.
A. D. 325.

On learning that his letter had been without any good effect, Constantine resolved, by the advice of his bishops, to assemble an Ecumenical or universal council, in order to condemn the heresy and reprimand its followers. During the reigns of the pagan Emperors, these large assemblies could not be held; but Constantine, who ruled over the whole empire, was able to immediately execute this project, so worthy of his faith and piety, and we cannot refrain from admiring the Providence of God, who facilitated this good work, by uniting so many countries under the dominion of one sovereign. The city of Nice was chosen for the council, on account of its proximity to Nicomedia, where the Emperor resided. Constantine, therefore, sent letters of invitation to all the bishops, requesting their attendance, and ordered that all the necessary expenses for the journey should be paid from the royal treasury.

This council was of so much importance, that the bishops eagerly responded to the imperial summons, and assembled at Nice, to the number of three hundred and eighteen, representing all the provinces of the empire, without counting the priests and deacons. Osius, bishop of Cordova, presided, as the deputy of the Pope St. Sylvester, who sent two priests, being unable to attend in person on account of his great age. St. Alexander, bishop of Alexandria, was accompanied by the youthful deacon, Athanasius, whom he greatly esteemed and found of much assistance. The assembled council was a grand and imposing spectacle; several of the bishops were of eminent sanctity, and still bore the marks of wounds received for the faith during the last persecution, among whom was St. Paphnutius, bishop of Upper Egypt, who had lost his right eye.

The Emperor frequently invited the holy prelate to the imperial palace, conversed upon religous topics with him, and showed every respect and honor to this heroic soul who had suffered in the cause of truth. The appointed day having arrived, all who were to assist at the council repaired to a large hall, and after the bishops were all assembled, Constantine entered, thus manifesting his reverence for this august body. He informed the bishops that he did not wish his presence to interfere with their discussing freely, all questions appertaining to the dogmas of faith. They commenced by examining the doctrine of Arius, who was summoned before the council, and who dared to avow and defend his blasphemous creed. The bishops were unmoved by his sophistries, expressed the holiest indignation, and refuted by powerful arguments the impious heresy, opposing the authority of the Holy Scriptures, and the writings of the early fathers, which are the foundation of the true faith, to his abominable errors.

The council then declared that Jesus Christ is the true Son of God, equal to His Father, possessing the same divine attributes, in a word, God Himself. As the subtle Arians were so artful as to evade the real meaning of these expressions, and admit them without renouncing their error, the council could devise no other term which would more clearly express the nature of indivisible unity than the word "Consubstantial;" and this word, which banished all subterfuge, became the terror of the Arians, as it distinctly declares that the Son is equal in every thing to His Father, and is one and the same God with Him. The Arians withdrew from the assemblage, but the Fathers of the council always adhered to this term, which afterward became a distinctive mark of catholicity. The solemn profession of faith which is known as the Nicene creed was then declared. All the bishops, with the exception of a few Arians, subscribed to this document, and pronounced an anathama against Arius and his followers. In virtue of this sentence, which the secular power supported without the slightest hesitation, the Emperor condemned Arius to banishment. Such was the conclusion of this celebrated council, which is still held in the greatest veneration by the Church.

CONSTANTINE RECALLS THE HERETICS AND EXILES ST. ATHANASIUS.

The spirit of heresy, which is restless and turbulent, was not repressed by the authority of the council of Nice; and the Arians, although condemned, soon caused new troubles in the Church. They wrote to the Emperor, and by pretending to admit the articles of the Nicene creed, succeeded in having themselves recalled from banishment. They then endeavored by different artifices to prejudice the Emperor against the Catholic bishops, particularly Athanasius, who, after the death of St. Alexander had become bishop of Alexandria, and whom they regarded as their most formidable adversary. They strove to exculpate Arius, by assuring the Emperor that he had only been condemned because he had not clearly explained the meaning of his doctrine, and they declared, also, that as Arius was now most excellently disposed, it would be pleasing to God if he commanded Athanasius to receive him back into the Church. This was only designed as a trap in which they hoped to ensnare the holy bishop, knowing that he would refuse acquiescence, and thus irritate the Emperor.

Constantine followed the advice of the heretics, and ordered Athanasius to receive Arius, under pain of being deposed from his office. The Arians were not satisfied with this success, but published all kinds of calumnies against Athanasius, which were so widely circulated that it became at least necessary to examine whether such grave accusations had any foundation in truth. The Emperor, therefore, convened an assembly of bishops in the city of Tyre, for the purpose of inquiring into the conduct of Athanasius, and commanded the accused to appear before it. The Arians had been careful to select the judges from the bishops of their own party, and St. Athanasius was treated by these heretical prelates in the most insulting manner; not being permitted to sit with them, but obliged to stand like a criminal who waits for his sentence to be pronounced. The holy bishop listened quietly to the charges brought against him, and then answered their calumnies in an admirable defense, which clearly proved his innocence and confounded his enemies.

The Arians, being unable to refute his able argument, were transported with rage and hatred, and would have torn him to pieces if an imperial officer had not interfered. St. Athanasius, seeing that his life was in peril, proceeded to Constantinople, in order to justify himself in the presence of the Emperor. During his absence the Arians hastened to depose him from his bishopric, and were not ashamed to repeat the very same calumnies he had so clearly refuted; then following him to Constantinople, they added another accusation which they believed would make a great impression on the mind of the Emperor.

They said that Athanasius had threatened to prevent the usual transportation of corn from Alexandria to Constantinople. The holy bishop vainly protested against the palpable falsehood. Constantine, deceived and blinded by prejudice, judged him guilty, and banished him to Treves, a large city of Gaul, eight hundred leagues from Alexandria. Athanasius immediately obeyed the sentence of exile, and arrived in Treves in the beginning of the year 336. What a sad destiny is the heritage of royalty! Actuated by the best motives, sovereigns sometimes commit the greatest acts of injustice, through the artfulness of wicked courtiers who obtain an undue influence over their minds.

DREADFUL DEATH OF ARIUS.
A. D. 336.

The Arians, emboldened by the success of their plot against St. Athanasius, undertook to establish Arius as bishop of Alexandria; who, profiting by the absence of the holy prelate, repaired to that city and attempted to enter the Church; but the Catholics would not suffer him to remain, and his presence caused so much excitement that the Emperor was obliged to recall him to Constantinople. In order to avenge the rejection of their leader by the faithful of Alexandria, the Arians determined to give him a brilliant reception in the Church of Constantinople. The bishop of that imperial city was a venerable old man, and a devoted soldier of Jesus Christ; the Arians endeavored to persuade him to admit Arius to communion, but he peremptorily refused their request.

Enraged at their failure, the heretics threatened to depose him, or force him by command of the Emperor to receive Arius into the Church. They succeeded in obtaining the royal order, and a Sunday was chosen for the return of the wicked Arius, so as to render their victory the more conspicuous. In this fearful emergency, the holy bishop had recourse to prayer, and, retiring into his church, prostrate at the foot of the altar, all bathed in tears, he addressed this humble and fervent petition to the throne of justice: "If the wicked Arius is to be received into the Church, I implore thee, O Lord, to take me hence; but if thou lovest thy faithful children, do not permit us to become objects of scorn and contempt to the Catholic world!" The following day the disciples of Arius met together, and prepared to conduct their leader to the church, notwithstanding the opposition of the lawful bishop. They accompanied him through the streets in triumph, in the mean time heaping the most opprobrious epithets upon the holy prelate.

When the cortege arrived in sight of the church, Arius was stricken with a sudden deadly palor, and obliged to retire from the procession. Not returning for some time, a search was instituted, and he was found extended dead on the ground, bathed in his blood. This horrible spectacle inspired every one with horror, causing even his followers to tremble; and the spot where he lay was instantly deserted, no one daring to approach one who was considered the object of divine vengeance. The dreadful tidings soon spread abroad, and the next day the holy bishop returned solemn thanks to God — not for the death of Arius, whose unhappy end he deplored, but for His deigning to prevent in so signal a manner the entrance of heresy into the sanctuary.

The Emperor was deeply impressed by the event, recognizing in it the hand of God; and, from that time, he conceived the greatest aversion for the wicked sect, which, in the person of Arius, had been publicly condemned by God Himself. He acknowledged his error in exiling St. Athanasius, and was about to recall him from banishment, when death overtook him; not, however, before he had given an order to that effect.

THE RECALL AND JUSTIFICATION OF ST. ATHANASIUS.

A. D. 339.

The Emperor Constantine left three sons — Constantine, Constantius, and Constans, who divided the empire between them. Constantine, Emperor of Gaul, reinstated St. Athanasius in his bishopric, and sent him to Alexandria, with a letter containing many expressions of admiration and esteem, and, at the same time, expressing indignation and disapproval of the manner in which the bishop had been treated by the Arians. He said, that, in restoring St. Athanasius to his flock, he was only executing the pious wish of his father, who would have recalled the holy prelate himself, had not death prevented the performance of this duty. "When, therefore," he added, "Athanasius returns, you will know how much we honor him, and respect his many virtues."

The holy patriarch passed through Syria, and finally arrived in Alexandria, where he was received with transports of joy; the clergy and faithful running in crowds to meet him, and all the churches resounded with joyful hymns of thanksgiving. The Arians were greatly incensed at this ovation, and declared his return to be contrary to the canons, as they declared that he could not be reinstated but by the authority of a council. His enemies invented new calumnies against him, and resorted to every means in order to secure his ruin; they endeavored to prejudice the mind of Constantius, the Emperor of the East, by representing Athanasius as being very restless and impetuous, as having excited rebellion among the faithful; and falsely accused him without the slightest evidence, of having appropriated the grain destined for the maintenance of the widows and clergy.

The holy prelate easily refuted these allegations, but his defense did not remove the suspicions aroused in the mind of Constantius, who espoused the cause of the Arians, and would not listen to any justification of the bishop. These wicked men obtained the imperial permission to elect a new patriarch in Alexandria, and as they had complete control, they immediately convened a council, deposed Athanasius, and appointed a suspended priest named Pistus, as his successor. This bad priest, and the bishop who consecrated him, had been excommunicated by the council of Nice. On hearing of this schismatical ordination, the Pope refused to communicate with the usurper, all the Catholic churches pronounced anathema against him, and Pistus was deprived of the office he wished to wrest from the rightful incumbent.

The Church has always regarded schisms with the utmost abhorrence, and scornfully rejected those wicked ambitious men, who aspire to the Episcopal dignity, while the legitimate prelate is still living, and approved of by the See of Rome. She has declared in all ages, that such a usurper is without power or jurisdiction; that he is not a bishop but an imposter, not a shepherd but a robber and a wolf, who enters the fold in order to scatter and destroy the flock. Thus persecuted by his enemies, St.

Athanasius wrote to the Pope demanding justice, and afterward proceeded to Rome in order to give a correct account of the whole affair to the Pope.

The pontifical chair was occupied at that time by St. Julius, who received the prelate very kindly, and convened a council for the examination of his grievances, by which St. Athanasius was justified in the course he had pursued and confirmed in the possession of his diocese. The letter which his Holiness wrote on this occasion is still extant, and he there defends the truth with an earnestness and power worthy of the Vicar of Jesus Christ. Thus, we see, from the first ages of the Church that it was to the Pope, the successor of St. Peter, appointed by Jesus Christ Himself, pastor of His flock, that decisions of grave matters concerning the doctrines or discipline of the Church were referred. The most celebrated bishops of antiquity addressed the Holy See, to obtain a release from the unjust sentences often pronounced against them by Kings and Emperors. The whole Catholic world recognizes the pre-eminence of the sovereign pontiffs, and regards their jurisdiction and authority as extending over the entire Church, which superiority is received as an article of faith by her children.

OUTRAGES PRACTICED BY THE SCHISMATICS.

The ill success which attended the claims of the usurper did not disconcert the enemies of St. Athanasius; but they used more artful means in electing another bishop of Alexandria. Having the authority of the Emperor to do so, they selected a native of Cappadocia, named Gregory, whom they placed in the episcopal chair, and they obliged St. Athanasius to leave the city. The schismatics then gave themselves up to all kinds of excesses; without any fear of punishment, sustained as they were by the sovereign power. The violent usurpation of Gregory had spread alarm throughout Alexandria, and the Catholics hastened to seek shelter within the sacred portals of the churches. One of the imperial officers went among the people and incited the Jews and the depraved, wicked men, who are always to be found in large cities, to insult and molest the Catholics who had sought refuge within the precincts of the sanctuary.

Some of the faithful were trampled upon, others knocked down with loaded clubs or stabbed. The priests were dragged before the tribunal of the governor where Gregory was seated, and struck in the face when they refused to acknowledge the impious heretic as their bishop. Holy virgins were despoiled of their garments and beaten with rods; and the ministers of religion were deprived of food, in the hope of causing their death by starvation. These frightful scenes were rendered still more horrible, as they took place during Holy Week. On Good Friday, Gregory, accompanied by an escort of pagan soldiers, entered a church, and some thirty-four persons, principally women, whom he found in the sacred inclosure, were publicly beaten and then sent to prison.

In this manner he took possession of all the churches, so that the Catholic clergy and their congregations were either banished from the holy table or forced to communicate with the schismatics. The Pope undertook the defense of St. Athanasius, and in a council composed of a hundred and seventy bishops, declared the ordination of the usurper to be null and void, which sentence, however, did not prevent the schismatics from nominating a successor after the death of Gregory, and renewing all the shocking outrages of the first usurpation. They disturbed the faithful when they assembled for prayer; carried off several maidens from their homes, and insulted others in the street; the wives of the heretics, participating in their husband's acts of violence, heaped all kinds of indignities upon the Catholic women.

The persecution not only raged in Alexandria, but extended throughout Egypt. An edict was issued by the Emperor, banishing all the Catholic bishops from their churches, and appointing young profligates as their successors, who managed ecclesiastical affairs according to the dictates of their wicked hearts. These usurpers corrupted the faith in Egypt, where the Catholic doctrine had heretofore been taught in all its purity, and, as the faithful would have no communication with the heretics, they were again insulted, thrown into prison and their property confiscated. Schism had subsequently appeared in the Church, always bearing the same characteristics, and the same outrages and acts of violence have taken place, thus showing plainly its opposition to truth and religion, as the persecutors were always schismatics, and the persecuted Catholics.

THE EMPEROR CONSTANTIUS CAUSES TROUBLE IN THE CHURCH.

A. D. 365.

Constantius, by the death of his two brothers, having become sole master of the empire, published an edict obliging all the bishops to sign the condemnation of Athanasius, under pain of banishment. He believed that he could not abolish the Nicene creed without first silencing its most generous defenders; in order to accomplish this object, he assembled the bishops at Arlés, and afterward at Milan, appearing on both occasions as the principal accuser. The bishops declared that they could not condemn Athanasius without violating the holy canons. "Obey my will instead of the canons," said the haughty Emperor, "or else go into exile." The prelates told him that the empire did not belong to him, but to God, who had confided it to his care; and they begged him to fear the judgments of the Lord, and not confound the government of the Church with that of the State.

This bold response, so worthy of these courageous bishops, enraged Constantius, who, drawing his sword, swore that some of the prelates should be immediately executed, but he was persuaded to modify the sentence into one of banishment. Those, therefore, who refused to sign were driven from their dioceses, and Arian bishops appointed as their successors. Pope Liberius was at first strenuous in opposing the imperial mandate, and was banished to Berœa in Thrace; but, being overcome by the hardships of his exile, he consented to sign the document condemning Athanasius. He soon, however, repented of this fault, and promptly repaired the scandal his conduct had occasioned the faithful. Shortly afterward, the Emperor, who was more occupied in causing troubles in the Church than in governing his empire, convened a council at Rimini, Italy, at the same time that one was in session at Seleucia, in the East. The latter, which was not largely attended, was of no effect, and the bishops separated without having come to any conclusion.

As perfect liberty of speech was allowed in the council of Rimini, the Catholic doctrine was zealously defended, and the prelates refused to accept a new profession of faith; declaring their determination to retain the Nicene Creed, which required no retrenchment or addition, and anathematizing Arius and his followers. The bishops to the number of three hundred and twenty subscribed to this decree, and the Arians who refused to sign were condemned, and deposed from their dioceses. But the Emperor, prejudiced by the heretics, sent an order to the prefect of Taurus, forbidding the dispersion of the council, until the bishops had signed an artfully worded formula, in which the term "consubstantial" was omitted, and banishing those who refused to obey his commands.

Then the greater part of the prelates, wearied by so long a separation from their flock, and intimidated by the threats of Taurus, allowed themselves to be deceived by the wily Arians, and, believing that the sense of the word "consubstantial," was merely expressed in another form, signed the document without perceiving the gross imposture. Soon, however, discerning the fraud, they loudly testified their indignation, boldly rejected the perverted sense of the formula, and declared their adherence to the doctrine of Nice. It was on this occasion that St. Jerome uttered his celebrated speech, "that the world was astonished to find itself Arian." The only error of the bishops of Rimini consisted in having, through surprise and a want of reflection, allowed Arianism a momentary triumph; a number of the bishops were not imposed on, but, with Pope Liberius at their head, energetically opposed the scandal, and annulled the proceedings of the council of Rimini.

It is certain that the doctrines of the Church remained unchanged, as was remarked by St. Athanasius two years afterward, in a letter to the Emperor Jovian. "The Nicene creed, which we profess, has always been taught in all the churches; it is accepted by those of Spain, Great Britain, Gaul, Italy, Dalmatia, Dacia, Mysia and Macedonia, those of Greece, and Africa; the Islands of Sardinia, Crete, Cyprus, Pamphylia, Lyconia, and Isauria; Egypt, Lybia, Pontus, and Cappadocia, all have the same faith, as well as the majority of the Eastern Churches." Thus, not only the whole Roman empire, but the entire universe, including the most barbarous tribes, were of one faith and doctrine; the few who embraced the error, the council of Rimini, and the long, cruel persecutions of Constantius, could not corrupt the pure belief of the Catholic Church.

ST. HILARY OF POITIERS ZEALOUSLY DEFENDS THE NICENE CREED.

A. D. 353.

God raised up in Gaul an illustrious defender of the Catholic faith, in the person of St. Hilary of Poitiers; this holy prelate effected in the West what St. Athanasius accomplished in the East, opposing, with an invincible courage, the teachings of the Arians, and preserving his country from the contagion by maintaining the doctrine of Nice. As the Emperor Constantius had endeavored for several years to extend Arianism, he presented a petition to this prince, supplicating him to cease his unjust persecution of a number of churches, which were deprived of their legitimate pastors, and governed by the usurpers who had been appointed to succeed the rightful incumbents. The unhappy state of affairs had rendered his bold remonstrance very necessary; and he energetically opposed the plots of Saturninus, bishop of Arles, as famous for his vices as for his connection with the Arians. Constantius, on being informed by Saturninus of the zeal and courage of St. Hilary, banished this holy prelate to Phrygia. This sentence was destined to produce much good, as divine Providence often uses the perverse will of man in the execution of His designs.

The Emperor soon after convened a council at Seleucia, with the intention of destroying the canons of Nice. As the heretics were divided among themselves, and formed into two parties, St. Hilary was invited to attend the council by one of these parties in the hope of winning him over to their side, and thus confounding their opponents. The holy prelate repaired to Seleucia and there defended the Nicene creed with so much eloquence and boldness, as to abash the enemies of truth. He then proceeded to Constantinople, and asked permission of the Emperor to hold a public conference in his presence, in which he proposed to answer the heretics and demonstrate the falseness of their doctrine by their continual changes and alterations. "Since the holy council of Nice," said he, "those in whom you repose your confidence do nothing but invent new creeds, their faith is not the faith of the Scriptures, but simply mere conjecture; last year they altered their creed four times, thus showing a want of unity and stability. They advance new doctrines almost daily, which oppose and anathematise those they held previously. They speak of the Holy Scripture and the apostolic faith, in order to deceive the weak and give an appearance of truth to their sophisms."

These admirable words could be applied to the different heresies which have sprung up since the time of St. Hilary. The Arians, who dreaded his ardent zeal and unanswerable arguments, avoided the discussion he asked for; and, in order to escape further exposure, induced the Emperor to send him back to his church. The holy bishop when returning to his diocese traveled through Illyria and Italy, everywhere reanimating the weak and lukewarm Christians with new faith and courage. His first care, on arriving in Gaul, was to remedy the evils which had befallen the Church; and he excommunicated and deposed Saturninus and several others, who were guilty of heresy. The presence of the holy bishop produced the happiest effects; the faith was restored in all its purity; the discipline of the Church recovered its pristine vigor, scandals were abolished and peace succeeded to persecution; and the death of Constantius, which occurred in the year three hundred and sixty-one, deprived the Arians of their most powerful support.

ST. MARTIN, BISHOP OF TOURS.
A. D. 360.

The most illustrious of the disciples of St. Hilary was St. Martin, bishop of Tours, who was much attached to this great prelate; ardently admiring his virtues and always ready to participate in his combats for the faith. Martin was born at Sabaria, a city in Pannonia, of idolatrous parents. This holy child, destined by God to lead a holy and saintly life, at the age of ten years, went to the Christian Church and enrolled himself in the ranks of the catechumens.

Being the son of a tribune, he was obliged to enter the military service; and this profession, which is generally a very dangerous school for youth, became for him a career of virtue and mortification. He was especially distinguished for his tender love of the poor, to whom he could refuse nothing, distributing nearly all his pay among the destitute and indigent. One day, during a severe winter, he encountered at the gate of the city of Amiens, a wretched beggar almost insensible with cold; this deplorable spectacle excited the charity of the holy Martin, but he found he had nothing to bestow upon the mendicant. He suddenly remembered his cloak, and drawing his sabre he divided the mantle in twain and gave one half to the suffering man. So beautiful an action was soon rewarded; the next night in a dream Martin beheld Jesus Christ robed in this portion of his cloak, and heard him say to the Angels who surrounded their Lord: "Martin, although but a catechumen, has clothed Me in this garment." This consoling vision caused him to ask for baptism, and after the reception of the sacrament he determined to quit the army.

Attracted toward St. Hilary of Poitiers, by his great reputation for sanctity, he built a monastery two leagues from that city, whither he retired with some followers. Martin occasionally emerged from his seclusion, in order to preach the faith to the idolaters, who were still quite numerous in the villages, and God approved of the zeal of His servant by bestowing upon him the gift of working miracles. The fame of his sanctity soon spread throughout Gaul, and he was considered worthy of the episcopal dignity. The people of Tours desired to make him their bishop, but it was only by means of the greatest persuasion that he was induced to leave his solitude.

St. Martin still continued his mortified and austere life after his elevation to the office of bishop, making no change in his dress or table, but only desiring to be worthy of his new position by the zealous practice of every virtue. The destruction of idolatry was the object of his indefatigable labors, and he traveled through Touraine, where he converted many of the pagans by his sermons and miracles. Being one day in a small town filled with idolaters, after exhorting them to abandon their superstitious practices, he said he could completely destroy an old tree which they were in the habit of worshipping. The pagans consented to the trial, on condition that he should stand on the spot where the tree was to fall. Martin seized an ax and gave a powerful blow, which severed the tree from the root; but when about to fall upon him he made the sign of the cross over the swaying mass, when it immediately raised its drooping boughs, stood upright for a moment, and then fell heavily upon the opposite side, striking awe and terror into the minds of the assembled pagans, who not only beheld the overthrow of their idol, but also witnessed the hand of God, who had thus plainly protected His servant.

St. Martin, in addition to his missionary labors, performed many other acts of charity; sometimes interceding with princes for the redress of wrongs and grievances. An object of this nature induced him to repair to Treves to use his influence with Maximus, to whom he presented his petition in so dignified a manner as to impress even the Emperor, who was much pleased with his deportment and appearance. St. Martin, who received several invitations to dine at the palace, at first declined these attentions, but subsequently deemed it expedient to accept the kindness, and Maximus was so delighted with his acquiescence, that he assembled all his court to meet the distinguished guest.

The holy prelate sat next to a priest of Tours, who always accompanied him on his missions. When the wine was served the Emperor signed to an officer to present the cup to St. Martin, whom he expected would immediately pass the goblet to him; but the holy bishop offered it to the humble priest, as being the most worthy of the company present, and passed the wine to him before he did to the Emperor. This action elicited the applause of Maximus, who praised St. Martin for honoring the priesthood of Jesus Christ in preference to the imperial power. His holy, austere life, great virtues, and numerous miracles, rendered the bishop of Tours very celebrated in the Church.

THE EMPEROR JULIAN WISHES TO RE-ESTABLISH PAGANISM.

A. D. 363.

Julian, who succeeded Constantius, renounced Christianity, and for this reason was called the Apostate. On ascending the throne he began his reign by granting perfect liberty with regard to religion, and recalling all those who had been exiled on account of their faith. His motive for this course was less to win popularity than to cast odium on the government of his predecessor.

St. Athanasius, profiting by this clemency, returned to Alexandria, which city he entered in triumph. The people ran to meet him in such crowds, that it seemed as if the whole of Egypt had assembled to welcome its beloved pastor. The trees and the roofs of the houses were filled with eager spectators, and others thronged the streets, and endeavored to approach near enough to walk within the shadow of the Saint. This joy, however, was not of long duration. The Emperor, who, to great qualities united a false and capricious disposition, had conceived the insane idea of abolishing Christianity and restoring idolatry. To accomplish this object he banished St. Athanasius from Alexandria, and the holy bishop was once more forced to conceal himself in order to escape further insults.

Julian, however, did not resort to violence, but used all kinds of artifices; he fomented the division between the Catholics and heretics, so as to weaken both parties, and thus finally crush them with a single blow. The religious freedom he ostensibly allowed the Christians was, in reality, a state of strict bondage; not condemning them to death by a general edict, but adopting other and surer means to accomplish their ruin. Every honor and favor were lavished on the pagans, while the Christians were scorned, insulted, and oppressed. Julian particularly desired to humble the clergy, and all that appertained to a religion he hated, and with this view, he deprived the priests of all their privileges, and abolished the annual pension devoted to the maintenance of the acolytes and virgins consecrated to the service of God. This, he said derisively, was in order to remind them of the perfection of their state of life, and oblige them to practice evangelical poverty.

He plundered the churches, and used the spoils

for the adornment of the pagan temples, which he had rebuilt at the expense of the Christians. The priests also suffered many indignities, being imprisoned and tortured in order to force them to give up the sacred ornaments of their respective churches; and they were insulted and calumniated without being allowed the slightest defense. The churches were pillaged, desecrated or demolished; the tombs of the saints opened, their bones dishonored, and their ashes scattered to the winds. The wily Emperor endeavored to win over the lukewarm Christians by specious promises; the faithful who resisted these snares were regarded as enemies of the State, whereas, those who sacrificed their consciences to the love of riches were loaded with honors. Apostacy was a sure path to every dignity, and the greatest talent and merit displayed by the Christians was of no avail at the imperial court; apostacy concealed every crime, and sanctioned the most shameful outrages. Julian issued a law excluding the Christians from holding public offices, under the pretext that the Gospel forbade them to use the sword; deprived them of all their rights, and would not allow them any defense when called before the tribunals. "Your religion," said he, "prohibits all quarrels and dissensions."

The cities that declared in favor of idolatry were assured of his protection, while those that remained faithful to Christianity were denied even common justice; refusing, as he did, to grant audiences to their deputies, and rejecting all their petitions. He forbade the Christians to teach the arts and sciences, for he knew that knowledge and learning served to confound error, and defend the truth; but the ostensible pretext assigned was, that the Christians should remain in ignorance, and believe without reasoning. This species of persecution would, perhaps, have been more fatal to the Church, than were the cruelties of Nero and Dioclesian, if God, who always protects His children, had not shortened the life of this prince, and destroyed his infernal project by annihilating its author.

JULIAN UNDERTAKES TO REBUILD THE TEMPLE OF JERUSALEM—HIS DEATH.

A. D. 363.

The Emperor Julian, while striving to overthrow the Christian religion, furnished a new proof of her divine origin, and of the truth of her doctrines. He was acquainted with the prophecies which announced the destruction of the Temple of Jerusalem, and declared its ruin irreparable, and he knew that Jesus Christ had predicted that not a stone should remain on a stone. In order to falsify the Holy Scriptures, he determined to rebuild the Temple, and, although an enemy of the Jews, he invited them to participate in the enterprise; promising to defray all the necessary expenses, and sending one of his most confidential officers, named Alypius, as his representative, to hasten the execution of his commands.

The Jews soon assembled from all parts of the country; and an immense number of workmen gathered on the site where the Temple had formerly stood. They cleared away the rubbish and stones and labored arduously to demolish the old foundations. Venerable men, delicate women, and little children lent their assistance in removing the ruins. Cyril, bishop of Jerusalem, however, laughed at their futile efforts, and loudly declared, that the time for the accomplishment of the Saviour's prediction had arrived, and their human plans would all be frustrated by the hand of God Himself. Accordingly, when the foundations of the old Temple were demolished, a horrible earthquake destroyed all their labor, scattered the materials they had collected, overturned neighboring houses, and killed or wounded all the workmen. Although thus visibly punished for their presumption, the obstinacy of the Jews was not overcome; and soon recovering from their fright, they again renewed their efforts. Then globes of fire issued from the earth, throwing back the stones the workmen were endeavoring to place on the walls, and consuming the iron tools.

This terrible phenomenon was renewed several times; that it was the avenging power of God was evident from the fact of the fire reappearing whenever the work was recommenced, only vanishing when all further attempt was abandoned. So wonderful an event astonished all the eye witnesses; and a great many Jews and numerous Pagans confessed the divinity of Jesus Christ, and earnestly asked for baptism. The Emperor, blind in the midst of light, was disconcerted without being convinced.

This extraordinary fact is incontestable, and is certified to by the unanimous testimony of ecclesiastical writers of the third century, and also by pagan authors, such as Ammianus Marcellinus, etc. St. Gregory, of Nazianzen, and St. John Chrysostom, spoke of it publicly in the presence of a vast audience, several of whom had witnessed the prodigy. A famous Rabbi, who wrote in the following century, although interested in suppressing the miracle, copied an account of the supernatural event from the Jewish archives. Julian himself acknowledged that he attempted to rebuild the Temple, and his silence concerning the obstacles which forced him to relinquish his undertaking is a tacit avowal of what is related by the historians of his time.

THE EMPEROR JOVIAN PROTECTS CATHOLICITY.

A. D. 363.

Immediately after the death of Julian, the principal officers of the army held a council, and unanimously elected Jovian as Emperor. He was the commander of the imperial guards, and his personal qualities gained him universal esteem. Possessed of undisputed courage, he was capable of meeting critical emergencies with admirable coolness and judgment. As the Roman army was at that time in the interior of Persia, a man of this character was needed to hold the reins of government, and his attachment to the Christian religion inspired confidence and hope in the hearts of the faithful; the following occurrence showed the strength and purity of his faith.

When the Emperor Julian was preparing to make war upon the Persians, he summoned Jovian to his presence, and said to him in a peremptory manner:

"Sacrifice to the gods, or return me thy sword." Jovian unbuckled the weapon and presented it to the prince without the slightest hesitation. The Emperor, however, soon restored it, as he did not wish to lose the services of so distinguished an officer at a period when he most required his assistance. Before receiving the imperial insignia, Jovian assembled the whole army, and proclaiming himself a Christian, said that he would not command idolatrous soldiers whom the God of battles would not protect. The troops immediately cried out with one voice: "Fear not, Emperor, you command a Christian army! The most aged among us were instructed by the great Constantine, and the rest by his son! The reign of Julian was of too short a duration to entirely alienate from the faith those whom he persuaded to apostatize, and we all declare our faith in the Crucified Jesus, who died on the Cross for mankind!" Jovian was much pleased with this noble answer; he readily assumed the sovereign power, placed himself at the head of his troops, and by his wise measures soon extricated the army from its critical position, and in a short time found himself once again in his own dominions.

The pious Emperor then applied himself to the task of remedying the evils inflicted by Julian on the Church, and one of his first acts was to recall St. Athanasius from exile and re-establish him in his diocese. The letter containing the welcome intelligence expressed the profoundest veneration for the holy bishop and the sincerest sympathy for his unmerited sufferings. Athanasius once more left his solitude and returned to Alexandria, where he was received with acclamations of joy and gratitude by his loving children. His enemies, the Arians, endeavored to prejudice Jovian against the Saint, but their malicious efforts happily proved unsuccessful, as the esteem of the Emperor only increased in his regard, and Athanasius was often honored with the imperial confidence. In order to strengthen his faith, and preserve the pure doctrine of the Church, Jovian begged the holy prelate to send him a clear and precise exposition of the Catholic belief. Athanasius promptly acceded to his pious request, and wrote a lucid explanation of the faith of the Nicean council, and demonstrated plainly that the only means of obtaining a remedy for the evils which distracted the Church was by a perfect submission to the decrees of this council.

The Church began to breathe once more after so long a period of trial, and found in Jovian a pious son and valiant champion. The Emperor restored the rights and privileges of the acolytes, virgins and widows, and ordered the governors of provinces to protect the assemblies of the faithful, to honor the divine worship, and attend to the instruction of the people. The faithful, however, did not long enjoy this peace and calm, for Jovian's sudden death deprived them of a just and merciful sovereign, and the Church of a zealous defender.

VALENS RENEWS THE TROUBLES OF ARIANISM.

A. D. 367.

Valentinian, who was elevated to the imperial throne after the death of Jovian, divided the empire with Valens, his brother. The former was sincerely attached to the true faith, and the Church enjoyed perfect peace throughout his empire, but Valens, who ruled over the East, commenced a violent persecution against the Catholics, and began by banishing St. Athanasius, who was always the principal object of hatred to the Arians and the first victim of their fury. The outrage offered the holy prelate was the signal for a general persecution. From that time the Catholics suffered all kinds of trials and shameful treatment; their property was confiscated; they were loaded with chains, and dragged to execution without being allowed to utter a word of remonstrance or defense. Among many others is related the following instance:

The faithful of Constantinople, refusing to believe that the Emperor authorized the persecutions, deputized eighty virtuous ecclesiastics to present a petition to the throne, demanding redress from their grievances. Valens listened to their representations, while he concealed his rage at their boldness; but when he dismissed them from the royal presence, he commanded Modestus, prefect of the pretorium, to put them all to death. The prefect, fearing a revolt in the city, if they were publicly executed, sentenced them to exile, and placed them on board of a ship, which was to conduct them to their destination. But this wicked man, dreading the imperial displeasure, privately instructed the captain of the vessel to set it on fire as soon as they were out of sight of land, and all the eighty priests perished either by fire or water.

Hearing of the sufferings of the Eastern Church, the hermits resolved to lend her all the assistance in their power, and emerged from their loved solitudes in order to encourage their afflicted brethren. One of their number, a venerable saintly recluse, attracted the attention of the Emperor. "Whither goest thou?" said the prince. "Why dost thou not remain in thy cell, instead of traveling through the cities, exciting our subjects to revolt, and disobedience of our mandates?" The recluse, sustained by an ardent zeal, boldly answered: "Prince, I remained in solitude as long as the flocks of the Heavenly Shepherd were in peace; but now that I see them about to fall a prey to ravening wolves, is it proper for me to dwell tranquilly in my seclusion? If I were a daughter, who, having retired to rest in my father's house, discovered an incendiary about applying a flaming torch to the paternal mansion, should I continue in quiet repose, and allow the house to be destroyed? Should I not, rather, give the alarm, throw water on the burning structure, and use every effort to extinguish the conflagration? This is now my purpose: thou hast kindled a fire in the house of the Lord: from my cell I descried the flames, and I have come to quench them."

The Emperor could not answer this noble and generous speech, and even showed signs of relenting towards St. Athanasius, whom he permitted to return to his diocese; but he was only prompted to this course for fear of irritating his brother Valentinian, who esteemed and respected the holy bishop. St. Athanasius, therefore, was once more restored to his see, and breathed his last in Alexandria, six years afterward, having won the admiration and affection of the whole Church by his eminent virtues and severe trials. Five times had he been sent into banishment, and five times recalled from exile during his eventful life.

FEARLESSNESS OF ST. BASIL, BISHOP OF CESAREA.

A. D. 370.

Valens was unceasing in his endeavors to establish Arianism in his dominions, and traveled in person through several provinces in order to expel the Catholic bishops from their dioceses, but he invariably encountered generous defenders of the faith in all the cities and country places.

St. Basil, bishop of Cesarea, in Cappadocia, was especially distinguished for his boldness and courage. This great prelate was an impregnable bulwark, defeating all the efforts of heresy against the faith. Before proceeding to Cesarea, the Emperor sent Modestus, prefect of the pretorium, to visit St. Basil, in the hope of winning over the Saint, or else so to intimidate him as to oblige him to receive the Arians into his Church. The prefect accordingly summoned the holy bishop to his presence, and apparelled in all the insignia of his rank, the highest in the empire, ascended his tribunal surrounded by his lictors. Basil appeared perfectly composed and tranquil.

The prefect at first was kind and gentle, and urged him to yield to the imperial wish, and admit the Arians to communion. This artful course proving unavailing, Modestus assumed a threatening air, and exclaimed in an angry tone: "Art thou not afraid of incurring the displeasure of Valens? Dost thou think to oppose so great a prince, whose commands are obeyed by the whole world? Can he not confiscate thy possessions, condemn thee to banishment, and even deprive thee of life?" "These threats do not terrify me," replied Basil, "he who has no property has nothing to lose; unless thou deprivest me of these miserable garments I wear, and a few books, which alone constitute my wealth. As for exile I know of none, not being attached to any place. The whole earth belongs to God; all parts are my country, or rather my temporary abode. With regard to death, I have no fear, it is but the passage from time to a blessed eternity, and I should hasten joyfully to the presence of the Lamb; having long renounced the world, and practiced many austerities, tortures cannot intimidate me; my body is so emaciated and feeble it could not endure much suffering; the first blow of the executioner would terminate my life and trials."

This sublime language, so new to the ears of a courtier, amazed the prefect. "No one," said he, "has ever spoken to me with so much audacity." "Because," replied the holy prelate, "perhaps thou hast never before encountered a bishop." The prefect was forced to admire this intrepid soul, superior to both promises and threats; he relinquished his efforts to gain the Saint's submission, and left Cesarea for the purpose of relating his unsuccessful mission to Valens." "Prince," said he to the Emperor, "we are conquered by one man. Smiles and frowns are equally unheeded by this bold Christian; violence is the only means left!" The Emperor, however, did not deem it advisable to follow this advice, as he was fearful of exciting the rage of the Cesareans, and the courageous prelate commanded his involuntary respect.

ADMIRABLE COURAGE OF A CHRISTIAN WOMAN.

Bishops and priests were not the only victims who suffered, during the persecution of the Emperor Valens, but persons of all ages and both sexes testified their allegiance to Jesus Christ. The following is an example of the faith and courage of a Christian woman: The bishop of Edessa had been banished to a city of Mesopotamia, on account of his attachment to the Nicene doctrine, and a successor appointed by the Emperor governed his diocese. Valens had charged Modestus to compel the priests and deacons to receive the new bishop, and if they refused their consent, to send them into exile.

Having convened an assembly of the clergy, the prefect endeavored to gain their acquiesence to the imperial commands; but one of the priests nobly responded, in the name of the whole meeting: "We have a legitimate bishop, and we do not recognize any other!" They were all sentenced to banishment according to the royal order. The laity were encouraged by the example of their pastor's refusal to acknowledge the usurper, and when the hour for public prayer arrived, left the city and assembled in a country place, where they performed their devotions. When the Emperor heard of these proceedings, he was much incensed against Modestus, and reprimanded him severely for not preventing these meetings, which he ordered him to disperse with his soldiers.

Although opposed to Christianity, the prefect disliked vigorous measures, and secretly warned the faithful not to repair to the usual place of assembly, as he had been commanded by the Emperor to punish all he should find there. He hoped by this threat to frighten them into obedience, and thus appease the angry Valens; but the Christians only hastened more eagerly, and in greater numbers, to the appointed place. In this emergency the prefect was at a loss how to act, but finally concluded to advance noisily with his troops toward the spot, in hopes that the faithful would receive timely intimation of their approach and disperse.

In passing through the city, he saw a poor woman hurry out of her house, without even closing the door, holding a child by the hand, and suffering her mantle to drag carelessly on the ground, instead of fastening it, according to the custom of the country. In this guise she crossed through the file of soldiers that preceded the prefect, walking very rapidly, without manifesting the least sign of fear. Modestus ordered her to stop, and asked her whither she was hastening. "I am hurrying," said she, "to the field where the faithful are assembled." "Dost thou not know," exclaimed the prefect, "that a decree has been issued, sentencing all those who are found there, to be put to death?" "I am perfectly aware of it," replied the woman, "and for that reason am eager to arrive there, fearing to lose the opportunity of winning a martyr's crown." "But why dost thou take thy child with thee?" "That he may participate in my happiness, and, while still pure and innocent, enter into the Kingdom of Heaven," was her answer.

Astonished at the woman's extraordinary courage, Modestus returned to the palace, and informed Valens of the occurrence, and persuaded him to renounce a useless enterprise, which, even if successful, would not redound to his glory. This fact is a sufficient illustration of the sentiments of the Christians with regard to the schism. Always faithful to this precept of Jesus Christ: "I am the good Shepherd; and I know mine, and mine know me;" they were ever submissive to the bishop appointed by the Church, ready to sacrifice all they held most dear, and even suffer death itself rather than recognize a usurper.

VALENS REPRIMANDED BY ST. BASIL.

As the Feast of the Epiphany occurred during the Emperor's visit to Cesarea, Valens attended divine service at the church where St. Basil officiated. He entered the building accompanied by all his guards, in order to astonish the holy bishop by the imposing spectacle. On beholding, however, the beautiful order and modest deportment of the immense congregation, the profound recollection of St. Basil, who was standing motionless before the altar, his eyes fixed on Heaven, his thoughts raised up to God, and the pious demeanor of the priests who surrounded the bishop, resembling angels rather than men, he was deeply impressed by the edifying sight, and stood transfixed with amazement.

Overcoming his emotion, he presented an offering, but, as none of the attendants advanced to receive it, not knowing whether St. Basil would accept alms from a prince who had proved so hostile to Christianity, the Emperor was so much affected that he nearly fell to the ground, and was obliged to be supported by one of the priests who observed his weakness. The holy prelate deemed it advisable on this occasion to relax the strictures of ecclesiastical discipline and consented to receive the imperial offering. Valens became more lenient toward the Christians, and endeavored to win over St. Basil, by sending magistrates, officers of the army, and other distinguished personages to converse with him; he finally summoned the holy bishop to his presence, who spoke to him with apostolic courage, and he even silenced a courtier who addressed some insulting remark to the Saint. This conference proved very advantageous to Basil, and the Emperor donated him a piece of ground for founding an hospital in Cesarea; but the Arians soon perverted the royal mind and induced him to alter his intentions; and Valens was about to banish St. Basil, when his son was attacked with a violent fever, which the physicians could not abate.

The Emperor, convinced that this illness was a just punishment of his wicked designs against St. Basil, sent for the holy prelate. No sooner had the Saint entered the palace than the young prince began to recover, and the bishop assured Valens the child would not die if he promised to instruct him in the Catholic doctrine. This condition being accepted, he knelt and prayed, and the child was immediately cured; but the Emperor was not faithful to his word, and allowed an Arian bishop to baptize his son, who was again taken ill and died in a short time. This affliction did not soften the obdurate heart of Valens, and the holy prelate was a second time condemned to banishment; but when about to sign the sentence, the pen fell three times from his hand and he was so much agitated that he was unable to trace a single character. Finally the wrath of God descended on the head of this impenitent prince, who perished in battle, and whose body was never recovered, it being believed that he was carried in a disabled condition to a cottage, which was burned by his enemies.

VIRTUES OF ST. GREGORY OF NAZIANZEN.

St. Basil was united by a tender friendship to St. Gregory of Nazianzen, who was a zealous and ardent defender of the faith. This intimacy, which commenced during the period of their studies in Athens, lasted until the end of their lives. "We were both animated by the same desire," says St. Gregory in his beautiful account of this holy union; "we were steadfast in the practice of virtue, and strove to render our friendship eternal by preparing earnestly for a blessed immortality; we exercised a pious vigilance over each other, had no intercourse with dissipated companions, but visited those students, who, by their modesty, circumspection and wisdom, sustained and encouraged us in the practice of holiness and sanctity; knowing that a bad example, like a contagious disease, is easily communicated. We were acquainted with but two roads in Athens, the one leading to the Church, and the other to the schools; being perfectly ignorant of those which conducted to worldly feasts, spectacles and public games."

What more beautiful example can be proposed to youth than the edifying lives of these young Saints? Happy those, who, while still in the morning of life, form virtuous and pious friendships, thus escaping the evil influence of the vain and worldly votaries of fashion! St. Gregory of Nazianzen passed the greater part of his life in solitude, to which he was much attached; he was drawn from his retirement by St. Basil, and elevated against his wishes to the episcopacy, and was sent about the year 379 to Constantinople, to assume the government of that diocese, and oppose the progress of Arianism, which was making rapid strides in that great city.

His virtues, learning and eloquence all promised success, and he had the boldness to attack the heresy in the very abode of the Emperor who protected it. Gregory bore the greatest insults with meekness and patience; was charitable to all, led a penitential, austere life, weeping over his sins, and preparing by prayer and meditation on the Holy Scriptures for the exercise of the holy ministry. This deportment, so worthy of a bishop, won him the affection of the people of Constantinople, who soon learned to respect and venerate so saintly and learned a man. His extensive knowledge of the Bible, acute judgment, brilliant imagination, wonderful facility of expression, and pure, concise style of preaching, excited the admiration of the whole city. Truth found in him a zealous defender, and the faithful a bright example of every virtue; but the little regard he entertained for the great, and the jealousy his talents excited, were the cause of so many trials to him, that he determined once more to seek retirement, and he hastened to his loved seclusion, which now possessed new charms for him, as he wrote to one of his friends: "I cannot sufficiently prize the happiness my enemies have procured me; they have delivered me from a fiery furnace by relieving me of the cares and responsibilities of a bishopric."

The discourses of this holy Doctor constitute the greatest portion of his writings. Nothing is more sublime, more noble or more worthy of the grand mysteries of the Catholic faith, than these admirable sermons, which have acquired for St. Gregory the title of "the Theologian" of the Church of God.

THE MACEDONIAN HERESY.

The death of Valens terminated the outrages which Arianism, supported by the imperial authority, had committed in the East; but from the bosom of this heresy sprang another, which was also contrary to the dogma of the Holy Trinity, as it attacked the divinity of the Holy Ghost. The author of this new scandal was Macedonius, a semi-Arian, who had usurped the diocese of Constantinople. For several years the new doctrine was hidden under the cloak of Arianism, and had not attracted much attention during the great troubles occasioned by this factious sect.

From the beginning of the reign of Valens, however, St Athanasius, who was ever watchful over the interests of the faith, had received an intimation of the impending evil, and wrote an able treatise refuting the wicked heresy. The holy Doctor proves in this document that the Church has always believed and taught the existence of three persons in One God, that the Holy Trinity has but one and the same nature, and is but One and the same God. He shows, by the Holy Scriptures, that the Holy Ghost is God; that His attributes of sanctity, vivification, immutability and infinity belong to God alone, and concludes the eloquent defense by affirming that all his arguments are based on the doctrine of the Apostles. When the Arian influence began to decline, the Macedonians rose in favor and appeared under a new guise. Their morals were pure, their exterior very grave and their life austere; and as the populace were deceived by this appearance of piety, the Macedonians formed a large and powerful party in a short time in the city of Constantinople.

This new heresy extended as far as Thrace, Bithynia, and the Hellespont. The Emperor Theodosius, the successor of Valens, was distinguished in the beginning of his reign for his zeal in arresting the progress of error. This prince, who, by his daring exploits, and especially through his fervent piety and ardent love for the Church, has merited the title of Great, shortly after his baptism published a celebrated law, in which he declares that communion with the Roman Church is a sure mark of Catholicity. "We desire," said he, "all our subjects to profess the religion taught the Romans by the Prince of the Apostles, whose present successor is the Pontiff Damasus; that, according to the doctrine of the Gospel and teaching of the Apostles, we may believe in the divine nature of the Father, the Son and the Holy Ghost, equal in majesty and power, being one adorable Trinity. We declare those who accept this pure doctrine to be Catholics, and designate those whose rash and shameful impiety we condemn, by the ignominious title of heretics, and command that their places of meeting shall not be honored with the name of church, lest we incur the divine wrath."

In fine, the Catholic faith is the one taught by Jesus Christ, proclaimed by the Apostles, and preserved intact by the Fathers of the Church. The Church is founded on this faith, and whosoever departs from it, is not a Catholic but a heretic. The true religion is older than any of the heresies; the

Apostles lived before the authors of these sects appeared; truth precedes error; in a word, the really divine doctrine is the one which was received the first; those which have subsequently arisen are necessarily false, and unworthy of credence.

ECUMENICAL COUNCIL OF CONSTANTINOPLE.
A. D. 381.

Theodosius was aware that a stronger power than the imperial authority was necessary, to effect a complete reunion of all parties, and, on his accession to the throne, he determined, like the great Constantine, to convene a universal council, but waited until peace was restored before executing his design. He, therefore, wrote to all the Eastern bishops, inviting them to repair to Constantinople, which was the city appointed for the assembly, as he wished to attend the sessions in person. The necessary arrangements for the reception and entertainment of all the bishops were made, and Theodosius was not less lavish in his preparations for their comfort during their sojourn, than Constantine, who spared no expense in his generous hospitality toward the prelates, who assisted at the council of Nice.

The bishops hastened from all parts of the East, to the number of one hundred and fifty. Meletius, bishop of Antioch, was to preside over this august assembly. The Emperor was very desirous to see him, not only on account of his reputation for sanctity, but also because of a dream, in which he had seen him presenting him a sceptre with one hand and the crown with the other. The Emperor entertained the warmest feelings of respect and veneration for the holy prelate, from the time of this vision, although he had never met him. As soon as the bishops arrived they proceeded in a body to the royal presence; as the Emperor wished to ascertain whether he could recognize Meletius among the others, he would not allow him to be pointed out, and the features of the venerable man being indelibly impressed on his mind, he immediately discovered him in the crowd, and, hastening toward him, embraced him with respect and tenderness, reverently kissing the hand which had crowned him in advance. Theodosius then entreated all the bishops to seek the most effectual means of restoring peace to the afflicted Church, promising to support their decisions with the imperial authority.

The council was opened with a great deal of solemnity. The proceedings began by attempting to reclaim the Macedonians, the Emperor himself exhorting them to return to the faith and communion of the Church; but they absolutely refused, and withdrew from the council, thereby publicly avowing themselves heretics. The decrees of the council of Nice were approved, and in confirming the Nicene creed a few words were added, in order to explain more fully the Incarnation of the Son of God, and the divinity of the Holy Ghost. In speaking of the Incarnation, this creed said: "He came down from Heaven, was incarnate, and was made man; suffered, rose again the third day, ascended into Heaven, and will come to judge the living and the dead." The creed of Constantinople adds: "Who for us men, and for our salvation, came down from Heaven, and was incarnate by the Holy Ghost of the Virgin Mary, and was made man. He was crucified also for us, suffered under Pontius Pilate, and was buried. He rose again, according to the Scriptures, and ascended into Heaven, and sitteth at the right hand of the Father; and he shall come again with glory, to judge both the living and the dead, of whose Kingdom there shall be no end." With regard to the third person of the Holy Trinity, the Nicene creed explained the doctrine in these few words: "We believe in the Holy Ghost." That of Constantinople, on account of the Macedonian heresy, says: "And we believe in the Holy Ghost, the Lord and life-giver, who proceedeth from the Father and the Son, who, together with the Father and Son, is adored and glorified, who spake by the prophets."

The Emperor Theodosius accepted this decree as issuing from the mouth of God Himself, and made a law commanding the immediate execution of all the decisions of the Council. Although this assembly was only composed of the Eastern bishops, nevertheless the approbation of the Pope and the Western prelates caused it to be recognized as an Ecumenical council.

CLEMENCY OF THEODOSIUS.
A. D. 387.

Theodosius was naturally impetuous and easily moved to anger, but his piety enabled him to restrain his temper. A revolution broke out in Antioch, because a tax which the people hated had been imposed upon them. The populace, in their mad frenzy, threw down the statues of the Emperor and Empress, and dragged them in contempt through the streets. On being informed of this outrage, Theodosius flew into a violent passion, and in the heat of his anger threatened to destroy the city and bury the inhabitants under the ruins. Becoming cooler, however, he appointed two commissioners to inquire into the disturbance, investing them with authority to condemn the guilty to death. Meanwhile the people became conscious of their great crime against the imperial dignity, and dreaded a well-merited punishment, not daring to leave their homes, and constantly fearing a summary execution.

Flavian, bishop of Antioch, was plunged in the deepest affliction at the conduct of the infatuated mob, but his tender heart was filled with sorrow at the thought of their sad fate, and he passed whole days and nights in tears at the foot of the altar imploring the God of Mercy to soften the heart of the Emperor. Finally, this old man, more venerable on account of his sanctity than his years, sought the imperial presence in order to intercede with Theodosius in behalf of his culpable brethren. When he appeared before the Emperor, he did not advance toward the throne, but stood with his eyes cast down, as though he were the sole criminal who had committed the outrage. Noticing his embarrassment, Theodosius approached him, and after recalling the favors he had generously lavished on the city of Antioch, added, after each recital: "And it is for conferring these benefits that I have merited such shameful insults?"

Flavian, overcome by his just reproaches, sighed deeply. "Prince," said he, "we deserve every chastisement; destroy Antioch even to its foundations; reduce the city to ashes and still we should not be sufficiently punished. Our grievous fault can, however, be remedied; thou canst imitate the goodness of God, who, although constantly outraged by His ungrateful creatures, grants pardon and forgiveness to repentant sinners. Deign to overlook our offense, and we will owe our salvation to thee; thy clemency will add a new luster to thy honor and glory. The infidels will exclaim: 'How great is the God of the Christian! He raises men above weak human nature, and transforms them into Angels. Do not fear that exemption from punishment will corrupt other cities; alas, our fate will terrify them; the consternation into which we are plunged is the most cruel of punishments. Be not ashamed to listen to the prayers of a feeble old man, as God Himself speaks in my entreaties. He sends me to remind thee of the precepts of the Gospel, and to say to thee in His name: 'If thou wilt not forgive others, thy Father who is in Heaven will not forgive thee. Think of that terrible day when princes and their subjects shall appear before the tribunal of supreme justice, and remember that thy sins will be pardoned through the merits alone of Jesus Christ, who suffered every insult and indignity at the hands of the ungrateful and perfidious Jews.'"

Theodosius was moved to tears by this eloquent appeal, and answered: "Can I refuse forgiveness to men like myself, when the Master of the world, overwhelmed with shame for love of us, prayed to His Father to have mercy on His cruel executioners? Go, Father, hasten to thy flock, restore calmness and tranquillity to the affrighted city of Antioch; tell the offenders I grant them pardon, and entreat them to repair their error by future loyalty and respect for their lawful monarch.

FALL AND REPENTANCE OF THEODOSIUS.
A. D. 389.

Theodosius shortly afterward forgot the moderation he had shown in the affair of Antioch, and allowed himself to be overcome by his natural impetuosity of disposition. The city of Thessalonica, the capital of Illyria, revolted against its governor, who lost his life during the excitement. The news of this disturbance aroused the indignation of the Emperor, who immediately ordered a massacre of all the inhabitants of the city, without regard to age, sex, or condition. Seven thousand fell victims to this severe edict; St. Ambrose, bishop of Milan, wrote to the Emperor, who was in that city, and represented to him the crime he had committed, in condemning the innocent with the guilty; he exhorted him to repentance; terminating his letter by warning him that he should not assist at divine service until he had expiated his grave offense.

The Emperor, however, was deaf to this prohibition, and at the customary hour proceeded toward the Church; the holy bishop met him when within a few yards of the sacred edifice: "Go no further, Prince," cried he, "thou dost not yet feel the enormity of thy crime; reflect a moment—with what eyes dost thou look upon the holy Temple? Dost thou dare enter into the sanctuary of an angry God, thy hands still reeking with innocent blood? Canst thou, a murderer, presume to receive the body of the Lord? Withdraw, O Theodosius, from these sacred precincts, and add not the crime of sacrilege to that of murder!" The Emperor strove to excuse his conduct by quoting the example of David, who was guilty of adultery and murder. "Thou hast imitated him in his sin," said Ambrose, "imitate him in his repentance."

Theodosius received this reprimand with sentiments of humility and contrition, and returned to the palace, where he remained in seclusion for six months. The approach of the joyous festival of Christmas seemed to augment his grief. "Alas!" he exclaimed, "the Temple of God is open to the least of my subjects, and I am denied admission!" He sought the presence of the holy bishop, and with prayers and tears entreated him to grant him absolution. Ambrose replied, that he could not allow him to assist at the divine mysteries until he had first performed a public penance, which condition was cheerfully accepted by the contrite and repentant Theodosius. The Saint also commanded him to publish a law, suspending all sentences of death for thirty days; the Emperor immediately obeyed, and affixed the imperial signature to the decree, promising a faithful observance of the mandate. Then St. Ambrose, touched by his docility and ardent faith, pronounced the sacred words which restored the humble monarch to the communion of the Church, and permitted him to enter the holy Temple of the Lord, where Theodosius fell prostrate before the altar, bathed in tears, and striking his breast, uttered these words of David: "My soul hath cleaved to the ground; quicken thou me according to thy promise."

Touched by so great an example, the people mingled their prayers and tears with the supplications of their prince; and this mighty sovereign, whose violent rage had made his empire tremble, inspired the liveliest sentiments of compassion and love in the hearts of his subjects. St. Ambrose was deeply affected, and deemed it expedient to relax the strict ecclesiastical discipline, which granted absolution only at the time of death in cases of murder. The heartfelt contrition of the illustrious penitent was still more augmented by this act of clemency, and during the eight remaining years of his life, he continued to evince the sincerest repentance. This great prince has always been reverenced by the Church, and religious authors cite the Emperor Theodosius as the model of Christian princes.

SCHISM OF THE DONATISTS.

The schism of the Donatists, which distracted the African Church for two centuries, commenced in the reign of Constantine. It was at first entirely unnoticed, but finally proved itself to be a most formidable enemy to the faith. The schismatics began by inquiring if Cæcilian, bishop of Carthage, was legitimately ordained; and several prelates, headed by Donatus, on the pretense that his ordination was not valid, refused to recognize Cæcilian as their lawful bishop. The affair was referred to the Pope, who decided in favor of Cæcilian, whose innocence he proclaimed, and this judgment was subsequently confirmed by decree of the Emperor Constantine. Donatus and his partisans, however, absolutely refused to submit to the sentence, and fomented the disturbance by appointing another bishop of Carthage, and sending letters to all parts of Africa, warning the faithful against acknowledging Cæcilian as the lawful incumbent.

This unhappy division was the cause of innumerable evils in Africa. The sentence of excommunication pronounced by the Church against her rebellious children, did not terrify the Donatists, who were desirous of separating from her, and thus form a distinct society; so that this punishment passed unheeded, by men who sought only to destroy the unity of the Church. The schismatical party increased imperceptibly, and, when sufficiently strong, committed the most horrible acts of violence. In fine, the obstinacy of the Donatists degenerated into perfect fury; they took forcible possession of the churches, drove away the bishops, and destroyed the altars and sacred vessels. Their impiety went so far as to rebaptize, against their will, those who had been baptized in the Catholic church. If the faithful refused to receive a second baptism from their sacrilegious hands, they were treated in the most barbarous manner. Not satisfied with using every species of torture, these wretches were so inhuman as to pour vinegar and lime into the eyes of their victims. It is related that, on one occasion, they rebaptized forty-eight persons, who had not strength to endure the torments.

The Catholic bishops, at first, only opposed mildness and patience to the cruelties of the schismatics, hoping by these lenient measures to reclaim their unfortunate brethren. St. Augustine, bishop of Hippo, who afterward became so celebrated, labored assiduously to create a better feeling and reunite the contending parties. He succeeded in converting a great number, but the majority only became still more infuriated, and even endeavored to seize the person of the holy bishop. One day he nearly fell into their hands, and would have perished but for a blunder of his guide, who, inadvertently, strayed from the street where the assassins were concealed. Their audacity daily increased, and the Catholic bishops deemed it necessary to solicit the protection of the Emperor, who issued a severe law against these sectarians, forbidding them under pain of death to hold public assemblies.

CELEBRATED CONFERENCE AT CARTHAGE — TERMINATION OF THE SCHISM.

A. D. 411.

The Catholic bishops, who were more anxious for the conversion than for the punishment of the Donatists, entreated the Emperor to employ milder measures, and proposed to try the effects of a conference, to which Constantine finally consented. All the African bishops, Donatist as well as Catholic, received orders to repair to Carthage, so that prelates chosen from both parties could confer together. The tribune Marcellin was appointed by the Emperor to maintain order and tranquillity. On the sixteenth of May, in the year four hundred and eleven, this celebrated conference was inaugurated. Seven bishops were selected from each side to discuss the affair, and four ecclesiastical notaries appointed to record their proceedings.

When these preliminaries were satisfactorily arranged, the Catholic bishops gave an admirable example of moderation and generosity, proclaiming verbally and by writing the following magnanimous promise: "If our adversaries gain the advantage over us in this conference, we consent to resign our office and submit to their guidance; if, on the contrary, the Donatists being conquered, return to the Church, we will share the episcopal dignity with them. If, however, the faithful object to the unusual sight of two bishops in one diocese, we will retire and leave them in undisturbed possession of our sees. We can work out our salvation by living as simple

Christians; and therefore, if the resignation of our office will promote the spiritual welfare of the faithful, we will cheerfully retire."

Among nearly three hundred Catholic prelates, who assisted at this conference, only two at first objected to this generous resolution; but they soon concurred in the general opinion. St. Augustine, who was the instigator of this movement, was not only one of the seven chosen by the Catholic bishops to defend the cause of the Church, but the six others depended on him to refute the sophistries of the Donatists. The most perfect order was maintained in this celebrated conference, which lasted three days.

St. Augustine proved incontestably that there could be no legitimate reason for separating from the Catholic Church, and eloquently depicted the criminality of those who endeavored to destroy her unity. He demonstrated the necessity of being in communion with our holy Mother the Church, without which there is no hope of salvation; because, outside of this One, Only, Church, there can be no true sanctity or real holiness; that the true Church, the spouse of Jesus Christ, is, according to His divine promise, spread over the whole world, and not confined to an obscure corner of Africa; that the good and bad are mingled together while on earth; that the faithful should avoid all participation in the crimes of her unworthy children, but not separate exteriorly from them. God rewarded the zeal of the holy Doctor. Those ecclesiastics who still retained a love for truth, and the people, who were informed of the proceedings of the conference, were finally convinced by his able arguments, and from that time great numbers returned to the Church.

THE PELAGIAN HERESY.
A. D. 412.

The schism of the Donatists had quietly disappeared, when the Church was attacked by new enemies, who caused her much sorrow and grief. Pelagius, a native of Great Britain, was the author of the heresy; he was a subtle, artificial and hypocritical character, and without changing his opinion could use different modes of expression, and thus deceive the unwary. He went to Rome, and there introduced a new doctrine, the offspring of inordinate pride, denying, as he did, original sin, and salvation through the merits of the Redeemer. He dared not explain himself openly at first, for fear of exciting opposition, by combating the ancient and universal belief of the Church; but, in order to gradually prepare the people for the reception of his wicked doctrine, he clothed his errors in equivocal and artful language. He attached to himself a disciple, named Celestius, who greatly contributed toward the extension of this impious sect. Celestius proceeded to Africa, and, being of a bolder and more enterprising nature than Pelagius, taught openly, in direct opposition to the doctrine of St. Paul, that the sin of our first parents is not communicated to their descendants, and that man, without supernatural grace, can, by his own power, obey the commandments of God.

This new profanity caused many disturbances. St. Augustine in learned treatises admirably refuted it, and proved by the express words of Scripture, and by the sacrament of infant baptism, that we are all born in original sin; quoting the beautiful prayer which emanated from the divine lips of a God-man, as conclusive evidence of our daily need of grace, to direct and aid our will in all that appertains to the salvation of our immortal souls. Celestius was therefore condemned at Carthage, and excluded from all ecclesiastical communion.

In the meantime, Pelagius, who had proceeded to Palestine, and succeeded by his dissimulation and falsehoods, in deceiving the bishops of that country, becoming bolder, sent his apology to St. Augustine, in which he boasted of the favorable opinion he had won in the East. This scandalous conduct excited the zeal of the African bishops, by whom two councils were convened — one at Carthage, and the other at Milevis — in which were declared, according to the Catholic doctrine, that the sin of Adam had descended to his posterity, and that, without an interior grace which inspires the love of virtue, we cannot perform any spiritual action conducive to salvation.

The Fathers of these councils wrote to Pope St. Innocent, requesting him to confirm this decision by the authority of the apostolic See. The sovereign Pontiff replied to the synodical letters of the African bishops, approving of their zeal in preserving the purity of the faith, and firmly establishing the old doctrine of original sin, and the necessity of supernatural grace for the worthy performance of all acts of Christian piety. He solemnly condemned Pelagius, Celestius, and their followers, declaring them separated from the communion of the Church, unless they abjured their errors.

After the publication of the pontifical decree, St. Augustine considered the affair terminated. "Rome has spoken," says the holy Doctor; "the decision of the African bishops has been sent to the Holy See, the letters of the Pope, confirming it, have been received; the controversy is finished, and may it please God to exterminate the error as well!"

INTRIGUES AND OBSTINACY OF THE PELAGIANS.

The desire of St. Augustine was not gratified, the error continuing to exist, notwithstanding the condemnation it had received. Pelagius and his followers refused to submit to the sentence pronounced against them, and strove to efface in the eyes of the world their disgraceful defeat. Pope Innocent, who had condemned them, was dead, and Pelagius wrote in a forcible and respectful manner to his successor, Zozimus, in order to prove his innocence. Celestius then repaired to Rome, and presented an artfully worded confession of faith to the Pontiff, promising to abjure all that the Holy See anathematized.

The new Pope asked him several questions, to which Celestius replied with that appearance of simplicity and candor, deceit can so well assume.

Zozimus did not pursue his investigations, but pronounced him innocent; not that he approved of his errors, but because this imposter had previously declared himself willing to abide by the judgment of the Holy See. Zozimus wrote a letter to the African bishops, in which he appeared convinced of the sincerity of Pelagius, and spoke a little reproachfully of their conduct in his regard, without, however, uttering a word in favor of the heresy.

The African prelates immediately saw that the Pope had been deceived by these artful impostors, and hastily convened a numerous council. Two hundred and fourteen bishops composed the assembly; they gave a more minute account of the schism, explained all that had taken place in Africa, exposed the venomous doctrine concealed under the profession of faith, as well as the hypocrisy of the heretics, and they drew up certain canonical laws which they sent to Rome, accompanied by a letter expressed in these terms: "We have decreed that the sentence pronounced by Innocent against Pelagius and Celestius is in full force, until they frankly acknowledge that the grace of Jesus Christ is necessary, not only to know, but in order to follow, the paths of righteousness, as without this supernatural aid we can neither think, say, nor perform any pious thought, word, or action. The vague submission of Celestius to the Holy See is not sufficient reparation for the scandal he has caused; he must anathematize, without the least equivocation or ambiguity, whatever is at all doubtful in his profession of faith, lest some may infer — not that the schismatic has abandoned his errors, but that the Holy See has approved of them."

These representations produced the desired effect. Zozimus attentively examined the whole affair, and, becoming convinced of the deception of Celestius, pronounced a sentence which confirmed the decisions of the African bishops and condemned Pelagius and his followers. This decree was received with respect and obedience by the whole Christian world; but the heretics then showed the insincerity and falseness of the promises they had previously made to the sovereign Pontiff. They appealed from the judgment of the Pope to a general council, but St. Augustine opposed them, and asserted that the assembled Church would only ratify the decision of Zozimus and the African bishops; that the heresy was sufficiently condemned; and that no further examination was needed, but, on the contrary, every effort should be made to repress the schism. The Emperor Honorius approved of this decree, and pronounced a sentence of banishment against those who obstinately persisted in countenancing the condemned doctrine.

ERRORS OF THE SEMI-PELAGIANS.

The Pelagian heresy was gradually extinguished, but from its ashes arose another sect, which softened all that was most revolting in the first, and adopted a medium course between the doctrine of Pelagius and the orthodox faith. This milder form of error was introduced by some priests of Marseilles, who were called Semi-Pelagians. They attributed the commencement of faith and the first good impulses of the human heart to free will. According to their teachings, God, in consequence of these holy emotions, gives an increase of faith, and the grace to perform good works. Thus the Semi-Pelagians, like the Catholics, admit original sin, and the necessity of an interior grace to practice virtue, but they contended that man could merit this grace by a commencement of faith and a first good emotion, of which God is not the author.

St. Augustine ably refuted this pernicious error, and directed all his zeal against this insidious heresy. He composed two works on this subject, in which he clearly shows, that not only the increase, but even the beginning, of faith is a gift of God; that the first movements of grace cannot be founded on our own merits, and do not emanate from us in any way whatever. To prove this, he quotes several passages from the Bible, which teach that it is God Himself, who directs the human will and disposes it to good, and he also dwells particularly upon these words of the Apostle: "What have you that you have not received?" words clearly showing that man has need of the grace of God in order to commence to perform good actions conducive to salvation; that God does not call men because they are righteous, but that they may become righteous. He affirms, that the Church has always declared, in her prayers, that she expects divine mercy, not in consequence, however, of any intrinsic merit of ours, and that grace would cease to be grace were it not gratuitous. Finally, he demonstrates this truth by the baptism of infants, who are called to this grace without any merit of theirs; "for," said he, "where is the faith or good works of these infants?"

The Pope St. Celestin, hearing of the erroneous doctrine of the priests of Marseilles, condemned them, and declared, in opposition to their heretical teachings, that God operates in such a manner in the human heart that a holy thought or pious desire — in short, every good emotion, is of a supernatural nature; and that if we are capable of a meritorious action it is through the merits of Jesus Christ, without whom we can do nothing.

These disputes were at length terminated by the celebrated canon of the second council of Orange, over which presided the illustrious St. Cesarius of Arles, and is expressed in these words: "If any one says that either the increase or commencement of faith, and the first good impulses of the heart, by which we believe in Him who justifies the sinner, is not the effect of supernatural grace, but a natural tendency toward good, he contradicts the belief of the Apostles themselves, since St. Paul says: 'We are confident that He who has commenced the good work in you, my brethren, will perfect it until the day of Our Lord;' and again: 'You have received the grace to believe in Jesus Christ; . . . it is by this grace that you will be saved through faith which does not come from you, but is a gift of God.'"

ST. JEROME.

St. Jerome, one of the most illustrious Doctors of the Church, united with St. Augustine in combating the Pelagian heresy. Born in Dalmatia, of wealthy Christian parents, at a very early age Jerome showed so much aptness for learning, that his father considered it his duty to carefully cultivate this happy disposition, and accordingly sent him to Rome, where he made wonderful progress in his studies and oratory; but, as the esteem and praise of men was rather the object of his wishes than any desire of advancing in the way of salvation, God permitted him to fall into great excesses. He soon, however, returned to the path of virtue, and, toward the year 374, retired into the desert of Chalcis, in Syria, a vast solitude scorched by the intense heat of the sun, but nevertheless inhabited by a few hermits, whose love of a penitential life led them to choose this wilderness for their abode.

Seized with fear of the judgments of God, Jerome's only desire in leaving the world was to escape the divine anger, when suddenly Pelagius appeared in Palestine, and endeavored to promulgate his errors in that country. The holy recluse, alarmed at the danger which menaced the faith, strenuously opposed the new doctrine. Pelagius became infuriated, and not only wrote in defense of his errors, but excited his followers against St. Jerome to such an extent, that they committed the most horrible acts of violence, attacking, plundering, and burning the monastery in which he resided. St. Jerome repaired to Antioch, where Paulinus, the bishop of that city, ordained him priest; but he did not remain here, or become connected with any Church, as it was still his desire to lead a life of solitude and penance.

Proceeding to Constantinople, he remained for some time with St. Gregory of Nazianzen, and, under the guidance of this able master, applied himself to the study of the Holy Scriptures. From thence he went to Rome, where Pope Damasus detained him, in order to reply to those who wished to consult his Holiness upon scriptural matter or points of moral theology. After the death of the Pontiff he returned to Palestine, and resided in Bethlehem; here it was that the holy Doctor, in the enjoyment of his long desired rest, wrote the greater number of those admirable works on the Holy Scriptures, which are of inestimable value to the Church. He also undertook to translate the Bible into Latin, adhering carefully to the original text, and with this view, devoted himself to the study of the Hebrew language, receiving lessons from a learned Jew, whom he converted, and who also became his disciple. He not only enriched the Church with a new translation, but also wrote treatises elucidating the meaning of the sacred volume.

Several commentaries of St. Jerome are still extant. In the preface of the one on the prophet Isaiah, who lived seven hundred years before our Lord, he says, that he not only regards Isaiah as a prophet, but also as an evangelist and apostle, as his prophesies contain an account of the whole life of our Saviour; His being born of a virgin, His ignominious death, the glory of His Resurrection, and the establishment of His Church, throughout the world. "Isaiah," says this learned translator, "spoke so plainly of all these things, that he seems rather to record a history of past events, than to predict what was to be accomplished in the future."

VIRTUES AND SUFFERINGS OF ST. JOHN CHRYSOSTOM.

A. D. 407.

At this period St. John Chrysostom, archbishop of Constantinople, rendered glory to God by his apostolic zeal in the reformation of the clergy and inhabitants of that great city. He boldly reprimanded the inordinate love of riches, the luxurious habits of the women, and the overweening pride of the great. The court itself did not escape his vigilance, and he frequently reminded the Emperor and his wife Eudoxia, of the weighty obligations of their high position. This courageous conduct made him powerful enemies; the Empress especially was displeased with a sermon in which she imagined that he alluded to her. She sought for means of revenge, and, in the person of Theophilus, bishop of Alexandria, found a willing instrument to carry out her plans. St. Chrysostom was accordingly deposed and exiled, but the very next day a terrible earthquake occurred in Constantinople, which was regarded as an evidence of divine wrath.

Eudoxia herself was so much alarmed, that she implored the Emperor to recall the holy bishop, who returned in triumph to the city. A new disturbance, however, soon arose; a silver statue of the Empress had been erected near the principal church of Constantinople; and public games, interspersed with superstitious practices, were celebrated in its vicinity. The holy bishop preached against this irreligious custom, which sermon exasperated Eudoxia to such a degree that she determined upon the ruin of the holy prelate; she deposed and banished him to Cucusus, a small city in Armenia; having chosen this barren country in order to make the Saint feel the full weight of her anger. The journey occupied seventy days, and was attended by many hardships and inconveniences, occasioned by his ill health and the harshness of the soldiers who accompanied him. As soon as he recovered, St. John labored still more zealously for the welfare of the Church; instructing the people of the country, assisting the poor and ransoming the captives. His enemies, although successful in their efforts against him, became jealous of his good works, and banished him to Pythyus, an obscure city on the extreme borders of the empire, and near the eastern shore of the Euxine sea. He was conducted to this new place of exile by two brutal soldiers, who treated him in the most cruel and violent manner, for a reward had been promised them if the Saint died on the journey.

The holy bishop, weak and exhausted, finally sank under so many sufferings; and after a toilsome march of three months, arrived near Comana, in Pontus, and was attacked with a malignant fever, which obliged him to stop in that city in the presbytery of St. Basiliscus, bishop and martyr. That night Basiliscus appeared to him and said: "Courage, my brother, to-morrow we shall be together." The next day the Church lost one of her holiest bishops and most illustrious Doctors. His extraordinary eloquence, which equaled the most celebrated orators of antiquity, won for him the surname of Chrysostom, or the "Golden Mouth."

THE NESTORIAN HERESY.

The spirit of error, after attacking the mystery of the Holy Trinity, the doctrine of original sin and that of grace, strove to undermine the belief in the mystery of the Incarnation. The Church had always taught that Jesus Christ is the Word made flesh, and that accordingly, there are two natures and but one person in Jesus Christ; whereas, Nestorius, Patriarch of Constantinople, declared there were two persons in the Son of God. Not venturing to openly assail the Catholic doctrine, he pursued another plan, and said that the Blessed Virgin ought not to be called the Mother of God, but simply the Mother of Christ, thus distinguishing between the person of Christ and that of the Word.

This impious heresy, entirely contrary to the faith and tradition of the Church, greatly scandalized the clergy and laity. The first time this blasphemy was proclaimed in Constantinople, the faithful left the Church in order to show their disgust for the sacrilegious Nestorius. Thus the voice of faith is always raised in opposition and condemnation of every heresy, that is to say, whenever the doctrines of the Church are attacked. Nestorius, who was in favor at court, endeavored to influence the Emperor, and by this means promulgate his errors; but God provided a remedy against the danger which threatened the Church, in the person of an illustrious defender of the dogma assailed. St. Cyril, bishop of Alexandria, was the invincible bulwark which Providence opposed to the wily efforts of the heretic.

As soon as the holy prelate was warned of the progress of the impious doctrine, he published a work, clearly explaining the truth of the mystery of the Incarnation. "I am amazed," he writes, "how it can be doubted that the Blessed Virgin is the mother of God; for if our Lord Jesus Christ is God, the Blessed Virgin, His mother, is unquestionably the mother of God. The Apostles have taught us, and the early Fathers declare, not that the nature of the Word or the divinity originated in Mary, but that the sacred body, to which the Word is hypostatically united, was formed in her womb, and animated with a rational soul; thus it is said the Word was made flesh. In the order of nature, although the mother has no part in the creation of the soul, still we do not hesitate to say that she is the mother of the entire man, and not simply of the body." This defence of St. Cyril became very celebrated in the Eastern churches, and was most consoling to the faithful, who had been scandalized by the pernicious doctrine of Nestorius. St. Cyril wrote to the heretic, mildly endeavoring to reclaim him from his errors, and exhorting him to atone for the scandal he had given, by calling the Blessed Virgin by her rightful title of mother of God. "Be assured," he adds, "I am ready to suffer every thing — imprisonment and death itself, in defense of the teachings of our Lord Jesus Christ."

This letter was of no avail, as the author of a heresy is rarely converted or convinced of his criminality, in attacking the pure faith of the Catholic Church. The holy bishop finding his hopes frustrated with regard to Nestorius, appealed to Pope St. Celestine, to whom he gave an account of what had occurred, and of the existing state of the Church of Constantinople, imploring his Holiness to use every means to exterminate the heresy. Nestorius also sent his written profession of faith to Rome. The sovereign Pontiff convened an assembly of bishops, in which the writings of Nestorius were carefully examined, and, being found contrary to that of the Fathers, were unanimously condemned. Celestine wrote to the bishops of the principal Eastern dioceses, notifying them of this decision, and addressed a letter to St. Cyril, praising his zeal and vigilance, and expressing his approval of his explanation of the mystery of the Incarnation, assuring him that if Nestorius continued to assail the Catholic doctrine, and within a given time did not abjure his errors, he should be excommunicated from the Church.

GENERAL COUNCIL OF EPHESUS.
A. D. 431.

Nestorius refused to submit to the sentence pronounced by the Holy See, and, like all other heretics, was only the more eager to spread his impious doctrine. Although he had partisans at court, the Emperor Theodosius, the younger, who was sincerely attached to the faith, was astonished at hearing of the tumult raised by the faithful of Constantinople, and he resolved to convene a general council at Ephesus. This intelligence infused joy into every Catholic heart, and the bishops assembled from all parts of the Christian world to the number of two hundred — St. Cyril presiding in the name of the Pope. Nestorius also repaired to Ephesus, accompanied by the Count Candidian, whom the Emperor had appointed for the protection of the council, but who, nevertheless, openly sided with the heretic. Nestorius refused to appear at the council, although three times officially summoned; giving for a pretext the absence of John, bishop of Antioch, and the suffragan bishops who had not yet arrived. As the delay of these prelates seemed intentional, and as fifteen days of the time appointed by the Emperor for the opening of the council had elapsed, the first session was finally held.

In the center of the church, on an elevated throne, was placed the book of the Gospels, representing the presence of Jesus Christ in their midst, in accordance with His divine promise of being with those who assemble together in His name. The bishops were seated on either side, according to their respective rank. As Nestorius positively refused to appear, it was necessary to examine his teachings through his writings, which were read aloud. When the reading was concluded the bishops exclaimed: "Anathema to these impious errors! anathema to whoever holds this doctrine, which is contrary to the Holy Scriptures, and the traditions of the Fathers!" The letter of Pope Celestine to Nestorius was then read, and several passages from the writings of the most illustrious Fathers, such as St. Cyprian, St. Athanasius, St. Ambrose, and St. Basil were cited, in opposition to the heretical assertions of Nestorius. Then, after each bishop had solemnly testified to the faith of his Church, the Blessed Virgin was declared to be the mother of God, and a sentence of excommunication was pronounced against Nestorius.

When the people of Ephesus heard of this decree they were transported with joy, and loaded the Fathers of the council with thanks and benedictions, the whole city resounding with the name and praises of the mother of God. The prelates wrote to the Emperor, informing him of this decision, but Count Candidian intercepted the letters, and, in concert with Nestorius, prejudiced Theodosius against them by a false account of the proceedings of the assembly; preventing the deputies of the council from reaching the Emperor by guarding the vessels and roads, so that truth would have succumbed for a while beneath this vigorous resistance, if God had not overcome every obstacle, and defeated all the conspiracies formed against his Church. One of the deputies, disguised as a beggar, carried the true version of the proceedings of the council concealed in a hollow staff, and succeeded in effecting an entrance into the palace. Upon receiving a correct account of the council, the Emperor banished Nestorius to a monastery of Antioch, and, as he there continued to promulgate his errors, he was exiled to Oasis, in Egypt, where he died a miserable death three years afterwards.

THE EUTYCHIAN HERESY.

The Nestorian heresy gave rise to another which appeared soon after, and was not less opposed to the mystery of the Incarnation. Eutyches, while opposing Nestorius, fell into error himself. He taught that there was only one nature in Jesus Christ after the Incarnation. Thus does the human mind only avoid one extreme to fall into another; but the Church, guided by the spirit of truth, condemns all doctrines opposed to faith. Nestorius had divided the persons of Jesus Christ, and Eutyches confounded the two natures. He was the superior of a monastery near Constantinople, and had been very zealous in maintaining the unity of persons in opposition to the teachings of Nestorius; but this aversion to Nestorianism threw him into still greater error, which caused as much scandal as the one preceding. Eutyches at first only explained his views to some friends in private conversations, but subsequently strove to diffuse his doctrine throughout the monasteries of Constantinople. His friends used every effort to undeceive him, and prevent the slightest appearance of scandal, but all their efforts were in vain, as he was of a most obstinate nature; they were then obliged to denounce him to St. Flavian, patriarch of Constantinople.

This holy prelate, after employing mild and gentle means to reclaim the heretic, assembled the bishops, who were then in the imperial city, and summoned Eutyches before them. He at first refused to appear, and, as he persisted in his opinions, the prelates condemned his doctrine, and deposed him from his position of superior of his monastery. Eutyches, nevertheless, found partisans at court, who encouraged him in his rebellious conduct; Chrysaphius, one of the principal ministers of the Emperor, sustained him with all his influence; he was a barbarian, whose handsome face was his only merit; avaricious, cruel and irreligious, he possessed the confidence of the Emperor and governed the affairs of State. Chrysaphius obtained from Theodosius permission to have the doctrine of Eutyches examined in another assembly of bishops, and appointed Dioscorus, bishop of Alexandria, president, as he was a friend of Eutyches, and prejudiced against St. Flavian. Constituting himself master of the convention, Chrysaphius conducted the proceedings in the most violent manner, making it resemble a meeting of brigands, rather than an ecclesiastical assembly. Two commissioners of the Emperor entered accompanied by soldiers bearing chains in their hands, and threatening the most dreadful fate to those who would not accede to the commands of the imperial favorite. In the midst of this tumult Eutyches was absolved and St. Flavian condemned.

As several bishops refused their approval of this iniquitous sentence, the doors were closed and they were forced to sign the decree. Those who would not yield to these violent measures were banished, among whom was St. Flavian, who, during the journey to the place of exile, was severely beaten, and died a few days afterwards. The Emperor Theodosius, who had allowed himself to be influenced in so weak and criminal a manner, did not long survive him. The blind confidence he reposed in his favorite, tarnished the glory of his reign, the end of which was as sad as the beginning had been bright and promising. Marcian, a religious prince, succeeded him, whose first care was to preserve the purity of the Catholic faith without spot or stain.

GENERAL COUNCIL OF CHALCEDON.
A. D. 451.

St. Leo, who was at this period the worthy occupant of the chair of St. Peter, felt most keenly the injury the Church had sustained, and he earnestly endeavored to restore peace. The most prompt and efficacious remedy was a general council, which the Emperor Marcian, according to the desire of the Holy Pontiff, convened at Chalcedon, a suburb of Constantinople, as this prince wished to attend in person in order to maintain decorum and tranquillity. The bishops assembled to the number of three hundred and sixty in the church of St. Euphemia, and the first session was held on the 8th of October in the year 451. St. Leo, not being able to go, sent three legates, who presided in his name. The book of the Gospels was, as in the council of Ephesus, placed on a raised dais in the midst of the assembly. They commenced by examining the violent and unjust conduct of Dioscorus with regard to St. Flavian, and reproached him with having trampled on every rule of the Church, and they concluded by deposing him from the episcopal dignity.

An admirable letter, written by St. Leo to St. Flavian at the beginning of this heresy, was then read, in which the holy Doctor explained in a clear and forcible manner the Catholic doctrine concerning the mystery of the Incarnation; that is to say, the unity of persons, and distinction of natures in Jesus Christ. This belief, found to be in perfect conformity with the Nicene creed and that of Constantinople, was unanimously approved, and regarded as an infallible rule of faith. "We all believe this," exclaimed the bishops. "Peter, himself, the great Prince of the Apostles, speaks to us by the mouth of St. Leo; this doctrine must be received as orthodox; anathema to all who differ from us." The prelates then drew up a confession of faith, in which, after referring to the creeds of Nice and Constantinople, they continue as follows: "We declare that it is necessary to believe in one and the same Jesus Christ, Our Lord, true God and true man, perfect in both natures; consubstantial to the Father according to the divine nature, and to man according to the human nature; engendered by the Father, before all ages, according to the divine nature, and born of the Virgin Mary in time according to the human nature; one and the same Jesus Christ, Our Lord, in two natures, without contradiction, without change, without separation, without the union destroying the different natures. On the contrary, the properties of both are preserved, and unite in one single person, in such a manner as to form one and the same only Son, God, the Word, our Lord Jesus Christ." The Emperor assisted in person at the sixth session, assuring the Fathers that, like the great Constantine, his only desire in being present was to sustain the decisions of the Council with the imperial authority, and not to alter their decrees. All the bishops cried out: "Long live the new Constantine! Long live our Catholic Emperor and Empress! God grant many years and a prosperous reign to Marcian, the servant of Christ!"

The Emperor desired the confession of faith to be read aloud to him, and when it was concluded asked if all agreed on what they had just heard. The prelates exclaimed: "We have but one faith and one doctrine; such was the belief of the holy Doctors; such was the faith of the Apostles, and it is this faith which has saved the world!" Acclamations of joy resounded on all sides; they called the Emperor and Empress the new Constantine and the new Helena, with many other titles of respect and affection. Marcian enforced the execution of the decrees of the Council by a law, saying that whoever made further inquiries after this decision, evinced a love of falsehood and a desire to disagree.

GREAT QUALITIES OF ST. LEO.

St. Leo had been raised up by divine Providence principally to combat the Eutychian heresy; but this was not the only service he rendered the Church. This great Pontiff rescued his flock on two critical occasions, when all seemed lost. Attila, king of the Huns, who called himself the scourge of God, after ravaging Italy with fire and sword, advanced towards Rome, which city he intended to destroy. The Emperor, who was not prepared to defend it, consulted with the senate as to what course he should pursue. They could devise no other plan than to send a deputation to the barbarian, offering terms of peace. St. Leo, convinced that God can change the most obdurate heart by His almighty power, undertook in person this dangerous mission, which he executed so boldly as to impress the savage conqueror, who, although not at all imposing in appearance, was still terrible to behold, showing his barbarous origin in every feature. He was of small stature, but very broad, an immense head, bright eyes, a very slight beard and thin hair, which the hardships of war had whitened at an early age, a flat nose, swarthy complexion, and a haughty and threatening manner, made him a very repulsive and alarming object to approach.

St. Leo, sustained by an invisible power superior to all human strength, appeared boldly and confidently before this mighty prince, whose glance alone caused the most powerful kings, his vassals, to tremble. The Pontiff spoke respectfully but forcibly to

Attila, asking him to restore peace and tranquillity to Italy. The courage of the prelate astonished the barbarian, who, turning to his attendants, said: "I know not why, but the words of this priest have touched me." Becoming more tractable, he listened to the proposals of the Emperor, and ceasing his hostilities, withdrew his army from Italy. How potent is the charm of virtue which can thus soften the most ferocious nature.

About three years after, the Pope was subjected to a similar trial, when Genseric, king of the Vandals, in his turn desolated Italy, leaving traces of his cruelty wherever he passed. On entering Rome, St. Leo sought his presence, and asked him to spare the lives of the inhabitants. He spoke with so much dignity and wisdom, that he succeeded in obtaining a promise from Genseric, that neither the fire nor the sword should be employed against the city, thus securing the safety of the people and the public edifices; but the holy Pope only retarded for a short time the fall of the Roman empire in the West. The different provinces of which it was composed became, soon after, the prey of several barbarous tribes, who successively invaded them. Finally, Odoacer, king of the Heruli, conquered Italy in 476, crowning his victory by the capture of Rome, and extinguishing even the name of empire in the West, by assuming the title of king of Italy, which he considered more glorious than that of Emperor.

In the general confusion which followed this great event, the barbarous tribes invaded the surrounding provinces, loading themselves with rich spoils. Thus the most powerful empire in the world was destroyed about 1280 years after Romulus, its founder — a striking example of the instability of the grandest structures of human greatness. Not only kings and their subjects pass away, but the most powerful kingdoms are swept from the face of the earth — the Church which Jesus Christ has established through His sufferings and death being the only edifice that will exist until the end of time.

ESTABLISHMENT OF THE CHURCH IN IRELAND.
A. D. 431.

Very little is known concerning the early history of Ireland. According to some accounts, Milesius with a colony of Phœnicians from the coast of Spain, landed in Ireland in the year 1300 B. C.; but others assert it to have been at a much later period. The island was divided by the Milesians among several princes, who governed the provinces with the title of kings. The religion of the inhabitants resembled that of the Eastern nations; they adored the sun under the name of Baal or Bel, and the moon under that of Re; the adoration of fire also formed a part of their worship.

The most important event in the history of Ireland, was the introduction of Christianity into the island, by the great and glorious St. Patrick, in the year 430, under the pontificate of Pope Celestin, whose attention had for some time been directed to the conversion of the Irish. He therefore appointed Palladius bishop, and instructed him to undertake the difficult mission; but Palladius dying soon after his consecration, St. Patrick was chosen to succeed him.

VIRTUES OF ST. PATRICK.

It is the generally received opinion that St. Patrick was born in Gaul, of noble parents, in the year 387. At the age of sixteen he was captured by a wandering band of robbers, and taken as a slave to Ireland. He was placed by his master in charge of large flocks of sheep, and being exposed at all times to the cold and heat on the mountains and in the valleys, he often suffered cruel hardships, but the grace of God sustained him and dwelt in his heart. At the end of six years he escaped from his bondage, and returned to his native country. After spending a short time with his parents, he entered the famous monastery of St. Martin, near Tours, and when he had made the necessary studies he was elevated to the dignity of the priesthood.

Upon the death of Palladius, St. Patrick was consecrated bishop, and at once proceeded to the scene of his labors. He arrived in Ireland in the first year of the pontificate of Sixtus III, A. D. 432. He went from province to province in order to instruct the people in the truths of religion, and his efforts were everywhere crowned with success. The entire island was soon christianized, and before his death he had founded three hundred and fifty-five churches, and consecrated the same number of bishops. He died on the 17th of March, A. D. 465, which day is still celebrated by the Irish with great solemnity. He was the means used by God to convert a whole nation to the Catholic faith, and his memory is held in benediction and grateful remembrance by those for whom he labored.

CONVERSION OF SCOTLAND.
A. D. 431.

Great diversity of opinion exists among historians, in regard to the precise period of the introduction of Christianity among the Scots. Tertullian and Eusebius assert, that the Gospel was preached to them very near the time of the Apostles; but eminent ecclesiastical writers represent Scotland to have been in a rude and barbarous state, even in the fourth and fifth centuries. The Scottish people claim St. Palladius as their first Apostle; it is certain, that, although Ireland was the scene of his early missionary labors, he, in the year 431, arrived in Scotland, where he preached with great success and founded many churches.

The saint died at Fordun, near Aberdeen, in the year 450. The Scots venerate St. Andrew as principal patron of their country, and their historians tell us that the Abbot Regulus brought thither from Constantinople, in the year 369, certain relics of this Apostle, which he deposited in a church he built in his honor with a monastery attached, where now stands the city of St. Andrew's.

CONVERSION OF THE FRENCH.
A. D. 493.

When the Roman empire was declining in the West, God did not abandon Gaul to the government of idolatrous princes, but called Clovis, king of the French, to a knowledge of the Gospel. This people, issuing from Germany, had already established themselves in Gaul. Clovis, though still a pagan, had espoused Clotilda, a Christian princess of great piety. The queen frequently conversed with the king about the Christian religion, and convinced him of the absurdity of the pagan worship; but Clovis could not summon courage to renounce his idols. Nevertheless, Clotilda obtained his consent to the baptism of their infant son; but as the child died a few days afterward, Clovis reproached the queen, and attributed his son's death to the anger of the gods. The pious princess, however, was not disheartened; faith in the Providence of God dried the tears maternal tenderness drew forth, and sustained her in her bereavement. Their second son also received baptism, and as the child became ill, the king declared he would die like his brother, as he had also been baptized. Clotilda had recourse to prayer, and God, satisfied with having tested her faith and confidence in the divine mercy, rewarded her piety by restoring the young prince to health.

The great qualities of Clovis, and the hopes entertained of his conversion, won him the affection of his new subjects. The most fervent prayers were offered for him throughout the kingdom, and the Holy Spirit was implored to enlighten his mind and touch his heart. These supplications were at length heard, and divine Providence decreed that the conversion of this prince, upon which that of the whole nation depended, should be occasioned by a miracle similar to the one which, in former times, had caused the great Constantine to declare his allegiance to Jesus Christ. A miraculous victory was the means by which these two princes were induced to embrace Christianity. The Allemani, a warlike people of Germany, had crossed the Rhine, and advanced toward Gaul, with the intention of invading that country. Clovis marched against them, and encountered them on the plain of Tolbiac, in the duchy of Julien. Before his departure, Clotilda told him that if he desired a victory, he must invoke the God of the Christians.

The battle commenced, the French troops began to falter and disperse, and this appearance of panic redoubled the ardor of the Allemani, who considered the day theirs. In this extremity Clovis remembered the words of Clotilda, and addressing the throne of grace and mercy, exclaimed: "O God, whom Clotilda adores, come to my help. If thou wilt give me the victory, I will adore no other God but thee!" God had chosen this moment to make Himself known to Clovis, by granting an immediate answer to his earnest and touching petition. Hardly had the prince ended his supplication, when the French rallied, and, rushing on the Allemani, put them to flight; nearly all those who escaped the carnage which ensued, surrendered at discretion.

BAPTISM OF CLOVIS.

It could not be doubted, but that Heaven had blessed the French arms by turning the tide of conquest in their favor, and this warlike nation acknowledged the God of Clotilda to be the God of battles and of victory. Clovis recrossed into Gaul, in order to fulfill the solemn vow he had made. Even during the march he was eager to receive instruction in the faith, and, for this purpose, when passing through Toul, he persuaded a worthy priest to accompany him. Clotilda was much rejoiced when she heard of the victory, and especially at the happy intelligence of the conversion of Clovis. She went as far as Rheims to meet him, and congratulated him more on his holy dispositions than on the conquest he had gained.

St. Remi, bishop of that city, whom God had adorned with talents and virtues, in order to render him worthy of becoming the Apostle of Gaul, continued to instruct the king in the truths of the Catholic faith. Clovis no longer delayed his profession of faith, and assembling his soldiers, exhorted them to follow his example — renounce their false idols and adore the God who had blessed their efforts against the enemy. He was suddenly interrupted by the acclamations of his troops, who cried out: "We reject our mortal gods, and are ready to serve the God of whom St. Remi preaches." Clovis, delighted to find his army animated with these Christian sentiments, consulted St. Remi as to what day should be appointed for the baptism, and they finally decided on Christmas eve. Remi, who wished to impress the French by allowing them to witness the most august ceremonies of the Church, omitted nothing which could add to the splendor of the occasion. The church and baptistry were hung with the richest tapestries, and a great number of deliciously perfumed wax tapers lent their brilliancy to the scene, which diffusing an exquisite fragrance caused the holy place to be everywhere pervaded with a celestial odor. Nothing can be more magnificent than the description of the reception of the new Catechumens, which is still extant. The streets and public places were draped with rich cloths of gorgeous hues, and they marched in procession, carrying the Holy Gospel and the Cross from the royal palace to the Church, singing beautiful hymns and solemn litanies. St. Remi led the king by the hand, the queen following with two princesses, sisters of Clovis, and accompanied by three thousand soldiers, principally officers, whom his example had won to Jesus Christ.

On arriving at the baptistry, the king asked for baptism, and the Saint replied: "Bow thy neck humbly, Sicamber; adore that which thou hast burnt, and burn that which thou hast adored." The king, having thereupon confessed his faith in the Trinity, was baptized in the name of the Father, the Son, and the Holy Ghost, and was anointed with the holy chrism. The three thousand warriors who were present, without counting the women and children, were then baptized by the bishops and priests, who had repaired to Rheims for the ceremony. One of the sisters of Clovis received baptism, and another sister, who was a Christian, but who had fallen into the heresy of the Arians, was reconciled, and received the holy chrism. The conversion of Clovis caused universal joy and thanksgiving throughout the Christian world. Pope Anastasius I was the more rejoiced, as he hoped to find in this prince a powerful protector of the Church, Clovis being at that period the only Catholic sovereign. From the time he embraced the true faith he became its most zealous defender — an example which his successors have imitated for twelve centuries — thus meriting the title of Christian kings.

VIRTUES OF ST. GENEVIEVE.

Clovis greatly venerated a holy maiden named Genevieve, who lived during his reign, and was celebrated throughout Gaul for the purity of her life and her extraordinary miracles. She was born at Nanterre, near Paris. St. Germain, bishop of Auxerre, in passing through this place, discerned something very remarkable in this young girl. He advised her to consecrate her virginity to God, conducted her to Church, and bestowed upon her the blessing of the Virgins. The following day he asked her if she remembered her promise; and when she replied that she would fulfill it with the grace of God, he gave her a copper medal, on which a cross was engraved, advising her to wear it around her neck, and forbidding her all ornaments of gold, silver or precious stones.

From this time Genevieve made great progress in

virtue, and practiced the most austere penances. She ate but twice a week, her food consisting of a small quantity of barley bread and a few roots, moistened with a little water — this rigorous fast being sustained by means of fervent and almost continual prayer. She would prostrate herself in the presence of God, and bathe the ground with her innocent tears. Her many virtues, however, did not avert the shafts of calumny, but these trials only increased her sweetness and patience. God was not unmindful of His faithful servant, and proclaimed her sanctity by bestowing upon her the gift of working miracles and uttering prophecies. The cruel Attila having turned his devastating march in the direction of Paris, the city was thrown into the greatest consternation. Genevieve exhorted the citizens to appease the divine wrath by earnest prayers, vigils and fasts. She united her supplications to theirs, and it was revealed to her that this scourge of God would not enter Paris, which prediction was verified. Thus delivered from such imminent peril, the grateful inhabitants rushed in crowds to implore the aid of the Saint, and the holy maiden refused nothing which contributed to the service of God or the salvation of souls.

Through her efforts and influence a church was erected in honor of St. Denis and his companions; and during a time of famine Genevieve undertook a long voyage, and after many difficulties and obstacles, succeeded in procuring food for the starving people. The admirable virtue of holiness was never more fully displayed than in this remarkable girl;

and the envious, who had at first calumniated her, were finally compelled to acknowledge the sanctity of her penitential and mortified life. Notwithstanding her great austerities she lived to an advanced age, and after passing ninety years in the practice of all kinds of good works, died in the year 511. Her remains were interred near the body of Clovis in the church of the Apostles SS. Peter and Paul, which, at the present day, is called in her honor the church of St. Genevieve. The timely assistance this virtuous maiden procured for the city of Paris did not cease after her death, but she continues to protect the capital which venerates her as its patroness, and treasures her precious relics as a safeguard against all public calamities.

ORIGIN OF ST. BENEDICT.

A. D. 480.

Benedict, whom Providence had destined to become the founder of the monastic life in the West, or at least to perfect this holy state, was born of noble parents at Norcia, in Italy. At an early age he was sent to Rome, where he remained three years, living in the greatest retirement, having no acquaintances, with the exception of a holy monk named Romain, who supplied him with the small quantity of bread necessary for his sustenance. His reputation for sanctity soon became known, and he acquired so great a celebrity in that city, that the Religious of a neighboring monastery asked him to become their Abbot. St. Benedict refused to accept the invitation for a long time, telling them they would not be satisfied with his mode of life.

Overcome by their earnest entreaties, he finally consented to assume the charge of the monastery; but some wicked men among the Religious, unable to endure his regular and penitential discipline, resolved to get rid of the Saint by means of poison, which they placed in a glass of water which they knew he would drink at one of his meals. During the repast, St. Benedict, according to his custom, made the sign of the cross over the glass, and it immediately fell to pieces. Benedict divined the cause and saw from what danger he had been delivered; quietly rising from his seat, he said to the guilty monks: "Brethren why have you treated me in this manner? I predicted that you would not be satisfied with your choice; seek then a superior who will please you."

Leaving the convent he resumed his solitary life, but notwithstanding his endeavors to remain concealed from the eyes of men, his reputation for sanctity spread abroad, and the desert was soon filled with recluses. As several persons entreated his guidance in the way of salvation, he was obliged to receive them as his disciples. Benedict erected twelve monasteries, in each of which he placed twelve monks, subject to the rule of a superior, retaining himself those who still needed his instructions. Young men went in crowds to seek him, and the most illustrious families of Rome confided their children to his care, among whom particular mention is made of Maurus and Placidus, sons of two distinguished senators. Educated in his school these youths became great saints, and were the means of attracting many souls to the path of virtue.

One day the young Placidus while drawing water fell into the lake. St. Benedict, who was in the monastery, received a supernatural warning of what had occurred, and said to Maurus: "Hasten, brother, Placidus has fallen into the lake!" Maurus eagerly ran to the spot, found Placidus gasping for breath, and seizing him by the hair dragged him on shore. On recovering from his alarm, Maurus looked at the scene of the accident, and was terrified at perceiving that he had walked on the water. On recounting this phenomenon to his superior, St. Benedict attributed the miracle to his prompt obedience; but the humble Maurus contended that it was owing to the prayers of the Saint.

FOUNDATION OF THE MONASTERY OF MONTE CASSINO.

The principal institution of St. Benedict was the monastery of Monte Cassino, which was situated in the kingdom of Naples. When the holy Abbot first visited this mountain, an ancient temple of Apollo stood on its summit, where the people were accustomed to worship. On beholding this remnant of paganism, Benedict destroyed the statue, and succeeded by his discourses and miracles in effecting the conversion of these poor people. God then granted His servant the gift of prophesy, and proclaimed his sanctity by a great number of miracles. Totila, king of the Goths, struck with astonishment at all he heard concerning the holy Abbot, was seized with a great desire to visit him. He accordingly proceeded to Monte Cassino, and in order to ascertain if Benedict could really predict future events, sent word to the Saint that he intended visiting him; but instead of going himself, he dispatched one of his officers to the monastery, appareled in his royal robes and accompanied by numerous attendants.

Benedict, who had never met Totila, was not, however, deceived, but on seeing the officer exclaimed: "My son, take off the garments which do not belong to you!" The officer and his retinue, lost in astonishment, hastened to inform Totila of what had occurred. Then this prince, no longer doubting that there was something wonderful about this extraordinary man, solicited an audience. On being admitted he approached St. Benedict with respect and fear, and prostrating himself at his feet, remained in this position until the holy Abbot assisted him to rise. The Saint then gave him most salutary advice, and predicted the principal events of his future life. Totila begged his prayers, and adopted a more humane course of conduct. Shortly after, capturing the city of Naples, he treated the prisoners with a kindness totally unexpected, and unusual in a barbarian conqueror.

St. Benedict sent several of his disciples to France, for the purpose of founding monasteries in that country. He foretold his death, some time before he was attacked with his last illness, prepared his grave and was soon after seized with a violent fever. As his disease increased rapidly he desired to be carried to the church, and there received the body and blood of Jesus Christ, then raising his hands toward heaven, he expired, in his sixty-third year. St. Benedict left his disciples so admirable a rule of life as to merit the eulogiums of Pope St. Gregory; and we behold in this holy monk a man profoundly versed in the science of salvation, and endowed by the Holy Ghost with the grace to conduct souls to the highest state of perfection. His rule of life was found to be so full of wisdom and prudence, that it was adopted by all the Western monks. The celebrated Cosmo de Medici, and several other able lawgivers, frequently referred to this rule, which they regarded as a rich treasury of invaluable precepts, most useful in the art of governing mankind. This pious institution also became a source of many other inestimable advantages; besides the beautiful examples of virtue it has produced, we are indebted to the monks for the preservation of the most important facts of history; the sciences and literature were also cultivated in the secluded shades of the cloister, to the fullest extent the times allowed.

FIFTH ECUMENICAL COUNCIL.
A. D. 553.
THE THREE CHAPTERS.

After the death of the Emperor Marcian, the Eutychians reappeared in Egypt, and committed the most horrible acts of violence. No opposition was ventured on, because of their great number and immense influence. They used every means to weaken the Council of Chalcedon, by which they had been condemned; and the following is an account of the efforts used to accomplish their object. Since the time of Nestorius, three works in favor of that heresy had appeared, viz., the writings of Theodoret, bishop of Cyrus, against St. Cyril; the letter of Ibas, bishop of Edessa, and the works of Theodore, bishop of Mopsuestia. These three publications, called the Three Chapters, were of a most reprehensible nature; but their authors, apparently, retracted their errors, by making a profession of orthodox faith in the Council of Chalcedon.

The Fathers of this Council, being assembled for a different purpose, did not examine the Three Chapters, and were contented with obliging their authors to anathematize Nestorius; to which Theodoret and Ibas consented, the third bishop having died. The declaration of the two bishops was approved without any reference being made to their works. The Eutychians, who wished to attack the Council of Chalcedon, complained of its silence in regard to the Three Chapters, and for having received its authors as orthodox Catholics. They warmly insisted on the condemnation of the Three Chapters, and secured the protection and authority of the Emperor Justinian. This prince, who wished to increase his power in religious affairs, published an edict condemning the three works. The Catholics, although disapproving of the doctrine advocated in these writings, and acknowledging them to be most pernicious, feared, in attacking them, to assail and weaken the authority of the Council of Chalcedon, and thus augment the triumph of the Eutychians. This affair created a great sensation. Pope Vigilius, at first, rejected the edict of the Emperor against the Three Chapters, then, in hopes of promoting peace, condemned them himself, with this reservation: In accordance with the authority of the Council of Chalcedon.

Finally, they determined to convene a general council at Constantinople, in order to terminate the dispute. The three works which excited so much disturbance were then examined and condemned, but without the least reflection on the Council of Chalcedon. The Fathers expressly declared that they held the same faith as the four first Councils, thus placing that of Chalcedon in the same rank as the three others. It was also decided that the works of an author could be justly censured without condemning him personally. Pope Vigilius, after some opposition, confirmed this decision, and all the Eastern and Western Churches testified their approbation. This Council of Constantinople was, therefore, regarded as the fifth general Council; and we here see a remarkable proof of the power possessed by the Church to condemn heretical works, explain the sense of doubtful writings, and compel the faithful to submit to her decrees. This supreme authority is absolutely necessary for the protection of the faith, since one of the most effectual means of preserving the integrity of the holy doctrines she teaches, is to guide the faithful to the pure fountain of truth, and guard them from the poisoned stream of error. Charged by her Divine Spouse to promulgate the truth, she always strives earnestly to warn her children against falsehood and the wicked machinations of corrupt men.

CONVERSION OF ENGLAND.
A. D. 596.

The Gospel was preached in England during the second century, but had become extinct at the time that kingdom was conquered by the Saxon idolaters, who banished the first inhabitants. St. Gregory the Great, when still but a deacon, conceived the idea of re-establishing Christianity in this country. One day, while passing by a market in Rome, his attention was attracted by the fair and beautiful complexion of some English slaves, who were exposed for sale, and he asked the merchant if they were Christians. "No," was the reply; "they are pagans." "It is a pity," said the Saint, "that so handsome a race should be under the dominion of the devil." He was unable to undertake this mission himself, but when elected to the chair of St. Peter he immediately proceeded to execute his long cherished project. Accordingly, forty missionaries were sent to England, under the charge of Augustine, prior of the monastery of St. Andrew. This apostolic band courageously went forth to announce Jesus Christ to a new people, and landed on the coast of Kent.

The king, who was named Ethelbert, granted the missionaries a public audience, and they marched to the palace in procession, carrying a silver cross, adorned with the image of the Saviour, whilst reciting fervent prayers for the salvation of this nation, in whose spiritual behalf they had journeyed from so great a distance. The king bade them be seated, and lent an attentive ear to their discourse. "We come to announce to you the happiest tidings," said St. Augustine, "the God who sends us here offers you, after this life is ended, a kingdom infinitely more glorious and lasting than your beautiful England." "That is an inviting promise," said Ethelbert, "but as it is something entirely new to me, I cannot abandon the worship I have so long practiced, together with the whole English nation. Nevertheless, I do not prevent you from converting to your religion all those whom you can convince; and as you have come from a distance, in order to benefit us by what you believe to be the truth, I will have you furnished with all that is necessary for your subsistence."

The holy missionaries began to preach the Gospel, faithfully imitating the life of the Apostles. The purity of their morals, their abstemiousness, disinterested piety, and the gift of working miracles which God had bestowed on them, deeply impressed a great number of idolaters, who renounced their superstitions and embraced Christianity. The king himself, astonished at the wonders performed by these extraordinary men, was converted to the faith. His conversion was followed by that of an immense number of his subjects. From this period, Ethelbert showed the greatest zeal for the promulgation of the faith throughout his dominions, but used no compulsion, as he was taught by the missionaries that the service of Jesus Christ should be free and voluntary; he therefore contented himself with reposing the greatest confidence in those who professed Christianity, and manifested the utmost kindness towards them.

ST. AUGUSTINE CONSECRATED BISHOP OF CANTERBURY.

In order to give some form to the rising church in England, and firmly establish the faith in this country, Augustine crossed over to France, and received the Episcopal consecration from the hands of the bishop of Arles, who was the vicar of the Holy See in Gaul. He then returned to England, where he effected the most wonderful change, and God sustained his preaching by numerous and extraordinary miracles, for he had the happiness of baptizing over two thousand persons at Canterbury on Christmas day. The fame of the prodigies worked by St. Augustine in England spread as far as Rome, and St. Gregory wrote him letters of counsel and advice, and warned him to use with fear and trembling the great gift of miracles God had vouchsafed to bestow upon him.

After congratulating the bishop on the conversion of the English, he says to him: "This joy, my dear brother, should be mingled with fear; for I know that God has accomplished great things through your ministry in this nation. Remember then, that when the Apostles joyfully said to their divine Master, 'Lord, we have conquered the devils themselves through thy name,' He replied: 'You should not rejoice at that, but rather because your names are written in Heaven.' While God thus acts outwardly in your regard, you should, my dear brother, severely scrutinize your conscience, and learn the state of your soul. If you find you have offended God, by word or action, always keep the remembrance of your sins before your mind, in order to repress any secret self-complacency which may unwittingly creep into your heart. Remember that the gift of miracles is not given in your behalf, but for those whose salvation you are to secure. You know the words of Truth itself contained in the Gospel: 'Many will come and say to me, we have wrought miracles in thy name, and I will declare to them that I know them not.'" Nothing so surely proves the miracles of St. Augustine as these solemn words of St. Gregory.

As the conversions in England daily increased, the Pope sent new laborers to cultivate this rich soil, which divine grace had rendered so fruitful. He invited English youths to Rome, where they were instructed in the monasteries, and then returned to their native country as ministers of the Gospel of Jesus Christ. The zeal of the holy Pope extended over the whole Church, guarding and watching his flock with the most untiring vigilance. Notwithstanding a very weak constitution, Gregory was ever faithful in the exact performance of his apostolic functions, correcting abuses and maintaining the strictest discipline. He protected the defenseless and assisted the poor, upon whom he showered such an abundance of alms, as sometimes to deprive himself of the barest necessaries of life. Although overwhelmed with business, he always personally instructed the people by oral teaching and written discourses.

Gregory wrote a great number of works, in which he explains the principles and maxims of Christian morality in a clear and comprehensive manner. Such arduous labors and continual application finally undermined his health, and terminated his useful life. St. Augustine, his loved disciple, survived him but three years, and then hastened to receive the same bright crown of everlasting glory promised to those who labor for the salvation of souls.

MAHOMET APPEARS AS A PROPHET.
A. D. 622.

The conversion of the North to Christianity in some measure repaired the losses the Church had experienced in the East. We often have occasion to remark the wisdom and justice of God, who thus passes the torch of faith from one nation to another, so that the Church regains in one country what she has lost elsewhere, and thus remains always Catholic.

Mahomet, who deprived her of the most beautiful of the provinces of the East, was born at Mecca, in Arabia, of a pagan father and a Jewish mother. Both parents died when he was still a child, and Mahomet was educated by an uncle, who established him in business. He married a widow, whose agent he had been. When about forty years of age he

MAHOMET APPEARS AS A PROPHET. 271

commenced his course of deception and imposture, and asserting that God inspired him, without furnishing the slightest proof of a divine mission, he introduced a new religion, which was a mixture of Judaism and Christianity, adding some dogmas peculiar to the inhabitants of Arabia. He taught that there is only one God, but without any distinction of persons in the divinity; rejecting the Incarnation and the other mysteries of the Christian religion, while accepting the rite of circumcision, and prescribing abstinence from wine and pork: allowing, however, every man as many wives as he wished, having himself sometimes ten at once. This impostor exhorted the people to take up arms in defense of the religion, promising those who fell in battle, a paradise, where they would be steeped in every sensual pleasure. When asked to perform miracles in proof of his mission, he replied that he was not sent to work miracles, but to promulgate his doctrine by means of the sword.

As Mahomet could neither read nor write, he employed an amanuensis to transcribe his impious teachings, which work when completed, he called the Koran. Being subject to epileptic fits, he represented them as ecstasies occasioned by the visits of the angel Gabriel, who revealed his doctrine to him. Robbers and fugitive slaves became his most attached followers, as he promised them perfect license in their conduct and morals. After raising a small army, Mahomet placed himself at their head as commander and lawgiver; he began his pretended mission by attacking the caravans which traversed the desert for trading purposes, thus enriching his disciples and himself with the plunder, and providing the requisite means for accomplishing his designs. When his party augmented in numbers, he marched toward the city of Mecca, which he captured, and he subsequently conquered the Arabian tribes, forcing them to submit to his authority and embrace his religion.

His progress was so rapid, that when he died in 631, nearly the whole of Arabia was under his dominion; his successors continued his conquests, and in a short time acquired a vast empire. It is very plainly seen, by what means this sect was so widely spread; violence and the love of pleasure being the two powerful causes which secured its success. Mahomet established his religion by allowing free scope to the passions, and by putting to death those who refused to accept his doctrine; whereas the Apostles, following the footsteps of their Divine Master, established Christianity by preaching and practicing a pure code of morals, and shedding their blood in defense of the faith. The one is all material in its origin, and the other is manifestly of divine growth.

TAKING OF JERUSALEM BY CHOSROES, KING OF PERSIA.

A. D. 614.

The Persians, under the command of Chosroes, their king, attacked the Eastern empire with terrible violence. Having crossed the Euphrates, they seized the city of Apamea, and advanced in the work of destruction as far as the gates of Antioch. A Roman army which they encountered in their march was cut to pieces. They penetrated into Palestine and crossed the Jordan, and the banks of this river were covered with ruins wherever they appeared. The people of the country fled before them, but the hermits, who could not consent to leave their cherished solitudes, at first suffered the most horrible tortures, and finally were cruelly massacred. The army then marched toward Jerusalem, which they entered without encountering the slightest resistance; the garrison had abandoned the city, and a general consternation filled the minds of the unfortunate inhabitants.

The Persians destroyed every thing by fire and the sword, and a great number of priests and Religious perished; it was against these that the idolaters principally directed their rage. The rest of the citizens, men, women and children, were loaded with chains and dragged beyond the Tigris. The Jews alone were spared, on account of the hatred they bore the Christians, which they signalized on this occasion by carrying their atrocities to greater lengths than even the pagans themselves. They bought all the Christian captives they could obtain from the Persians, in order to enjoy the barbarous pleasure of putting them to death. Eighty thousand were thus massacred by the Jews, and the bishop Zacharias was carried into captivity.

After pillaging the Holy Sepulchre and the other churches of Jerusalem, they applied the torch to them, and these noble edifices soon fell a prey to the devouring flames. They carried off the sacred vessels, and all the splendid ornaments that the piety of the faithful had accumulated in those holy places; but the most severe loss to the Christians was that of the true Cross, which each one of them would have ransomed with his heart's blood. The Persians carried away this sacred relic in the very state in which they found it, that is to say, enclosed in a case, and marked with the seal of the bishop. The Christians succeeded in saving the sponge which had been saturated with vinegar and presented to Jesus Christ while on the cross, and the lance that had pierced His sacred side. An officer of the Emperor took these holy relics from the sacrilegious hands of a Persian soldier, who exchanged them for a large sum of money, and carried them back to Jerusalem, where they were exposed during four days to the veneration of the faithful, who bathed them with their tears.

The Holy Cross was deposited at Tarsus, in Armenia, and the ruins of a castle are still shown where this sacred relic was placed, as it appeared less valuable to the Persians than the other spoils they had secured. After the departure of the Persians, the inhabitants of Jerusalem who had escaped by flight returned to the holy city. The priest Modestus, in the absence of the Bishop Zacharias, assumed the government of this desolated church, and assiduously labored to restore the demolished edifices. In this pious enterprise he received great assistance from John, patriarch of Alexandria, surnamed the Almoner. It was in this capital of

Egypt, that a great number of the inhabitants of Palestine had taken refuge. The holy prelate received them with paternal tenderness, placed the wounded in hospitals and supplied the wants of all in necessity. To those remaining in Jerusalem he sent money, wheat, and clothing, and alleviated by every means the unhappy condition of these suffering people.

THE HOLY CROSS DISCOVERED AND RETURNED TO JERUSALEM.

A. D. 628.

The Emperor Heraclius sent an embassy to Chosroes, to treat with him regarding terms of peace; but this idolatrous prince exacted as a condition, that he should abjure Christianity and adore the sun, the principal divinity among the Persians. Heraclius rejected this impious proposition with horror, and determined to strain every nerve for the preservation of religion and the empire. He raised an army and marched against the enemy. God aided His people, and in the very first campaign the Emperor gained the advantage over the Persians. This success raised the courage of his troops, and war was waged against these pagans during a period of four years. Heraclius resolved then on a decisive battle, and having assembled his soldiers, he animated them to combat by enumerating all the evils the Persians had brought on the empire — the country ravaged, villages sacked and plundered, the altars desecrated, the churches reduced to ashes. "Behold," he said to them, "the enemies with whom you contend; they declare war against God Himself, and they have gone so far as to burn His altars and temples. God will combat for you; take up your arms with confidence and courage; faith surmounts all obstacles, and triumphs over death itself!" These glowing words made a powerful impression on the troops, who with the greatest impetuosity attacked the Persians. The Emperor was conspicuous in the thickest of the fight; he received several blows, which fell upon his shield, and thus saved his life. The contest lasted a whole day; the Persians lost three of their principal officers, and more than half their soldiers, while only fifty men perished in the Roman army.

Chosroes fled, and after a retreat of eight leagues passed the night in a miserable cottage, the roof of which was so low that he was obliged to crawl into it on his hands and knees. Weakened by these unaccustomed hardships, and attacked by a violent disease, he named a favorite son for his successor, thus depriving his eldest son of the throne, who, in consequence, revolted against his father, took him prisoner, and kept him in close confinement, where he died of starvation. The new Persian king proposed a cessation of hostilities, and sent back all the Christians who had been dragged into captivity: among others, the patriarch Zacharias, to whom he gave the Holy Cross, which had been carried off fourteen years before. During all this time this holy relic remained enclosed in its case, the Persians not having sufficient curiosity to break the seal. This seal was recognized by the patriarch, and the sacred relic was returned to his hands in the same condition as when it had been stolen. Thus we see that God Himself protected this precious relic from the sacrilegious hands of the pagans.

The Emperor Heraclius returned to Constantinople in triumph, seated in a chariot drawn by four elephants, preceded by the Holy Cross — the most glorious trophy of his victory. At the beginning of spring Heraclius left Constantinople for Jerusalem, there to return thanks to God for his success, and to replace the Holy Cross in the church of the Resurrection. He desired to tread in the sacred footsteps of the Saviour, and to bear the Cross on his shoulders to the summit of Mount Calvary, in imitation of his divine Master. This day was observed by the Christians as a solemn festival, and the Church still celebrates its anniversary on the fourteenth of September.

HERESY OF THE MONOTHELITES.
A. D. 630.

The joy which the Church experienced at the recovery of the true Cross, was interrupted by a violent storm, which broke out in the East, where a new heresy, or, rather, that of Eutyches, a little disguised, reappeared under another name. The secret followers of this heretic taught, that there is only one will and one operation in Jesus Christ, which is the signification of the Greek word Monothelism, the name of this sect. The Catholic Church, on the contrary, which recognized two natures in

Jesus Christ, recognized also two wills: the divine will and the human will, which are never in opposition, but are also perfectly distinct. The Monothelites were firmly supported by Sergius, the patriarch of Constantinople, who used all his influence in their behalf. He skillfully insinuated his views into the mind of the Emperor Heraclius, who protected him by publishing a famous proclamation under the title of the Ecthesis, or Exposition.

St. Sophronius, the patriarch of Jerusalem, zealously combated this new heresy, and published a work, in which, after proving the distinction of natures in Jesus Christ, he clearly explained the doctrine of the Church concerning the two wills, and the two distinct natures. Sergius, who feared that the Pope Honorius would be prejudiced against his new creed, was the first to write to him, in order to win him over to the same belief. This letter was flattering, and artfully worded. In it he stated that the question which had arisen placed an obstacle in the conversion of heretics, and asked that there should be no mention of either one or two wills of Jesus Christ, as silence was the only means of uniting the factions. Honorius fell into the snare, and entered into a dangerous agreement with him. He consented to a silence, in which truth and falsehood were equally suppressed; and by this weakness, without actually promulgating the error, he gave rise to a suspicion that he was favorably inclined toward the heresy. Finally, the artifices of these heretics were discovered by the vigilance of St. Sophronius, who informed the Pope of the progress of the new sect.

Honorius was dead, but his successor condemned both the error and the proclamation issued by the Emperor in its favor. This first sentence was subsequently confirmed by the Pope St. Martin, and the zeal which he manifested in preserving the purity of the faith cost him his liberty and his life.

The Emperor Constans, the successor of Heraclius, having published a second proclamation in favor of Monothelism, removed the holy Pope from Rome, and had him brought in chains to Constantinople, where he endured the most shameful insults and indignities. St. Martin was afterward exiled, and died after ten years of captivity and suffering, without uttering a single complaint, or relinquishing any of the duties of his sacred office. A holy abbot of Constantinople, named Maximus, imitated the zeal of the saintly Pope, and received the same treatment from the hands of the heretics. He was cruelly beaten, his tongue cut out by the roots, and he terminated his martyrdom in a state of banishment.

THE SIXTH GENERAL COUNCIL.

A. D. 680.

The Emperor Constantine, surnamed Pogonatus, assuaged the grief of the Church, and repaired the wrongs which had been practiced against her by his predecessors. This prince thought he could not make a better use of his authority than by convening a general Council. He wrote on the subject to Pope Agatho, who informed the western bishops of the pious intentions of the Emperor, and appointed three legates to preside over the Council in his name. The new error had not penetrated as far as the West, and all the bishops united in the recognition of two wills in Jesus Christ as well as two natures. The Emperor received the legates of the Holy See with every honor, and the opening of the Council took place in one of the halls of the palace, the book of the Gospels being placed, as was the custom, in the middle of the assembly.

The Emperor was present, accompanied by thirteen of his principal officers. The legates of the Pope spoke first, and proposed the subject for the consideration of the Council. "For more than forty years," said they, "Sergius and others have taught that there is only one will and one nature in our Lord Jesus Christ. The Holy See has rejected this error, and exhorted them to renounce their pernicious belief, but without any good result; this, then, is the reason why we demand of them an explanation of their doctrine." The Canons of the preceding Councils, and the authority of the early Fathers, were then carefully examined, and the new Creed was found to be contrary to Scripture and tradition. The Monothelites were convicted of having altered the passages quoted from the Fathers in defense of their errors. The letter of St. Sophronius, which they had opposed, was produced, and proved to be in exact conformity with the true faith, the doctrine of the Apostles and the traditions of the early Fathers.

After this examination, the confession of faith was proclaimed, in which their adherence to the doctrines of the preceding Councils was declared, and then sentence was pronounced in these words: "We decide that there are two wills and two natural manifestations in Jesus Christ, and we forbid the teaching of a contrary doctrine. We abhor and detest the impious belief of the heretics who only admit one will and one nature in Jesus Christ, as these dogmas are in opposition to the doctrine of the Apostles, the decrees of the Councils, and the opinions of the early Fathers." The holy Council afterward anathematized the authors of the sect, and even censured Honorious, who had seemed to be their partisan. The Emperor Constantine, who was present at the conclusion of the council, received the same honors as had formerly been paid the great Constantine, Theodosius and Marcian. The decisions were signed by the legates, all the bishops to the number of one hundred and sixty, and the Emperor himself, who ordered the decrees to be immediately executed, and he enforced them with all his authority; in short, the error was now completely conquered, and the troubles ceased.

CONVERSION OF GERMANY.

A. D. 723.

The torch of faith, like the sun, only leaves one country for a time, to enlighten another. In proportion as the light of the gospel was dimmed in the East by the conquests of the Mohammedans, it shed its saving rays on the pagan North through the apostolical labors of missionaries. The most celebrated of them all was St. Boniface, Archbishop of Mayence, and the Apostle of Germany. He was of English birth, and from his earliest infancy gave tokens of his high destiny. Several missionaries visited his father and spoke to him of heavenly things, and the youthful Boniface was so much affected by their edifying instructions, that he was seized with an ardent desire to imitate them and consecrate himself to God. Although still but a child, the virtuous impressions he then received were never effaced from his mind. He entered a monastery, where he was trained in the duties of the holy ministry; and, having been ordained priest at the age of thirty, his zeal for the instruction of the people and the salvation of souls daily increased. He lamented unceasingly over the unhappy condition of the nations still plunged in the darkness of idolatry.

Overcome by these reflections, he had recourse to Pope Gregory, who, recognizing his divine vocation, invested him with authority to announce the Gospel to the Germans. The holy apostle found it very difficult to awaken in the hearts of these barbarous people the sentiments of meekness and piety taught by the Scriptures; but, finally, his labors were rewarded, and the harvest was abundant. He first went to Bavaria and Thuringia, where he baptized a great number of infidels. The pagan temples were everywhere destroyed, and Christian churches erected on their sites. The holy apostle, nevertheless, endured many trials, especially in Thuringia, a country that had lately been devastated by the Saxons, and where the people were so poor that they were obliged to procure their necessary subsistence by the hardest manual labor. From thence he proceeded to Friesland, where, for three years, he exercised the functions of the holy ministry, and converted a multitude of souls to Christianity.

The Pope, hearing of the immense harvests his apostolic labors were reaping, commanded him to come to Rome, in order to receive the episcopal dignity. On his return from this journey, St. Boniface began to preach the faith in Hesse, where he was rewarded by extraordinary success, and he there founded several churches and monasteries. Summoned to Bavaria by the duke of that province, he was the means of reforming the abuses which had crept into the Church; and, finding that impostors had sprung up, who deceived the people by their artifices and scandalized them by their disorderly lives, he silenced some and expelled others, thus restoring the original purity of faith and morals in this country. The Pope appointed him his legate in Germany, and allowed him to make whatever regulations he pleased for the welfare of the infant Church.

MARTYRDOM OF ST. BONIFACE.

The reputation of St. Boniface spread over the greater part of Europe, and his Apostolic labors were so much venerated, that a great number of holy men associated themselves with this mission, and thus mitigated its hardships and trials. Then the holy archbishop, weighed down with age and infirmities, thought of choosing a successor. After consecrating a new archbishop of Mayence, he charged him with the care of this particular church, so that he might be at liberty to follow the vocation he had received from Heaven, and devote himself to the conversion of infidels. He could not rest while so many souls were still ignorant of Jesus Christ; moreover, he was inflamed with a desire to shed his blood for the faith, and he had a presentiment that his death was near at hand. Having, therefore, arranged all the affairs of his church, he departed, accompanied by several zealous co-operators, to preach the Gospel to an idolatrous nation on the most remote coast of Friesland, and there converted a great number of pagans, whom he baptized. He appointed a day on which to administer to them the sacrament of confirmation, and, as they could not all assemble in the same church, he named an adjoining field, where they should meet for the reception of this sacrament. Tents were erected, and the day for the solemnization of the ceremony arrived.

While waiting for the newly made Christians, St. Boniface was engaged in prayer; but, instead of the converts appearing, a troop of pagans arrived armed with swords and lances; they immediately destroyed the tents, and then rushed upon the holy bishop. His attendants armed themselves to repel the attack of the barbarians; but the bishop, hearing the noise, summoned his clergy, and holding in his hands the relics he always carried with him, thus addressed his companions: "My children, lay down your arms, the Scripture forbids us to return evil for evil; the day I have so long expected has arrived; hope in God, He will save our souls." He then exhorted them to suffer courageously a momentary death, which would conduct them to life eternal.

The example of the holy prelate strengthened them more than his words. He had scarcely finished speaking when the barbarians assailed him; but the bishop was immovable. The infuriated wretches instantly massacred the saint, together with his companions, to the number of fifty-two. St. Boniface thus terminated by a glorious death, a life which had been a continuous martyrdom, as it had been entirely devoted to the conversion of the pagans. His immense labors, and the benefits which the Church received from his exertions, entitled him to the precious crown. The body of the holy martyr was carried to the Abbey of Fulda, which he had founded, and God there honored His servant by the great number of miracles which were wrought at his tomb.

HERESY OF THE ICONOCLASTS OR IMAGE-BREAKERS.

A. D. 727.

The Eastern Church was frequently disturbed by new heresies, which succeeded each other after short intervals of repose. Those which arose in the eighth century were the more dangerous in having a prince for their author. It has already been seen that Emperors sometimes protected error; but now we behold an Emperor who is the leader of the sect. Leo, the Isaurian, had risen to the imperial dignity through his warlike qualities. Born, and we may say nurtured, in the camp, he was entirely without education; nevertheless he had the foolish vanity to assume the office of a religious reformer. He allowed himself to be prejudiced against the veneration of holy images, which he called idolatry; and issued a proclamation, in which he commanded all the images of Jesus Christ, the Blessed Virgin and the Saints to be removed from the churches. This order, so contrary to the constant and universal practice of the Church, occasioned intense excitement, and the inhabitants of Constantinople openly murmured against it.

Germanus, the patriarch of this city, zealously opposed the heresy, heedless of the anger of the Emperor; he at first endeavored privately to disabuse the mind of the prince of its error, by explaining to him that the veneration paid the holy images referred to those they represented, in the same manner as the statue of an Emperor is honored, that this relative homage had always been rendered to the images of Our Lord and His Holy Mother from the time of the Apostles, and that it was the rankest impiety to attack so ancient a custom. But the Emperor, who was ignorant of the elements of the Christian doctrine, clung obstinately to his heretical opinions. The patriarch then wrote to the Pope of all that had occurred in Constantinople.

The sovereign Pontiff replied to the holy bishop, congratulating him on his courage in combating the' rising heresy, and an assemblage of bishops was held, in which it was condemned. The Holy Father wrote also to the Emperor, exhorting him to revoke the edict, warning him that it was not the place of a prince to decide in matters of faith, or to alter the discipline of the Church. These remonstrances had no effect on the Emperor, who only became more determined upon the immediate enforcement of his law. He had all the images destroyed, and the walls of the churches, which had been ornamented with pictures, were painted white. He ordered a large Crucifix which Constantine, after his victory, had placed at the entrance of the imperial palace, to be broken to pieces. The women who were present essayed at first by their entreaties to induce the officer who had been empowered to carry this order into execution to desist from this impious act; but their prayers were of no avail, as the officer himself ascended the ladder and struck the figure three times with a hatchet.

The pious women, fired with a holy indignation, overturned the ladder, and the sacrilegious officer died from the effects of his fall. The women were condemned to be executed with six other persons, whom the Emperor suspected of instigating this opposition to his edict. The patriarch St. Germanus was driven from his see, and died in exile at the advanced age of ninety years.

VIOLENCE OF THE ICONOCLASTS.

Constantine, surnamed Copronymus, son and successor of Leo, followed in the footsteps of his father, and went even to greater lengths. Educated in impiety, of a passionate and fiery nature, increased by an insolent and bold demeanor, he furiously persecuted those who persisted in honoring the holy images. Constantinople became a scene of bloodshed; the Catholics were tormented in every way; their eyes were put out, they were severely whipped, and then cast into the sea. The Emperor was particularly incensed against the monks, who were made to endure all kinds of sufferings; their beards were soaked in pitch and then set on fire, and pieces of wood, ornamented with pictures of saints, were then broken over their heads. These atrocities only diverted Constantine, and his chief amusement during his respasts was to listen to the recital of the cruelties that had been practiced during the day. Not content with the outrages perpetrated through his officers, he presided himself at executions, gratifying thus his sanguinary taste. He caused a tribunal to be erected at one of the gates of the city, and there, surrounded by the executioners, he tortured the Catholics, and feasted his eyes on spectacles too horrible for any but himself and his courtiers to witness.

There lived near Nicomedia a holy abbot named Stephen, who was held in great veneration on account of his sanctity and many virtues. The Emperor, wishing to win him over to his party, summoned him to

Constantinople, and undertook to question him himself, in the hope of convincing him by his arguments, as this prince considered himself a most logical reasoner. He accordingly entered into a controversy with the holy bishop. "Oh, stupid man," said the Emperor, "canst thou not trample on the image of Jesus Christ without offending Jesus Christ Himself?" St. Stephen approached him, and showed him a piece of money stamped with his portrait. "I can, then," replied the holy abbot, "treat this image in the same manner, without failing in the respect I owe you as the Emperor!" and, throwing the money on the ground, he trampled on it.

The courtiers rushed upon him to punish him for his boldness. "What," said St. Stephen, sighing deeply, "is it a crime to dishonor the image of an earthly prince, and no sacrilege to cast into the flames the image of the King of Heaven!" No answer could be made to this appeal, but his destruction was resolved upon. He was accordingly imprisoned, and shortly afterward put to death. Nineteen officers, accused of an intimacy with the holy martyr, and of having praised his constancy, were tortured, and two of the most distinguished were beheaded by command of the Emperor. The persecution extended to the provinces, and the governors, in order to please Constantine, signalized themselves by practicing the greatest atrocities against the Catholics throughout the whole empire. They not only desecrated the images of the Saints, but profaned holy relics, which they tore from the sanctuaries, and then threw them into the sewers and rivers, or burned them with the bones of animals, so that the ashes could not be distinguished.

SEVENTH GENERAL COUNCIL, AND SECOND COUNCIL OF NICE.

A. D. 787.

After the death of Constantine Copronymus and his son Leo, the sovereign power fell into the hands of Irene, who governed as regent during the minority of her infant son Constantine, and the suffering Church, so long tormented by the Iconoclasts, began to taste the sweets of peace. This princess, who was attached to the Catholic doctrine, undertook to repair the evils caused by the bad government of the last Emperors. By the advice of Tarasius, patriarch of Constantinople, she wrote to Pope Adrian, asking for the convocation of a general Council. The Pope approved of her request, and sent two legates to preside over the Council in his name. Constantinople was first chosen as the place of assembly, but as the Iconoclasts, who were very numerous in this city, began to create disturbances, the place of assembly was transferred to Nice, a city already celebrated for the holding of the first general Council. The bishops of the different provinces of the empire assembled to the number of three hundred and seventy-seven. Two imperial officers were appointed to maintain order, and the bishops were allowed perfect freedom of speech. Eight sessions were held. In the first a letter from the Pope was read, in which he vindicated the traditions of the Church concerning the veneration of holy images. He explained, also, the object of this homage.

The profession of faith of the Eastern bishops, who could not attend the Council, as they were under the dominion of the Mahomedans, was read, and their doctrine was found to be in perfect conformity with the pontifical letter. The testimony of the Holy Scriptures and of the early Fathers was then produced, and the arguments of the Iconoclasts refuted, the heresy crushed and silenced, and, finally, the bishops, after declaring their entire concurrence in the decisions of the preceding Councils, pronounced sentence in these words: "We decree that images and pictures shall not only adorn the churches, the sacred vessels, the vestments and the walls, but also be placed in houses, and on the roadside, because the oftener the images of Jesus Christ and His holy mother, the Apostles and Saints, are seen, the more frequently are we reminded of those whom they are intended to represent: honor and reverence should be rendered to these images, but not supreme worship, which belongs alone to the Deity. Incense and lights may be burned before these holy images, as was the custom with regard to the cross and Gospel and other sacred things, as the homage paid to the image referred to the object it represented. Such is the doctrine of the holy Fathers and the Catholic Church."

Anathemas were pronounced against the Iconoclasts, which decree was signed by the legates and all the bishops. The bishops afterward repaired to

Constantinople, where the eighth session was held in the presence of the Emperor and his mother, who signed the decision of the council amidst the acclamations of the audience. Thus this heresy was extinguished for a time, but subsequent reformers, following in the footsteps of these early fanatics, revived the error in the sixteenth century, committing the same acts of destruction and violence.

BEAUTIFUL CHARACTERISTICS AND HOLY ZEAL OF CHARLEMAGNE, KING OF FRANCE.

A. D. 768.

The piety of Charlemagne, king of France, was a subject of great joy to the Church, which this prince unceasingly protected during the course of a long and glorious reign. He ascended the throne while very young, but he was only youthful in his vigorous constitution and activity; prudence governed his career, and his imperial power was employed in extending the religion of Jesus Christ. During the first years of his reign he published, by the request of the bishops, a code of laws, in order to maintain the ecclesiastical discipline, and he protected the Holy See from the usurpations of the king of the Lombards. For a long time the Saxons had invaded his dominions, and to punish them, he waged a lengthy war against them, which terminated in the conversion of the nation; and this was the most precious fruit he derived from his conquest, as it was not submission to his authority he desired, but the enlightenment of these ignorant pagans.

This idolatrous people made a long resistance, but finally embraced Christianity, which procured their pardon for their continual inroads. As Charlemagne distrusted their constancy, and as several among them appeared to be actuated only by political motives, he sent zealous missionaries to strengthen them in their faith; nevertheless, Witikind, the most influential of their chiefs, refused to accept the faith, and was more exasperated than vanquished by their defeat. Charlemagne, who failed to conquer him by belligerent means, did not despair of gaining him by a treaty, and proposed, therefore, that a conference should be held. Witikind repaired to Attigny, where the court was held, and then, what terrible combats had failed to effect, was accomplished by the majesty and goodness of Charlemagne; these noble qualities disarmed this leader of the rebels, who now cheerfully acknowledged the power of this great prince.

During his sojourn in France, Witikind carefully examined the truths of Christianity, and when he understood them he believed; thus, suddenly awakening to the grace which spiritually enlightened him, and detesting paganism, he asked for baptism, which he received, Charlemagne standing as his sponsor. Witikind, not less candid than honorable, gave striking proofs of the sincerity of his conversion, by manifesting as much zeal for the propagation of the faith, as he had formerly shown in arresting its progress. Charlemagne referred the glory of his success to God, to whom he rendered solemn thanksgiving, for the conversion of the Saxons and their leader.

25*

CHARLEMAGNE REVIVES LITERATURE.

When Charlemagne ascended the throne, ignorance was universal throughout France. The taste for letters had been entirely lost, and there were neither masters nor public schools where learning could be acquired. Charlemagne, who knew that the cultivation of the arts and sciences contributed not only to the good of religion, but to the glory of the empire, determined to revive literature in his kingdom. In order to succeed, it was necessary to establish schools and excite emulation, and to find masters capable of giving instruction. Of the latter, France was very deficient. Charlemagne invited to his court the most learned men and most renowned personages of foreign countries, and induced them to remain in his empire, by conferring on them rewards worthy of the monarch, and of the scholars who had left their native land to benefit his people. He did not consider any price too dear which procured him the services of men, who, by their talents, reflected honor and glory upon France and upon religion.

The celebrated Alcuin, a learned Englishman, whom he loaded with honors and favors, assisted him greatly in his laudable endeavors. Alcuin was the most intellectual man of his age, and had taught the sacred and profane sciences in his own country with immense success. He accepted the invitation of Charlemagne, and advised that prince to establish schools in the principal cities and large monasteries of the kingdom. Charlemagne followed this counsel, and wrote a circular letter to the bishops and abbots, exhorting them to begin this most useful and necessary work. As oral teaching was not sufficient, and as it was necessary to have books, which are in a measure the guardians and depositaries of knowledge, the king used great precaution to prevent this source of public erudition from being corrupted by the negligence of copyists, whose services were employed before the discovery of the art of printing.

He published a law, by which he commanded that only intelligent and venerable men should be appointed to transcribe books. The study of religion was the principal object of his attention, and he caused the manuscripts of the Old and New Testament to be revised and corrected with the utmost exactness. He also undertook the correction of the prayers of the divine office, so that they should be free from any expression which did not refer to the honor and majesty of God. He obtained choristers from Rome, who taught the French the plain Roman chant, and he ordered all books of vocal music to be examined and corrected. He also appointed these choristers the principal masters of music throughout the kingdom. In order to set an example of application to study, and to excite emulation, he established an academy within the precincts of the palace, where the youthful princes and the children of his courtiers were educated.

Charlemagne, himself, condescended to enter the ranks of the disciples of Alcuin. France derived the greatest advantages from this institution. The thirst for knowledge became universal, and every one was desirous of receiving instruction. In a short time Charlemagne gathered together a band of learned men, whose united efforts furthered the cause of science, and whose brilliant intellects brought literature to a high state of cultivation. It is believed that this academy was the commencement of the University of Paris, the oldest and most celebrated in Europe.

PART SECOND.

CHARLEMAGNE IS CROWNED EMPEROR OF THE WEST.

A. D. 800.

Charlemagne was now master of nearly all the provinces composing the Western empire. Germany, Gaul, and the greater part of Spain and Italy being under his dominion, the title of Emperor was the only thing wanting to complete his glory. The Romans had conferred upon him the dignity of patrician of Rome, and his subjects could not more worthily acknowledge the signal services he had rendered the Church and State, than by offering him the imperial crown. During a visit which he made to Rome, Pope Leo III, in concert with the principal Roman lords, determined to proclaim him Emperor of the West. They did not give him the slightest intimation of their intention, lest it might be supposed that he had solicited the dignity, and in order to render his promotion more glorious and honorable.

On Christmas day the king went to the church of St. Peter to assist at the divine sacrifice, and when kneeling at the foot of the altar the Sovereign Pontiff placed the imperial diadem on his head, amid the joyous acclamations of the thousands who had assembled for mass. "Life and victory to Charles the most pious and august, crowned by God, the great and pacific Emperor of the Romans." Leo then anointed the king and his son, prince Louis, with holy oil, and was the first to render homage to the new Emperor, by prostrating himself before Charlemagne. It is thus that the Western empire, which had been abandoned by its former rulers, passed into the hands of the French, in the person of a prince, capable by his valor and piety of augmenting the glory Constantine and Theodosius had won during their prosperous reigns. The modesty manifested by this great prince, on this occasion, lent a new lustre to his dignity, and gave him another claim to imperial honors.

Eginhard, his secretary, relates, that, on returning from the ceremony, Charlemagne declared, that, if his absence could have defeated the plan, he would not have attended divine service, notwithstanding the solemn festival. He made magnificent presents to the church of St. Peter, and the other churches of Rome, and returned after Easter to Aix la Chapelle. Finding himself at peace with all the neighboring nations, Charlemagne desired to mark the beginning of his imperial rule by redoubling his zeal for the welfare of his subjects, and by severely punishing crime and vice. He accordingly sent officers of the royal household into the different provinces, to inquire into abuses and render justice to the weak and oppressed. It was by making one of these acts of reparation that he prepared himself for death. The time appointed by God for recompensing his virtues had arrived, and this great prince was attacked by a fever. As his disease hourly increased, he received the holy viaticum with the most fervent piety, and yielded his soul to God, in the seventy-second year of his age. Such was the Christian death of the greatest and most valiant king of France; one of the most zealous defenders of the Church; a prince whom the world numbers among her heroes, and whom religion has placed in the rank of the saints.

CONVERSION OF THE DANES AND SWEDES.

A. D. 829.

The conversion of the Saxons was followed by that of several other nations, which were gradually enlightened and civilized. St. Ansgarius preached the faith in Denmark and Sweden. This holy Apostle was born in France, and had been educated in a monastery of Corbie. After acquiring the Apostolic spirit in this holy retreat, he was sent by his superiors to Denmark, in order to announce the glad tidings of salvation to these barbarous and idolatrous people. His labors were crowned with success, and the number of converts daily increased. The most effacacious means he employed to perpetuate the first of his teachings was, by purchasing young slaves, and inculcating in their youthful minds the fear of God and the practice of virtue, and he thus succeeded in establishing a flourishing school. While this work was prospering, the King of Sweden asked the Emperor, Louis Debonnaire, to send missionaries to announce the Gospel in his dominions.

Louis appointed Ansgarius, and another religious of Corbie, who volunteered his services, to undertake the mission. The two priests departed, loaded with rich presents from Louis, to the King of Sweden, but were attacked during the voyage by pirates, who appropriated the gifts, and they consequently arrived in Sweden empty handed. The king, nevertheless, received them very kindly, and they made a great many conversions. The governor of the city was one of the first who embraced the faith, and this lord, who was one of the royal favorites, erected a church in honor of the true God. When the number of Christians had considerably increased, an Archiepiscopal see was established at Hamburg, and St. Ansgarius appointed archbishop. He labored most zealously for the salvation of souls, while leading an austere and mortified life; his food consisting of only bread and water. Ansgarius frequently retired to a little hermitage which he had built, as an asylum from worldly cares and distractions, and in this peaceful abode he would shed tears of penitence before God, when he was not occupied with his pastoral duties.

God bestowed the gift of miracles on his servant, who cured a great many sick persons by his prayers; but his humility was so great, that on one occasion, when several persons were speaking in his presence of some miraculous cures he had effected, he said: "If my prayers were of any avail before God, I would offer them to obtain one miracle, and that is, to make me His faithful servant." The holy prelate always desired to shed his blood for the faith, and, when attacked by his last illness, was inconsolable at the thought of losing this happiness. "Alas!" he exclaimed, "my manifold sins have deprived me of a martyr's crown." When near his end, he employed his failing strength in exhorting his disciples to serve God with fidelity, and persevere in the mission which was dear to him. This infant Church was exposed for some time to a violent storm through an invasion of barbarians; the precious seed, sown by the holy Apostle, was not lost, however, but produced abundant fruit, owing to the labors of his successors.

CONVERSION OF THE SCLAVONIANS AND RUSSIANS.

A. D. 842.

The Sclavonians, a barbarous people who inhabited a portion of the country known at the present day by the name of Poland, frequently made incursions beyond the limits of the Western empire; they thus were brought in contact with the Christian religion, and soon evinced a desire to embrace the faith. With this intention they had recourse to the Empress Theodora, who governed as regent during her son's minority, begging of her to send them missionaries, promising in return for this inestimable benefit, to be henceforth docile and obedient subjects of the empire. A priest, named Constantine, was chosen for this mission. When he arrived at his destination, he applied himself to the study of the language of the country, and translated into this tongue the Gospels and other parts of the Scripture which he considered the most useful for the instruction of the converts.

God blessed his labors, and the whole nation became christianized, and their neighbors, the Russians, followed their example, and the light of faith soon penetrated these heathen countries. The Emperor Basil took advantage of this happy change to conclude a treaty of peace with them, and after propitiating them by handsome presents, induced them to receive a bishop ordained by Ignatius, patriarch of Constantinople. A striking miracle wrought by this Saint caused his teachings to yield abundant fruit. The Russian prince had assembled the people in order to deliberate whether they should abandon their old worship; the bishop was summoned and interrogated as to his creed; the holy prelate in reply exhibited the book of the Gospels, and related several miracles from the Old and New Testament. That of the three children in the fiery furnace made a deep impression on the assembly, and they said to Ignatius: "If thou canst perform a similar wonder, we will believe that thou speakest the truth." "We are not permitted to tempt God," answered the bishop; "if, however, you are resolved to behold His power, ask what you will, and He will manifest His omnipotence through the ministry of His servant."

The Russians demanded that the holy volume he held in his hand should be thrown into a fire kindled by their own hands, and they promised, if it was not consumed in the flames, to become Christians. Then the bishop, raising his eyes to Heaven, said: "Jesus, Son of God, glorify thy holy name in the presence of this incredulous people." The book was accordingly cast into a red-hot furnace, and allowed to remain for some time. On extinguishing the fire it was found to be as perfect and unharmed as before it was thrown into the flames. The heathens instantly asked for baptism, and eagerly received the saving waters of regeneration. Thus God has worked from age to age, and renews at the present day, extraordinary miracles in behalf of the Church. This miraculous power is not weakened; and, when missionaries are sent to new countries, prodigies and wonders are wrought in testimony of the religion our Lord Jesus Christ has established, through His sufferings and ignominious death on the Cross.

CONVERSION OF THE BULGARIANS.

A. D. 855.

The Bulgarians, during a war against Theophilus, Emperor of the West, were defeated in battle, and the sister of the vanquished king was found among the captives. This princess was carried to Constantinople with the other prisoners of war, and detained in that city for thirty-eight years. During this long captivity she was instructed in the faith and received baptism. After the death of Theophilus, Theodora, his widow, governed in the name of her son. The king of Bulgaria, thinking this a favorable moment to retrieve his loss, made a declaration of war. Theodora courageously replied, that, if he crossed the limits of the empire, she would march against him, and hoped to conquer the invader of her dominions; but that even if he were to gain the victory, he should be filled with shame at having overcome a mere woman. The king, astonished at so bold an answer, conceived the highest esteem for Theodora, and offered her peace on certain conditions, which she accepted. One of the stipulations was that his sister should be liberated from captivity.

On returning to her brother's dominions, the princess frequently spoke to him of the Christian religion, exhorting him to embrace the true faith. Her entreaties touched the king's heart, and Heaven itself seemed to act in concert with the pious princess. A contagious disease having spread through Bulgaria, the monarch had recourse to the God his sister worshiped, and the dreadful pestilence instantly disappeared. After this miracle the king was convinced of the truth of Christianity; but the dread of offending his subjects, who were strongly attached to their superstitious practices, prevented him from a public profession of faith. A severe warning finally brought this stubborn prince under the mild yoke of the Gospel.

A gallery was being decorated in the palace, and as the king was naturally of a fierce and stern disposition, he had expressly commanded the painter to choose some terrible subject. The artist, who was a Christian, represented the Last Judgment, and portrayed most vividly the sufferings of the damned, with all the frightful circumstances which are capable of inspiring terror. The explanation of this picture caused the sovereign himself to shudder with horror; he resolved to abandon idolatry, and sent word to Theodora that he only waited for a minister of the Christian religion to receive baptism. The Empress sent him a bishop, who secretly baptized him at night; but, notwithstanding his precautions, the rumor of his conversion soon spread abroad.

The Bulgarians revolted and attacked the palace; but the king, animated with confidence in the power of God, sallied forth at the head of his retainers and soon dispersed the mob. He pardoned the rebels, who were finally won over to the faith. The monarch then sent ambassadors to the Pope, asking for ministers of the Gospel, and he consulted him on several questions concerning religion and morality. Pope Nicholas I was deeply moved at the sight of these new Christians who had come from such a distance to receive the instructions of the Holy See. After cordially welcoming them, he satisfactorily explained whatever they did not understand, and finally dismissed them, filled with joy and accompanied by two worthy bishops.

PHOTIUS USURPS THE SEE OF CONSTANTINOPLE.

A. D. 853.

God, who consoled His Church by the progress of Christianity in the countries of the North, allowed her to be disturbed by the scandalous usurpation of Photius in the See of Constantinople. This man, equally distinguished by his noble birth, great qualities and profound erudition, had been appointed to several important posts in the imperial court, but he disgraced his talents and position by his impostures and frauds. He was the favorite of Cæsar Bardas, uncle of the young Emperor Michael, and his principal minister. Bardas, whose profligate and corrupt life had caused him to be excommunicated by St. Ignatius, patriarch of Constantinople, plotted the destruction of this holy prelate. Having great control over the mind of the Emperor, his nephew, he persuaded him to banish Ignatius, and then used every artifice to induce the patriarch to resign his bishopric voluntarily; but, not succeeding in his designs, he appointed Photius, who was a layman, bishop of Constantinople.

So extraordinary a promotion created a great disturbance. The suffragan bishops at first refused to recognize Photius, but some were finally pursuaded to receive him, and the others were exiled. The approbation of Pope Nicholas was now the next thing to be gained, and Photius wrote, informing the Sovereign Pontiff of his elevation to the Patriarchal See. The usurper employed every means to prejudice the Pope in his favor; pretending that it was entirely against his wishes that he had been chosen to fill so high an office; that he had strenuously resisted the appointment, but had been forced to accept it, and that he had shed tears when he unwillingly consented to be consecrated bishop; adding, that Ignatius had voluntarily retired into a monastery, there to end his days in holy seclusion and prayer, his advanced age and infirmities being the cause of this step. His letter was accompanied by another from the Emperor, confirming all these falsehoods.

During this time, St. Ignatius was confined in a filthy dungeon, where every insult and indignity was heaped upon him. In order to hasten his ruin, he was accused of having conspired against the State, although no proof could be produced, and he was loaded with chains and banished to Mitylene, in the island of Lesbos.

Nicholas, who had not received any account of the affair from Ignatius, was on his guard, and refused to ratify the election of Photius without a careful examination of the facts on both sides. For this purpose, he sent two legates to Constantinople, to ascertain the true state of the case, and render him an exact account of all that had transpired. During their journey the legates received rich presents from the Emperor and Photius, who thus endeavored to gain their influence. On arriving in Constantinople, they were placed under a strict guard and forbidden all visitors, so as to prevent them from learning of the violence which had been employed toward St. Ignatius. The legates were then threatened with the most frightful torments if they refused to acknowledge Photius as bishop; they resisted for a long time, but were finally overcome by solicitations, promises, and threats, and they yielded to the imperial command.

INFAMOUS DECEPTIONS OF PHOTIUS.

St. Ignatius at length found means of informing the Sovereign Pontiff of all that had happened in Constantinople. Nicholas was much grieved at the criminal weakness of the legates, and condemned all their proceedings. He wrote to the Emperor and Photius, saying that he recognized Ignatius as the legitimate Bishop, declaring the nomination of Photius to be null and void. This base impostor suppressed the original letters, substituting forgeries of his own, written as if coming from the Pope, in which Nicholas assured him of his regret at having opposed his wishes, and after having learned the truth, promised perpetual friendship and regard.

This fraud proving unsuccessful, the wicked Photius attempted another most unheard of and extraordinary deception. He affirmed that a general council had been held, in which Nicholas was condemned, giving this falsehood so truthful an appearance as to deceive many persons. The acts of this pretended council were so skillfully composed as to deceive even the most incredulous minds. Photius was well informed in regard to the proceedings of a council. He, therefore, prepared an account, in which was given the accusations brought against the Pope, the testimony of the witnesses against him, as well as a speech of his own, in which he played the part of defender of the Pope, as he was unwilling that the absent Pontiff should be condemned without a hearing; but the Fathers of the pretended council had refused to listen to the arguments in his defense, and Photius, finally yielding with reluctance to their authority, had pronounced a sentence of deposition and excommunication against Nicholas.

The impostor induced several corrupt bishops to sign these false decrees, adding himself nearly a thousand signatures; among others the names of the deputies of the three Eastern patriarchs. Photius had the audacity to send these forgeries to Louis le Débonnaire, King of France, in order to persuade that prince to assist him in depriving Nicholas of the pontifical dignity. He also addressed a circular letter to the Eastern bishops, filled with complaints against the Latin Church, and declared the doctrine which teaches that the Holy Ghost proceeds from the Father and the Son to be an erroneous belief, although this Catholic dogma was held by both the Latin and Greek Church, and ratified by several councils. He censured the Roman Church upon some points of discipline which he had himself hitherto regarded as irreproachable. Thus a poisonous seed was planted, which subsequently produced a grievous heresy that even exists at the present day.

RE-ESTABLISHMENT OF ST. IGNATIUS — EIGHTH GENERAL COUNCIL.

A. D. 869.

Photius found that he was not regarded by the Emperor Basil with the same favor as by Michael, his predecessor. The new emperor, far from protecting the usurper, assembled in his palace the bishops who were then in Constantinople, and by their advice removed Photius from the Patriarchal see and sent him to a monastery. It was at this time that the acts of the false council, forged by this wicked man, commenced to excite suspicion. The fraudulent decrees were carried to the senate and publicly exposed before all the people, who were horrified at so extraordinary an imposture.

Immediately after the expulsion of the usurper, Ignatius, the lawful bishop, returned to his diocese, and in order to repair the many scandals which disgraced the Church, induced the Emperor to convene a general council. Basil despatched deputies to the Pope, begging him to send his legates, and wrote at the same time to the three eastern patriarchs, and to all the other bishops of the empire, inviting their attendance at the council, which was held in Constantinople in 869. Pope Adrian III, the successor of Nicholas, appointed three legates, to whom he gave two letters, one for the Emperor and the other for Ignatius. They were received in Constantinople with the greatest pomp and splendor; and these prelates, by their admirable behavior, sustained with dignity the primacy of the Holy See; they presided over the council, while Ignatius and the deputies of the other Eastern patriarchs came next in rank. Eleven of the principal officers of the court assisted at all the sessions, in order to maintain order and decorum. The legates read a formula of reunion, which was accepted by the whole council.

The primacy of the Roman Church was therein recognized, and a sentence of excommunication pronounced against all heretics, Photius in particular, as well as his followers. The bishops, who from violence or fear had espoused his cause, humbly asked pardon for their criminal weakness and were instantly forgiven. Photius hypocritically pleaded innocence, and enacted the part of an oppressed victim. He refused to answer the greater part of the questions asked him; and when forced to speak, used the very words our Lord Jesus Christ pronounced before His judges at the time of His Passion.

This impious conduct excited universal indignation, and he was ignominiously expelled from the assembly. The last session was the most largely attended, the Emperor and his two sons being present. The decrees of the Popes, Nicholas and Adrian, were then confirmed, and as the usurper obstinately adhered to his heretical opinions, he and his followers were anathematized. Basil then declared, that, if any one objected to the decisions of the council, he should proclaim his reasons at once, as, after the closing of the assembly, all its proceedings were to be accepted with implicit obedience, under pain of incurring the displeasure of the Church. Finally, two letters were written in the name of the council to Pope Adrian, asking him to confirm the acts of the council, and cause them to be received by all the Western churches; the other was addressed to all the faithful, exhorting them to submit, without murmur, to the decrees of the assembly.

REFLECTIONS ON THE HERESIES.

Heresies and schisms were the second trial through which the Church was to pass. "Heresies must arise," says the Apostle, "in order to try the virtue of the faithful." The efforts of the heretics were never more violent than when the pagans ceased to persecute the Christians. Hell then employed every artifice for the destruction of the still bleeding Church, which had so successfully repulsed the attacks of her first enemies, and she had hardly commenced to enjoy the peace occasioned by the conversion of the great Constantine, when Arius excited a more violent disturbance than had hitherto troubled the tranquillity of the spouse of Jesus Christ.

Constantius, son of Constantine, won over by the Arians, oppressed all the Catholics in his dominions. This new persecutor of Christianity was the more to be dreaded, as it was in the name of Jesus Christ that he attacked our Divine Lord Himself. After him came Valens, also an Arian, and more implacable in his hatred than Constantius. Several other Emperors protected the different heresies that appeared at intervals, with similar vindictiveness. The Church learned by sad experience that she had not less to suffer from Christian Emperors than she had endured from infidel princes, and that the blood of the martyrs was not only to preserve her doctrine inviolate, but also every separate article of faith, which was successively assailed by her unworthy children. The Divinity of Jesus Christ, His grace, the sacraments, in short, all the dogmas of religion, have been the subjects of different heresies, and have occasioned most unhappy divisions in the Church.

In this confusion of sects, all of which claimed to be Christian, Almighty God did not forsake the Church He had Himself built on a rock, but rendered her as invincible against internal disturbances as against external enemies. Each dogma has been solemnly defined by the whole Church; that is to say, she has confirmed the belief which was held by good Catholics at the time of the appearance of the heresy; and those who attacked this creed by introducing new doctrines, have been expelled from her bosom. The Church has seen heresies arise in her midst, and she has seen them successively crushed, according to the promise of our Divine Lord, although they were often supported by Emperors and Kings. Constantius and Valens were no more able to change the faith of the Church, than Nero and Dioclesian could prevent its establishment.

In order to try those who remained faithfully attached to the truth, God has permitted certain heresies to make some progress; but error has never prevailed, and the true faith has always been universally and publicly promulgated. The Church has always exercised an undisputed authority, which could never be assumed by heresy. She has never ceased to be Catholic and Universal, as her dominion extends over the whole world, and, although compelled at times to excommunicate her unworthy children, she does not lose her universality. By reading attentively the history of the Church, we find that, whenever attacked by a heresy, she speedily repaired her loss by making new conquests.

The Church resembles a great tree, which has been deprived of some of its branches; its vitality is still uninjured and it puts forth new leaves, the pruning of the withered branches only rendering the fruit the more abundant and excellent. She is Apostolic, that is to say, she goes back through an uninterrupted succession of Pontiffs to St. Peter, who was established the chief of the Apostles by Jesus Christ Himself, whereas each of the new sects necessarily fail in a continuation of their ministry, being unable to go beyond its author, who was a member of the Catholic Church before he formed a separate society. These divisions caused a great sensation at the periods they occurred; the pagans regarded the Church as the parent stem from which all the different sects detached themselves, never losing her strength or power through the loss of these corrupt members.

The idolaters called her the Great Church, the Catholic Church, as it was impossible to bestow any other name upon this divine work, whose founder was the Son of God, our Lord Jesus Christ. The heretics, on the contrary, bear an unmistakable mark of novelty and rebellion which they cannot conceal. They can never rid themselves of the names of their originators; the Arians, Pelagians and Nestorians, vainly endeavored to abolish the title bestowed upon them against their wish; the world very naturally calls each sect after the one who first introduced the new creed. The visible fact of their separation from the great Church, which is both universal and apostolic, is most apparent; this mark of human origin, which is ineffaceable, will always be against them, and plainly demonstrates to the whole world that their sects are the work of fallible men. These rotten branches, cut off from the living tree, have never borne fruit, never attained any growth, and have finally perished in obscurity. Being merely human inventions, they have disappeared, notwithstanding the support of the powers of the world and hell; while the edifice created by God has remained firm and immovable.

The Church has triumphed over heresies, as she triumphed over idolatry, and this will be the fate of all the schisms which shall arise in the fold of Jesus Christ, who will crush and destroy them by His almighty power; the past victories of the Church are a sure presage of the conquests she will gain in the future; the promises she has received are eternal, and will continue to be fulfilled throughout all ages.

INVASION OF THE BARBARIANS—SCANDALS— TENTH CENTURY.

During the tenth century the Church suffered greatly from the cruelty of the northern tribes, who ravaged successively all the provinces of the Western empire. The Normans, Hungarians, and other savage people, devastated Germany, England, France, Italy and Spain, leaving everywhere traces of their destructive and sanguinary march. The cities were reduced to ashes, monasteries plundered and destroyed, schools abolished, and the arts and sciences almost entirely abandoned. Ignorance produced a relaxation of discipline and corruption of morals; scandals increased; the most holy laws were publicly violated, and the evil extended even to the heads of the Church, Rome itself not escaping the contagion.

The Church groaned and wept over these disorders, this trial being much more painful than the persecutions she had formerly endured. These unhappy scandals, however, should not weaken, but strengthen our faith; for the sustaining hand of God was never more manifest than at this mournful period, showing incontestably that the divine purity of the spouse of Jesus Christ cannot be tarnished by the wickedness and malice of her unworthy children. In the midst of so many excesses the faith remained the same as in the first ages of the Church, and in the public instructions, God did not permit the least attack to be made upon Christian morals and Catholic belief. Vices and abuses were continually opposed; the councils renewed the laws of discipline, and endeavored to enforce obedience to their decrees. Divine Providence raised up illustrious Saints, who zealously combated the progress of impiety. Finally, the Church gained sufficient strength, not only to heal the wounds she had received from the barbarians, but also to convert these new persecutors, and bring them under the mild rule of the Gospel. Thus the savage tribes, who overthrew the Roman empire, instead of destroying the Church, were conquered by her. It is true, that the germ of their wild origin was only gradually eradicated, and their ignorant minds but slowly enlightened; but God finally caused the Church to triumph over ignorance and barbarism, as she had already overcome persecution and heresies.

The arts and sciences found an asylum in the monasteries and among the clergy; the episcopal residences and religious houses became places of public instruction, where the taste for study and the love of knowledge were fostered. While the nobles devoted themselves to the profession of arms, disdaining the cultivation of letters, the priests and monks were occupied in transcribing the ancient works they had saved from the ruthless hands of the barbarians. These precious monuments of learning would have certainly perished if the Church had not transmitted them to posterity. It was in her bosom that the dying embers of literature were rekindled, the darkness of ignorance dispelled, and the arts and sciences gained a new luster. Thus religion has not only carefully preserved the ancient and incontestable traditions which regulate our creed and morals, but also revived letters at a time when the whole of Europe seemed indifferent to learning.

RE-ESTABLISHMENT OF DISCIPLINE IN ENGLAND.
A. D. 912.

The Church, which is never forsaken by the Spirit of God, discovered in herself, during this corrupt period, a new principle of life, which refreshed and invigorated her. St. Odo was placed by Providence over the first see in England, for the purpose of restoring the discipline of this kingdom. When made archbishop of Canterbury, he framed wise laws for the regulation of the clergy, nobles and people.

King Edward seconded the efforts of the holy prelate, and issued excellent proclamations, enforcing law and order throughout his dominions. A zealous bishop cannot fail to effect a great amount of good, when protected by a religious prince; thus St. Odo reformed a great number of abuses, and the work so happily commenced was fully accomplished by his successor, St. Dunstan. This holy prelate, animated by the same spirit, finding himself obliged, in virtue of his office, to watch over all the English churches, traveled through the different cities of the kingdom, instructing the faithful in the rules of a Christian life, and exciting them to the practice of virtue by his earnest and touching exhortations, speaking with so much unction and power that it was impossible to resist his eloquence. He was indefatigable in his labors; continually occupied in abolishing scandals, settling disputes, and reuniting those who were at variance. Dunstan only rested from this perpetual toil during the time of prayer, and when forced to take the necessary repose, exhausted nature demanded.

The principal object of his zealous efforts was the reformation of the clergy; he induced the king to inflict severe punishment upon those who desecrated the holy ministry by their excesses, and he restored the priesthood to its original dignity and sanctity, so that the most illustrious houses of England considered it an honor for their children to enter religion. St. Dunstan was both firm and energetic in the exercise of his duty, as will be seen by the following example: One of the most powerful lords in the kingdom had married his first cousin, and although remonstrated with by the bishop, refused to separate from her. The holy prelate forbade him to enter the church; upon which the baron complained to the king and obtained an order addressed to St. Dunstan, requesting a removal of the punishment.

The Saint, astonished that so pious a monarch should allow himself to be deceived, exhorted the baron to repentance, but finding that he only became more enraged, courageously said: "When I see you truly penitent, I will cheerfully obey the king, but as long as you obstinately continue in your sin, no man shall cause me to violate the law of God and bring contempt on the decrees of the Church." The firmness of the archbishop finally touched the heart of the culprit, who expressed sincere contrition for his fault, submitted to the authority of St. Dunstan, and not only dissolved his unlawful alliance, but as a national council was then in session, appeared in the midst of the assembly barefooted and clothed in sackcloth, holding a bunch of rods in his hand, as a sign of humility and obedience to the commands of God and the Church. He then threw himself at the feet of the Saint, who, mingling his tears with those of the penitent, received the contrite baron once more into the saving fold of Jesus Christ.

The firmness of St. Dunstan was again demonstrated on another occasion. Although a sincere

Christian, the king committed a great sin; the holy archbishop immediately went to him and forcibly represented the enormity of his crime; Edward, overcome by his reproaches, tearfully asked him what he should do to obtain forgiveness; Dunstan imposed a suitable penance upon the monarch, who performed it with sentiments of the deepest contrition.

RESTORATION OF DISCIPLINE IN GERMANY.
A. D. 901.

At this same period saintly and illustrious bishops, supported by the powerful authority of the Emperor Otho, labored successfully to reform the abuses in Germany, but none more effectually than St. Bruno, archbishop of Cologne, and brother of the Emperor. At four years of age he was sent to Utrecht, where Bishop Baudri, a very learned man, gave him excellent masters. Bruno made great progress in his studies, and advanced daily in the practice of virtue; his thirst for knowledge did not diminish his piety; he was most punctual in his attendance at the holy offices, where his recollection and modesty edified the assistants. The slightest irreverence during divine service excited his pious indignation. One day he saw Prince Henry, his brother, speaking during mass to Conrad, Duke of Lorraine. After the service he spoke to them of the impropriety of conversing in the presence of the Blessed Sacrament, assuring them they would incur the divine wrath if they continued such irreverence.

RESTORATION OF DISCIPLINE IN GERMANY. 321

The love of religion was a sure claim to his regard, and he joyfully lent his influence and protection to all enterprises undertaken for the glory of God, and the salvation of souls. On returning to court he found every encouragement to sanctity of life within its precincts; the palace being at that time an edifying school of royal and Christian perfection, St. Matilda, mother of the Emperor Otho, and Adelaide his wife, giving, by their excellent example, eloquent lessons of mortification and holiness to the courtiers and attendants. Thus, while scandals increased, God adorned His Church with saintly monarchs, who consoled and edified the faithful.

Bruno was prepared for the Episcopal dignity by being appointed superior of several monasteries, where he displayed the greatest wisdom and prudence, and restored exact discipline. Being subsequently raised to the see of Cologne, he gave a wider scope to his zeal, and labored to extend piety and religion throughout Germany. His first care was to re-establish peace and concord in his diocese, and regulate the proper celebration of the divine offices.

The Emperor, his brother, when leaving for Italy, confided the royal authority to Bruno during his absence, who faithfully acquitted himself of the charge, understanding the duties of a prince as well as those of a bishop. He only used his authority for the establishment of good institutions, the protection of the weak, the succor of the poor, the intimidation of the wicked, and for the encouragement of the faithful; and he also built and renovated a great number of churches and monasteries. This holy prelate announced the word of God, and explained the Scriptures in a clear and comprehensive manner; but his principal care was to place wise and virtuous bishops in the provinces where laxity of morals and other abuses had been introduced, as he was persuaded that the most powerful means for correcting and reclaiming those who had wandered from the path of duty, was for their pastors to give not only good instructions, but good examples also.

RE-ESTABLISHMENT OF MONASTIC DISCIPLINE IN FRANCE.

A. D. 910.

Nothing contributed so much to the restoration of ecclesiastical discipline in France as the foundation of the celebrated monastery of Cluny, which became the nursery of many apostolic men. This congregation owed its origin to the zeal of the virtuous Bernon, who was its first abbot. Descended from one of the noblest families of Bourgogne, Bernon embraced the monastic life in the Abbey of St. Martin of Autun, from which he was soon removed, and appointed superior of the monastery of Beaume, where he enforced regularity and order.

Several officers of William, duke of Aquitaine, having visited this edifying institution, spoke of it in such high terms that the duke determined to found a similar house in his dominions, and place it under the charge of the holy abbot. He, therefore, invited St. Bernon to Cluny, for the purpose of choosing a proper locality for the erection of a convent. Bernon accordingly repaired thither, accompanied by St. Hugh, then a monk of St. Germain of Autun, his particular friend. The duke received them with great kindness, and acquainting them with his intention of building a monastery in his domains, requested them to find a proper site for this new establishment. The two Religious, charmed with the situation of Cluny, replied that they could not choose a more agreeable spot than the one they were then occupying. The duke at first objected, as it was here his hounds were kept. "Very well, my lord," pleasantly answered Bernon, "dismiss the dogs and receive the monks!" William, finally, graciously consented, and desired that the monastery should be dedicated to SS. Peter and Paul. He also drew up a deed of gift, which is still extant, explaining his motives. "Wishing," he says, "to make good use of what God has given me, I consider it a duty to endeavor to win the affection of the poor of Jesus Christ, and render this work perpetual, by founding a religious community. I give for the love of Jesus Christ, our Lord and Saviour, my estate of Cluny, for the erection of a monastery in honor of SS. Peter and Paul, which will always be an asylum for those who, destitute of the riches of this world, come to seek in religion the treasures of virtue."

The intentions of the pious founder were fulfilled; the community accomplished an immense amount of good, and was distinguished for its regular discipline and the extraordinary merits of its abbots. The true spirit of the religious vocation emanated from this house, and soon spread throughout France.

The holy abbot at first only placed twelve monks at Cluny, but their reputation for piety and fervor soon extended abroad; other communities were desirous of securing the guidance of the saint, and he governed seven religious houses at the same time. This celebrated monastery has given several great Pontiffs to the Church, and produced holy bishops who revived Christian piety in the different dioceses of France.

THE WORK OF REFORMATION IS CONTINUED BY THE SUCCESSORS OF ST. BERNON.

St. Odo, who succeeded the saintly founder, completed the establishment of the new congregation, and arranged all the minor details of the convent. Odo was born in the province of Maine, of a noble family; he studied in Paris, where, notwithstanding the unhappy state of morals, the doctrine of the Church was perpetuated by a continual succession of excellent teachers. The desire of consecrating himself to God induced him to go to Rome, in the hope of finding some community where he could advance in the way of perfection and holiness. Passing through Boulogne he was struck with the spirit of piety which prevailed in the house of Cluny, and finding in France what he intended seeking in Italy, he remained in this monastery and asked to be admitted among the monks.

The great qualities of the new Religious were soon discovered, and the care of the youthful pupils who were educated at the convent was confided to him.

The satisfactory manner in which he acquitted himself of the duties of this important office, and his talents and virtues, which commanded universal admiration, caused him to be chosen by his brethren as their abbot. Odo resisted for a long time, and only yielded to the express command of the bishop, who threatened him with excommunication if he persisted in his refusal. Finally he obeyed, and received the abbatial benediction. Under his wise rule the Abbey of Cluny was distinguished for the exact observance of discipline, the virtuous spirit of emulation among the Religious, the study of the doctrines of the Church, and charity toward the poor. This edifying life attracted a great number of noble and illustrious persons to Cluny; not only laymen of the highest rank repaired thither to practice penance, but bishops even left their dioceses in order to embrace a monastic life. Counts and dukes were eager to submit the monasteries in their domains to the guidance of Cluny, so that the holy abbot might reform whatever was amiss in these communities. It was for this reason, that St. Odo did not confine himself to one convent, but labored indefatigably for the restoration of discipline throughout France, and even Italy, whither he was called by the sovereign Pontiff.

Odo was forced to strain every nerve to accomplish this formidable task, but his brilliant success consoled him in all his efforts, and he demonstrated to the world what great things can be effected by a single man for the glory of God, when he is actuated by supernatural motives. The successors of St. Odo inherited his virtues and zeal: Maïeul, Odilo, the venerable Peter and Hugh edified the whole Church by their sanctity, and put the last stroke to the work of reformation. Through their care and example, religious fervor was rekindled in all the monasteries, and the good they accomplished without any assistance inspired others with a desire to imitate them. St. Gerard established a strict discipline in Belgium, and Adalberon, bishop of Metz, met with the same success in Lorraine.

REFORMATION OF THE CLERGY.

Pope Leo IX zealously applied himself to the abolishing of evils which had crept into ecclesiastical discipline, directing his efforts against the two prevailing vices — simony and immorality, which at that time afflicted the Church. With this intention he made several journeys to France and Germany, undaunted by any dangers or obstacles which beset his path. He assembled councils, and drew up wise rules for the extirpation of abuses; all guilty priests were deposed from their office, and when they refused submission to this sentence, were excommunicated.

The successors of the holy Pontiff followed in his footsteps, and imitated his firmness in reforming the morals of the clergy. Their endeavors were wonderfully seconded by a remarkable man, whom Providence seemed to have raised up at this unhappy period for the revival of religious fervor. St. Peter Damian, who rendered the Church this important service, was born at Ravenna, in Italy. Deserted by his unnatural parents, he was brought up by a charitable woman, who treated the unfortunate child with maternal tenderness. God, who had destined him for great things, gave him the means of education, and he made extraordinary progress, both in learning and virtue, leading a mortified and studious life. Finally, Peter renounced the world, and entered the monastery of Fontavelle, in Umbria, where the monks lived in separate cells, and devoted themselves to prayer and reading. They subsisted on bread and water four days in the week, and partook of a few roots on Tuesday and Thursday. Peter gave a bright example to all the monks, by his fervor in penitential exercises, and he became a model of every virtue.

The Pontiffs, seeing of what great service his piety and learning would be to the Church, elevated him to the highest ecclesiastical dignities, and appointed him cardinal and bishop of Ostia. The holy prelate labored with unwearied zeal and undaunted courage in opposing the laxity of morals, and strove to enforce the laws of the Church. Having been sent on several embassies, he neglected nothing which could repress scandals, correct abuses, and re-establish everywhere the most exact discipline. The reformation of ecclesiastical communities, which was accomplished in a Council held at Rome by Alexander II in 1063, was one of the fruits of his labors.

Since the fourth century communities of priests had existed, whose members possessed every thing in common, and lived together under the immediate jurisdiction of the bishop. In the midst of large cities, surrounded by the tumult of the world, they practiced, as well as their sacred duties would permit, the retirement and austerities of hermits. This institution merited the approbation of St. Ambrose, who speaks of it in these terms: "It is a company of celestial and saintly warriors, who spend day and night in chanting the praises of God, without neglecting the flocks intrusted to their care; they are continually occupied, either in pious reading or in manual labor. Can there be any thing more admirable than this life, in which pain and self-denial are recompensed with a heavenly peace, sustained by mutual example, alleviated by constant habit, and soothed by holy employments? This life is neither troubled by temporal cares, nor distracted by the pleasures of the world; neither molested by the visits of idle people, nor weakened and degenerated by intercourse with mankind."

St. Augustine also held it in great esteem, as is seen by two discourses which he composed on the excellence of communities, and it has served as a foundation for the rules observed by the canons of the Church. This strict discipline gradually became weakened, and was almost abolished by the incursions of barbarians, who destroyed and plundered the churches in the tenth century. It was restored to its first state of perfection by St. Peter Damian, and his successors were called canons regular.

CONVERSION OF THE NORMANS.
A. D. 912.

Nothing gives more honor to the Church, and renders the powerful protection of her Divine Head more apparent, than does the conversion of barbarous tribes. We are edified and confirmed in our faith when we see, that, during a period which was disgraced by so many disorders, the Church, instead of being weakened, made new conquests, and subdued savage nations who had desolated her sanctuaries and persecuted her children. The Normans had ravaged France for seventy years, when suddenly, God was pleased to arrest this devastating torrent.

The time destined by Providence for the conversion of this people had arrived, and still nothing seemed prepared for this great event. Rollo, the bravest of their chiefs, appeared more determined than ever on continuing the war; King Charles the Simple then entered into treaty with him, offering the province of Neustria and the hand of his daughter in marriage, if he would receive Christian instruction and baptism. These conditions were accepted and peace declared. The archbishop of Rouen instructed Rollo in the mysteries of religion and baptized him in the beginning of the year 912. This conversion, which seemed to be actuated by political motives, was nevertheless very sincere; the conditions of the treaty being the means appointed by Providence to bring this prince and his subjects to a knowledge of Christianity.

The new duke, immediately after his baptism, asked the archbishop which were the most venerated churches in the province of Neustria. The prelate named the churches of Our Lady of Rouen, Bayeux, and Evreux, those of Mount St. Michael, St. Peter of Rouen and Jumièges. "And what saint is most loved in our immediate neighborhood?" asked the duke. "St. Denis, Apostle of France," replied the archbishop. "Very well," said Rollo, "before sharing my lands with the nobles of my army, I wish to give a portion to God, the Holy Virgin and the saints whom you have named, so as to merit their protection." In effect, for a week after his baptism, during which time he wore a white garment according to the custom of the times, he each day donated ground to some one of the churches indicated; and then divided his lands among his vassals. Rollo did not neglect the instruction of his officers and subjects, nearly all of whom received baptism; divine grace perfecting and sanctifying whatever of human respect or worldly motive had prompted them when first embracing Christianity.

A sudden and extraordinary change was effected in the morals of these people; it is only the faith of Jesus Christ that could subdue so warlike and savage a nation as the Normans. Rollo appeared after his conversion as gentle and religious as he had hitherto been ferocious and barbarous; this great warrior became a wise lawgiver, and he proved that it was as easy for him to obtain the respect and obedience of his subjects, as it had been to terrify the world by his military prowess. He at first established laws for the government of his new dominions, and as the Normans had formerly been addicted to plundering, he issued very stringent decrees against theft; his commands being so scrupulously observed that no one dared to pick up any thing he found on the roadside.

The following is a remarkable example: The duke one day hung one of his bracelets upon the branch of an oak tree, under which he was resting from the fatigues of the chase, and forgot to remove it. This bracelet remained suspended from the bough for three years, during which time no one dared to appropriate it, so firm was the popular belief that nothing could escape the vigilance and severity of Rollo. His name alone inspired so much terror, that it was sufficient for any one who had been assailed to pronounce it, and all within hearing would be obliged to go in pursuit of the criminal.

CONVERSION OF THE HUNGARIANS.
A. D. 1002.

The Hungarians, a savage tribe from Scythia, devastated Germany, and penetrated as far as Lorraine, leaving everywhere traces of their cruel and destructive march. They burned churches, massacred priests at the foot of the altar, and carried a great number of Christians, without distinction of age, sex, or condition, into captivity. The grace of God, however, softened these monsters, and inspired them with sentiments of humility and virtue. One of their kings became favorably disposed toward the

Christians who were living in the vicinity of Hungary; and he published an edict allowing them entrance into his dominions, promising them a hospitable reception.

This lenient step brought him to a knowledge of the sanctity and truth of the faith, and finally effected his complete conversion. He and his whole family received baptism. St. Adalbert, bishop of Prague, baptized his infant son, who was called Stephen. This young prince was most carefully educated; from his earliest infancy he showed the most pious dispositions, and afterward became the Apostle of Hungary. On ascending the throne he strove to convert his subjects, and establish Christianity in his kingdom. He was opposed in this design by some rebellious vassals, whose attachment to idolatry induced them to take up arms against their sovereign; but Stephen, full of confidence in the assistance of God, advanced to meet them, bearing on his standards a picture of St. Martin, for whom Hungary has always had great veneration, as he was a native of that country. Stephen conquered the rebels, consecrated their lands to God, and founded a monastery in honor of St. Martin.

When peace once more reigned in his dominions, the king used every effort to propagate the faith; and, in order to attain this object, distributed abundant alms and offered up fervent supplications to the throne of grace; frequently prostrating himself before the altar groaning and weeping over his own offenses. This pious monarch sent everywhere for evangelical laborers, and God inspired some zealous priests to leave their homes and devote themselves to the spiritual welfare of this country. Innumerable conversions were made, and Stephen succeeded in abolishing idolatry from his territories. Then, in order to give a proper form to the Hungarian Church, it was divided into ten bishoprics; Strigonium, on the Danube, being the Metropolitan diocese, of which St. Sebastian, a holy Religious, was chosen archbishop. The king sent a bishop to Rome, asking for the confirmation of this appointment, and the deputy related to the Pope all that the prince had effected for the good of religion and salvation of souls. The sovereign Pontiff was much rejoiced at this consoling intelligence, and granted all Stephen's requests; he sent a crown to the king, and also a cross, to be carried before him as a sign of his apostleship, from which originated the title of "apostolical," conferred upon Hungarian monarchs.

On the return of his deputy, Stephen was solemnly crowned, with his wife, a princess of eminent piety, who eagerly participated in all the good works of her saintly husband. Stephen was particularly devoted to the Mother of God, and placed himself and his kingdom under her powerful protection; an example subsequently imitated by one of the kings of France. The fervor of this religious prince increased as he grew older, and when he felt his death approaching, he called for the bishops and nobles, and earnestly solicited them to protect and promulgate the faith in Hungary.

THE HERESY OF BERENGARIUS.

A. D. 1050.

The Church of God is not destined to enjoy the sweets of perfect peace here below; for she is nearly always afflicted by heresy, schism or scandals. During the eleventh century she endured all these different trials. Berengarius, archdeacon of Angers, desiring to distinguish himself and acquire celebrity, dared to attack the mystery of the Eucharist, and taught that the body and blood of Jesus Christ are not contained therein in reality, but only figuratively.

A universal outcry arose on every side against this impious doctrine, entirely contrary to the belief of the Church. The Catholic Doctors zealously refuted this pernicious creed, and wrote to all parts of the Christian world in defense of the truth. Lanfranc, archbishop of Canterbury, and Adelman, bishop of Brescia, addressed letters to the heretic, endeavoring to reclaim him from his error. "I conjure you," said Adelman, "not to disturb the peace of the Catholic Church, for which so many millions of martyrs and holy Doctors have shed their innocent blood. We believe that the true body and blood of Jesus Christ are contained in the Eucharist. This is the doctrine taught from the earliest ages, and still preached by our holy mother the Church, which is spread over the whole world, and bears the title of Catholic. All those calling themselves Christians glory in receiving, in this sacrament, the real body and blood of Jesus Christ. Interrogate those who have studied our holy books, ask the Greeks, the Armenians, in fine, the Christians of every nation, and they will all acknowledge this as their belief."

He then establishes the truth of this Catholic dogma by quoting the words of Scripture; and as Berengarius replied by saying, that he could not understand how the bread could become the body of Jesus Christ, Adelman added: "The just man, who sees with the eyes of faith, does not doubt the word of God, nor endeavor to investigate a mystery which is above human reason; he is happy in believing in heavenly mysteries, so as one day to merit the reward of his faith, instead of vainly striving to penetrate that which is incomprehensible to finite man. It is as easy for Jesus Christ to change the bread into His body, as to change water into wine, or create light by His single word." In order to silence Berengarius, a council was immediately held at Paris, where his letters upon this subject were read aloud. The Fathers were horrified at the impious doctrine they contained, and testified their indignation against the wicked author by unanimously condemning him.

Pope Nicholas II convened another council at Rome. Berengarius attended, but dared not persist in his error, and promised to sign the profession of faith drawn up by this assembly, and expressed in these words: "I anathematize all heresies, especially the one of which I am accused. I protest with my heart and with my lips, that in regard to the Eucharist, I hold the same faith as the Pope and the council have commanded me to believe on the authority of the Scriptures, and the teachings of the apostles, viz., that the bread and wine which are offered at the altar become after consecration the true body and the true blood of Jesus Christ." Berengarius confirmed this declaration by an oath, and consigned the books containing his heresy to the flames.

Soon after, it was noticed that he became unsettled in his belief, and asserted that the substance of the bread is not changed into the body of Jesus Christ, but that the bread remained in union with the body of our Lord. This was the last effort of the heretic; but the Church, who follows up heresies step by step, so as to condemn error as soon as it appears, after so clearly establishing the real presence in the first profession of faith, issued a second, in which the change of the substance was more distinctly expressed. Berengarius again subscribed to this, and confessed that the bread and wine which are placed on the altar are, in virtue of the all powerful words of Jesus Christ, substantially changed into the true and real body and blood of our Lord, in such a manner, that the body which is received is the same that was born of the Virgin Mary, suffered on the cross, and is now seated at the right hand of the Father in Heaven.

Berengarius thus condemned himself a second time, and this heresy, anathematized by its own author, was suppressed for a while, and did not reappear until several centuries later, when it was revived by the Protestants.

SCHISM OF MICHAEL CERULARIUS, PATRIARCH OF CONSTANTINOPLE.

A. D. 1053.

About the period that Berengarius was agitating the Western Church, Michael Cerularius, patriarch of Constantinople, revived the unhappy division commenced by the heretic Photius. The wound he had inflicted on the Church had never entirely healed; a hidden jealousy still rankled in the hearts of the bishops of Constantinople; they envied the prerogatives of the See of Rome, the fountain head of Catholicity, for it was to St. Peter, first bishop of Rome, that our Lord Jesus Christ addressed these words: "Thou art Peter, and upon this rock I will build my Church."

Nevertheless, Michael Cerularius, more violent than Photius, presumed to set at defiance the Church of Rome, and separate himself from the union of which she is the center. In order to palliate this scandalous rupture, he renewed the unjust accusations and absurd reproaches made by Photius against the Latins. He prohibited all communication with the Pope, closed the Latin Churches in his diocese, and carried his fanaticism so far as to re-baptize such as had received baptism in those churches. Pope Leo IX, hearing of these outrageous proceedings, used every effort to calm the disturbance and settle the difficulty, refuting by admirable arguments all the accusations of the patriarch, and assuring him that a difference of forms was not a sufficient reason for destroying the unity of the Church.

Most earnestly desiring the restoration of peace among his distracted fold, Leo sent three legates to Constantinople to confer with the patriarch and endeavor to re-establish tranquillity and union; they were intrusted with two letters, one for the Emperor and the other for Michael. The legates were kindly received by the Emperor, but the patriarch refused to hold any intercourse with them. Indignant at such insolent behavior, the legates excommunicated Michael, depositing the written sentence on the altar of the principal church in the presence of the clergy. Then shaking the dust from their feet as they left the church they uttered these words, "May God witness and judge our act." They bade farewell to the Emperor, who blamed the patriarch, but had not the courage to reprimand his unworthy conduct.

Michael Cerularius, enraged at the condemnation of the legates, had the audacity to excommunicate the Pope; and endeavored, by letters filled with falsehood, to separate the Eastern patriarchs from the Roman Church. His fraud deceived several bishops, who fell into his artful snare; but the schism was not general, and did not make much progress for more than a century afterward, when the Latins became odious to the Greeks by seizing the city and government of Constantinople.

TROUBLES IN EUROPE ON THE SUBJECT OF INVESTITURES.

A. D. 1075.

Shortly after the scandalous attempt of Michael Cerularius in the East, Henry IV, Emperor of Germany, gave rise to a quarrel, which occasioned great evils in the Church and Empire. It was one of the established customs of Germany for the Emperors to bestow their benefices on the bishops and abbots, by presenting them with the cross and ring, which was called the right of investiture. Henry IV was not satisfied with following this ancient custom, but, on this occasion, made a shameful traffic of the ecclesiastical dignities, conferring them, not on the most worthy, but on those who offered the highest price for them. Pope St. Gregory VII, filled with zeal for the discipline of the Church, desired to correct this abuse. As the ring and crosier are the symbols of spiritual power, which cannot be conferred by laymen, he condemned the practice of investitures, and threatened to excommunicate those who gave or received the dignities of the Church in this manner.

The Emperor disregarded this menace, and, on persisting in his obstinacy, was excommunicated. The Pope not only inflicted this spiritual punishment, but declared Henry to be deprived of the imperial dignity, and his subjects absolved from their oath of allegiance. After this sentence of the Pope was promulgated, several nobles, dissatisfied with the government, elevated to the imperial throne

Rudolph, duke of Suabia, who was consecrated at Metz ten days after his election. This prince raised an army, and obtained a victory over Henry, but this first success did not continue. Rudolph perished in a second battle, and Henry, finding himself in a condition to revenge himself on the Pope, marched into Italy, deposed Gregory, and placed Guibert, archbishop of Ravenna, in the papal chair. Guibert assumed the name of Clement III. This Pope, who lived until the end of that century, caused great trouble to Gregory VII and his successors.

FOUNDATION OF THE CARTHUSIAN ORDER.
A. D. 1084.

The Church, in the midst of the discords by which she was agitated, was not without consolation. A new order of solitaries sprung up, who, by their examples of sanctity, lives of recollection, mortification, and prayer, were a source of great edification to the faithful, and of honor to religion. St. Bruno, the founder, was born in Cologne, of noble parents. His childhood was marked by an extraordinary piety, which developed with his years; his progress in learning was not less wonderful, and he became so able a theologian that his renown spread far and wide. He was the rector of studies, and chancellor in the church of Rheims, but, dreading the dangers of the world, he formed the resolution of living in solitude, and consecrating himself to a penitential life. He communicated his design to several of his friends, and, by his fervor, inspired them with the same sentiments. They applied to St. Hugh, bishop of Grenoble, who led them into a frightful desert in his diocese, called La Chatreuse, where St. Bruno and his companions established themselves.

The wonders which formerly excited the admiration of the faithful in the Thebais were renewed in France. "These new solitaries resembled angels more than men," wrote a cotemporary. Another thus describes their manner of life: "Each one has his separate cell, and receives one loaf and a small quantity of vegetables for his nourishment during the space of one week; but all assemble on Sunday and pass this holy day together. They wear a simple habit, and underneath it a hair shirt; extreme poverty reigns among them, even in their church; with the exception of the chalice, there are no gold or silver ornaments. They keep perfect silence, and ask by signs for what they absolutely need. They are supported by the work of their hands, and are generally occupied in copying books," which was the only method of preserving literature in those times, before the art of printing was discovered. Their reputation for sanctity spread on every side, arousing men from their indifference, and inducing many to join them.

Persons of all ages and every condition hastened to the desert to embrace the Cross of Jesus Christ, and monasteries were founded in different countries. Hardly six years had elapsed since the foundation of this holy society, when Pope Urban II summoned St. Bruno to Rome to assist him, by his advice, in ecclesiastical affairs, but the distractions of the world soon caused him to regret his cherished solitude, and he asked permission to return to the desert. The sovereign Pontiff, in order to retain him, offered to appoint him archbishop of Rheims, but the servant of God was only the more determined in his resolve, and finally obtained the Pope's consent. He went to Calabria with some companions who became attached to him in Italy, and founded a new monastery.

St. Bruno passed the remainder of his life in prayer and penitential exercises. Feeling his end approaching, he assembled his community, and made a profession of faith against the heresy of Berengarius, in these words: "I believe in the sacraments of the Church, and particularly that the bread and wine consecrated on the altar are the true body of Our Lord Jesus Christ, His true body and true blood, which we receive for the remission of our sins and in the hope of eternal salvation." The spirit of the holy founder was perpetuated by his disciples; his order, with rare fidelity, did not relax from its first fervor; it has subsisted for eight centuries, and has never required reformation in its rules, discipline or morals.

FIRST CRUSADE.
A. D. 1095.

Toward the end of the eleventh century the crusades commenced, that is to say, the wars undertaken to deliver the Holy Land from the Mahometan yoke. The Emperors of the East, whom the infidels had deprived of their most beautiful possessions, particularly of Palestine, supplicated for a long time the assistance of the Latins. In order to obtain succor, it was necessary to impart a religious motive to their entreaties. A priest of the diocese of Amiens, called Peter the Hermit, having made a pilgrimage to Jerusalem, was much grieved at beholding the holy places profaned by the infidels. He conferred with Simon, patriarch of Jerusalem, and, during their consultations on this subject, conceived the idea of delivering Palestine from the servitude under which it had groaned for so long a period. They agreed that the patriarch should write to the Pope, and that Peter should endeavor to win his consent to the project.

Peter went to Italy, and gave a touching description of the deplorable condition of the Holy Land to the Pope. Urban II was much affected; he resolved to persuade the Christian princes to unite their forces for the deliverance of Palestine; he appointed a council at Clermont, which was attended by a number of princes. Urban addressed them in so pathetic a manner, that the auditors burst into tears, and exclaimed, "God wills it!" These words, which were unanimously pronounced as if by inspiration, seemed a happy augury, and afterward became a watchword. The greater number of those present enrolled themselves for this expedition, and adopted as the sign of their engagement and as their insignia, a cross made of red cloth and worn on the right shoulder; this was the origin of the title "Crusader."

The bishops at the same time preached the crusade in their dioceses, with a success which surpassed all their hopes. Peter the Hermit traversed the provinces in order to animate the faithful to this great undertaking. His zeal, disinterested spirit, and penitential life, gave him the prestige and authority of a prophet. Preparations were soon made in France, Italy and Germany; the nobles and common people all evinced the utmost eagerness to assume the cross. Great edification was given by the sudden cessation of enmities and civil wars, which had hitherto universally prevailed in all the provinces. Peace and justice seemed to have returned to earth in order to prepare mankind for the holy crusade. Among the French nobles who exhibited the most distinguished zeal, were Godfrey of Bouillon, duke of Lorraine, Hugh the Great, count of Vermandois, Raymond, count of Toulouse, Robert, count of Normandy, and Robert, count of Flanders. Heroes like these were capable of conquering the world, had there been more union among the commanders, and more discipline among the troops.

Godfrey of Bouillon, who deserves all the honor of this crusade, united prudence to the ardor of youth, and the most intrepid courage to the tenderest piety. Although he was not the highest in rank among the Crusaders, his army was the best, as his reputation had attracted to his standard a great number of youthful nobles, who wished to acquire, in his excellent service, the science of war. The Crusaders divided themselves into several bands, taking different routes to Constantinople, in which city they had agreed to meet, but large numbers perished on the way in consequence of their excesses and insubordination.

EXPEDITION OF THE CRUSADERS.

Godfrey of Bouillon, who maintained strict discipline among his troops, was the first to arrive at Constantinople, and waited there for the rest of the Crusaders. When they were all assembled they crossed the Hellespont and besieged Nicæa, the capital of Bithynia, in order to open a passage to the Holy Land. This city was strongly garrisoned, but could not hold out against the besiegers, it therefore surrendered at discretion. A few days afterward the Crusaders, who resumed their march, found themselves surrounded by enemies. A dreadful combat took place; the Christians fought like lions, and the infidels fled, amidst great carnage. This victory did not remove every obstacle, as the Christian army was exposed to the horrors of famine, the whole country being devastated by their enemies. The scarcity of food and the fatigues of the march carried off great numbers, and destroyed nearly all the horses.

They finally arrived in Syria and determined to attack Antioch, which was then one of the strongest fortified cities of the East. The enemy, who expected this assault, had provided for a long resistance, and assembled a large army for its defense. The siege lasted seven months, and the Crusaders began to despair of success, when a happy occurrence rendered them masters of the city. The son of one of the principal inhabitants of Antioch was taken prisoner, and the father offered a large sum of money for his ransom. The Crusader who captured the youth returned him without ransom. This generosity won the heart of the father, and induced him to admit the Christians into the city. After this success, the way was open to them through Palestine, and the army advanced, without further obstacles, toward Jerusalem, the great object of the expedition. The city resisted for a long time, the enemy having neglected nothing which could assist in its defense; but the Crusaders performed prodigies of valor, and at the end of five weeks stormed the city at three o'clock on Friday: a remarkable coincidence, as this was the day and hour in which Jesus Christ had died on the Cross.

In the first heat of victory, nothing could resist the soldiers. The infidels were put to the sword, and the carnage was horrible; but this outburst of rage soon changed into the tenderest piety. The crusaders threw off their blood-stained garments, and, weeping and barefooted, visited all the holy places consecrated by the sufferings of the Saviour. The few Christians who lived in Jerusalem uttered cries of joy, and returned thanks to God for delivering them from their oppressors. Eight days after, the princes and lords assembled to elect a king, capable of retaining this precious conquest. Godfrey of Bouillon, the most valiant and most virtuous prince of the whole army, was chosen. He was conducted to the church of the Holy Sepulchre, and there solemnly proclaimed king. When presented with a crown of gold, this prince refused to receive it. "God forbid," said he, "that I should be crowned with gold, in the place where the King of Kings was crowned with thorns."

ESTABLISHMENT OF THE MILITARY ORDERS.

A. D. 1098.

The crusade gave rise to the establishment of the military orders, the most ancient of which are the Hospitallers of St. John, who exist at the present day, under the name of the Knights of Malta. The first house of this celebrated order was in the beginning only a hospital, erected in Jerusalem for the reception of pilgrims who came to visit the holy places, and for the accommodation of the sick. It had been founded by Neapolitan merchants, at the time Jerusalem was still in the hands of the infidels. The blessed Gerard, a native of Provence, and a person of great prudence and rare virtue, was the director of this hospital when the Crusaders entered the city.

Godfrey of Bouillon, being elected king, protected this establishment, and bestowed many benefits on it. Several young gentlemen who had followed him in his expedition, edified by the charity practiced in the hospital toward the pilgrims and the sick, voluntarily renounced all idea of returning to their country, and devoted themselves to this good work. They did not limit themselves, as had been formerly the case, to the peaceful exercise of charity, but took up arms against the enemies of their religion. These brave warriors were inspired with renewed piety and courage for the sacred cause in which they combatted. Dreaded by the Mahometans of Jerusalem, on account of their military prowess — in the hospital they were the humble servitors of the pilgrim. Austere in their own lives, they were filled with generous charity toward others; they ate bread made of the coarsest flour, reserving the better quality for the sick. In order to perpetuate this beneficent institution, they resolved to bind themselves by solemn vows. The patriarch of Jerusalem approved of this determination, and they took the three usual vows of religion in his presence, to which they added a fourth — the promise to fight against the infidels.

Pope Paschal afterwards sanctioned this order, and endowed it with many privileges. They thus formed, at the same time, a religious and military body, where, without foregoing the rites of hospitality, their especial object was to defend Christians against the insults and attacks of infidels. This new order increased rapidly, and accomplished immense good in all the kingdoms of the East. A great number of the youthful nobility hastened from all parts of Europe to enlist under its banner. These brave knights signalized their zeal and courage on a thousand occasions, and became the strongest support of the throne of Jerusalem during its brief existence. After the fall of this kingdom, which lasted only ninety-six years, they crossed over to the island of Rhodes, where they sustained the ever memorable siege against Soliman, the Turkish Sultan. They afterwards repaired to the island of Malta, which became the principal house of the order and the residence of the grand master, to whom the Emperor Charles V yielded the sovereignty of the island, of which they retained posession until it was captured by the French, and ultimately taken by the English.

INSTITUTION OF THE PREMONSTRANTS.
A. D. 1120.

The Church, which had established in the East a society of religious heroes, saw with increased joy several new orders formed in France, destined to produce another species of good works. St. Norbert seemed to have been raised up by God, in order to be a perfect model of virtues to the priesthood, and to institute the order of canons regular. St. Norbert was born in the Duchy of Cleves, of a noble family. Placed at an early age in the Church, he at first did not appreciate the holiness of his vocation.

He had been the incumbent of several benefices, the revenues of which were wasted in luxury and pleasure, but God, who destined him to become a vessel of election, terrified him as He did St. Paul, in order to raise him to a higher pinnacle of glory. One day when Norbert was riding through a pleasant meadow, a great cloud suddenly gathered, and a thunder-bolt fell at the feet of his horse, who, plunging violently, threw him to the ground and nearly killed him. Norbert remained insensible for an hour, but, consciousness at length returning, he cried out like Saul, "Lord, what wilt thou that I shall do?" God replied interiorly to him, that he should lead a life worthy of the state he had embraced.

From that time he was completely changed; discarding his fine apparel, he robed himself in coarse sackcloth, renounced all the church livings he possessed, sold his patrimony, distributing the proceeds to the poor, and went barefooted in search of Pope Calixtus, who was then holding a council at Rheims. The Pope received him kindly, and gave him in charge to the bishop of Laon.

This bishop, at the close of the council, proceeded to Laon, accompanied by Norbert, and kept him with him during the winter in order to re-establish his health, which his austerities had very much weakened. As Norbert frequently avowed a wish to retire into solitude, the prelate, who wished to retain him in his diocese, carried him to different places, so that he might choose a retreat. The Saint was attracted to a very secluded spot called Prémontré, where he fixed his abode. His eloquent sermons and his sanctity of life soon gained him a number of disciples; in a short time forty ecclesiastics and several laymen joined him. They all seemed animated by his penitential spirit, and strove to imitate the virtues of their master.

Norbert now thought of establishing a rule of life. After some deliberation he concluded to adopt that of St. Augustine, to which all his followers consented, and they made a solemn profession, with a promise of fidelity. The holy founder afterward proceeded to Rome to petition the sovereign Pontiff to confirm his order. Pope Honorius granted his request, and God bestowed His benediction on this infant institution, which very soon spread over the whole Christian world. The greatest eagerness was everywhere manifested to obtain admission into this holy society. Thebaut, count of Champagne, touched by the discourses and virtues of the pious founder, determined to renounce the world, and offered himself and his possessions to Norbert, but the Saint, who cared less for his personal aggrandizement and the promotion of the order than for the general good of the Church, advised him to remain in the world, where he could advance the interests of religion, by teaching his vassals to honor and serve God.

The pure origin of the many religious orders of the Church is well worthy of remark, the austere life and self-abnegation of those devoting themselves to this mode of life, prove clearly that they never solicited donations.

ST. NORBERT IS CREATED BISHOP OF MAGDEBURG.

God, who had raised St. Norbert to a high degree of sanctity, destined him for the government of a great nation and the edification of Germany. Obliged to visit that country on affairs of importance, Norbert arrived at Spire while the Emperor Lothaire was holding a council for the election of an archbishop of Magdeburg. He was invited to preach, which he did so eloquently that the deputies of the church of Magdeburg proposed him for the vacant chair; and, without giving him time for consideration, seized hold of him, exclaiming, "Here is our Bishop, here is our Father!" They presented him to the Emperor, who approved of the choice of the council.

After the confirmation of his election by the legate of the Pope, who was present, the new archbishop was conducted to Magdeburg. As soon as Norbert came in sight of the city of which he was to be the pastor, he proceeded the remainder of the way barefooted. On his entrance into the city, a great concourse of people eagerly hastened to meet the holy man; a universal joy pervaded the city; he was conducted in procession to the church and from thence to the Episcopal palace. He was very poorly clad, and wore nothing which could distinguish him from the common people; when he was about to enter the palace, the porter, who did not know him, mistook him for a beggar, and roughly repulsed him, saying, "The other poor people came in long ago — go away, and do not disturb these lords!" The crowd cried out, "Wretch, what are you doing; it is the archbishop, your master, whom you reject." The porter, overwhelmed with shame at his blunder, endeavored to hide himself, but the archbishop stopped him and said, smilingly, "Fear not, my friend, I am not displeased, you appreciate me better than those who force me to inhabit a palace, which is entirely unsuited to so poor a man as myself."

St. Norbert governed his diocese with admirable wisdom, but endured many and severe trials. The church of Magdeburg had become very lukewarm and indifferent, and he was earnestly desirous of effecting an entire reformation. His efforts were very successful with regard to some, but his pious zeal exasperated others into bitter enmity. "Why," said they, "have we called this stranger, whose morals are so contrary to ours, among us?" They loaded him with insults, and tried every means to lower him in the esteem of the people, and, in their rage, even threatened his life.

Norbert endured their insults with marvelous patience, and on one occasion said to his friends: "Is it surprising that the devil attacks me, when he attempted the destruction of Jesus Christ, our Lord and King?" His charity, mildness and perseverance finally triumphed over all obstacles, and he terminated his austere and laborious life after having perfectly fulfilled all the duties of a good pastor.

FOUNDATION OF THE ORDER OF CISTERCIANS.

A. D. 1110.

The order of Cistercians, established about the same time as that of the Premonstrants, was not less celebrated and useful to the Church. St. Robert, its founder, had entered a religious life at the age of fifteen. With the design of living in perfect solitude, and rigidly practicing the rules of St. Benedict, he and several companions established themselves in the forest of Citeaux, fifteen miles from Dijon. Their abode was in a wild, uncultivated region, the resort of wild beasts, and altogether repulsive to nature. For this very reason it appeared to them the most suitable spot for the accomplishment of their wish to retire from the world and live entirely for God. They commenced to cultivate the ground, and to build small huts in which to dwell. Here these holy Religious unceasingly immolated their bodies to God by the exercise of penance, and their hearts by the fire of charity. They frequently suffered for the want of bread, and, with all their efforts, they could not procure the common necessaries of life from the barren soil surrounding them. Nevertheless, they refused all the rich presents offered them by the duke of Burgundy, so attached were they to their holy vow of poverty.

Although this new institution was renowned for its fervor, several years elapsed before it made much progress; it was a tree which became firmly planted, before it spread forth its sheltering branches. God was pleased to adorn it with all the virtues which most attract the admiration of men. A young lord named Bernard embraced the ascetic life, together with thirty companions whom he had persuaded to join him, and whom he brought with him to Citeaux, as precious spoils which he had captured from the world. Bernard, born in the castle of Fontaine, in Burgundy, of noble parents, united extreme beauty of person to the most brilliant mental qualities, giving promise of a distinguished career in after life. His prospects for worldly happiness appeared bright and alluring, but he formed the generous determination of sacrificing every thing to God.

His brothers and friends, learning his intention, used every means to deter him, but he was only the more firm in his resolution, and, finally, by his holy zeal and arguments, inspired his most bitter opponents with the same desire. He was followed to Citeaux by all his brothers, except the youngest, who remained with his father to be the solace and comfort of his declining years. When about departing, the eldest, seeing his young brother playing with some children, said to him: "You will be the sole heir of our house; we leave you all our possessions." "Yes," replied the child, "heavenly treasures are your portion, and earthly goods are my inheritance; the division is not equal." This child remained for a short time at home, and then, relinquishing his bright earthly prospects, joined his brothers.

Upon the retirement of Bernard to Citeaux, the most sublime virtues were exhibited in his holy life; he practiced such severe mortifications, that he seemed to become an entirely spiritual man; he partook of the necessary food with the greatest reluctance, and his meals were always an occasion of penance to him. His spirit of recollection was so profound, that, after living a whole year in the noviciate, he left without knowing the shape of the house; he spent the greater part of the night in prayer, regarding the time given to sleep as so much time lost. His fervent example animated his companions, and he derived new strength by recalling to mind the causes of his conversion, often saying to himself, "Bernard, for what purpose didst thou come hither?" These few words inspired him with courage to fulfill all the duties of a religious life.

ST. BERNARD IS MADE ABBOT OF CLAIRVAUX.

The reputation of St. Bernard attracted so great a number of Religious to Citeaux, that, in order to accommodate them all, several abbeys were founded, among others that of Clairvaux. The place where it was built was formerly called the valley of Wormwood, the surrounding woods having been for a long time the retreat of robbers; it now became the abode of sanctity. Bernard was appointed abbot of this new house, and removed thither with twelve companions, but the number rapidly increased. The holy abbot was accustomed to say to those admitted to the novitiate, "If you desire to enter this door, leave behind you the body you have brought from the world, this portal is only opened to the soul." It must be understood that the rule they observed was extremely severe. As the monastery was at first very poor, their only food was barley bread and a small quantity of soup made of roasted beech leaves. Notwithstanding this meager diet, the holy society lived in perfect contentment, for the love of penance seasoned this rude fare.

The only occupation at Clairvaux was prayer and manual labor, and although the community was very numerous, the silence of night reigned during the day. This holy silence so impressed their worldly visitors, that they dared not hold even the most innocent conversation while in this holy sanctuary. Men who had been rich and honored in the world gloried in the poverty of Jesus Christ, who cheerfully suffered the inconveniences of hunger, thirst, heat and cold, and all kinds of humiliation, as an example for His followers. The holy abbot was foremost among them, and practiced much more than he exacted. He entertained so high an idea of the religious state at the beginning of his administration, that he was shocked at the smallest imperfections unavoidable in this life, desiring his monks to live not like men, but angels. God, however, undeceived him, and he afterward made allowances for human weakness, leading his Religious to perfection by different means according to the amount of grace he recognized in them.

St. Bernard sanctified his whole family; his brothers were with him, and his father, Tescelin, in his old age, received the monastic habit at Clairvaux. One married sister, much attached to the world, was the only member of the family who had not entered religion. Experiencing, however, a desire to see her brother, she repaired to the monastery, superbly dressed, and accompanied by a numerous retinue. The holy abbot refused to see her in all this splendor, which circumstance filled her with shame and compunction. "Although I am a miserable sinner," said she, "Jesus Christ has died for me. If my brother detests my body, the servant of God will not despise my soul. Tell him to come and give me his commands, and I am ready to obey!" St. Bernard then consented to see her, and she was induced by his exhortations to renounce the pleasures of the world. Two years afterward, having obtained the consent of her husband, she entered the monastery of Jully, founded for women, where she died in the odor of sanctity.

CELEBRITY OF ST. BERNARD.

St. Bernard daily became more celebrated for his talents and virtues, which were soon rewarded by the gift of miracles. The first was wrought in favor of a gentleman, a relative of the holy abbot. This person became ill, and suddenly lost his speech and consciousness. His family were very much alarmed, as the sick man had not been considered very just in his dealings. St. Bernard was sent for. He assured them that consciousness would return to the sick man if they would repair the wrongs he had committed on others. Restitution was immediately made, and the holy abbot left him to offer up the holy sacrifice of the mass. Before the mass was concluded, the sick man began to speak freely, and asked for a confessor. He wept while making his confession, received the sacrament with very holy dispositions, and, three days afterward, died a most saintly and contrite death.

One day a woman went to see the abbot, carrying her child, whose hand was withered and the arm completely twisted. St. Bernard was moved to pity by the deplorable sight, and told the woman to place the child on the ground. Then, addressing a fervent prayer to God, he made the sign of the cross on the arm of the child, who was instantly cured, and ran to embrace his happy mother.

The report of his miracles spread abroad, and sick persons were brought to him from great distances. The blind, paralytic, and diseased, were healed by his simple touch, or by his making the sign of the cross over them. The conversions he effected were not less surprising; no one could resist his persuasive eloquence, or rather the divine spirit which breathed forth in all his words. A band of youthful nobles, devoted to pleasure and amusement, were curious to see him, especially as they were passing near his abbey of Clairvaux. The holy abbot received them very kindly, and, in order to turn them from their worldly and dangerous pursuits, invited them to sojourn with him for a few days, until the coming of Ash Wednesday, which was near at hand; but they declined his hospitality. "I hope," said he, "that God will grant me that which you refuse." At the same time, presenting them with some wine, he told them to drink to the health of their souls. They laughingly complied, and shortly afterward took their departure; but they had scarcely lost sight of the Abbey when, remembering what St. Bernard had said to them, they were entirely changed in their feelings, and returning to Clairvaux, joyfully embraced the religious life.

The holy reputation of St. Bernard induced many churches to desire him as their pastor. The archbishoprics of Milan and Rheims, and the bishoprics of Langres and Chalons, were offered him. He rejected all those dignities, and the sovereign Pontiff respected his virtues so highly, that he refrained from forcing any office on him. The humble recluse only sought seclusion and retirement, devoting himself to the instruction of his Religious, and the service of God; but the reputation his sanctity and mortifications acquired for him, was often the means of disturbing his solitude. His advice was applied for by all the provinces, and he was obliged to assist in ecclesiastical affairs. He was the solace of the unhappy, the defender of the oppressed, the scourge of heretics, the oracle of the sovereign Pontiff, and the counselor of bishops and kings,—in a word, a man of the Church, always ready to sustain her rights, to maintain unity, and to combat error.

ST. BERNARD PREACHES THE SECOND CRUSADE, HIS DEATH.

A. D. 1146.

St. Bernard was afterward engaged in an affair which drew upon him many reproaches and greatly tried his patience. The Holy Land was in danger of falling again into the hands of the infidels, who had already gained possession of the city of Edessa, and put the Christians to the sword. The King of Jerusalem applied to the Western princes for help. The Pope, alarmed at the unhappy condition of Palestine, endeavored to rekindle in Christian hearts the same enthusiasm Pope Urban had excited half a century before. He wrote to the King of France on the subject, exhorting the French nation to take up arms in defense of the holy faith.

St. Bernard was appointed to preach the crusade. The King of France had invited him, and the Pope had written to him, suggesting this course, but the holy abbot did not comply until he received a formal command. He then preached, not only in France, but in Germany, with wonderful success. His sermons were sustained by miracles, and princes and nobles rushed forth with such eagerness to assume the cross, that all Europe seemed hastening to the Holy Land. Although an immense number of crosses had been prepared, they were not sufficient for the multitude who applied for them; the holy abbot was obliged to tear up his garments to supply the demand. King Louis set the example to his subjects by assuming the cross, and he prepared to march in person at the head of his army.

The Emperor Conrad, of Germany, who also joined this expedition, led the van, and started on the festival of the Ascension in the year 1147. This army was composed of seventy thousand armed knights, without counting the light infantry and cavalry. The army of the French King, which commenced its march fifteen days after that of the Emperor, was not less considerable, but nearly all perished through the want of a proper military discipline. When the German army, with the remnant of the French, arrived in the Eastern empire, they committed so many depredations, that the indignation of Manuel Comnenus, Emperor of Constantinople, was aroused. This prince, who feared for the safety of his dominions, determined upon the ruin of the Crusaders, and gave them infidel guides, who led them into the deserts of Asia Minor, where they fell into the hands of their enemies. It was with the greatest difficulty that Louis and Conrad crossed into Syria with the remainder of their armies. They attacked the city of Damascus, but were obliged to abandon the siege and return to Europe.

Thus terminated this unfortunate expedition, in which two of the finest armies the world ever saw, utterly perished. The shame and regret this terrible loss occasioned, induced the people to break out into reproaches against St. Bernard who had preached the crusade, and who had prophesied a great success; but he defended himself by saying that the Crusaders had merited the wrath of God by their disorders, and thus prevented the fulfillment of His promises to them, in the same way as the Israelites in the desert had been excluded from the promised land on account of their sins. Debilitated by hardships and austerities, he did not long survive this ungrateful return for his pious exertions. St. Bernard is regarded as the last of the Fathers of the Church. His eminent virtues and extraordinary talent render any eulogy unnecessary.

FOUNDATION OF THE ORDER OF THE TRINITARIANS.

A. D. 1166.

Shortly after the death of St. Bernard, France produced a new institution, which was very useful to the Church, and reflected much glory on religion. During the crusades a great number of Christians had been captured by the infidels; they languished in irons, exposed to the danger of losing the faith, when a holy priest was inspired by God to undertake their deliverance. John de Matha was born in Provence, of virtuous parents; he received a Christian education, and was strenghened by divine grace in his pious disposition. Study and prayer were the ordinary occupations of his childhood; his only recreation consisted in reading works of piety; from his youth he chastised his body by fasts and other mortifications, and distributed all the money his parents gave him, in alms to the poor. After completing his studies, he retired for some time to a neighboring hermitage, in order to live in uninterrupted communion with God. Finding himself disturbed by the visits of his family, he went to Paris, where he passed through a course of theology, and attained the rank of Doctor in the Church.

Maurice de Sully, bishop of Paris, hearing of his learning and piety, ordained him priest. While celebrating his first mass, he became aware of the designs of God in his regard, and he immediately prepared to follow his vocation by retirement and penitential exercises. Having heard of a recluse, named Felix of Valois, who lived in the diocese of Meaux, in a place called Cerfroi, he went to see him, and informed him of his intention. They formed together the plan of a religious society, whose object would be the deliverance of captives, and they proceeded to Rome, where they explained their project to Pope Innocent III, who approved of it in a bull, and raised it to a religious order under the name of the Holy Trinity for the Redemption of Captives. Returning to France, they founded the first monastery of the order, on the site of the hermitage of Felix of Valois. Their mode of life was so holy, the object of the institution so noble, and their efforts so laudable, that they soon won the esteem and veneration of the faithful.

The number of those who asked for admission into the community daily increased. The saintly founder was obliged to build several monasteries, and voluntary contributions poured in. He then began the special work of charity to which he had devoted himself, and sent two of his Religious to Africa, who were the first to redeem from the hands of the infidel one hundred and eighty-six Christian slaves. John made several voyages to Spain and Barbary, where he procured the liberty of one hundred and twenty captives. He endured the greatest hardships in his different journeys, and encountered dangers of every kind, but nothing could daunt his burning zeal. During all these journeys, hardships and trials, he did not lessen his austerities. Feeling his strength diminish, he retired to Rome, where he passed the two last years of his life in visiting prisoners, nursing the sick, and solacing the poor. It is only in the Christian religion that we find such noble examples of generous charity, sacrificing repose, health and life itself, for the happiness of others.

Natural sensibility and human benevolence can effect some little good, but are incapable of that heroism which dreads neither danger, labor, nor death. In order to acquire and perpetuate this spirit of self-abnegation, it is necessary to be actuated by higher motives and more powerful reasons.

MARTYRDOM OF ST. THOMAS OF CANTERBURY.
A. D. 1170.

The Church, which St. John de Matha honored in France, was glorified in England by the courage and martyrdom of St. Thomas of Canterbury. Born in London in 1117, he evinced from his infancy the most excellent dispositions. He attained the dignity of Chancellor of England, and was a great favorite of King Henry II. The See of Canterbury being vacant, the king wished to bestow this office on Thomas, who refused it, and told the monarch that if he became archbishop, he would undoubtedly incur his displeasure, as he would consider it his bounden duty to reform certain abuses which disgraced England. Henry disregarded these representations, and the Chapter of Canterbury elected Thomas archbishop. The prediction of the holy prelate was verified. The king appropriated to his own use the revenues of vacant benefices, and purposely delayed appointing new incumbents. Thomas energetically opposed this shameful abuse; he also objected to a practice of the civil judges of summoning the clergy before their tribunals, without regarding the higher power of the church in England. He courageously condemned the nobles and officers who oppressed the Church and usurped ecclesiastical possessions.

Henry was much incensed, and commanded the bishops to take an oath to maintain all the royal customs. The holy archbishop understood, that under the title of "customs," the prince meant the abuses of which we have spoken; he accordingly refused to take the oath. From that time the archbishop was persecuted to such a degree that his life was endangered, and he was obliged to cross over to France. Arriving on the coast, he dispatched two of his companions to Louis VII, asking for an Asylum in his dominions. On relating all that their master had suffered, Louis said to them, with great kindness, "Has the King of England forgotten these words, 'be angry and sin not?'" "Sire," replied one of the deputies, "he would perhaps have remembered it, if he had assisted at the divine office as often as your majesty." The king smiled, and promised his protection to the archbishop, saying, "it is in keeping with the ancient dignity of the crown of France, that the unjustly persecuted, and especially ministers of the Church, shall find safety and assistance in our kingdom." He afterward endeavored, in concert with the Pope, to bring about a reconciliation between the archbishop and Henry.

Thinking that all his difficulties were ended, Thomas returned to England; but three months had not elapsed before he again incurred the king's displeasure, who said, in a fit of passion: "What! is there no one who will rid me of a priest who disturbs my whole kingdom?" These words were equivalent to a sentence of death against the holy prelate. Four of the king's officers formed a horrible plot for the destruction of the archbishop; they repaired secretly to Canterbury, and assassinated him while he was officiating at the altar. Henry was filled with dismay when he heard of this murder, and swore that he had not commanded it. He remained three days, locked in his chamber, scarcely partaking of any food, and refusing all consolation; and he consented to perform any penance that might be imposed on him. God soon manifested the sanctity of his servant by the number of miracles wrought at his tomb, and by the terrible punishments he inflicted on Henry, until this prince appeased the Divine wrath by a most sincere repentance.

THE THIRD CRUSADE.

A. D. 1191.

Henry II, king of England, in order to atone for his sins, resolved to go in person to the Holy Land, to the assistance of the suffering Christians. Syria was at this time in the most unhappy condition. Saladin, Sultan of Egypt, had invaded it at the head of an army of fifty thousand men, and had gained a great victory over the Christians, in which he captured Guy of Lusignan, king of Jerusalem, Renard of Chatillon, the grand master of the Hospitallers, and many other distinguished nobles. But the most important loss was that of the Holy Cross, which had been carried to the field of battle, and which fell into the sacrilegious hands of the infidels. After this defeat of the Christian army, nothing could arrest the progress of Saladin, nearly all the cities voluntarily opening their gates to him. He besieged the city of Jerusalem, and entered it in triumph; thus this holy city fell again under the Mahometan yoke, eighty years after it had been captured from them by the Christians.

Three important places, Antioch, Tyre and Tripoli, were all that remained to them. The intelligence of this disaster spread universal consternation throughout the West, and Pope Urban III died of grief. The kings of France and England, who were then at variance, were so much afflicted that they forgot their private quarrels, in order to fight against the infidel. Henry II died before the accomplishment of his vow, and his son Richard, he who afterward became so distinguished for undaunted courage as to receive the title of "Cœur de Lion," (Lion-heart) took up the cross with Philip Augustus, king of France. In order to defray the expenses of this crusade, a tax, called the "Saladin tithe," was imposed on all ecclesiastical property, as it was the tenth part of the property, and was destined to carry on the war against Saladin.

The two kings embarked with their respective armies. Philip Augustus arrived first in Palestine, and joined the Christians who were besieging the city of Acre. This most welcome re-enforcement placed the assailants in a position to renew the siege, but Philip, out of deference to the king of England, waited for his arrival, in order to share with him the honor of taking the city, which finally surrendered at discretion; the principal article of the treaty being a demand for the restoration of the Holy Cross. There was every reason to hope that this first success would be followed by other conquests, but his ill health and the dissatisfaction of the king of England, determined Philip to return to France. Nevertheless, for fear of being accused of deserting his ally, he left

Richard ten thousand infantry and five hundred knights, with money sufficient to maintain them for three years.

Richard remained in Palestine with a splendid army, animated with zeal, and desirous of accomplishing a great enterprise; he gained a victory over Saladin, and, if he had marched directly upon Jerusalem, would have easily captured the city; but he did not profit by his advantage, and gave the enemy time to re-enforce it. Being subsequently obliged to abandon the projected siege, he departed for Europe, after concluding a three years' truce with Saladin. The only fruit of the third crusade was the taking of the city of Acre, which became the refuge of the Christians of the East; here they waited patiently, but in vain, for an opportunity of re-establishing the kingdom of Jerusalem.

THE FOURTH CRUSADE.

A. D. 1195.

The slight success of the third crusade did not prevent its being followed by a fourth, a few years after the return of Philip Augustus, but this prince took no part in the undertaking. The new expedition was set on foot by some French and Italian lords, commanded by the Marquis of Montferrat, and by Baldwin, count of Flanders. They agreed to assemble at Venice, and that republic promised to furnish the vessels necessary for the transportation of the Crusaders to the Holy Land. The Venetians, faithful to their engagement, soon collected a sufficient number of ships, and nobly offered their assistance in a war which concerned the faith; they equipped at their own expense fifty galleys for the accommodation of five hundred Venetian nobles, who enlisted in the crusade. They were waiting for favorable weather to set out, when the young Alexis, son of the Emperor of Constantinople, came to implore their aid for his father, whom a usurper had dethroned and imprisoned after putting out his eyes. He promised to re-establish union between the Greeks and Latins, to furnish one hundred thousand silver marks, and provisions for a year, to facilitate the conquest of the Holy Land, and to provide, during his life, for knights wounded in its defense.

These propositions appeared so advantageous that it was thought unwise to refuse them, although, by carrying the war into Turkey, they would deviate from the route first proposed. Thus, instead of proceeding to Palestine, they embarked for Constantinople, and in three days the Crusaders were masters of the city. The usurper fled, and the young Alexis was crowned Emperor. This unfortunate prince was shortly afterward strangled by one of his officers, who placed himself on the throne. In this crisis, the Crusaders held a council to determine on their course of action; they considered themselves authorized to avenge the death of the prince whom they had protected, and, once more besieging Constantinople, they carried it by storm.

The authority of the commanders could not restrain the soldiery, who committed the greatest excesses, plundering and devastating the whole city.

Having entire possession of Constantinople, the Crusaders resolved to elect one of their number Emperor. The choice fell on Baldwin, count of Flanders, whose many virtues won the admiration of the Greeks themselves. This prince was solemnly crowned in the church of St. Sophia, and from that time assumed the title and insignia of the Eastern Emperors. The nobles then divided most of the European provinces among themselves, and were so occupied in maintaining their possessions as completely to abandon the expedition for the deliverance of the Holy Land, to which they had pledged themselves. Thus commenced the Latin empire in Constantinople, but it was not of long duration. At the expiration of fifty-seven years the Greeks succeeded in placing on the imperial throne Michael Paleologus, a descendant of their former emperors.

The conquest of the Latins, far from facilitating the re-union of the Greeks to the Roman Church, completed their separation. The excesses committed at the taking of Constantinople inspired them with a violent hatred against the Latins, and it was at this period that the entire rupture and schism of the Greek Church was consummated.

THE ESTABLISHMENT OF THE MINOR BROTHERS.

A. D. 1204.

The establishment of two celebrated orders soon after the fourth crusade, is a more interesting object to the eye of faith, than the conquest of an empire. Francis, a native of Assisi, a small town in Italy, founded the first of these orders, and gave to his disciples the name of "Minor Brothers." His father, who was a merchant, destined him for the same business, and did not devote much time to his education. Although the youthful Francis showed more taste for the vain amusements of the world than for the exercises of piety, he manifested from his earliest years a tender compassion for the poor, and always assisted them to the utmost of his ability. On one occasion, however, he refused to bestow his accustomed charity, but he experienced such deep remorse, that henceforth he determined to give to all who asked for succor in the name of God.

During a dangerous illness, he resolved to renounce the world and devote himself to the service of God. Shortly afterward, encountering a ragged beggar, he took off a new garment and gave it to the poor man. One day, when on a journey, he found on the roadside so disgusting a leper, that he was at first filled with horror; but, remembering that to serve Jesus Christ we must conquer ourselves, he descended from his horse, kissed the leper, and bestowed alms on him. With such dispositions, progress in virtue was very rapid, and Francis became a changed man. He sought the greatest retirement, and meditated continually on the passion of Jesus Christ.

The secluded life of Francis displeased his father, who often ill treated him, and finally disinherited him. Francis never considered himself so rich, as at the moment when he had lost all earthly riches. He endured all these trials with the most angelic patience. "Deserted by my earthly father," said he, "I shall the more confidently adhere to my Father in Heaven!" He took up his abode near a small church called the "Portiuncula," or "Our Lady of the Angels," and devoted himself to nursing lepers, and practicing the most mortifying works of mercy and humility. Having heard one day those words which our Saviour addressed to His disciples, "Possess not gold nor silver, nor two coats, nor shoes, nor a staff," "Behold," he joyfully exclaimed, "this is what I seek and desire with my whole heart!" He immediately took off his shoes, threw away his staff; never possessed money, and wore only a simple garment, which he fastened with a rope around his waist, thus following to the letter the divine precept.

From that time he commenced to preach penance, in simple but solid discourses, which made the deepest impression on his hearers. He soon attracted a number of disciples, who imitated his mortified life, zealously announcing the word of God, exhorting all whom they encountered to the fear and love of the Saviour, and a strict observance of His commandments. Some listened with attention, but the greater number were shocked at their extraordinary appearance, coarse habit, and the austerity and singularity of their mode of life. They were interrogated as to their country and profession, and were frequently refused hospitality, as though they were criminals, and they were often obliged to pass the night without other shelter than the portico of a church. They were often grossly insulted, men, women and children jeering and scoffing at them as they passed through the streets, and throwing mud and stones at the humble servants of God, who patiently endured these affronts while exercising their evangelical functions.

Finally, through their self-abnegation and supernatural patience, they succeeded in overcoming all prejudice, and everywhere won public veneration and respect.

THE ORDER OF ST. FRANCIS CONFIRMED. HIS APOSTOLIC LABORS.

St. Francis, seeing the number of his disciples daily increasing, obliged them to practice the evangelical counsels, adding only a few especial rules in order to preserve uniformity in their mode of life. He went to Rome and submitted his rule to Innocent III, who approved of his discipline. On his return, the servant of God conducted his little community to the church of Our Lady of the Angels, which was given him by the Benedictines, to whom it belonged, and there he founded the first house of the order.

He endeavored to qualify his followers for the worthy exercise of the apostolic functions, encouraging them in the path of perfection, and instructing them how to gain souls to Jesus Christ; especially exhorting them to a strict adherence to the faith of the Roman Church. After speaking to them of the kingdom of God, of contempt for the world, the renunciation of their own will and the mortification of the body, he added : "Do not repine, because we appear despicable; place your confidence in God who has overcome the world. You will encounter unfeeling men, who will insult you; learn to suffer, with patience and humility, every species of opprobrium and ignominy." He then sent them to different countries, reserving for himself the mission to Syria and Egypt, in the hope of meeting with martyrdom among those people. He embarked with one companion, and landed at Damietta, where the Sultan Meledin resided.

This monarch ordered him to appear before him, and asked him who had sent him to his dominions. "Almighty God has sent me," boldly replied Francis, "to point out the way to heaven to you and your subjects." This courageous answer astonished the Sultan, who invited him to remain with him. "Most willingly," said Francis, "if you and your people will consent to embrace Christianity. In order that you may not hesitate to renounce the law of Mahomet, and receive that of Jesus Christ, kindle a large fire, and I, together with your priests, will throw ourselves into the flames, so as to show you which is the true religion." "I doubt very much," said the Sultan, "whether any of our priests would submit to this trial, and, moreover, it might create a disturbance." The Sultan was so charmed with the discourses of Francis that he offered him rich presents, which the holy man would not accept. This generous refusal rendered him still more estimable in the eyes of Meledin, who dismissed him with these words: "Pray for me, Father, that God may reveal to me the true faith, and give me the courage to embrace it."

On his return from Egypt, Francis convened a general chapter at Assisi. He found that his order had increased to the number of five thousand Religious. As some of the members urged him to obtain from the Pope the privilege of preaching everywhere, without being obliged to ask permission of the bishops of the dioceses, he indignantly replied, "What, my brethren, do you not know the will of God? He wishes us at first to gain the approbation of superiors, by humility and respect, and then to win those who are subject to them by our discourses and good example. When the bishops see that you strive to lead an exemplary life, and have no desire to interfere with their authority, they will solicit you themselves to labor for the salvation of the souls under their charge. Our especial privilege should be, the absence of all privileges." When St. Francis felt his end approaching, he redoubled his penances and austerities; on the day of his death he read the passion of our Saviour, and commencing to recite the one hundred and forty-first Psalm, expired while uttering these words, "The just wait for me, until thou reward me."

CONGREGATION OF THE PREACHING FRIARS.

A. D. 1216.

The second order, which sprung up at that time, was founded by St. Dominic. Descended from an illustrious Spanish family, St. Dominic from his earliest years was animated with a great desire to labor for the salvation of souls, and particularly for the conversion of those who were plunged into the darkness of error. He soon found an opportunity to exercise his zeal; he was canon-regular of the Church of Osma, when Diego, the bishop, was appointed by Innocent III to instruct and reclaim to the true faith the Albigenses, whose errors infected the city of Albi and its vicinity. Dominic accompanied his bishop in this Apostolic mission, and ardently applied himself to the conversion of these heretics.

The name of Albigenses had been given to different sectarians, who, although divided in sentiments, agreed among themselves to reject the authority of the Church, abolish the sacraments, and, in short, destroy the whole ancient discipline. These fanatics ravaged and desolated the whole country, and sometimes bands of thousands of men attacked and plundered cities and villages, massacred the priests, desecrated the churches and destroyed the sacred vessels. The missionaries were aware of the dangers and difficulties of their enterprise, but were not in the least daunted by them, being ready to sacrifice their lives in a holy cause. God delivered them several times from imminent danger. Two assassins waited in a street through which Dominic was to pass, intending to kill him, but he escaped from their hands; on being asked what he would have done had they attacked him, "I would have thanked God," he replied, "and would have prayed him to let my blood flow, drop by drop, and my limbs be torn one from another, so as to have prolonged my sufferings, and thus enrich my heavenly crown." This sublime answer made a deep impression on his enemies.

The holy missionaries held several conferences with the heretics, all of which terminated in the triumph of faith over error. Not a day passed without extraordinary conversions taking place; this only exasperated the Albigenses; and, as these sectarians were supported by Raymond, count of Toulouse, they committed the greatest cruelties. Violent remedies were necessary to check these proceedings, and a new crusade was set on foot against these heretics, as much because they disturbed the public tranquillity, as for their errors. Simon, count of Montfort, had command of the army raised against the Albigenses. This noble carried on a vigorous war against them, and, if we find in the course of his exploits traces of excessive severity, it must be remembered that he was endeavoring to deliver poor desolated provinces from inhuman wretches who were guilty of every crime.

St. Dominic did not participate in this military expedition; mildness and patience were his only weapons. When he beheld the army of Crusaders approaching, he used every effort to arrest the punishment which threatened these obstinate people; and, finding among the Crusaders some who had enlisted only for the sake of booty, and who abandoned themselves to every excess, he undertook their reformation, and labored as zealously for their conversion as for the reclaiming of the Albigenses.

ST. DOMINIC OBTAINS THE CONFIRMATION OF HIS ORDER.

A. D. 1216.

The Crusade undertaken against the Albigenses, was not the only and best means of re-establishing and maintaining the faith in Languedoc, as God wished to effect good by persuasion, more than by terror. He inspired St. Dominic, therefore, with the design of founding an order of Apostolic men, who, in sanctifying themselves by a religious life, would labor successfully, through their preaching, to spread the light of faith, and effect the conversion of the wicked. With this view he received several companions, who consented to live together according to a plan he drew up for their guidance. Foulques, the bishop of Toulouse, highly approved of this project, and facilitated its extension with all his authority. He took Dominic to Rome, in order to obtain the approbation of the sovereign pontiff. After a few objections, which were soon answered, the Pope approved of this new institution, and affixed his official seal to its constitution and rules. Bishop Foulques gave St. Dominic and his followers their first church, founded in honor of St. Romain, in the city of Toulouse. A pious emulation was manifested by the citizens, in contributing toward their permanent establishment.

This laudable generosity soon spread throughout the whole province, and foundations of this order were rapidly erected at Montpellier, Bayonne, Lyons and several other cities. The high reputation of these new Religious, known under the name of "Preaching Friars," attracted men of the highest order of intellect and virtue to their community. The holy founder sent several of his disciples to different countries to preach penance, and to defend the purity of the faith against heretics. Seven proceeded to Paris, to whom the University and a pious Doctor, named John, dean of St. Quentin, gave the house of St. Jacques, from which they took the name of Jacobins. This little community increased so rapidly, that St. Dominic found there thirty Religious, when he visited Paris in 1219.

The holy founder was much rejoiced to see the work of God prospering, and prayed the more fervently for the conversion of heretics and sinners. Nothing would have gratified him more than to have had the opportunity of announcing the Gospel to heathen nations, and to shed his blood for Jesus Christ, if the will of God had not detained him among his brethren. It was owing to these sentiments that he made preaching the primary object of his order, and he desired all his Religious to pay particular attention to this branch of their studies. The importance of this sublime function caused him to use the utmost care in preparing his disciples for missions, exhorting them to the practice of every virtue. He taught them to preach extemporaneously, and inspired them with an ardent love for their neighbor. One day, after preaching, he was asked from what book he had studied his discourse? "The book which I use," he replied, "is the book of charity."

He predicted the hour of his death long before it occurred. Toward the end of July, he said to several of his friends: "You perceive that I am at present in good health, nevertheless I shall leave this world before the feast of the Assumption." He was seized with a violent fever, and, after exhorting his Religious to edify their neighbors, and honor their state of life by the practice of virtue, he calmly expired on a bed of ashes, upon which he had caused himself to be laid. If the important services rendered by religious orders were properly appreciated, and their efforts for the conversion and instruction of the world recognized, as well as the great assistance they have been to pastors in the exercise of the holy ministry, it would be impossible to deny that these establishments have produced men, alike honorable to the Church, and to the State.

BIRTH AND EDUCATION OF ST. LOUIS, KING OF FRANCE.

A. D. 1213.

God crowned the signal favors He had bestowed on this period, so fruitful in saints, by the birth of a great prince, who sanctified the throne by his virtues, and honored it by his rare qualities. Louis IX was not twelve years of age when his father died; he was educated under the guardianship of his mother, Blanche of Castile, who governed the kingdom of France, as regent, during the minority of her son. This princess inculcated a love of virtue and piety in the mind and heart of her infant son; she often repeated these beautiful words, so worthy of a Christian mother: "My son, although I love you tenderly, I would rather see you deprived of the throne, and of life itself, than stained by one mortal sin." The young Louis listened attentively to the wise counsels of his mother, which were never obliterated from his mind.

Blanche did not undertake the entire education of the youthful king, but procured men of great learning and wisdom to assist in forming his character, which subsequently developed the noble qualities of a hero, and the virtues of a saint. They taught him the holiness and grandeur of Christianity, and how infinitely superior were the precepts of Jesus Christ to the false maxims of a deceitful world. The natural disposition of the prince seconded the efforts of his instructors, and his rapid progress in all the branches of a royal education repaid all their care. He manifested during his whole life an extraordinary veneration for the holy sacrament of Baptism, by evincing a marked attachment for the place where the saving waters of regeneration had been poured upon his infant head; he frequently signed himself Louis of Poissy, thus signifying his preference for the glorious title of Christian, to that of king of France.

He was anointed king at Rheims, on the first Sunday of Advent, 1226. This consecration was not looked upon by the prince as a simple ceremony, but regarded as a solemn engagement on his part to promote the happiness and welfare of his people. He prepared himself for it by exercises of piety, supplicating the Lord to diffuse in his soul the holy unction of grace. He appeared deeply impressed with the words of the Psalm which is chanted at the beginning of the office, and applied them to himself: "To Thee, O Lord, I have lifted up my soul; in Thee, O God, I have put my trust." The mind of Louis was not neglected; he was taught the art of government and the science of war; he studied history, which has always been regarded the text-book of princes; in short, nothing which could contribute toward the formation of kingly virtues was neglected in his education. He was sufficiently acquainted with Latin to understand the writings of the Fathers which he was accustomed to read daily in order to sanctify his other studies.

When the young king commenced to govern alone, he assiduously applied himself to the exact and faithful accomplishment of the high duties of his responsible office. Surrounded by magnificence and splendor, he was never extravagant in his habits, but preferred simplicity in every thing; his apparel, his table, his court, all announced a prince opposed to luxury and ostentation. After devoting the greater part of his time to affairs of state, he would enter into conversation with some pious person; he every day consecrated several hours to religious exercises, and when some wordly-minded courtier once remonstrated with him on this practice, he mildly answered: "My love for prayer is looked upon as blamcable, while nothing would be said if the time I give to God was employed in gambling, hunting and other dissipations."

ST. LOUIS OBTAINS THE CROWN OF THORNS FOR FRANCE.

A. D. 1239.

Shortly after St. Louis assumed the reins of government he found an opportunity to testify his piety and profound respect for religion. Baldwin III, Emperor of Constantinople, went to France to ask for assistance in sustaining his throne. This empire had never been firmly established since its conquest, and was at this period strongly assailed by the Greeks, who hoped to overthrow the Latin rule. Baldwin, loaded with favors by the holy king, showed his gratitude by offering him the crown of thorns worn by our Saviour on the cross. This crown had been preserved from time immemorial in the chapel of the palace of the Emperors of the Eastern empire. The religious prince was transported with joy at this proposal, and sent deputies to Constantinople, to whom the Emperor gave letters commanding that this sacred relic should be placed in their hands.

On arriving at Constantinople, the deputies found that the Venetians, who had lent a considerable sum of money to the people of Constantinople, had demanded the holy crown as a pledge of repayment. It was necessary to cancel the debt before the deputies could obtain possession of the sacred relic. On being informed of this difficulty, Louis furnished the requisite sum, and the sacred crown was brought to France, secured with the seals of the empire, and the Republic of Venice. When the king learned that the ship carrying the precious freight was approaching the coast of Sens, he advanced to meet it as far as the town of Villeneuve, accompanied by his court and a procession of priests. On beholding the holy crown, he burst into tears, and every one present testified the deepest emotion; then the king and his brother Robert took charge of the case in which it was placed, and carried it to Sens, marching barefoot in the midst of an immense concourse of people, to the church of St. Stephen in that city. The pious king received it with the greatest splendor in Paris, and placed it in his palace.

Some years after, several other relics were sent to Louis from Constantinople, including a large piece of the true cross, the lance which pierced the side of our Lord, and the sponge which was presented to Him saturated with vinegar and gall. Louis caused them to be inclosed in silver shrines enriched with jewels; he built a chapel for their reception on the site of the old Oratory, and appointed canons who should there celebrate the divine office. The dedication of the Holy Chapel was celebrated with great solemnity, the king frequently repaired to this holy place, and sometimes passed whole nights within its sacred precincts; but these religious exercises never encroached upon the time he owed to the duties of his position. Louis was convinced that the piety which prevented the accomplishment of duty is contrary to the precepts of religion. The attention he paid to every branch of government is attested by the monuments which still exist, and prove that the care of his kingdom was his principal occupation. France owes to St. Louis some of her noblest establishments and her wisest laws.

FIRST CRUSADE OF ST. LOUIS.

A. D. 1248.

A dangerous illness which attacked St. Louis was the cause of the first crusade he undertook for the recovery of the Holy Land. He was seized with a violent dysentery, which reduced him to the lowest extremity, and at one time his attendants thought life had fled. His people, overwhelmed with sorrow at their approaching loss, addressed fervent supplications to God, praying Him to spare their king and father. The piece of the Holy Cross and the other valuable relics brought from Constantinople were applied to the dying prince, and he immediately recovered consciousness. The first word he uttered, was to call for the bishop of Paris and ask him for the Cross, as he wished to go to the relief of the Holy Land. The prelate made many objections, but the king insisted with such heartfelt earnestness, that the bishop finally acceded to his request. On receiving the sacred relic, he kissed it with great veneration, and said that he had been cured through its supernatural qualities. When he first appeared in public he was much affected at the joy testified by his subjects on his happy and miraculous restoration to health.

He prepared himself by the performance of all kinds of good works for the accomplishment of his vow. A great number of his friends received the Cross, and their example was followed by the nobility and common people. The king set sail with the intention of carrying the war into Egypt, and thus attack, in his own country, the Sultan who had subjugated the Holy Land. The fleet arrived safely at the island of Cyprus, whither the king had previously sent stores of provisions. War was then declared against the Sultan of Egypt in the event of his refusing to restore to the Christians the places sanctified by the Passion of Our Lord, and of which the infidels had obtained possession. The haughty Mussulman refused to yield them, and made preparations for the defense of Egypt. The fleet of the Crusaders therefore sailed from the island of Cyprus and arrived in sight of Damietta, one of the strongest fortified cities in Egypt. The enemy guarded the coast to prevent the Christians from landing. Then the king appeared on the deck of his ship and his nobles gathered round him. "My friends," said he, "this voyage has been directed by a special providence; we cannot doubt but that God has some great object in view; we will be invincible, if we are united, but whatever the issue, it will be for our advantage. If we die, we shall obtain the immortal crown of martyrdom; if we are victorious, God will be glorified. Let us combat for Him, and He will secure our triumph. Do not think of any danger to which I may be exposed, for I am but a mortal, whose frail threads of life are in the hands of God."

These touching words, and the intrepid courage of the king, inspired the Crusaders with renewed ardor, and they boldly advanced toward the shore. The legate, who was in the same ship with the king, held the Cross aloft, in order to animate the soldiers by the sight of this sacred symbol. A small boat led the way, carrying the oriflamme, the standard borno by the French kings in battle. As the water was too shallow to allow a nearer approach of the vessels. Louis jumped into the sea, sword in hand, and was immediately followed by the whole army. The enemy let loose a shower of arrows upon the advancing host, but could not resist the impetuous attack of the French, and fled in great disorder.

The inhabitants and governor of Damietta abandoned the place, and St. Louis entered the city without opposition; not, however, with the pomp and splendor of a conqueror, but with the humility of a truly Christian monarch, returning thanks to God for this signal victory. St. Louis walked with the princes and clergy, and proceeded in this manner as far as the principal mosque, which the legate transformed into a church, by the solemn celebration of the holy sacrifice of the mass.

CAPTIVITY OF ST. LOUIS.
A. D. 1250.

Having thus taken the city of Damietta, St. Louis determined to proceed to Cairo, the capital of Egypt. In order to reach this place, he was obliged to encounter the infidel army, which was encamped on a spot called the Massoure. The king advanced with his troops and attacked the enemy, who made a vigorous resistance. The rashness of the Count of Artois, who, contrary to the command of the king, his brother, pressed forward to the Massoure, brought on himself and the whole French army all the misfortunes which followed this disastrous day. The enemy rushed upon the count with the greatest fury; the French troops flew to the rescue of the prince, and a bloody combat ensued in which he perished. The loss was considerable on both sides, but the enemy could easily re-enforce themselves, while the Crusaders labored under every disadvantage.

In addition to this unhappy defeat, a contagious malady appeared among them, and kept them inactive for the space of several months; and as their provisions were exhausted, a dreadful famine ensued. They were therefore obliged to return to Damietta, but the enemy followed in close pursuit, the whole march being a continued fight. St. Louis made the most incredible exertions to save his army, but, being forced to stop in a small city, the king, his two brothers, and the greater part of the army fell into the hands of the enemy. The saintly monarch in captivity was the same as when surrounded by all the pomp of royalty; as great in chains, as when victorious in the field of battle. The infidels themselves were astonished at his courage, and said he was the bravest Christian they had ever known. Although inhumanly treated, he always deported himself with dignity, rising superior to all the reverses of fortune; with a Christian faith he intrusted every thing to providence, and with heroic courage, he trampled on all vicissitudes—"You are in irons," said the infidels, "and yet you treat us as if we were your captives."

This extraordinary firmness made such an impression on the Sultan that he offered St. Louis his liberty, provided he would give a large sum for the ransom of himself and the other prisoners. "A king of France cannot be ransomed with money," replied the king. "I will give the city of Damietta for my freedom, and pay the required sum for the redemption of my subjects." The Sultan, filled with admiration, only exacted the fifth part of the stipulated amount. The conditions were all settled, but before they were put in execution, the Sultan was killed by his enemies, and his untimely end was productive of the most disastrous consequences to the French monarch. The enraged assassins of the Sultan rushed to his prison, but Louis met them with perfect serenity, and abashed them by his calm demeanor. They eventually agreed to the treaty previously arranged, and even thought of making Louis their Sultan, but the dread of seeing their mosques destroyed by so religious a prince deterred them from offering him this dignity. On being restored to freedom, the king faithfully adhered to his promises. He evacuated Damietta on the appointed day, paid the ransom, and as the infidels had miscalculated the amount to their disadvantage, he informed them of their mistake.

JOURNEY OF ST. LOUIS TO PALESTINE.

The infidels, contrary to the stipulations of the treaty, retained a great number of French prisoners, and used every effort to induce them to renounce their religion. This treachery prevented Louis from returning to France, although his presence was very necessary in his kingdom. In order to secure the freedom of the remaining captives, and to preserve the Holy Land from entire destruction, he set sail for Palestine, and arrived safely at the port of Acre. He was received with great joy by the inhabitants, who went in procession to meet him when he landed. Scarcely six thousand men remained of his magnificent army, too small a number to undertake any great enterprise. Nevertheless, at the request of the Christians of this country, he concluded to remain at Acre for a short time, but he sent his brothers, Alphonsus of Poitiers, and Charles of Anjou, back to France.

During the sojourn of this prince in Palestine, he visited the holy places with the tenderest sentiments of piety, and the most edifying marks of respect. He visited Nazareth on the day of the Annunciation, and when within sight of the sacred spot, he descended from his horse and prostrated himself on the ground, and although fatigued and fasting, he finished the journey on foot. He was extremely desirous of going to Jerusalem, and the Sultan, who was master of the city, readily consented to receive him; but he was told that if he entered the Holy City without accomplishing its deliverance, all the monarchs who should subseqently visit Palestine would consider themselves released from their vow, satisfied with his example of a simple pilgrimage of devotion; this argument induced him to relinquish his design. While in Palestine he employed himself in adjusting the affairs of the resident Christians, and he repaired and fortified, at his own expense, the fortresses they still held.

He was occupied with these works of charity, when he heard of the death of his mother Queen Blanche of Castile. On receiving this sad intelligence, he wept bitterly, but bowed in humble Christian resignation to the will of God, and kneeling at the foot of the altar, he uttered the following words: "I thank thee, O Lord, for having preserved until now a mother so worthy of my affections, it was a proof of Thy mercy in my regard; and now that Thou claimest her as Thy own, I will not murmur. I loved her most tenderly, but since it has pleased Thee to take her from me, may Thy holy name be blessed forever and ever, Amen!" The death of his mother caused him to think of returning to France, from which he had been absent nearly six years. He therefore issued his last orders, and, having placed the fortresses in Palestine in a state of defense, sailed from the port of Acre in the month of April, 1254, loaded with the blessings of the bishop, the nobility, and the inhabitants, who accompanied him to his vessel.

During the voyage the holy king was continually engaged in prayer, nursing the sick, and in instructing the sailors; his example produced most beneficial results, and the exercises of religion were performed with monastic regularity. He landed at Provence, and from thence proceeded to Paris, where he arrived on the fifth of September. His first act was to proceed to the church of St. Denis, and there return thanks to God for his safe voyage, and he made magnificent presents to the church in token of his pious gratitude.

SECOND CRUSADE OF ST. LOUIS—HIS DEATH.
A. D. 1270.

St. Louis, on his return from Palestine, did not resign the Cross, as he meditated a second expedition for the same object; he was confirmed in this intention by the news he received from that country. After his departure from the East, the infidels had retaken several of the places he had fortified, and perpetrated inhuman cruelties upon the Christians who refused to renounce Christianity and embrace Mahometanism. When he had regulated the affairs of his kingdom, Louis announced his determination to go to their assistance, and asked the lords and princes of his dominions to enlist with him in the sacred cause. His appeals and example made the deepest impression on the people, and he soon found himself at the head of a powerful army.

He embarked in the month of July, 1270, and directed his course toward Tunis. The king of this country had given him cause to think that he would embrace the Christian religion, if it were not for fear of the revolt of his subjects. This conversion, which Louis ardently desired, would greatly facilitate the recovery of the Holy Land. "Oh," he exclaimed sometimes, "if I could have the consolation of standing god-father to a Mahometan prince." But this sweet hope speedily vanished, for as soon as the Crusaders landed in Africa, the king of Tunis arrested all the Christians who were in that city, and threatened to have them beheaded if the French army approached the place. As the city of Tunis was very strongly fortified, and defended by a numerous garrison, Louis did not consider it prudent to make any advance until the re-enforcements he expected should arrive, and he contented himself with protecting his army from the assaults of the enemy by surrounding his camp with ditches and palisades. But soon malignant fevers and other diseases, occasioned by the excessive heat of the climate and the bad water, spread among the soldiers with such violence that nearly half the army perished. The saintly king was himself attacked, and foresaw from the first day of his illness that it would terminate fatally. The king never appeared more truly grand than at this critical time; notwithstanding the excruciating pains he suffered, he neglected none of the duties of royalty; he issued his commands with the same accuracy as when in perfect health, and more solicitous for the good of others than for his own relief, spared no pains for the solace and comfort of the sick. He was finally obliged to yield to the violence of the disease, and retired to his bed.

Philip, his eldest son, remained continually beside his royal father; and St. Louis, who loved him fondly, and intended him for his successor, collected his failing energies to give him admirable instructions, which are still extant, and commence thus: "My son, the first thing I enjoin you is, to love God with your whole heart, and be ready to suffer every thing rather than commit a mortal sin." This counsel had been inculcated into his own infant mind by his virtuous mother, and he had made it his own rule of life. St. Louis then asked for the sacraments, and received the last rites of the Church with a pious fervor which drew tears from the eyes of all the assistants. When his last moments approached, he had himself placed on a bed covered with ashes, where, with his arms crossed on his breast and his eyes raised to heaven, he expired, while distinctly pronouncing these words of the psalmist: "Lord, I will enter into Thy house, I will adore Thee in Thy holy temple, and I will glorify Thy name!" Thus died this most saintly king, whose virtues we cannot admire without blessing the religion which produced them.

VIRTUES OF ST. THOMAS OF ACQUIN.

St. Louis testified much esteem and affection for the Religious of the two new orders established by St. Dominic and St. Francis. He admired their zeal for the salvation of souls, their profound humility, their penitential and austere lives, and their entire self-abnegation. He said if he could divide himself into two parts, he would give one to the children of St. Francis and the other to the followers of St. Dominic. St. Thomas of Acquin, descended from a noble family in the kingdom of Naples, was at that period the ornament and glory of this last order. He received an education in accordance with his birth and the position he was to occupy in life; his parents sent him to the most celebrated schools in Italy—first to Monte-Cassino, and afterward to Naples, where there was a flourishing university.

The youthful Thomas soon manifested a great

talent for the sciences, and developed the most admirable traits of character. Several conversations which he had with a Dominican monk, who was filled with the spirit of God, inspired him with an ardent desire to enter this Order, and he received the habit at seventeen years of age. On his family being informed of this step, they used every means to change his resolution, but without effect. They even went so far as to seize him, imprison and cruelly ill treat him, but nothing could shake his determination. Finally they employed an artifice which hell alone could have suggested. A profligate woman was introduced into his chamber, but the holy Thomas, terrified at the danger which menaced his innocence, appealed for succor to the God of purity, and, snatching a flaming brand, indignantly drove this infamous creature from his room. After returning thanks to God for this victory, he consecrated himself anew to His service, and entreated our divine Lord, with tearful eyes and an humble heart, for grace to avoid the slightest sin against this beautiful virtue of which the devil had sought to deprive him. His prayer was heard, and as a reward for his fidelity he received the precious gift of perfect chastity.

God now restored him to liberty, and he was allowed to follow his vocation without further obstacles. His superiors sent him to Cologne, to study theology with Albert the Great; under the guidance of this able master he made great progress in this branch, but his humility concealed his talents; and he seldom spoke for fear of becoming vain and proud. This silence passed for stupidity, and he was called, through derision, "The dumb ox." But his master, who knew him better, was of an opposite opinion, and said to the scoffers, that the learned bellowings of this ox would one day resound over the whole world, and his prediction was subsequently verified.

After finishing his career and receiving the degree of Doctor, Thomas taught in Paris with great success. He composed a number of excellent works, which soon attained for him a high reputation abroad. The holy Doctor attributed his learning less to study than to prayer. He always invoked the Holy Ghost before writing, and became more fervent in his supplications, when engaged in a difficult passage. Pope Clement IV offered him the archbishopric of Naples, but the humble Doctor refused this dignity. The Pontiff yielded to his entreaties on this point, but ordered him to repair to the council assembled at Lyons. Thomas obeyed, and, although suffering with fever, departed for Lyons, but, as his indisposition increased, he was obliged to stop on the road, and expired in the diocese of Terracina, at the Abbey of Fosse-Neuve.

VIRTUES OF ST. BONAVENTURA.

St. Bonaventura reflected as much honor on the order of St. Francis, as St. Thomas of Acquin conferred on that of St. Dominic. He was born in Tuscany, of parents remarkable for their piety. The name of Bonaventura was bestowed on him by St. Francis, who foresaw the graces which divine mercy would lavish on this child of benediction, in his after life. This chosen soul, when only four years of age, was attacked by a dangerous illness; his disconsolate mother went to St. Francis and asked his intercession in her son's behalf. St. Francis prayed for him, and obtained his recovery. When Bonaventura was told of this signal favor he had received from God, he testified the most fervent gratitude, and at the age of twenty he entered the order of the Friars Minors, in accordance with the vow he had made his mother. He was shortly afterward sent to Paris to complete his studies under the celebrated Alexander of Hales, who was one of the most learned Religious of the order.

Bonaventura made rapid progress, and was admitted to the degree of Doctor at the same time as St. Thomas, to whom he was devotedly attached. These two holy Doctors frequently visited each other, and entertained the highest mutual esteem. One day St. Thomas, finding his friend occupied in writing the life of St. Francis, did not wish to interrupt his work; "Let one saint work for another," said he, "it would be unkind to deter you from so laudable a task." At the end of seven years of profession, he was chosen to fill the chair of Theology in the place of Alexander of Hales, and he acquitted himself of the responsible duties of this high office with great ability. When teaching this sublime science, he endeavored less to form learned men than to produce perfect Christians, and, while inculcating the dogmas of faith, showed, by his example, the practical effects of religion. He was only thirty-five years of age when he was placed, against his will, at the head of his order, which he governed in the capacity of General, with great prudence and wisdom.

Pope Gregory X, who admired his virtues and talents, wished to elevate him to the dignity of cardinal. The holy Doctor, suspecting this design, hastened to prevent its execution by leaving Italy privately; but a command of the sovereign Pontiff obliged him promptly to return. He was in a convent of his order when two papal nuncios were announced, who found him engaged in one of the most menial employments of the community. At this sight they testified some surprise, but the Saint was not at all embarrassed, continuing in their presence the work he had commenced; and when he had finished he received the new dignity with great reluctance, not disguising the pain he felt at being forced to relinquish the peaceful life of the cloister for the responsible duties imposed on him.

A short time afterward the Pope consecrated him bishop of Albano, and commanded him to prepare himself for the discussion of whatever subjects would be brought up at the general council of Lyons. St. Bonaventura attended this council and preached at the second and third sessions, but he then fell into a swoon from which he never recovered. He has left a great number of works which breathe the tenderest piety, and he was especially regarded among the Doctors of his time as the most excellent guide of a spiritual life.

FIRST RE-UNION OF THE GREEKS—SECOND COUNCIL OF LYONS.

A. D. 1274.

The principal object of the council of Lyons was the reconciliation of the Greek to the Roman Church, from which they had long been separated. The assembly opened on the twenty-seventh of May, 1274, and remained in session until the seventeenth of July. The council was largely attended, five hundred bishops and seventy abbots being present. James, king of Arragon, was there in person; several princes and ambassadors from other countries also assisted at this solemn council. Michael Paleologus, Emperor of Constantinople, was very desirous for this re-union for political reasons, as he dreaded an attack from the Latin princes. After having deposed Baldwin III from the throne, he, in order to avert the storm which threatened him, wrote to the Pope, and promised to use all his authority in suppressing the schism in the Church. This proposal was received with much joy by the sovereign Pontiff, as the Greeks themselves consented to a reconciliation, which heretofore had been vainly urged and the present occasion seemed very favorable to the execution of this great design.

Michael, who had solicited Gregory X to convene this council, did not fail to send ambassadors to it, namely, Germanus, the patriarch of Constantinople, Theophanes, archbishop of Nice, and George, the grand treasurer of the empire. These deputies were intrusted with a letter to the Pope, in which he was called the head of the Church, the sovereign Pontiff, the common Father of all Christians. They also carried another, written in the name of thirty-five archbishops, and their suffragans. In this letter, the prelates expressed their gratification and concurrence in the re-union with the Roman Church. On the arrival of these ambassadors, all the Fathers of the council went to meet them, and conducted them to the palace of the Pope, who received them most cordially, and gave them the kiss of peace, with every sign of a truly paternal affection. The prelates, on their side, paid the sovereign Pontiff all the respect due the vicar of Jesus Christ, and head of the universal Church; declaring that they came in the name of the Emperor, and the Eastern bishops, to render obedience to the Roman Church, and to profess one and the same faith. This avowal excited the liveliest joy in every Catholic heart.

On the feast of St. Peter, the Pope celebrated mass in the Cathedral of Lyons, in presence of the whole council. After the Creed had been chanted, the Patriarch Germanus, and the other Greeks, repeated it in their own language in order to show the similarity of their belief. They attended the fourth session, and were placed on the right hand of the Pope, next to the cardinals, and read aloud the letters of which they were the bearers. Then the grand treasurer, in the name of his whole country, abjured the schism, accepted the profession of faith of the Roman Church, and acknowledged the primacy of the Holy See. Pope Gregory, after expressing, in a short discourse, the joy of the Church, who tenderly welcomed her children back to her fold, intoned the Te Deum, and all the assistants, uniting their voices, returned a solemn thanksgiving to Almighty God. Every thing seemed to promise a lasting reunion, but it was only maintained during the life of the Emperor Michael, as his son who succeeded him revived the schism.

WESTERN SCHISM — COUNCIL OF CONSTANCE.
A. D. 1378.

A still more scandalous schism afflicted the Church, shortly after the suppression of that of the Greeks. Pope Clement V, who was a Frenchman, fixed his residence at Avignon, and his successors also continued to live in that city. Italy suffered greatly from the absence of the Popes, and Rome especially was disturbed by different factions. The return of the Pope was ardently desired and earnestly solicited by the inhabitants. Gregory XI yielded to their entreaties and left Avignon. He was received in Rome with the acclamations of the people and the liveliest expressions of public joy. After the death of Gregory XI, the people, fearing that the new Pope, who was also a Frenchman, would return to Avignon, gathered around the place where the cardinals were assembled, and cried out, "We will have a Roman Pope!" and declared if the cardinals elected a foreigner, they would make their heads as red as their hats. The cardinals, intimidated by these menaces, hastily named the archbishop of Bari, who took the name of Urban VI. This Pontiff, who was of a hard and inflexible character, soon alienated, by his imprudent conduct, those who had supported him. Dissatisfied with their choice, the majority of the cardinals left Rome, declared their election null, as it was forced from them by violence, and elected another Pope under the title of Clement VII.

This unhappy occurrence threw the Church into a dreadful state of confusion, as the Christian world was divided between the Popes. Clement was recognized in France, Spain, Scotland and Sicily. Urban was acknowledged in England, Hungary, Bohemia and a part of Germany. They both sustained this spiritual war, and, by their violent conduct, increased the schism, and caused all the subsequent evils. The death of Urban did not restore peace, and the cardinals who had adhered to him appointed his successor. The opposite party also elected their own Pontiff, and these disgraceful scenes were repeated several times. Finally, the cardinals, sorely grieved at this unfortunate division, agreed to assemble in council at Pisa, and, in order to restore peace, deposed the two Popes, and unanimously named Alexander V as the head of the Church.

Notwithstanding all their efforts, the schism continued and the evils increased. The obstinacy of the Popes, the jealousy of the conflicting parties, and the clashing interests of the crowned heads, seemed to threaten an interminable continuance of the schism. But God has promised His Church that He will not forsake her in time of extreme peril. He overcame all the obstacles which human passion opposed to the re-establishment of unity, and peace was once more proclaimed at the general council of Constance, held in 1414. All the aspirants to the papacy either abdicated, or were deposed by the authority of the council, which elected Martin V to the chair of St. Peter, and he was recognized as the legitimate and only Pontiff.

Although some were divided as to the rights of the competitors, still they all were not less attached to the Apostolic See, and this schism, lamentable as it was in itself, was not as injurious to the Church as other scandals. The following is the opinion of St. Antoninus, archbishop of Florence, who wrote about the middle of the fifteenth century: "It is possible for one to have belonged to either party in good faith and with a safe conscience, for, although it is necessary to believe that there is but one visible head of the Church, if it should nevertheless happen that two sovereign Pontiffs are elected at the same time, it is not obligatory to accept either as the legitimate Pope; but only to acknowledge as the true Pope the one who has been canonically elected; and the people are not expected to determine which is the Pope, but can follow the opinion and guidance of their pastors." The great design of God, which is the sanctification of His elect, was accomplished even in the midst of those scandals, and holy souls were found numbered in the ranks of both parties.

CONDEMNATION OF WICKLIFF AND JOHN HUSS.

Besides the extirpation of the schism, the council of Constance was assembled for the condemnation of heresies which were spread through Germany in con-

WICKLIFF AND JOHN HUSS.

sequence of this unhappy schism. Wickliff, a Doctor of the University of Oxford, was the principal author of these errors. He had commenced by advancing some singular opinions which were condemned by Pope Urban V* and the English bishops. In revenge, this heretic attacked the whole priesthood. He taught that the Pope is not the head of the Church, that bishops have no pre-eminence over priests; that the ecclesiastical power was lost by the commission of mortal sin, and that confession was not necessary, but that contrition was sufficient. These errors did not flourish in England from whence they sprung, and after Wickliff's death, this sect gradually disappeared; but he had left writings infected with the poison of heresy.

These works were carried to Prague by a Bohemian gentleman who had studied at Oxford, and who gave them to John Huss, rector of the University of Prague, who adopted the pernicious doctrines contained in these works, and proclaimed them in his sermons with great vehemence, with the addition of new errors, among others, the necessity of communicating under two species. He attracted a great number of followers, the most ardent of whom was Jerome of Prague, and this sect spread rapidly through Bohemia. The archbishops and Pope John XXIII used every means to arrest the progress of error and to reclaim the heretic to truth and obedience; but their efforts were of no avail, and John Huss continued to promulgate his doctrine in the cities and villages, followed by an immense crowd of people who eagerly listened to his discourse.

Affairs were at this crisis when the council of Constance was convened, before which John Huss appeared in person to defend his doctrine. Previous to his departure from Prague, he caused placards to be placed on the doors of the churches, saying that he consented to be tried, and to suffer the punishment inflicted on heretics if he could be convicted of an error against the faith. After this proclamation, the Emperor Sigismund had promised him his protection, not to guard him against the sentence to which he exposed himself, but to secure him a safe journey and facilitate his justification, if he had been calumniated. Huss had scarcely arrived at Constance, when he began to inculcate his false creed, without waiting for the judgment of the council concerning him and his doctrine. It was thought necessary to arrest him, and the council named two commissioners to examine his writings. They found a number of errors which they vainly besought him to retract. Huss appeared before the session, held on the fifth of June. A great many passages in his writings, tainted with the errors of Wickliff, were rejected. After allowing him to explain every objectionable clause, he was exhorted to submit to the judgment of the council, and presented with a formula in which he renounced his errors. This formula he obstinately refused to sign.

The council, unwilling to resort to extreme measure, convened several times, endeavoring in vain to induce him to retract his heresy. They commenced by condemning his books to the flames, thinking thus to intimidate him; but he persevered in his obstinacy. Then this headstrong heretic was solemnly suspended from holy orders and delivered to the civil authorities of Constance, who, in accordance with the imperial laws, condemned him to be burned. Jerome, his disciple, as obstinate as his master, suffered the same fate. The council did not demand his execution, but left him in the hands of the sovereign, who, for the good of the empire, can punish those who disturb the public tranquillity by promulgating false doctrines.

A NEW INDUCEMENT FOR THE RE-UNION OF THE GREEKS. COUNCIL OF FLORENCE.

A. D. 1437.

When the Greek Church fell into a state of schism, the sovereign Pontiffs had offered several inducements for the re-establishment of unity, but without success. Finally, in the year 1437, the Greek Emperor, John Paleologus, and the Pope Eugenius IV, having resumed negotiations, agreed to assemble in the West a general council, composed of Greek and Latin bishops. In virtue of this agreement, the council was opened by the Pope himself, at Ferrara, in Italy. The Emperor and the patriarch of Constantinople repaired thither, accompanied by twenty Eastern archbishops and a great number of other ecclesiastics of distinguished merit and cultivated minds. The patriarchs of Alexandria, Antioch and Jerusalem also took their departure for the West.

It being found very inconvenient to continue the council at Ferrara, it was, with the consent of the

Greeks, themselves, transferred to Florence. After all objections had been satisfactorily settled, the Emperor, patriarchs and bishops presented a profession of faith in conformity with the belief of the Roman Church, in which they especially acknowledged that the Holy Ghost proceeds from the Father and the Son, and that the Pope is the head of the universal church. The reconciliation was then confirmed on both sides; a decree was issued, in which were inserted all the points formerly contested by the Greeks; and this document was signed by the Pope, the patriarchs and the other Greek prelates, with the exception of the bishop of Ephesus, who positively refused to add his signature. Thus ended this great council, whose successful termination spread universal joy throughout the Catholic Church, but which, unfortunately, was not of long duration.

When the Emperor and Greek prelates returned to Constantinople, they found the clergy and people strongly prejudiced against the re-union. These schismatics loaded with insults those who had signed the decree, and eulogized Mark of Ephesus, for having been the only one who had the courage to refuse his consent. Those who had assisted at the council of Florence, intimidated by the invectives of the citizens, retracted what they had done, and the schism was thus again revived in Constantinople.

Some years afterward Pope Nicholas V, a Pontiff of great piety, reflecting on the inutility of the efforts which had been tried for the conversion of the Greeks, wrote them a letter, in which, after speaking of the preparation which the Turks were making against them, he exhorted them to abjure their past obstinacy: "The Greeks," said he, "for a long time have abused the patience of God by persisting in their schism. According to the parable of the Gospel, God waits to see if the fig tree, after being cultivated with so much care, will finally bring forth fruit; but if in the space of three years, which God still grants it, it bears none, the tree will be cut down at the root, and the Greeks will be punished by the ministers of divine justice, whom God will send to execute the sentence he has already pronounced in Heaven." The literal accomplishment of the prediction soon followed.

CAPTURE OF CONSTANTINOPLE BY MAHOMET II.
A. D. 1453.

Mahomet, the Turkish Sultan, having determined to obtain possession of Constantinople, the capital of the Eastern empire, laid siege to that city in 1453, with an army of three hundred thousand men, and one hundred galleys, without counting a great number of smaller vessels. It was of course necessary for the Greeks to have an equal force to oppose him. The garrison of the city consisted only of five thousand Greeks and two thousand foreigners, whom the Emperor Constantine Paleologus placed under the command of Giustiniani, a Genoese officer of great experience.

The Emperor neglected nothing which could strengthen the fortifications of Constantinople, before the arrival of the Turks. As the city was surrounded by a double wall, Mahomet prepared fourteen batteries of artillery, among which there were several cannons of enormous size, which hurled masses of rock weighing two hundred pounds. These terrible machines fired, day and night, upon the city, with such success, that large breaches were made in the walls. In this critical situation, the besieged opposed a vigorous resistance, by repairing the damages as rapidly as possible, and by making successful sallies, in which they killed a great number of Turks and burned their works.

The disheartened Turks now clamored loudly for the abandonment of the enterprise, but, Mahomet having promised them the booty of the city, they resolved upon a general attack. Preparations being completed, Mahomet attacked the city by sea and by land. The Greeks made a courageous defense and performed prodigies of valor, but Giustiniani, having been wounded, was compelled to abandon his post; this fact so discouraged the Greeks that they began to waver in their defense. The Turks instantly rushed through the breach, pursued the cowards, and put the greater part of them to the sword. The Emperor, who was stationed near the breach, offered the most determined resistance, but he was hurried on by the fugitives and perished with them. After the death of the Emperor, the Turks met with no opposition, and took complete possession of the city, where nothing escaped the vengeance of the conqueror. A horrible carnage ensued, and the city was plundered for three hours, during which the most terrible acts of violence were committed.

Thus fell the empire of Constantinople, after an existence of eleven hundred and twenty-three years, counting from the time it had been made the seat of government by Constantine the Great in 350, A. D. Its destruction was a visible punishment of its adherence to schism. God had waited patiently for the schismatics, and they had not profited by the time which had been granted them to return to their allegiance; they had turned a deaf ear to the exhortations which had been addressed to them, and thus became victims of the divine wrath. They refused to recognize the authority of the Vicegerent of St. Peter, and fell under the yoke of the infidel, from whom they could expect nothing but oppression and slavery. Every kingdom opposed to the authority of Jesus Christ is threatened with the malediction of God, and is in danger of complete *annihilation*.

ESTABLISHMENT OF THE ORDER OF MINIMS.
A. D. 1507.

The Church, in her deep grief at the entire destruction of the Eastern empire, was a little consoled by the moderation of the conqueror, who tolerated the Christian religion in the country of which he had become master, and he even appointed a patriarch to the see of Constantinople when he heard that it was vacant. The church found another source of consolation in the extraordinary holiness of St. Francis of Paula, whom God raised up to found a new religious order, consecrated especially to penance and humility. This holy man was born in the little town

of Paula, in Italy, from which he took his name.
His virtuous parents inspired him at an early age
with a taste for piety, less by their precepts than by
their example. The youthful Francis felt himself
called to a life of austerity and mortification, which
he practiced from his childhood. He never ate meat,
fish nor eggs, nor drank milk, a rule he rigorously
observed during his whole life.

Having a great desire for solitude, he retired to a
cave on the sea shore, where he enjoyed uninterrupted
communion with his Maker. He slept on the bare
rock, and his food consisted of the herbs which grew
around his cave. Under his poor outer garment he
wore a hair shirt. The reputation of such rare virtue in so young a man attracted several persons, who
begged permission to join him in his retreat, and
that he would teach them how to serve God. They
built cells and an oratory near his grotto. This was
the cradle of the order which he founded a short
time afterward, and the daily increase of his community decided him to construct a monastery and a
church on the site of their present habitations, a
project which he put in execution with the assistance and contributions of the neighboring inhabitants. The rule he imposed on his disciples was to
observe a perpetual Lent; and, in order to teach them
that penance was of no avail without humility, he
desired them to make a particular profession of this
virtue, and to assume the title of Minims; that is to
say, the least of all Religious. This order was approved of by Sixtus IV in 1474.

Louis XI heard of the extraordinary virtue of

Francis of Paula, and, in the hope of obtaining through his prayers a cure from a sickness with which he had been attacked, he invited the holy man to visit him. The Pope commanded Francis to comply with the request of the king. The saint obeyed, and was received with the greatest veneration and respect at court. Louis threw himself at his feet, and entreated him to obtain from God the restoration of his health. Francis endeavored to instil in him a more Christian sentiment, and exhorted the king to submit to the divine will, and offer his life as a sacrifice to the throne of grace. Francis won the admiration of the whole court by his perfect detachment from all earthly vanities, and by his wise discourses, which, from a man without learning or education, could only be inspired by the Holy Ghost. He was always spoken of as the holy man, the man of God.

The successor of Louis XI loaded him with favors, and he had the consolation of seeing his order extend not only through Italy and France, but also in Spain and Germany. He was taken ill at the convent of Plessis-lès-Tours on Palm Sunday; he went to church on Holy Thursday, when he received holy communion with the most fervent sentiments of piety, barefooted, with a rope round his waist, and bathed in tears. He died the following day, after having exhorted his Religious to a faithful observance of their rule, and to fraternal charity.

THE HERESY OF LUTHER.
A. D. 1517.

God did not fail to console His Church and bestow proofs of His divine protection, in order to strengthen her under the different trials which continually assailed her. The storm excited by Luther, at the beginning of the sixteenth century, was the most violent and disastrous which the Church endured since the heresy of Arius. This heretic, who was born in Saxony, belonged to the order of the Hermits of St. Augustine, and was a Doctor of the university of Wurtemberg.

Of a quarrelsome, imperious disposition, and full of presumption, he was much incensed at the indulgences granted by Leo X, because their publication was intrusted to the Dominicans, and not to his order. He commenced by denouncing the abuse of indulgences, and afterward the indulgences themselves. He then attacked the doctrine of the Church concerning original sin, justification, and the sacraments. These impious opinions being condemned by a papal bull, Luther furiously assailed the primacy of the See of Rome, and losing all self-control, he passed from error to error, from one excess to another, even reviving the heresies of the Albigenses, of Wickliff and of John Huss. He wrote against purgatory, freedom of will, the merit of good works, etc. Such was the commencement of his unhappy apostacy from the true faith, which he qualifies by the title of the Reformation.

As it was necessary to procure assistance to sustain

so bold an undertaking, Luther exhorted the German princes to seize the ecclesiastical possessions, the only method by which to give them influence. The hope of securing such spoils, induced many of the most powerful princes to join his party. Frederick, the Elector of Saxony, and Philip, the Landgrave of Hesse, publicly declared themselves his protectors. Luther won over this last prince by a still more shameful inducement: Philip desired to contract another marriage, although his wife was still living, and he wished to obtain the acquiescence of the new reformer. He accordingly applied to Luther, who, having assembled the Doctors of the new reformation at Wurtemberg, gave the Landgrave, contrary to the express commands of Jesus Christ, permission to have two wives at the same time.

In order to attract more followers, he attacked the law of celibacy, concerning priests and Religious, and himself set the example of its infringement by espousing (priest and monk though he was), a young Religious whom he had enticed from her convent to instruct in the new creed, and thus accomplished her ruin. Such lessons, sustained by such examples, soon obtained a ready entrance into the minds of the people, and a sect so favorable to the corrupt inclinations of the human heart augmented daily. From upper Saxony, it spread into the northern provinces, the duchies of Brunswick, Mecklenburg, Pomerania and Prussia, where the grand master of the Teutonic order became a Lutheran.

Luther now finding himself at the head of a formidable party, threw off all disguise and openly vented his anger against the Pope and other distinguished personages, upon whom he lavished the grossest insults that the wildest frenzy could suggest to a maniac. The vulgar jests, scandalous levity, and vile language which sully his writings, can only be read with disgust and indignation; it is therefore difficult to imagine how this person attracted so many princes, and even kingdoms, to join his party. Cupidity and a love of pleasure—two powerful means employed—must have had great influence over the minds of men to have so completely blinded them, and to have so rapidly spread a heresy, contrary to reason and judgment.

CALVIN ADDS TO THE ERRORS OF LUTHER.
A. D. 1536.

When Luther set the example of making innovations on the ancient faith, a number of pretended reformers sprung up, who, while adopting some of his errors, added others of their own. Calvin, who is regarded as a second leader of the Protestants, was born at Noyon. After being educated at Paris, he went to Orleans and Bourges, in order to study law in their celebrated schools. His master, in this last city, was a man of ability and learning, but imbued with the heresy of Luther. Under his guidance, Calvin imbibed a taste for novelty, and took no pains to disguise his sentiments.

France was then striving to repel the contagion which began to insinuate itself within its limits. The King, Francis I, vigorously opposed the Lutherans. Fearful, therefore, of being arrested, Calvin retired to Basle, and there published his book of Christian Instruction, which is an abridgment of his whole doctrine. With the exception of the article concerning the Eucharist, they did not differ much from the opinions of Luther, but rather adopted some of his ideas. He taught that free will had been entirely destroyed by sin; that God has created the greater part of mankind for eternal damnation, not on account of their crimes, but because such was His pleasure; he rejected the doctrine of the invocation of the saints, purgatory and indulgences, and desired neither Pope, bishops, priests, festivals, external worship, nor any of those ceremonials of religion which are of such great assistance in elevating the soul to the adoration of the Supreme Being.

Notwithstanding the wish of Luther to deny the real presence of the body and blood of Jesus Christ in the Eucharist, he remained so firm in his belief, that he never was able to reject this dogma. Calvin, more presumptuous, dared to attack this great mystery. Impressed, however, with the force of these words: "This is my body, this is my blood," and restrained by the ancient and universal belief in this dogma, he showed a strange embarrassment in his mode of expression, and seems ashamed of his own doctrine; thus rendering an unwilling homage to the truth he was opposing. This sectarian adopted a different course in extending his pernicious creed; he established himself in Geneva, which city had sometime previous deposed its Catholic bishop, and embraced Lutheranism. Calvin there assumed the office of a preacher and professor of theology, and having acquired great influence, made this city the center of his sect, and it was from thence he fanned the flame of discord in France and other parts of Europe.

His power was absolute in Geneva, and no one dared resist him without incurring severe punishment. He would not allow the slightest difference of opinion; and, to show the inconsistency of reformers, this man, who taught that it was not necessary to listen to or obey the Church of God, exacted a blind submission to all the opinions he was pleased to advance. He ordered Doctor Michael Servetus to be burned at Geneva for having promulgated several erroneous ideas respecting the Holy Trinity; and, nevertheless, furiously exclaimed against the just severity that was exercised in France against heretics. When he could find no other mode of wreaking his vengeance, his fiery temper was vented on all occasions in a manner disgraceful, not only to a would-be reformer, but to a well-bred man, and he bestowed on his adversaries such epithets as sinner, beast, ass, madman. Singular expressions to emanate from the lips of a man calling himself an Apostle! If we compare this shameful language with the words of St. Paul, we can judge, by the striking contrast, of the difference existing between those sent by God as Apostles, and those who are but the corrupt instruments of the demon of heresy and impiety.

VIOLENCE OF THE PROTESTANTS.

Heresy is the inveterate enemy of all subordination. The Arians had caused great trouble in the Church, and practiced the most horrible acts of violence. The same course was pursued by the Protestants, who showed no more respect for the power of princes, than for the spiritual authority of the Pope. "If I am allowed," said Luther, in speaking to his sovereign, "through love of Christian liberty, not only to despise, but to trample under foot the decrees of the Pope, and the canons of the council, do you suppose I have sufficient respect for your commands to regard them as binding?" "The Gospel," said he on another occasion, "has always caused disturbances; blood must be shed in order to establish it." What horrible scenes has this seditious doctrine occasioned throughout Europe!

In Germany the Lutherans assembled, armed themselves, devastated the provinces of Suabia, Franconia and Alsace; they pillaged and burned the churches, destroyed the monasteries and castles, and massacred the priests and Religious. They soon raised an army of seventy thousand men, and the Emperor Charles V had great difficulty in subduing them. What torrents of blood did not the Calvinists shed in France! This kingdom, during the space of three reigns, was distracted by continued factions, civil wars and sanguinary battles. We cannot read the history of the pretended reformation without shuddering at the recital of the dreadful excesses perpetrated or instigated by these fanatics; twenty thousand churches were destroyed during these wars. In the single province of Dauphiny they murdered fifty-six priests, and one hundred and ten monks, and burned nine hundred cities and villages. Their fury was directed even against the dead, and they went so far as to profane with their sacrilegious hands the precious relics of the martyrs and confessors of Jesus Christ; desecrating the holy remains of the saints by consigning their bodies to the flames, and then scattering their ashes to the winds. We will only cite two examples of this inhuman conduct.

In 1562, they broke open the shrine of St. Francis of Paula, at Plessis-les Tours, and finding the body in a state of entire preservation, dragged it through the streets, and burned it in a fire kindled with the wood of a large cross. In the same year, they violated the shrine of St. Bonaventura, at Lyons, despoiled it of all its ornaments, burnt the relics of the saint, and cast the ashes into the river Saône. If the maxims of the pretended reformers authorize such enormities, can their Gospel be the Gospel of Jesus Christ? When our Lord sent His Apostles to convert the world, He said to them: "Behold, I send you as sheep in the midst of wolves; you must oppose to their cruelty only patience and gentleness."

Blood was undoubtedly shed in establishing the Gospel, but it was only the blood of the lambs shed by the wolves of paganism. The apostles taught patience and submission to legitimate sovereigns, a doctrine to which the faithful have always strictly adhered. St. Justin, in his apology, says: "Our hopes are not founded on this present world, and

THE PROTESTANT CHURCH. 421

thus we offer no resistance to our executioners." The early Christians said to the Emperors: "We adore one God alone, but we will cheerfully obey you in every thing else." Tertullian also remarks: "As Christians we pray God to grant the Emperor a long life and tranquil reign, prosperity at home, victorious armies abroad, docile subjects, universal peace, and whatever a man and Emperor can desire for his good." What a contrast does this Christian spirit present to the intolerance of the pretended reformers!

VARIATIONS OF THE PROTESTANT CHURCH.

One of the characteristics of heresy is a disposition to vary and change its opinions. As it is only the production of man, every individual member of a sect thinks himself authorized to change its doctrines. The originator of a sect has no more right to attempt an innovation than has his disciples to follow the fancies of their own brains. We have seen changeableness of belief in the Arians, Pelagians and other false creeds, and it is not less apparent in all Protestant sects. Luther and Calvin could not restrain their proselytes within prescribed limits, for it was the fundamental doctrine of the reformation that every one should enjoy perfect liberty to decide for himself in matters of faith. What was necessarily the result of this freedom? "Those who reject one doctrine," said the celebrated Vincent of Lerins in the fifth century, "will very soon attack others, and what will be the miserable consequence of this mode of reforming religion? It will result in there not being one article of the original faith left."

This was the case with the so-called reformation; after shaking off the salutary yoke of the authority of the Church, it had no principle of unity, for this is the only authority which can restrain the human mind. The reformation approved of the examination and judgment of each individual; it consequently assumed innumerable forms; it is now divided into Anabaptists, Quakers, Puritans, Armenians, Episcopalians, Presbyterians, Methodists, and hosts of others, all professing different creeds, rules and discipline, uniting only in one thing, and that is an intense hatred of the Catholic Church, and disregard of all authority. New doctrines and new preachers appear daily, promulgating new errors, from whence arise so many contradictory confessions of faith, the authors themselves adhering but for a short time to their original belief, destroying to-day what they established yesterday. The remarks of St. Hilary, of Poitiers, to the Arians, can be justly applied to them: "You resemble unskillful architects who are never contented with their work; you only build to demolish. There are now as many different confessions of faith as there are men, and as great a variety of creeds as of persons. Each year and each month, a new structure appears; you are ashamed of the ancient faith; but from it, you draw new ideas in order to reject them anew."

Their instability on this point was so palpable, that they could not refrain from complaining of it themselves. The following are the words of one of their theologians: "What kind of men are our Protestants, who go astray at every moment, and then retracing their steps are blown about by every wind of doctrine, as much on one side as on the other? You may perhaps to-day be cognizant of their opinions on religious matters, but you can never be certain what their belief will be to-morrow. On what article of religion do these churches, which are separated from that of Rome, agree? Examine all the points of their faith from the first until the last, and you will hardly find one single dogma supported by one minister that is not condemned by another as an impious doctrine."

It is not surprising that they differ thus, when they have neither guide nor reference. They have denied the Church which Jesus Christ commands them to hear, and, finding themselves without a leader, are lost in unknown paths, whither the spirit of opposition has ensnared them, losing entirely the straight and narrow path of truth which they have forsaken. It is not thus in the Catholic Church, where there is perfect uniformity of discipline and belief. Founded on Jesus Christ, and governed by Him, according to His divine promise, she will never vary her creed; her doctrine, which she has received from God Himself, is always the same, and is preserved with inviolate fidelity, as she permits no innovation on any single point.

THE SCHISM IN ENGLAND.
A. D. 1533.

The wicked passions of princes are generally the cause of the revolutions which occur in empires, and especially changes in religion. This was the case in England, where the faith at first flourished so wonderfully that it was called the Island of Saints. Henry VIII was remarkable for his zealous defense of Catholicity; in the beginning of Lutheranism he had published several edicts against the followers of Luther in order to prevent the budding heresy from spreading in his kingdom, and moreover wrote a work ably refuting the errors of the reformation; but a criminal attachment stifled these happy dispositions and occasioned the misfortune of his reign. Henry had espoused by dispensation Catherine of Arragon, his brother's widow; and this union had existed for eighteen years, when he allowed himself to become the victim of a passion which precipitated his kingdom into a deplorable schism. The king wished to bestow the title and rank of queen upon Anna Boleyn, with whom he had become enamored; and in order to accomplish this design it was necessary to dissolve his first marriage; accordingly, on the plea of illegality, he urged the sovereign Pontiff to grant the desired separation.

Clement VII, after thoroughly investigating the reasons alleged for the divorce, declared them to be without any foundation, refused to separate those whom God had joined, and threatened to excommunicate Henry if he did not take back Catherine, his lawful wife. The infatuated monarch disowned the authority of the Pope, and by a solemn act of the English Parliament proclaimed himself the supreme head of the Church in England; sustaining this schismatical step by a violent persecution against those who refused to sign this impious declaration. Sir Thomas More, the Chancellor of State, and Fisher, bishop of Rochester, were the first victims of his wrath; on declining to acknowledge his ecclesiastical supremacy they were beheaded. It was then that the chancellor made this beautiful answer to the sacrilegious king: "If I were alone in my faith, I would not rely on my own judgment in this matter, but unhesitatingly accept the decision of the great English Parliament, but I have on my side the whole Church, that vast body of Christians." The condemnation of these two illustrious men was only the prelude to a great number of horrible executions, and Henry, who until this period had not evinced a cruel disposition, became a violent and sanguinary prince.

In order to punish the Religious who persevered in the obedience due the Holy See, he suppressed the monasteries, and appropriated their revenues to his own use; and it is said that he only proclaimed himself the head of the Anglican Church, so as to have an excuse for plundering the ecclesiastical possessions. Henry espoused Anna Boleyn, the original cause of all these evils, but, soon becoming disgusted with her, had her beheaded, and contracted a new alliance, which was followed by four others.

Thus God punished the first crime of this unhappy monarch, by allowing him to fall into still greater excesses, and abandoned him to the corrupt desires of his heart. Henry died in the most terrible remorse of conscience, after a wicked and profligate reign. Notwithstanding, however, his grievous faults, he did not alter the doctrines of the Church, but the schism he had excited soon led to heresy; the new errors could not fail to be well received in a country ready for any kind of revolution.

During Henry's life Lutheranism had commenced to creep into his kingdom in spite of his efforts to crush it, and after his death Edward VI entirely abolished the Catholic religion, and established the pretended reformation in England. The holy sacrifice of the mass was forbidden, the sacred images destroyed, the churches plundered and profaned, and the pulpits occupied by preachers who publicly attacked the ancient dogmas and ceremonies of religion. In order to form a correct estimate of the Anglican reformation, it is sufficient to recall its disgraceful origin. Henry VIII, when stretched on his deathbed, was deeply sensible of the wickedness and impiety of what he had done, for, at the hour of death, illusions vanish and truth shines forth in all its brilliancy.

CONVERSION OF THE INDIES.
A. D. 1541.

The losses endured by the Church in Europe through schisms and heresies were amply retrieved by the zeal of Francis Xavier, who, about this period, won innumerable souls and vast countries to Jesus Christ. Xavier was descended from a noble family in the kingdom of Navarre. He studied in Paris, where he taught philosophy in the University; it was there that he formed an attachment for Ignatius, of Loyola, founder of the Society of Jesus, and he became one of his first disciples. Having been chosen by Pope Paul III to preach the gospel in the East Indies, where the Portuguese had formed settlements, he embarked at Lisbon in 1541, and landed, after a long voyage, at Goa, capital of the Portuguese dominions in that country.

The deplorable state in which he found religion filled him with grief, and inflamed his zeal for the conversion of this benighted people. As the scandalous lives of the Christians in the Indies was the great obstacle to the conversion of the idolaters scattered among them, Xavier began his apostolic labors by reclaiming these bad Catholics to the practice of virtue and religion. In order to secure permanent success he applied himself to the education of youth, exciting them to a love of piety and learning. He assembled the little children, and, leading them to church, taught them the Apostles' creed, the ten commandments, and instructed them in the exercises of a holy and Christian life. The fervor of these children edified the city, and very soon changed the sad state of things; sinners began to repent of their crimes, and, going to St. Francis, solicited his advice. He received them with the greatest kindness, instructed the penitents, exhorting and converting them by his sweetness and charity.

The saint then proceeded to the pearl-fisheries, where the people had been baptized, but were still attached to their superstitions and vicious habits. In order to secure a plentiful harvest, he studied their language; and with great labor translated into it the Apostles' creed, the decalogue, the Lord's prayer, and, finally, the whole catechism; he committed his translation to memory, and traveled through the country announcing the gospel in this simple manner. His preaching, supported by wonderful miracles, produced abundant fruit; and the fervor of the converts was most edifying and remarkable; from a nation plunged in all kinds of vices the great St. Francis Xavier raised up a people of saints. Sinners reformed their lives, and the multitude of infidels who asked for baptism was so immense, that Xavier, exhausted with fatigue, could hardly raise his arm after administering the sacrament. Encouraged by this success, he advanced into the neighboring countries where the inhabitants had no knowledge of Jesus Christ; and in a short time he enjoyed the consolation of seeing these pagans voluntarily destroy their idols and erect Catholic Churches on their sites.

The following year Xavier passed into the kingdom of Travancore, where he baptized, with his own hand, ten thousand idolaters in the space of one month. Forty-five churches were built in this country, and St. Francis, who relates all these circumstances himself, adds that it was a most touching spectacle when these converted infidels hastened to demolish their pagan temples. The reputation of the holy apostle spread throughout the whole

Indies, and he was earnestly entreated to visit the different provinces, so as to instruct and baptize the inhabitants. While gathering this rich harvest of souls, Xavier wrote to Italy and Portugal, asking for assistance in his labors; and in the excess of his zeal wished all the Doctors of the European Universities to become missionaries. St. Francis visited the island of Manar, Cochin, Meliapore, Malacca, Moluccas, and Ternate, everywhere effecting a prodigious number of conversions, and establishing in each place a flourishing church.

It was with incredible labor and amidst all kinds of perils that Xavier accomplished such wonders, it being impossible to recount all that he suffered in his different missions; but his interior consolations amply repaid him for the dangers he encountered. "The dangers to which I am exposed," he writes to St. Ignatius, "the labors I undertake for the glory of God alone, are sources of inexhaustible delight to me, and these supernatural consolations are so pure, delicious, and continual, that they cause me to forget any pain or weariness of body." In the midst of the celestial favors which were lavished upon him, he would entreat the divine mercy to moderate these heavenly gifts, as the happiness was too great for a mortal to enjoy.

CONTINUATION OF THE APOSTOLICAL LABORS OF ST. FRANCIS XAVIER.

St. Francis Xavier, whose zeal knew no bounds, sailed for Japan, and arrived, in 1549, in the kingdom of Saxuma. With the assistance of a Japanese, whom he had converted in India, he translated the creed, and explanations of each one of the articles, into the language of the country. The king having granted him an audience, he obtained the royal permission to announce the faith in his dominions. St. Francis made a great number of conversions, but his joy was troubled by the persecutions of the bonzas, or Japanese priests, who succeeded in prejudicing the king against him. He, therefore, took his departure for Firando, the capital of another small kingdom, where he was kindly received by the prince, who allowed him to preach the gospel to his subjects.

The effect of these discourses was most extraordinary; and more idolaters were converted here in twenty days than during a whole year in Saxuma. The saint left these converts under the care of a missionary, who had accompanied him, and set out for Meaco, the capital of Japan, passing through Amanguchi, a most immoral and wicked city. His preaching was of no avail, and he was even insulted and treated with great indignity by these licentious people. On arriving at Meaco, he met with the same reception; but was grieved to see the blindness and obstinacy of the inhabitants; he therefore returned to Amanguchi, and, as he perceived that the poverty of his dress had shocked the idolaters, and prevented him from obtaining an audience at court, he thought it his duty to conform to the customs of the country. He therefore presented himself at the palace in a rich dress, accompanied by an imposing retinue, and carrying some presents to the king. Through this means Xavier gained the protection of the prince, and permission to announce the gospel; three thousand persons were baptized in this city, which success greatly consoled him for his previous failure.

From Amanguchi the holy Apostle proceeded to Bongo, where the reigning monarch was most anxious to see the servant of God. St. Francis here confounded in a public argument the bonzas, who, through interested motives, used every effort to oppose him; several of them, however, were converted to the true faith. His public discourses and private instructions deeply impressed the people, who hastened in crowds to ask for baptism. The king himself was convinced of the truth of Christianity; but worldly considerations prevented him from embracing the faith at that time. He afterwards, however, remembered the instructions he had received from Xavier, and, overcoming human respect, asked for baptism. Finally, after a sojourn of nearly two years and a half in Japan, the saint was inspired with a desire to announce the gospel in China. Although foreigners were prohibited, under pain of the most severe penalties, from entering this vast empire, he endeavored to discover some way of executing his design; a thousand obstacles opposed this zealous Apostle; and he experienced all kinds of difficulties, but nothing could daunt him, and by means of great patience, he succeeded in penetrating as far as the Island of Sancian, near Macao, on the coast of China.

Eternal Wisdom sometimes inspires His servants with intentions they are not destined to fulfill, in order to reward their good will and zeal in His service. At this period, when the holy Apostle seemed about accomplishing his cherished wishes, he fell ill, and after twelve days of anguish, which he endured without any human assistance, died at the age of forty-six. He was buried on the sea-shore, and unslacked lime thrown on the body, that, the flesh being quickly consumed, the bones might be more conviently carried in a vessel which was to return to India in a few days; but two months afterward his body was found as natural and entire as when living, and the vestments in a state of perfect preservation. The sacred remains of St. Francis Xavier were then conveyed to Goa, and deposited in the church of St. Paul, with every tribute of respect and honor; a great number of miracles were wrought upon his tomb, testifying to the sanctity of this great Apostle of the Indies.

OPENING OF THE COUNCIL OF TRENT.

A. D. 1545.

When the pretended reformation began to spread in Germany, it was decided that a general council was the best means to arrest the progress of error, and remedy the evils heresy had brought upon the

Church. The Emperor Charles V ardently desired it, and Pope Paul III, after learning the sentiments of other Christian monarchs, issued a bull for the convocation of a general council. He chose the city of Trent for the place of assembly, as it is situated between Italy and Germany, and thus was of easy access to the Fathers who composed the council. The Pope had several obstacles to contend with, which prevented the opening of the council until toward the end of the year 1545.

The bishops commenced by designating the points upon which they were to treat, and the order in which they were to be proposed. After a solemn mass of the Holy Ghost, the creed was read, according to the custom of the previous councils, which opposed this divine shield to all the heresies, and which had often, by this means alone, converted infidels to the faith, and confounded heretics. The prelates then treated upon the canonicity of the sacred volumes which are the foundation of Christianity, and unanimously agreed that it is necessary to recognize as strictly canonical all the books of the Old and New Testaments. One of the legates spoke with great learning and eloquence upon this subject; showing that these books had been received as inspired by the councils and Fathers of the early ages.

The truth of tradition was also argued, that is to say, the doctrine of Jesus Christ and His Apostles, which is not contained in the Scriptures, but has been handed down by word of mouth, and is found in the writings of the Fathers, and other ancient ecclesiastical works. A decree was issued on these two points, expressed in the following words: "The holy council of Trent, ecumenical and general, legitimately assembled under the guidance of the Holy Ghost, and presided over by legates of the Apostolic See, considering that the doctrines of faith and regulation of morals are contained in the sacred writings and unwritten traditions received by the Apostles from the lips of Jesus Christ Himself, or revealed to the same Apostles by the Holy Ghost, have been handed down to us; the holy council, following the examples of the orthodox fathers, accept all the books of the Old and New Testaments, and also all the traditions concerning faith or morals as coming from the lips of Jesus Christ, or inspired by the Holy Ghost, and preserved in the Church by a continual succession of pastors; it receives them with respect and piety; and, that no one may doubt which are the books approved by the council, it is ordered that a catalogue of the volumes be inserted in this decree." Then came the list of all the canonical books as they are printed in the Vulgate. The council adds: "Whosoever refuses to receive as sacred and canonical these books in all their parts, or knowingly and deliberately rejects the traditions which have been mentioned, let him be anathema."

Finally, in order to restrain restless minds, the council commands, that, in matters of faith and morals which have reference to the maintenance of Christian doctrine, no one whosoever shall presume to rely on his own judgment in explaining the holy scriptures contrary to the interpretation of the Church, whose privilege it is to decide on the true sense and real meaning of the Bible, or contrary to the unanimous opinion of the Fathers. The council also decrees that those who employ the words of the gospel in a profane manner,—that is, in jesting, foolish applications, flattery or superstitious practices, shall be punished as violaters of the word of God.

DOCTRINE OF THE COUNCIL ON ORIGINAL SIN.

The holy council of Trent explained, in the fifth session, the Catholic doctrine of original sin, and the remedy for this sin. It teaches that Adam, after transgressing the command of God, lost the sanctity and justice in which he was created; by disobeying God he incurred the divine wrath, became the slave of the devil, and subject to death. By his prevarication, the first man not only sinned himself, but entailed misery on his whole posterity; in transmitting sin, which is the death of the soul, he has brought upon the human race the death and sufferings of the body, according to the words of the Apostle, "as by one man sin entered into the world, and by sin death; and so death came upon all men, in one of whom all have sinned." This sin cannot be effaced by natural means, but solely through the merits of Jesus Christ, the only mediator, who has reconciled us to God by shedding His precious blood; and these divine merits are equally applied to adults and infants through the sacrament of baptism, according to these words: "For there is no other name under heaven given to men whereby we must be saved." And these: "Behold the lamb of God, behold him who taketh away the sins of the world; you all who have been baptized have been clothed in Jesus Christ."

Thus the children born of baptized parents have need of baptism, because they inherit from Adam original sin, which can only be effaced by the waters of regeneration in order to obtain eternal life. It is for this reason, that, according to the apostolic tradition, infants, who are incapable of any actual sin, are really baptized to obtain the remission of sin, as this sacrament effaces the sin they inherit through a corrupt race; for whoever is not born again by water and the Holy Ghost cannot enter the kingdom of heaven. Through the grace conferred in baptism, original sin is wholly remitted and effaced, for there is no guile in the regenerated, and there is no condemnation for those who have been buried with Jesus Christ in baptism in order to die to sin, and who do not live according to the flesh, but, divesting themselves of the old man, and clothing themselves in the new, have become pure without stain, the heirs of God, and co-heirs of Jesus Christ, in such a manner that nothing can oppose their entrance into the kingdom of the Father.

The holy council, however, acknowledges and confesses that concupiscence, or the tendency to sin, remains in those who have been baptized; this concupiscence having been left, in order to be overcome, cannot harm those who do not yield to it; but those who, through the grace of Jesus Christ, courageously resist this vicious inclination, will be crowned as having fought the good fight. If St. Paul calls it sin, it is because it is a consequence of sin, and leads to the commission of sin. The holy council then declares, that, in its decision concerning original sin regarding all mankind, it does not include the Blessed and Immaculate Virgin Mary, Mother of God; testifying by this decree their zeal in maintaining the pious belief of the faithful with regard to the Immaculate Conception of the Blessed Virgin.

DOCTRINE OF THE COUNCIL ON THE JUSTIFICATION OF THE SINNER.

The subject of justification naturally follows that of sin. The holy council first remarks that each of the dispositions that lead to the remission of sin is the effect of actual and saving grace, which God does not owe the sinner, but grants through pure generosity. Man can commit sin, and entail death on himself, but he cannot by his own power, without the assistance of divine grace, either efface sin, or even conceive a salutary desire of repentance. He is thus obliged to ask and hope for every thing from the hands of God, through the saving merits of Jesus Christ. The first disposition for justification is to firmly believe in the truths God has revealed, and the rewards He has promised to the faithful soul. Among these truths some are alarming, others consoling, producing in the sinner dread of punishment and hope of pardon. The sinner, overwhelmed by fear of the judgments of God, is reassured when he considers His mercy which is unfailing, and through a lively confidence, founded on the merits of Jesus Christ, will finally cast himself into the arms of His infinite mercy, and begin to love God as the source of all justice.

After showing how the sinner obtains justification, the council then proceeds to explain its nature and effects. Justification does not consist merely in the remission of sin, but also renews the life of the soul, in such a manner that the sinner becomes truly righteous, the friend of God, and the heir of eternal life. The Holy Ghost operates this wonderful change, and instills into the heart of the sinner the holy virtues of faith, hope, and charity, which unite the soul intimately to Jesus Christ, and constitute it a living member of His divine body. Man, thus justified through the grace of our Saviour, is not limited to the degree of sanctity he has received, but may advance from virtue to virtue, and daily become more holy by prayer, mortification, the practice of all good works, the exact observance of the law of God, and the maxims of the gospel.

In fulfilling these precepts, man proves the truth of the words of the Bible, which declares that the commands of God are not hard to obey, that the yoke of Jesus Christ is sweet, and His burden light, because, being the child of God, he loves Him as a Father, and this filial affection renders it easy and agreeable to accomplish His holy will. If, in order to make us feel the need of His grace, God seems to desert us, we should not be discouraged, but rather increase in humility and fervor, knowing that He does not command impossibilities, but has promised to listen to our petitions; and we shall receive help from above which will enable us to persevere unto the end in the way of righteousness.

DOCTRINE OF THE COUNCIL CONCERNING THE SACRAMENTS.

The holy council then speaks of the sacraments, which are so many means of attaining perfection, augmenting piety, or recovering the grace we may have lost by sin. The council teaches that the sacraments of the new law have been instituted by Jesus Christ, and are seven in number, viz.: Baptism, Confirmation, the Holy Eucharist, Penance, Extreme Unction, Holy Orders and Matrimony; that each sacrament contains the grace of which it is the sign, and confers this grace on all those who have the requisite dispositions.

After condemning the heresies of Luther concerning the two first sacraments, the council explains the Eucharist. The pure doctrine always taught by the Catholic Church is, that, after the consecration of the bread and wine, our Lord Jesus Christ, true God and true Man, is present really and substantially under the form of these visible appearances. It is criminal and sacrilegious to presume to give a metaphorical sense to the words by which Jesus Christ has instituted this sacrament. The Church, which is the pillar of truth, condemns this impious assertion, ever remembering, with tender gratitude, this most precious gift she has received from Jesus Christ, her spouse. Our Saviour, when about leaving the earth to go to His Father, instituted this sacrament, in which He lavished, as it were, all the riches of His love upon mankind, and in which is contained a memorial of all His wonders. He desires us in receiving this sacrament to show forth His death, and He wishes it to be the spiritual food of our souls, causing them to live in Him, for He says: "He that eateth me, the same also shall live by me." He moreover desires this sacrament to be the pledge of our eternal happiness, and the symbol of our union with the body of which He is the head. The Catholic Church has always believed that, when the words of consecration are pronounced, the real body and blood of our Saviour, together with His soul and divinity, are present under the form of bread and wine, and that each of the sacred species contains the same as the two combined, for Jesus Christ is whole and entire under the form of bread, even to the least particle, as He also exists under the appearance of wine even to the smallest drop; that, by the consecration of bread and wine, the substance of the bread is changed into the body of our Lord, and the substance of the wine into His blood; which change has been most appropriately called Transubstantiation. All the faithful, therefore, are obliged to honor the blessed sacrament with the supreme worship which is due to God alone, for we believe the God whom all the angels adored when He entered into the world to be truly present, the same Lord and Saviour to whom the Magi presented gold, frankincense, and myrrh; the same Divine Master whom the Apostles adored in Galilee.

THE SACRIFICE OF THE MASS.   441

With regard to the use of this divine sacrament, the holy council, with paternal affection, warns, admonishes, prays and conjures all those who bear the name of Christians to unite under this standard of peace, this bond of charity and symbol of concord, always remembering the extraordinary love of Our Lord Jesus Christ, who has given us His sacred body to be the food of our souls after suffering an ignominious death on the cross for our salvation; to believe in the mystery of the Holy Eucharist with so firm a faith, so profound a respect, and so sincere a piety, as to be able to worthily receive this celestial nourishment; so that, being sustained by this heavenly manna, they may pass from their earthly pilgrimage to eternal bliss, there to partake, without a veil, of this bread of Angels which they now behold under the simple forms of bread and wine.

DOCTRINE OF THE COUNCIL ON THE SACRIFICE OF THE MASS.

The Eucharist is not only a sacrament wherein Jesus Christ gives Himself to mankind for their spiritual nourishment, but it is also a sacrifice in which He offers Himself to the Eternal Father as a victim for the sins of men. The doctrine of the Council of Trent, with regard to the sacrifice of the mass, is expressed in these terms: Although Jesus Christ, Our Lord, has offered Himself as a victim of propitiation for the sins of the world, by expiring on the altar of the cross, nevertheless, as the priesthood was not to be abolished by His death, He has left the

Church, His spouse, a visible sacrifice, such as the nature of man demands; an unbloody sacrifice representing the bloody sacrifice of Calvary, preserving its memory to the end of time, and obtaining the remission of our daily offenses. Thus, at the Last Supper, on the very night of His betrayal, in order to show that He was a priest forever, according to the order of Melchisedech, He offered to God, the Father, His body and blood, under the form of bread and wine, and, under the same appearances, He administered the sacrament of the Eucharist to the Apostles, whom He then, for the first time, established priests of the new testament, and by the words: "Do this in commemoration of me," commanded them and their successors to offer His body and blood in the form He Himself prescribed, which has since been the universal practice of the Catholic Church. For, after celebrating the ancient Pasch offered by the Israelites in memory of their deliverance from Egypt, He established the new Pasch by giving Himself to be offered by the priests in the name of the Church, under visible forms, in memory of His passage from this world to His Father, when, ransoming us by the effusion of His precious blood, He delivered us from the powers of darkness and transferred us to His heavenly kingdom. It is this same offering, which cannot be sullied either by the unworthiness or malice of those who offer it, that our Lord predicted, through the prophet Malachy, should be offered everywhere in His name, that would become great among all nations. It is the same sacrifice that the Apostle Paul, in writing to the Corinthians, clearly indicated, when he said, "that those who were defiled by partaking of the table of devils could not be partakers of the table of the Lord." Finally this sacrifice was prefigured and represented by different kinds of sacrifices, as containing all the benefits which were only signified by the others, of which it is the perfect fulfillment; and as the same Jesus Christ, who offered Himself once on the cross by shedding His precious blood, is contained and immolated in this divine sacrifice, which is accomplished during the Holy Mass without shedding His blood, the council declares, that this sacrifice is truly and really a propitiatory offering; that through its merits we obtain mercy, and receive grace and help in time of need, if we assist thereat with a sincere and contrite heart, lively faith, and ardent hope. Appeased by this divine oblation, God bestows the gift of repentance upon sinners, pardons offenses, and even the greatest crimes, because it is the same victim, the same Jesus Christ, formerly offered on the cross, who now offers Himself by the hands of the priest; there being only this difference, that the sacrifice of the cross was bloody, while that of the altar is unbloody. Far from the latter detracting from the former, it is only through the unbloody oblation that we receive the abundant fruit of the sacrifice on Mount Calvary. Thus, in conformity with the traditions of the Apostles, the mass is offered, not only for the sins, sufferings, satisfaction and necessities of the living, but also for those who sleep in Jesus Christ, and are not yet entirely purified from the stain of sin.

DOCTRINE OF THE COUNCIL ON PENANCE.

If all those who are regenerated by baptism remained always in the state of grace, no other sacrament would have been necessary for the remission of sin. But God, in His infinite mercy, knowing our frailty, has bestowed another means for renewing the spiritual life of those who after baptism have fallen into mortal sin, and under the dominion of Satan. This remedy is the sacrament of penance, by which the merits of the death of Jesus Christ are applied to those who have lost their baptismal innocence.

Penance has always been acceptable unto God, but before the coming of Jesus Christ it was not a sacrament, and since His coming, it is a sacrament only for those who have received baptism. Our Lord Himself especially instituted the sacrament of penance, when, after His resurrection, He breathed on His disciples, saying, "Receive ye the Holy Ghost; whose sins you shall forgive, they are forgiven them," communicating by these words to the Apostles and their successors the power of forgiving and retaining sins committed after baptism. There is a great difference between these two sacraments, for penance does not effect the entire and perfect regeneration accomplished by baptism, as it is only through many contrite tears and great labor that the justice of God is appeased, so that the holy Fathers, with much truth, have called penance, a painful baptism. The form of the sacrament of penance, in which principally consists its virtue and efficacy, is contained in the words of absolution pronounced by the priest;

the dispositions of the penitent, which are contrition, confession and satisfaction, being the substance of the sacrament; and the reconciliation of the sinner with God is the effect.

Contrition, which is the first disposition of a penitent, is a sincere sorrow and detestation of the sins he has committed, with a firm resolution to avoid sin in the future. The holy council declares that this contrition does not mean only a cessation from sin and a determination to lead a new life, but also a hatred for the sins committed in our past life. Although it sometimes happens, adds the council, that contrition is perfected by charity, and that in such a case man is reconciled with God before the reception of the sacrament of penance, this reconciliation nevertheless cannot be effected by contrition alone, but must be accompanied by an earnest desire to receive the sacrament.

Imperfect contrition, called attrition, because it is generally occasioned by the consideration of the vileness and deformity of sin, or the fear of punishment, if accompanied by a hope of pardon and a detestation of sin, is neither hypocritical nor criminal, but a gift of God and an inspiration of the Holy Ghost; not a natural impulse but a supernatural assistance in the preparation for the worthy reception of the sacrament, and although attrition alone, without the sacrament of penance, is not sufficient to justify the sinner, it nevertheless disposes the sinner to obtain the grace of God in the proper performance of this sacred duty.

DOCTRINE OF THE COUNCIL ON CONFESSION.

The Catholic Church has always taught that the confession of all mortal sins is a necessary consequence of the sacrament of penance, which was instituted by our Saviour for the salvation of all those who have fallen after baptism. When about ascending into Heaven, Jesus Christ established priests as His vicars, thus constituting them judges before whom the faithful are obliged to reveal all the mortal sins they may have committed, so that, according to the power they have received of remitting or retaining sins, they may pronounce sentence upon the penitent; but it is evident priests cannot exercise this power without knowing the cause of offense, nor observe justice in their judgment if the penitent only confesses his sins in a general manner, without explaining every particular detail; from which the council concludes that the penitent must accuse himself of all the mortal sins he may have been guilty of after a strict examination of conscience; even when there are hidden sins committed against the last two precepts of the decalogue which forbid all irregular desires; these sins being sometimes more dangerous and fatal to the soul than public offenses.

With regard to venial sins which do not deprive us of the grace of God, and into which we frequently fall, they are not necessarily comprised in the precept of confession, as they can be expiated by several other remedies. Nevertheless, it is very profitable to confess them, as is seen by the custom of pious persons; but every mortal sin, even of thought, renders us children of wrath and enemies of God, and we are, therefore, absolutely obliged to supplicate for pardon at the throne of grace by an unreserved, sincere confession, accompanied by contrition. Those who voluntarily conceal any one mortal sin, have no claim to the forgiveness of God or the absolution of the priest; for, if a sick man is ashamed to make known his disease to the physician, the greatest science and most consummate skill cannot cure the unknown malady. He must also explain in confession the circumstances, which alter the nature of sin; because, otherwise, the priest cannot acquire a sufficient knowledge of the state of the soul, or justly estimate the grievousness of the offense, so as to bestow a suitable penance on the penitent.

It is very wrong to say that confession such as is commanded by the Church of God is an impossibility, or regard it as a torture to the conscience, for our holy mother, the Church, only exacts that, after a careful examination, we accuse ourselves of all the mortal sins we can remember. The sins which may be forgotten by an exact and conscientious Christian are included in his confession, and it is for those sins that we exclaim with the prophet: "Purify me, O Lord, from my hidden sins." It must be acknowledged, however, that confession, by reason of the shame we feel in avowing our sins, would appear a heavy trial, were it not lightened by the advantages and consolation which absolution confers on those who approach this sacrament with the requisite dispositions.

DOCTRINE OF THE COUNCIL ON SATISFACTION.

The holy council declares that it is absolutely false, and entirely contrary to the word of God, to say that He never pardons sin without at the same time remitting all the punishment due the offense; for, besides the authority of sacred tradition, there are several remarkable examples in holy books which completely refute this error. It is certainly most reasonable to suppose that Divine justice will more readily pardon those who, before baptism, sinned through ignorance, than those who, after having been once delivered from the power of the devil and received the gifts of the Holy Ghost, have deliberately profaned the temple of God and grieved the Holy Spirit. It is a mark of Divine clemency that our sins are not remitted without satisfaction being made, lest we might regard them as trivial offenses, and finally commit the most horrible crimes, meriting thereby the wrath of God on the day of judgment. For it is certain that the punishment inflicted for the satisfaction of sin prevents its commission, and acts as a restraint upon sinners, in obliging them to be more vigilant and guarded for the future. Moreover, satisfaction is a remedy which heals the wounds caused by sin, and destroys, by the practice of contrary virtues, the bad habits contracted during a sinful and unchristian life.

The Church of God has always believed that there is no surer way of avoiding the chastisements our sins deserve, than the practice of these penitential works, accompanied by heartfelt contrition. Finally, when suffering for our sins, by this species of satisfaction, we become like Jesus Christ, who offered satisfaction for our offenses, and we have a certain assurance that we shall be partakers in His glory if we have participated in His sufferings. This satisfaction, however, which we offer for our sins is not our own work, but only performed and accomplished through the merits of Jesus Christ; for, though utterly unworthy ourselves, we can perform wonders with the assistance of supernatural grace. Thus, we should have no feelings of self-complacency but glory only in our Lord Jesus Christ, who is our life, our mediator and redeemer, who sanctifies all good works, and renders them efficacious for salvation through His divine merits.

The ministers of God should, therefore, according to the inspiration of the Holy Ghost, and their own judgment, impose satisfaction suitable to the nature of the sins and disposition of the penitent, lest by too great leniency they become participators in the sins of others; remembering that the satisfaction they impose not only serves as a remedy for the maladies of the soul, and a preservative against future offenses, but also expiates the punishment due past sins. The holy council also declares that the goodness of God is so great, that through the merits of Jesus Christ we are enabled to satisfy God the Father, not only by the voluntary mortifications we practice for the punishment of our sins, or by those the priest imposes, but also by the temporal afflictions the Lord sends us, when we bear these trials with patience and submission.

DOCTRINE OF THE COUNCIL ON EXTREME UNCTION.

The council has thought proper to add to what has been said with regard to penance the following explanations concerning the sacrament of Extreme Unction, which the holy Fathers consider as not only the consummation of penance, but of a Christian life, which should be a continual penance. The council, therefore, declares, that Our Redeemer, who, in His infinite goodness desires to provide His servants at all times with salutary remedies against the attacks of their numerous enemies, has prepared in the other sacraments powerful helps for Christians, in order to guard them during life from every spiritual evil; and He wishes also to strengthen and fortify the last hours of their mortal career by the sacrament of Extreme Unction.

This great sacrament is a certain and unfailing protection; for, although the devil, during the whole course of our life, seeks and watches for occasions to destroy our souls, there is no period when he employs his artifices and snares with more cunning, so as to deprive us if possible of confidence in the mercy of God, than when death is drawing near. Now this holy anointing of the sick was established by Our Lord as a sacrament, first used by St. Mark, and plainly recommended to the faithful by St. James, in these words: "Is any man sick among you? Let him bring in the priests of the Church, and let them pray over him, anointing him with oil in the name of the Lord. And the prayer of faith shall save the sick man; and the Lord shall raise him up, and if he be in sins, they shall be forgiven him." By these words, which the Church has received through apostolic tradition as if from the lips of the Apostle himself, she teaches the proper matter, form, administration and effect of this salutary sacrament; for the matter of the sacrament is the oil consecrated by the bishop on Holy Thursday; finally she assures us of the grace of the Holy Ghost, by which the soul of the sick man is, as it were, invisibly anointed.

The form consists in the prayer which accompanies the anointing: "Through this holy unction, and through His most tender mercy, may the Lord pardon thee whatever sins thou hast committed by hearing, sight, etc." The real effect of the sacrament is the grace of the Holy Ghost, which remits the punishment due to sin, and any sins which are still to be expiated; it solaces and strengthens the soul of the sick person, inspires him with great confidence in the mercy of God, sustains and enables him to endure with patience and fortitude the inconvenience and pains of sickness, and firmly resist the temptations of Satan. Sometimes through virtue of this anointing, health is restored to the body when expedient for the salvation of the soul.

The words of the apostle clearly designate those who are to administer this sacrament, and those who should receive it; the bishops and priests being the ministers, and the sick the recipients, those especially who are attacked by a dangerous illness and in their last agony. We should not wait, however, until the sick person is deprived of his senses and unconcious, adds the catechism, composed by command of the Council, it being a great sin to delay until the last moment the administration of this sacrament, as we thus deprive the sick person of a great part of the fruit he could have derived from extreme unction, if he had received it in a state of perfect consciousness by uniting with faith and piety in the prayers of the Church.

DOCTRINE OF THE COUNCIL ON PURGATORY, INDULGENCES, AND VENERATION OF THE SAINTS, ETC.

The holy council of Trent, after anathematizing the errors of Luther and Calvin, with regard to the sacraments of holy orders and matrimony, thus explains the Catholic doctrine of purgatory: "The Church, inspired by the Holy Ghost, has always taught, according to the Holy Scriptures and apostolic tradition, that there is a purgatory, and that the souls there detained, receive comfort from the prayers and good works of the faithful, particularly through the sacrifice of the mass, which is so acceptable to God." Consequently the holy council enjoins the bishops to be careful that the belief of the faithful regarding purgatory should be conformable to the holy doctrine transmitted to us by the Fathers and councils, and commands the same to be universally preached and taught throughout the Church.

The council then speaks of the veneration paid to the saints, and declares that the saints who reign with Jesus Christ offer their prayers for the spiritual welfare of mankind; that it is both advantageous and profitable to humbly invoke them, and implore their intercession and assistance in order to obtain favors from God, through His Son, our Lord Jesus Christ, who alone is our Redeemer and Saviour; that the faithful should respect the relics of the saints, because their bodies were formerly the living members of Jesus Christ and temples of the Holy Ghost, and will one day rise to eternal life; that God authorizes this veneration by working miracles through these holy relics, as in past ages, by the shadow of St. Peter, and the linen which had touched the body of St. Paul. Moreover, that we should have and preserve, especially in the churches, the pictures and statues of Jesus Christ, the Blessed Virgin Mother of God and the saints, paying the honor and veneration due to them.

"It is not," adds the council, "that we believe these images to possess any divine property or virtue which command our veneration, nor ask of them any grace, nor repose confidence in them like the pagans who adore idols, but we honor them on account of the originals which they represent; so that, in kissing statues or kneeling before holy pictures, we adore Jesus Christ and honor the saints of whom they remind us. The bishops should also endeavor to make the history of our redemption, represented by paintings or otherwise, serve as instructions to the people, and confirm them in the practice of always remembering the articles of faith; that another great advantage is also derived from the use of holy images and pictures, by their not only recalling to the minds of the faithful the memory of the favors and graces they have received from God, but also because they expose to the eyes of Christians the miracles He has wrought and the salutary examples He presents them in the persons of the saints, so that they may return Him thanks and be excited by the sight of these objects to love and worship God, and increase in piety and virtue."

The council of Trent terminates its instructions by explaining the nature of indulgences: "Jesus Christ," says the holy council, "having conferred upon His Church the power of granting indulgences, and the Church having from the earliest ages made use of the power she has received from her Founder, the holy council commands and enjoins her to continue this most holy practice, and confirms it by the authority of the councils. The council anathematizes those who assert that indulgences are useless or deny the power of the Church to grant them; which power, however, is to be used with care and moderation, according to the ancient and approved custom of the Church, lest ecclesiastical discipline may become enervated and weakened by too great license.

CONCLUSION OF THE COUNCIL OF TRENT—ST. CHARLES BORROMEO.

A. D. 1563-1584.

The council of Trent, whose first session was held in the year 1545, was finally terminated in 1563, under the pontificate of Pius IV. Every obstacle which the spirit of heresy and error could raise, was opposed to this assembly for the space of eighteen years, in order to prevent its decrees from being executed or to weaken its authority. But faith finally triumphed, and He who has promised to remain always with His Church, enabled His spouse to obtain a victory over the passions of men, and the very heresy which seemed to threaten immediate ruin contributed towards her conservation and effected the happiest reformation. The twenty-fifth and last session was held on the third of December, 1563. The secretary, after reading all the decrees of the council, proclaimed the last at the conclusion of this celebrated assembly. It was hardly ratified when the Fathers, returning thanks to God, testified their joy by tears and acclamations, as in the ancient councils. The Pope confirmed the decisions by a bull on the sixth of January, 1564, kings, princes, rulers, and all the faithful being exhorted to receive religiously and humbly the holy laws it had passed.

The Venetians were the first to submit, and their example was very soon followed by Italy, Spain, Portugal and Poland. The decrees were also published in Flanders, the kingdoms of Naples and Sicily, and through the greater part of Germany, where, however, the Lutherans refused to recognize their authority, as if their consent affected the infallibility of the Church, or their sanction was necessary for the execution of its laws. France also accepted the decisions of the holy council, whose decrees are received as rules of faith for the whole church, being held in the same veneration as the four great councils, according to the words of a holy pontiff, "I revere the four first councils as I do the four gospels." The discipline and wise regulations of the council were adopted and enforced but slowly; numerous obstacles arose on every side, and some of the principal churches at first opposed its decrees; but God raised up one of those great and generous souls who have appeared in every century in the Church, as her support and powerful defender.

Charles Borromeo, the model of bishops, and restorer of ecclesiastical discipline, was born in Arona, near Milan, of one of the most illustrious Italian families. From his earliest childhood he manifested the most pious dispositions, plainly indicating the wonderful designs of God in behalf of His chosen servant. Charles embraced the religious state at an early age, and his uncle, the Cardinal de Medicis, having ascended the Papal chair under the title of Pius IV, summoned him to Rome, where he was appointed Cardinal and Archbishop of Milan, and the principal administration of ecclesiastical affairs was confided to his charge. Thus raised to the first dignities of the Church, enjoying the favor of the sovereign Pontiff, covered with glory and honor, and still in the bloom of manhood, Borromeo escaped all the snares that beset youth and talent, and showed himself worthy, by his many virtues and exemplary deportment, of the high rank to which Providence had elevated him. Through his zealous efforts, the Council of Trent was at length terminated; the publication of the decrees accelerated by his urgent solicitations to the bishops and princes, and, as soon at this venerable assembly was dissolved, he convened a large synod at Milan, in order to receive and publish its decisions.

Not satisfied with his first success, Charles applied himself particularly to the work of reformation commanded by the council; having been the moving spirit and director of the last sessions, he was perfectly acquainted with the intentions of the assembly. In order to hasten matters, he began the reform by correcting in his own person and household whatever was derogatory to the dignity of the Episcopal office, replacing the most innocent pleasures by grave and serious occupations, devotional exercises, preaching, administering the sacraments, and watching over the affairs of the diocese. But Charles Borromeo was destined to give a still more striking example of virtue to the Church. The council of Trent had loudly exclaimed against those bishops who did not reside in their dioceses. St. Charles, detained at Rome, by the express command of the sovereign Pontiff, considered it his imperative duty to personally superintend the flock confided to his pastoral care. He, therefore, asked his uncle's permission to return to his diocese, and finally, after urgent entreaties, obtained his request.

Restored to his beloved children, Borromeo labored only for their sanctification and the glory of the Church of God. Gathering around him men eminent for learning and piety, he convoked a provincial council, and enacted, according to the decrees of Trent, the wisest regulations for the reception and observance of the decisions of the council, the reformation of the clergy, and the proper celebration of the divine office. While thus laboring for the welfare of his flock, Charles did not spare himself, but gave up all his benefices, refused to wear silk garments, and adopted a most austere mode of life. His household was so well regulated that it resembled a religious seminary, rather than the palace of an archbishop, and, during the last years of his life, he subsisted entirely on bread, water, and a few coarse roots.

The great sanctity and wonderful zeal of the Cardinal Borromeo spread throughout Italy. This exemplary bishop frequently visited every part of his vast diocese, traveled through his ecclesiastical province, and penetrated as far as Switzerland. During his apostolic missions he sometimes proceeded on foot, endured hunger, thirst, and the inclemency of the weather, climbed the steepest mountains, and descended the most frightful precipices, to seek for his stray sheep and restore them to the saving fold of Jesus Christ. His zeal was so active, and his charity so fruitful, that he neglected nothing which could contribute to the glory of God and the salvation of souls. Unadorned altars, or negligence and indifference in conducting the holy ceremonies of the Church, found in St. Charles a reformer, who, by the use of magnificent vestments, when celebrating divine worship, restored the grandeur and splendor of religion, and re-animated the piety and fervor of the faithful.

He was the first who established seminaries, five of which were founded in his diocese. The Cardinal drew up wise rules for the government of these holy asylums which have served for models in the formation of similar institutions that have subsequently been so happily multiplied in the Church. He erected colleges, hospitals, and monasteries, organized pious associations, revived the spirit of discipline and ervor among the regular and secular clergy of his diocese, convened as many as six councils, all of which were confirmed by the Holy See; and, fearing tha all these good works would fail to inspire his people with the true spirit of Christianity, he still reproached himself with not having commenced to sanctify the flock placed under his guidance. Divine Providence, however, sent Charles one of those great trials by which ordinary virtue is generally prostrated, but which fully develop a great and generous soul. The plague appeared in Milan; and the wealthy portion of the inhabitants immediately abandoned the city; St. Charles was advised to retire into a place of safety and preserve his life so valuable to his diocese, but the holy prelate indignantly rejected counsel so contrary to these words of the Saviour: "The good shepherd giveth his life for his sheep;" and, offering his life as a sacrifice for his flock, he devoted all his energies to assist those stricken with the pestilence.

His ardent charity knew no bounds; night and day he labored indefatigably for the temporal and spiritual welfare of the unfortunate victims, carrying peace and consolation wherever he appeared. His mere presence assuaged the acutest suffering, and his words of piety and resignation to the dying comforted agonizing souls in their departure from this world. The contagion, however, continued to spread, all resources were exhausted, and there was no possible assistance or relief for the afflicted; but Charles, in his unfailing charity, discovered new means for solacing the sick. He borrowed money, sold his possessions and furniture, even to his bed, and carried, with his own hands, nourishment and remedies to the sick, fearing neither danger nor death while alleviating the sufferings of his beloved children.

The divine wrath was finally appeased by the devotion of the archbishop, and before his death Charles enjoyed the happiness of seeing tranquillity and health restored to his diocese. Seven years after the disappearance of the plague, this heroic soul was summoned to receive the crown of immortal glory, in recompense for so many virtues and sacrifices; he died on the third of November, 1584. His flock, whom he had cherished with the tenderness and solicitude of a father, were overwhelmed with grief at the loss of their beloved and saintly father; his death was deeply felt by the Holy See, of which he had been a powerful support, and the Catholic world lamented in his demise one who, by his saintly life, wide-spread zeal and prudent reformation, had effected so much good, and excited the admiration and gratitude of the faithful. Happy Church in whose bosom models of such heroic virtue are formed! What other society separated from the Catholic communion has ever produced a man so eminent for sanctity, zeal, and charity, as St. Charles Borromeo?

REFORMATION OF THE ORDER OF MOUNT CARMEL — ST. THERESA.

A. D. 1582.

While St. Charles was laboring for the restoration of ecclesiastical discipline, zealous missionaries were announcing the glad tidings of the gospel to barbarous nations, and the implacable spirit of heresy was sending generous martyrs to Heaven; new religious institutions were being formed in the Church, entire reformation effected in the cloisters, and the primitive fervor of monastic orders restored. We can refer to this epoch, although it was established shortly before this period, the congregation of the Theatines, founded by Pope Paul IV; the Barnabites, organized by three Milanese gentlemen, and the society of the Jesuits, which was confirmed in 1540, and enjoyed at this time a reputation due one of the most holy and useful orders that has ever appeared in the Church.

These were not the only monuments of the sixteenth century, when, notwithstanding the efforts of heresy, religion still maintained a happy ascendancy over the civilized world; St. John of God founded the brothers of charity devoted to the service of the sick. The sovereign Pontiff approved of the reform of the Recollects, who observed the rule of St. Francis in all its purity, and France beheld the origin of the penitents of Picpus, and the reformation of the mendicant friars. But of all the institutions of this era the most illustrious is the one which claims St. Theresa as its reformer.

This ardent lover of Jesus was born at Avila, in Spain, and evinced from her earliest years the most wonderful piety. The lives of the saints, which was her principal reading, inflamed her young heart with a desire for martyrdom; but these happy dispositions were unfortunately weakened. Losing her mother at an age when the passions begin to develop, Theresa, free from all maternal restraint, occupied her time with romances, novels and other works of fiction, and imbibed from these poisoned sources sentiments of vanity and worldliness; this pernicious literature being most fatal to innocence and virtue. Before these inclinations, however, had made a deep impression on her youthful mind, she was placed in a convent, where good example and the exercises of religion revived her piety. Theresa then realized the magnitude of the peril to which she had been exposed, and, in order to guard against a recurrence of the danger, she resolved to consecrate herself to God.

At the age of twenty-one she embraced the religious life in the Carmelite order, and, like a generous victim, zealously practiced the most rigorous penances. This new spouse of Jesus Christ was the recipient of the signal favors of a God who never allows Himself to be outdone by the generosity of His children. The divine gifts Heaven showered upon this humble servant, and the ineffable graces with which her soul were inundated, was the theme of every tongue in the convent. These days of peace and consolation were however limited. Recalled to the world, in order to re-establish her feeble and delicate health, Theresa became lukewarm and indifferent, acquired a taste for worldly amusements, and formed intimacies, which, although innocent in their nature, kept her in a state of imperfection and frivolity, so contrary to a spirit of recollection and fervor. The death of her father, and the perusal of the confessions of St. Augustine, re-animated the heart of Theresa, revived her piety, detached her from earthly affections, and raised her to a state of the most sublime and perfect love of God. When attempting to describe the fire which inflamed her soul, and the ardor by which she was consumed, words failed her; and if in the height of her raptures a few sentences escaped her lips, she was heard to exclaim, "Enlarge, O my God! enlarge my heart or withdraw thy divine grace." These celestial favors were not conferred without a mixture of trials and sorrows. It was thought, by some persons, that the revelations with which God favored His servant were only mental illusions, and at one time they threatened to take her before the tribunal of the inquisition.

In the midst of these exterior persecutions, mental languor and interior trials, Theresa never murmured, but suffered with heroic calmness and resignation. Tranquillity of mind and peace of soul soon succeeded to the storm, her persecutors became her vindicators, and those who had refused to recognize in her the gifts of God were the first to proclaim her virtues. Theresa began about this time to labor for the reformation of Carmel; endowed with superior talents and a courage not often found in a woman, she surmounted every obstacle, and by dint of perseverance, labor and zeal, revived in her order a spirit of penance and regular discipline. Sixteen convents for females and fourteen for males, embraced during her life-time her austere rule, which shortly afterward extended throughout the Catholic world.

Theresa was seconded in her efforts by John d'Ypez, better known as St. John of the Cross. An humble, mortified Religious, animated by the true spirit of evangelical perfection, John d'Ypez sustained and encouraged Theresa, at the same time submitting to all she thought necessary for the restoration of the primitive spirit of Carmel. The sanctity of his life and the greatness of his miracles have placed him among the number of the saints. In the midst of her labors for the welfare of her order, St. Theresa was afflicted by frequent illness and excruciating physical pain, but she obtained strength to bear them patiently from that ardent love of suffering, which caused her to exclaim so often: "Let me either suffer or die!" She never complained of these severe maladies, but esteemed herself too happy in purchasing, by a momentary anguish a crown of never fading bliss, which bright recompense for her many and heroic virtues she received on the fourth of October, in the year 1582.

ERRORS OF BAIUS. RENEWED VIOLENCE OF THE HERETICS.

Baius, a Doctor of Louvain, with a view of uniting Catholics and Protestants, promulgated most erroneous opinions with regard to grace, free will, justification and original sin. He taught that the involuntary motions of concupiscence are sinful; that liberty, according to the Holy Scriptures, is a deliverance from sin; that man is laid under a law of necessity; that since the fall of Adam all the works of men not actuated by divine grace are criminal; and that a sinner before being justified can merit eternal life. This Lutheran doctrine had no sooner appeared than it found zealous opponents in the defenders of the Catholic faith. The theological faculty of Paris in 1560, censured eighteen propositions extracted from the works of Baius; and a few years afterward the holy Pope Pius V condemned seventy-six of his heretical opinions. Baius, at first, seemed to submit to the sentence, but soon published a long apology of his doctrine, in which he unhesitatingly asserted, that the teachings of the holy fathers were attacked in the bull in which he was anathematized. Pius V, with extraordinary condescension, ordered a new examination of the censured doctrine, and confirmed his first judgment. Baius refused to sign his condemnation, but finally obeyed, through fear of attracting too much notice if he persisted in his insubordination. After the death of the Pope, Baius and his followers again commenced to disturb the peace of the Church. He published the sixth apology of his doctrine, complained of having been condemned without a hearing, and used every argument which could possibly justify his course.

Gregory XIII, in order to put an end to the trouble, issued a bull in the year 1579, confirming that of Pius V. The university of Louvain and all the Doctors received it, and Baius was once more forced to retract by word of mouth, and by writings, the condemned propositions. He obeyed, but has left posterity in doubt as to whether his last recantation was more sincere than the preceding ones. He died in 1589, after having traced out the labyrinth of errors in which we behold semi-Calvinism seeking refuge and defending its heresies with so much cunning, that, notwithstanding the rejection and condemnation of the Church, it still desires to be looked upon as united to her communion. While Baius promulgated his errors and proclaimed his pernicious doctrine, the Calvinists devastated Flanders, revolted in Holland against the legitimate sovereign, and endeavored to overthrow the Spanish rule, at the same time that they separated from the Catholic communion.

About this period entire kingdoms suddenly renounced the true faith, embraced the errors of Protestantism and seemed to have completely abandoned the Church, to whom they owed their faith, prosperity and happiness; Scotland, Denmark and Switzerland abjured the creed professed by Rome, and heresy stalked abroad over the world. Wherever it prevailed, fire and sword destroyed the altars and profaned the temples of the living God, and cruel executioners inhumanly put to death the faithful who refused to recognize or embrace their errors. When resistance was offered and the danger partially averted, the wicked heretics endeavored to augment their numbers by exciting revolt and practicing unheard of cruelties. Thus we see heresy seated on the throne of England, and exercising its rage against the Catholics.

The inhuman Elizabeth, trampling under foot all law divine or human, immolated to her jealousy, and hatred of the religion of her fathers, the unfortunate Mary Stuart, Queen of Scotland, whose pure and innocent blood swelled the sanguinary stream which flowed for the same holy cause in every part of the kingdom. The Catholics, murdered and proscribed, without refuge or defense, were the unhappy victims of the rage and malice of these barbarous heretics. Thus in France, Calvinism attacked the sovereign, and, notwithstanding daily losses and continual reverses, devastated the provinces and prolonged a civil war, which was more disastrous in its effects than the invasions of the barbarous tribes were centuries previous. The heretics finally became more successful; a young prince, presumptive heir to the throne, placed himself at the head of the rebels; victory followed him everywhere, and his white plume was adorned with the laurels of repeated triumphs.

It was in vain that the League, a frightful mixture of human passion and false zeal for religion, strove to stem the progress of this impetuous torrent. He surmounted every barrier, and a decisive blow had already opened the gates of the capital to the conqueror, when He, who watches over the welfare of Christian nations, touched the heart of the son of St. Louis. Henry IV renounced his heretical opinions before entering Paris, and made a solemn abjuration of his errors in the church of St. Denis, in the presence of the archbishop of Bourges and a great number of prelates. His profession of faith was expressed as follows: "I promise and swear, in the presence of Almighty God, to live and die in the Catholic, Apostolic, and Roman Church, to protect and defend her at the peril of my life, and I renounce all heresies contrary to her doctrines." Before his recantation, Henry IV assembled the Protestant ministers, and asked them if they believed salvation was to be found in the Roman Church. They were obliged to acknowledge, that, according to their principles, it could be found in that fold. "Why, then," replied the king, "have you abandoned it? The Catholics contend that there can be no salvation in your Church, while you admit that you could be saved in theirs; my common sense prompts me to espouse the safest side, and to prefer a religion in which, according to the testimony of the whole world, I can secure eternal happiness."

Henry IV, when seated on the throne, used every means to repair the losses he had inflicted on the State and Church; he recalled the Jesuits who were banished by an act of parliament, adjusted difficulties, quieted civil dissensions, and labored throughout his entire reign for the welfare of his subjects. A most estimable prince, if his passions had not tarnished the purity of his morals. He met his death by the hand of an assassin.

ST. FRANCIS OF SALES.
A. D. 1622.

The Church preserved the decrees of the holy Council of Trent, while heresy, separating itself more and more from the Catholic faith, plunged into all kinds of errors, and embraced the most opposite and contradictory doctrines. Innumerable sects sprang up under the leadership of restless and violent men; each day witnessed new professions of faith, and the continual changes of the Protestants seemed to presage the speedy advent of a period when they would only maintain the appearance of christianity and the semblance of religion. Discord and dissension reigned in their conventicles, and all attempts at a reform, undertaken for the purpose of re-establishing the purity of morals and faith, only occasioned still greater troubles and scandals. We will not dwell longer upon the efforts of the heretics, but leave them to their endless broils and disputes; nor speak further of the Anabaptists, Libertines, Socinians, Monists, and other horrible sects, which Protestantism itself blushes to own; but we will direct our gaze to that living image of the Son of God, conversing with men, the illustrious bishop of Geneva, Francis of Sales, whose name is never pronounced without recalling the most beautiful and virtuous of souls.

He was born near Annecy, in Savoy, in 1567, and was indebted to his pious mother for a Christian education, and the germs of the many virtues which now expanded and developed his rare qualities of mind and heart. Count de Sales, his father, sent Francis to Paris to pursue his studies. In the midst of the corruption of a great city, and the dangers which surround the young, he escaped the general contagion, and continued to lead a most regular and pious life. He was several times, however, subjected to severe trials, and it is related, that, overcome by a frightful temptation to despair, Francis for a long time believed himself abandoned by God, and destined to eternal flames. What a punishment for a pure heart that served God with the most extraordinary fervor and fidelity! In this agonizing frame of mind he passed whole nights in groans and tears; nothing could console or calm his tortured soul; when one day as he was prostrated before a statue of Mary, and more than usually tormented by the dreadful thought of his hopeless doom, Francis addressed this touching prayer to God: "O my God! since I am condemned to hate Thee for all eternity, grant at least that I may love Thee with all my heart while on earth!"

Scarcely had he finished this heroic act of love, when a bright ray of hope illuminated the darkness of his soul, and his supplication was rewarded by a deliverance from the most dreadful of all temptations. Francis left Paris in his seventeenth year, and repaired to Padua where he studied theology and law with great success for several years. He then traveled through Italy, and, in accordance with the wishes of his father, visited all the monuments and places of historical or artistic interest, returning to his devoted family adorned with every virtue and possessed of great learning; they entreated him to accept the position of senator in the senate of Chambery; but he positively refused the office, declaring his determination to embrace the ecclesiastical state.

His design was at first opposed; the interests of his noble house, and the brilliant destiny which awaited him, being adduced as reasons for the relinquishment of his desire to retire from the world. Finally, however, after many contests and a long opposition, he obtained his father's consent, and we behold him in his chosen career, instructing the poor, converting heretics, and proclaiming his divine calling by the practice of every Christian virtue. Calvinism had appeared in a part of Savoy, and the ignorant and rude inhabitants embraced its tenets with great ardor. Francis de Sales commenced his ministry by opposing this heresy; he traversed Chablais and the neighboring country, and, in a few years, Catholicity reigned where Protestantism had formerly prevailed. No one could resist the sweet persuasive words of the saint: seventy thousand heretics returned to the Church; as many being converted by the example of his heavenly virtues and extraordinary mildness as through his eloquent discourses. Elevated to the Episcopal dignity, a few years after his ordination, he still labored indefatigably for the salvation of souls, undertook the conversion of the heretics of Gex, and his efforts were crowned with the most abundant success. Sovereign Pontiffs wrote him letters of praise and commendation, and monarchs frequently bestowed upon this humble servant of God flattering testimonials of their regard and esteem.

Henry IV offered him an annuity and a bishopric; Christine of France, who, through entreaties and prayers, induced him to act as her almoner, regarded him with the warmest affection, and the Duke of Savoy, his sovereign, seized every opportunity to manifest his reverence and love for the holiest and most illustrious bishop in his dominions. The episcopal career of St. Francis de Sales was an uninterrupted succession of charitable works and apostolic labors. He reformed his clergy, visited his diocese, preached in the towns and villages, crossing, at the peril of his life, the most rapid torrents, and descending the steepest mountains of the country. He conversed with the peasants and the poor who came to see him with so much paternal kindness that he won all hearts. He himself taught the first elements of Christian doctrine to the children, encouraging their efforts and animating their courage. His zeal was unbounded and universal, and was proof against the most formidable obstacles, and undiminished by his numerous duties. He labored for the establishment of the Order of the Visitation, counseled the illustrious St. Jane Frances de Chantal, its foundress, directed her course and composed the holy rules of this new community. So many arduous occupations, however, did not completely absorb his attention; the saints know how to regulate their lives according to a system of perfect order, and he found time to write several works.

In these productions, St. Francis of Sales shows

his angelic nature; they are full of sweetness and charity, and inspire the reader with a love of piety and religion. Virtue never appeared more lovely than when he described its beauties, and religion never more attractive than when he spoke of it in words of glowing eloquence.

This great bishop, after a truly apostolical career, died, in the prime of life, at Lyons, in 1622, and was canonized forty-three years after his decease.

STATE OF RELIGION IN JAPAN.

The Christian religion preached in Japan by St. Francis Xavier, in the middle of the sixteenth century, had made rapid progress in that country, and sixty years after his death the Catholic population was estimated at nearly two millions of souls. The greater number of the nobles were declared believers in the true faith, or were the protectors and friends of the Christians; several princes renounced the worship of idols, among the most fervent of whom were the sovereigns of Bongo, Arima, Fungo, Bugen and Omura, and their ardent faith and good works sustained and encouraged the neophytes. So wonderful a success seemed to portend that one more conquest would entirely christianize Japan, when suddenly a revolution broke out in the empire, and a severe persecution destroyed the peace and security hitherto enjoyed by the Christians.

Taï-Kosama, a usurper, began to harass the faithful, exiled those in authority whom he suspected on account of their integrity and piety, and unhesitatingly shed the precious blood of the courageous followers of Jesus Christ; this, however, was but a prelude to the barbarous persecution which subsequently desolated Japan. All who avowed themselves Christians, perished; no one escaped the rage of the persecutors; neither the infirmity of age, delicate women, the most elevated position, nor distinguished services, were exempted from the frightful carnage. These heroic martyrs were subjected to the severest trials; and hell invented the most horrible tortures to test the courage and faith of these generous confessors. They were arrested, not singly, but in numerous bands, not chained or manacled, but secured with sharp pointed instruments, which pierced and lacerated their limbs. The inhuman executioners dragged their victims by the hair, brutally assaulting and trampling upon their quivering and aching bodies. Such was the beginning of those awful scenes, from which the Christians, however, emerged victorious, ready to endure still more dreadful tortures for the sake of their crucified Lord and Master. At first the martyrs were beheaded and their bodies consigned to the flames, but this punishment appearing too lenient, fresh victims were put to death in the most frightful manner, until the diabolical rage of the persecutors was nearly exhausted.

These barbarous men employed every means cruelty and violence could invent for the destruction of the Christians, sometimes actually tearing them limb from limb. The legs of some were crushed between two heavy wooden beams, covered with sharp iron nails; the limbs of others stretched and extended by slow and exquisitely painful tortures; several were laid on their faces, and, after piling large stones on their bodies, they were elevated by ropes fastened to their hands and feet drawing them backwards, and in a moment, crushing the bodies to a thousand pieces. Numerous bands of executioners traversed the provinces seeking new victims, so as to prolong the persecution. Sharp bodkins were inserted under the nails of the martyrs, and then suddenly and violently withdrawn, occasioning the most excruciating agony; others were thrown into pits filled with vipers, their bodies pierced with pointed reeds, flaming torches were applied to the wounded flesh, and, in order to lacerate the heart as well as the body, tender mothers were struck with the heads of their infants who were held aloft by their feet, the inhuman fiends redoubling their cruelty at every agonizing shriek of the innocent lambs.

These dreadful sufferings, however, did not diminish the courage of the Christians, but seemed to animate them with an ardent desire for martyrdom; they hastened to the place of execution as though it were a great festival, and were never more joyous than when being dragged to the scaffold; the prisons resounded with beautiful hymns, and the darkest dungeons were transformed into bright sanctuaries, where the praises of the Lord were continually sung. When the decree proscribing the Christian religion throughout Japan was issued, the women assembled for prayer, boldly carrying some symbol of the faith; the maidens took the vow of virginity, and the little children ran to meet the guards, so as to be placed in the ranks of the martyrs. Seeing their parents distressed on account of their tender age and delicate bodies, these infant soldiers of the cross promised to entreat the executioners to put them to death the first; and in order to calm the fears of a fond father or loving mother, endeavored to become accustomed to suffering, anticipating by voluntary tortures the cruelties which awaited them at the hands of the inhuman tyrant, who thus ruthlessly destroyed these innocent babes. God, however, did not abandon His servants, but sustained them with a supernatural courage, and manifested His power as visibly as at the time of the first martyrs; the chains which bound the Christians were severed by invisible hands, their frightful dungeons transformed into abodes of bliss, and the persecutors either converted or punished. The fire of persecution, however, can never die out as long as any Christians remain, and it seems that new tortures will be invented and new cruelties practiced.

In the neighborhood of Nagazaqui there is a frightful mountain which vomits forth flames, fetid waters and burning lava; the persecutors resolved to cast the Christians into this horrible abyss; but as they would be immediately suffocated if thrown with force, they were lowered by degrees that through this insupportable agony their constancy might be overcome, or else they would expire in the most violent convulsions. Some of the martyrs were stretched naked upon the edge of the crater of the volcano, and exposed to the eruptions of lava and flames which, from time to time, issued forth, they were soon covered with pustules, which caused the most terrible suffering; when their poor bodies were reduced to one agonizing wound, they were abandoned as corpses ready for the charnel house. To this punishment was frequently added the torture of water and the pit. In the first, the victim was made to drink an immense quantity of water, and when dreadfully swollen, a plank was laid across his stomach, and by walking heavily upon it, all the water he had swallowed, accompanied by streams of blood, was ejected. In the second, the martyr was lowered, head downward, into a disgusting pit, reeking with filth, two sloping planks fastened over his back and stomach, shut out the light, and prevented any of the horrible odor from escaping.

In this frightful condition the generous Christians suffered a lingering martyrdom; their nerves shattered, muscles distended, the blood pouring from their eyes, ears, nostrils, and mouth, so copiously, that death would instantly have released them from their tortures, if their fiendish executioners had not rendered them a cruel assistance, which prolonged their lives in excruciating agony for nine or ten days. It was through these diabolical means that the Church was utterly destroyed in Japan. All the missionaries became successively the victims of these atrocious cruelties, and the executions were only suspended when there were no more Christians to be found in the empire. The tyrants abolished the slightest vestige of religion; every Japanese was obliged to wear some external sign of paganism; and all Europeans, with the single exception of the Hollanders, who were allowed to land at the port of Nangazaqui, were forbidden by the most stringent laws from penetrating within the limits of the empire. O profound wisdom of God! how inscrutable are Thy ways! Thou hast snatched the torch of faith from a soil, which was so carefully cultivated, so fruitful in virtue, watered by the innocent blood of so many martyrs, sanctified by the labors of numerous Apostles, and yet weak mortals seek to unveil Thy counsels and penetrate Thy judgments!

ORIGIN OF JANSENISM.

. D. 1630.

Baius, whose errors and condemnation have been elsewhere narrated, left disciples, who in secret spread his doctrine and propagated his pernicious belief. It now remains for us to show how they succeeded in reproducing his teachings, what efforts were made to sustain them, and for us also to demonstrate, by unmasking their obstinacy and artifices, how the least innovations in matters of faith are criminal and dangerous. Jansenius, who gave his name to this new heresy, was born in Holland, and had imbibed from James Jansen, a Doctor of Louvain, the errors of Baius. He became attached through the persuasive eloquence of his master to the heretical opinions, represented as being the pure doctrine of St. Augustine; and he applied himself for more than twenty years to the examination of the writings of this great

Doctor, hoping to discover therein the necessary authority for supporting the opinions toward which he was already favorably inclined.

The fruit of these labors and researches was a large work, which he entitled "Augustinus," as if containing only the doctrines of this great saint. His book was finished in 1638, and about being published, when he died of the plague, two years after his nomination to the bishopric of Ypres. He had confided his intentions to some friends, desiring them to publish his work, after inserting several protestations of submission to the Holy See, no doubt insincere, since the author could not ignore the fact, that, in reviving the errors of Baius, he would merit the same condemnation. Two years, therefore, after the appearance of the "Augustinus," Urban VIII anathematized the work as reproducing the heresies of Baius. The censuring voice of Rome, however, far from arresting the progress of the creed, irritated the pride of the partisans of the new doctrines, and rendered them more obstinate and persistent in their defense. Cornet, head of the faculty of Theology of Paris, presented five propositions, extracted from the writings of Jansenius, before the Sorbonne, and the faculty having condemned them, seventy Doctors exclaimed against the sentence and refused to submit to the decision. The affair was then carried before the bishops, who referred it to Pope Innocent X, and the sovereign Pontiff, after an examination of two years, at length solemnly condemned the five doctrinal points.

Completely conquered and crushed by this blow,

which they had striven to elude, the Jansenists declared that the propositions had been condemned according to reason, but not according to fact, that is to say, as heretical and impious in themselves, but not according to the meaning of Jansenius, an empty subterfuge of heresy, which only served to unmask the false teachings of Doctor Arnaud and his adherents. In fact, if this distinction could be admitted, the condemnation of heresy by the Church would be vain and useless; it could be obstinately defended, under the pretext that the author was misunderstood, and the true meaning of his words distorted and changed. Thus, in order to effectually destroy all the resources by which cunning seeks to sustain error, Alexander VII, in his decree of 1656, declared that the five propositions were taken from the work of Jansenius, and were condemned according to the meaning of this author.

Convicted by this sentence, which was sanctioned by the whole Church, the Jansenists pretended that the bull simply referred to the regulation of discipline, which only exacted a respectful silence and not entire submission; and in order to avoid signing the formula of faith which was prescribed at this period, they had recourse to equivocations and mental reservations of which they pretended to have a great horror. The heresy was finally attacked in its last stronghold; Clement XI, by his bull of 1705, declared that a respectful silence was not the proper mode of rendering the obedience due the Church; but that it was also necessary to condemn, as heretical and worthy of rejection, the real meaning of the writings of Jansenius, which had been formerly condemned in the five propositions.

It was in this way that the question of Jansenism and its condemnation arose, in the beginning of the seventeenth century. At first unknown, feeble, and servile, this new off-shoot of heresy assumed an appearance of piety, and an affectation of severity and rigor in morals. It soon extended and attracted followers, and although possessing no attractive attributes, whole judicial and religious corporations, through a spirit of revolt and opposition to legitimate authority, which is the distinctive characteristic of Jansenism, obstinately persisted in the defense of a doctrine which did not seem at all calculated to gain proselytes. In fact, far from lightening the yoke imposed by religion, it aggravated it, and it made the tribunal of penance a tribunal of terror and vengeance.

The Jansenists only spoke of mortifications, austerities, and self-renunciation, while maintaining at the same time that all good works are the gifts of God, as gratuitous and independent of the natural inclination of man, as the rain is of the earth. They described in glowing terms the charity and love of God, and still represented Him as a hard and cruel master, who wishes to reap where He has not sown, who punishes because we have not received what He does not judge proper to bestow, and even refuses to give. They teach that love only, and not fear, should attract us to a God who denies His grace not only to sinners, but even to the righteous, who blames them for faults it was impossible to avoid, and punishes them for not possessing virtues never conferred upon them. In short, a God who sent His only Son to die on the cross for the salvation of a few men, and not for the redemption of the whole human race; such is the substance of the pernicious doctrines of Jansenism.

A frightful combination of the most gloomy and despairing heresies, which makes man the mere sport of the anger of God, makes virtue a gift possessed without merit, acquired without effort, and lost without any fault; pictures crime as a fatality which cannot be avoided, a misfortune that overwhelms us, and a precipice down which we are dragged by corrupt nature. We will shortly see the disastrous consequences of this dangerous creed, which leaves nothing undone to oppose legitimate authority, which creates a disgust for the practice of virtue, destroys confidence in God, and plunges us into despair.

ST. VINCENT DE PAUL.
A. D. 1660.

There are few periods in the history of the Gallican Church so fruitful in pious institutions, and eminent personages renowned for the sanctity of their lives and the firmness of their faith, as in the first part of the seventeenth century. It seemed as if Heaven was pleased to unite during this golden age the most sublime virtues in opposition to the efforts of heresy, and show to the world that it was from the bosom of the true Church that zealous missioners came forth, as well as holy Pontiffs, pious founders, and so many useful institutions established for the glory of God, and the succor of the poor and unfortunate.

Berulle, Ollier, Bourdaise, Vincent de Paul, and so many others who participated in their labors, were all children of the Catholic Church. To recount their virtues and apostolic lives is to confound heresy and glorify the Holy Mother of all the faithful, who has received from her celestial spouse the power of producing saints.

Vincent de Paul, the most illustrious of the holy personages, who, at this remarkable epoch, reflected honor on the Church and glorified religion, was born in the diocese of Dax, in 1576, of poor and obscure parents, and during his childhood was employed in tending sheep. He afterward had the happiness of receiving an education, and finally entered the priesthood. Shortly after, when returning from Marseilles to Narbonne, he fell into the hands of the Turks, who carried him in captivity to Tunis; but Providence, who had particular designs of mercy in his regard, soon delivered him from prison. He succeeded in converting his master, who was a renegade Christian, and they both escaped in a small skiff, leaving the land of captivity to return once more to their native country.

On arriving in France, Vincent de Paul successively filled several positions where his rare humility concealed his worth and veiled the luster of his virtues. Finally, M. de Berulle placed him in the house of Emmanuel de Gondey, general of the galleys, where he began to manifest more openly the holy zeal which animated his pure soul. He first established country missions, and ardently applied himself to this most important work of the ministry. Being summoned to Marscilles, whither the general of the galleys had repaired in order to perform the duties of his office, he could not behold, without emotion, the frightful condition of the galley slaves; who, condemned by human justice, expiated their crimes, deprived of all consolation, in the midst of blasphemies and despair. Vincent lavished the tenderest care upon these unfortunate beings, and strove to soften and subdue their unhappy hearts, rendered fierce and ungovernable by the withering breath of sin.

Nothing seemed painful to him in the exercise of this most arduous ministry; he lived in the midst of these poor wretches so as to solace their griefs and assuage the hardships of their unfortunate lot. It is related, that, touched by the despair of one of the slaves, he took his place, carried his chain, and remained for some time in the prison. St. Francis de Sales, who said he could not find a worthier priest in the Church of God than Vincent de Paul, confided to him the direction of the Sisters of the Visitation, who for forty years enjoyed the happiness of receiving his intructions, and profiting by his beautiful example.

The moment had now arrived when St. Vincent de Paul was to develop the generous and noble inclinations of his holy soul. After the death of M. de Gondy, he retired to the college of the Bons-Enfants (Good Children), and there commenced the foundation of the congregation of St. Lazar, or the Priests of the Mission, which was approved in 1632;

and as if the establishment and direction of this budding institution was not sufficient for his zeal, he superintended the missions of Italy, Scotland, Barbary, and Madagascar; gave retreats to the young men preparing for holy orders, and organized those celebrated ecclesiastical conferences, which have produced so many illustrious bishops and holy personages. Being summoned to the Queen's council, he repaired to the court, in order to establish perfect equity and justice, and to show all the authority which can be exercised by a holy priest, who is only animated with a desire to promote the interests of God.

The moving spirit in all kinds of good works, which charity effected at this period, Vincent de Paul founded the order of the Sisters of Charity for serving the poor and sick; erected the hospitals of Bicêtre, Salpêtrière, Pitié; that of Marseilles for the galley slaves; and the Holy Name of Jesus for the aged and infirm. A zealous protector of virgins consecrated to God, he sustained the institutions of the Daughters of Providence, St. Genevieve and the Holy Cross. St. Vincent succeeded in effecting a reformation in Grammont, Prémontré and the Abbey of St. Genevieve. But an object particularly dear to his heart was the sad condition of so many infants, who, born in vice or misery, were found abandoned by their inhuman parents in the streets and alleys of the capital. Deserted by the whole world, they seemed to have only received life to endure sufferings, or drag out a wretched existence in sorrow and crime. Vincent de Paul could not behold these innocent victims without sentiments of the deepest compassion and tenderness; he commenced his charitable work by rescuing some of these babes, interesting in their behalf the energies of some pious souls, and in a short time the foundling hospital was established and endowed.

While solacing present misfortune, however, he foresaw the wants of the future, and organized the confraternity of the Daughters of Charity, and these worthy children of St. Vincent de Paul, also inherited his sublime charity, for no species of benevolence is unknown to them, and no infirmity or misfortune is unsolaced or uncared for by these holy women. Persons afflicted with the most loathsome diseases, hardened prisoners, destitute orphans, distant islands, foreign lands, nothing can weaken their courage or abate their charity; hastening as they do to comfort misery and wretchedness wherever it may be found. Utterly incapable of such generous devotion, heresy cannot behold the Sisters of Charity without admiration; and its envenomed lips, which utter the most horrible blasphemies against the Church of God, are eloquent in their praise of these truly Christian women. To all these good works performed or directed by St. Vincent de Paul is added the distribution, through his hands, of more than forty million of francs in alms, not only in France but even to the farthest extremity of the world!

Numerous provinces were rescued from the horrors of famine through his watchful care, and the unfortunate found in him a benefactor and father in times of war or of distress. In the midst of the prodigies wrought through his means, St. Vincent was ever poor, humble, and considered himself the least and most unworthy of men. Overcome by age, labor and suffering, he entered into a blessed eternity, on the twenty-seventh of September, 1660, in his eighty-fifth year, bitterly lamented by all, especially the afflicted and unhappy, who had lost an ardent friend and zealous protector; and leaving to posterity a name which is enshrined in the hearts of thousands, who are to-day benefited by his unwearied and indefatigable exertions, in the cause of suffering humanity!

PROGRESS OF THE FAITH IN CHINA, AND THE OTHER COUNTRIES OF THE EARTH.

God does not limit His watchful care to one small portion of the globe; for Jesus Christ, who has died for all mankind, provides every nation with the means of salvation, and leads them to a knowledge of the truth: "Who will have all men to be saved, and to come to the knowledge of truth." (1 Tim., 2, 4.) It is for this end that He has in all ages inspired apostolic men with a desire to carry the light of faith to the most distant nations, buried in the darkness of infidelity.

During this century, a numerous band of holy men devoted themselves to distant missions, one of the most flourishing of which was the Chinese empire. St. Francis Xavier, the Apostle of India and Japan, expiring within sight of this country toward which his zeal was directed, was only able to supplicate the throne of grace for the salvation of its benighted inhabitants. Toward the latter part of the sixteenth century, Father Ricci and two other Jesuits, animated with the same desire to accomplish the conversion of these infidels, succeeded in effecting an entrance within the limits of the empire, by joining some Portuguese merchants who were traveling thither. Ricci, who was well acquainted with the language, laws and customs of this nation, began by exciting admiration through his writings and learning; for it was by mathematics and astronomy that Christianity was introduced, and the influence acquired by missionaries versed in these sciences was the means of propagating the faith in this vast empire. Ricci first obtained permission to settle in Canton, and afterward at Nankin, where his admirers increased rapidly. He built an observatory, and profited by the consideration in which he was held, to announce the Christian religion, of which there scarcely remained the slightest vestige, although it had been preached in this country during the time of the Apostles, and subsequently in the seventh century.

The holy missionary, assisted by his companions, was so happy as to convert several of these infidels, and even some of the mandarins, which prepared the way for his entrance to the capital. He arrived at Pekin in 1600, and won the favor of the Emperor, who allowed him to reside in that city; some pictures of our Lord and the Blessed Virgin, which he presented to this prince, were accepted with pleasure, and placed in a conspicuous position in the palace, and every honor and respect was shown them. The zealous missionary profited by this auspicious beginning, to spread the light of the gospel, the end and aim of all his labors. He succeeded in converting a great number of Chinese, including some of the principal officers of the court; Ricci enjoyed the continual favor of the Emperor, erected a church, planted the germs of Christianity, which soon produced abundant fruit, and terminated his glorious career in 1617.

Father Schall, a Jesuit of Cologne, who was summoned to the imperial court, became the professor of mathematics, and was appointed one of the mandarins. His life was passed in alternate peace and the most violent persecutions; wasted and worn by sufferings, he died in 1666, after having zealously performed the laborious duties of a missionary for the space of forty years. The Religious of different orders, particularly those of St. Dominic, and the secular clergy, associated themselves with the Jesuits in the great work of the propagation of the gospel, and were rewarded with numerous conversions. Their success excited the envy of the bonzas, and several mandarins, who began a persecution; but the ardor of these laborers in the service of God, and the fervor of the converts, were only augmented by this painful trial.

Toward the end of the seventeenth century a revolution placed on the throne the dynasty of the Tartar princes, who during the remainder of this century were favorable to the Christians. Churches were erected throughout the whole empire, in honor of the one true God, and a magnificent temple built within the precincts of the imperial palace. The harvest was so abundant that the number of missionaries were insufficient for the work; but the courage, zeal, and activity, of this little band supplied the deficiency, and they carried the light of faith into the most remote portions of this vast empire. During the century, God raised up other apostolic men, who announced the glad tidings of the gospel on the coasts of Africa, in Egypt, Greece, the Levant, and throughout nearly the whole continent of America.

From the sixteenth century, missionaries visited all parts of the Western hemisphere, and while civilizing the people by instructing them in the true faith, used every effort to repair the ravages which ambition and the love of gold had made in the New World. We cannot but admire the zeal of these missionaries, who were not deterred by the ferocity of savage tribes, long journeys, strange climates, the dangers and hardships of sea voyages, or foreign and unknown tongues. They have braved the deep snows of the North, the burning sands of the South; the pride of civilized nations, such as the Chinese; the ignorance and stupidity of the Indians in America, and have often been exposed to frightful perils, and even death itself, while exercising the functions of the holy ministry.

It is evident that no human or interested motives are capable of inspiring such extraordinary courage; that it is only Christian zeal and supernatural charity which can infuse such noble sentiments into the hearts of Catholic priests, who have won more and greater triumphs than the most renowned of earthly conquerors. If these heroic men had not commenced to direct the route of navigators, and made the most important discoveries, the largest portion of the globe would be still unknown. Christianity is, therefore, victorious over every obstacle; always universal in not being confined to any particular country, but is spread through all parts of the known world, gaining everywhere believers and followers. Like a great tree planted, as St. Paul says, on the Apostles and prophets, and on Jesus Christ, who is the corner stone, she continually produces new branches, which flourish in the most arid soil and bears abundant fruit.

THE CAUSES OF INFIDELITY.

The despairing doctrines of Calvin and Luther touching predestination, free will and grace, caused the most disastrous consequences. Calvin made God the author of sin; as is testified by Bolsec, an apostate Carmelite monk, and Luther professed the most anarchical principles in his work on Christian Liberty. These pretended reformers, who revived the errors of the Albigenses and other heretics, as injurious to the welfare of governments, as hurtful to the true religion, excited in the minds of men a spirit of unbelief and insubordination. Their pernicious teachings produced the Socinians; the Deists approved of the creed and followed in the footsteps of the Socinians, and from this desire of change sprang the infidelity which prevails at the present day.

It was from the bosom of Protestantism, that in England there arose Hobbes, Tholand, Woolston,

Tindall, and so many others, who openly taught the most impious doctrines. Spinoza and Bayle appeared in Holland; one of whom established deism, or rather materialism; and the other proclaims in all his works a skepticism which caused him to say that "he was really a Protestant; since he protested against every religion;" but Catholicity was the principal object of all his attacks. These men can be regarded as the first of those writers who afterward in every country repeated and inculcated their sophisms under plausible forms.

But the principal support of infidelity was the conduct of the Duke of Orleans, regent of France during the minority of Louis XV. It seemed as if God manifested His wrath against this nation, when death removed the Dauphin, the father of Louis XV, and the pupil of Fenelon, a prince who inspired fond hopes of a prosperous and religious reign; and also when the father of Louis XVI was snatched from the useful career he was pursuing, the Church and State both suffered from his untimely loss. It was especially during the regency of the Duke of Orleans, that infidelity, until then fearful of exposure, began to extend and glory in its pernicious doctrines, which menaced the destruction of society as well as the ruin of religion. The palace of the regent was the resort of the wits and learned men of the day; it was within its precincts that they perpetrated their epigrams and ridiculed the most sacred things and persons most worthy of honor and reverence; and from its walls issued those sarcastic and irreligious speeches which circulated through the capital and provinces.

The regent was regarded as the protector of these unbelievers, who took the name of philosophers, and openly approved of the most shameful license, which began in the palace and spread through the entire kingdom. They began by publishing anonymous pamphlets and short essays; a lingering vestige of shame preventing them from prefixing their names to these articles, as the nation was still attached to the religion established by Jesus Christ. It was not until 1751 that Prades, a priest and member of the Sorbonne, dared to defend a thesis regarded as the first public assault of infidelity against the Church. Diderot, one of the most violent advocates of this philosophy, had assisted him in the composition of this work, which was a synopsis of all the impious creeds of the pretended freethinkers.

During this same year, appeared the two first volumes of the Encyclopedical dictionary, a huge compilation which, according to the prospectus, claimed to be the most complete receptacle of all human knowledge, and a perfect library in itself; in reality, however, it was only the depositary of all the errors, sophisms, and calumnies, which, from the earliest ages, heresy had uttered against religion; being, in short, an arsenal of infidelity. This Encyclopedia, by dint of influential supporters, and the laudations and praises of all the papers belonging to their party, soon became a popular book; and the learned men of the day gradually became tinctured by this pernicious work, which was evidently the end and aim of its unprincipled authors.

Voltaire, who derided every precept of morality,

had sworn to consecrate his life to the destruction of the Christian religion; he was then in the zenith of his genius. He boldly attacked the Catholic faith in a number of writings, wielding the pen of ridicule with the malice of a demon, and adorning his sophisms with a brilliancy of expression that dazzled the imagination, while it blinded the intellects of his readers. The wide-spread perusal of his insidious and impious works rendered Voltaire undeservedly famous, and attracted a great number of proselytes. Learned and able writers, however, immediately hastened to unmask his errors, and, while victoriously refuting his infidel creed, demonstrated the undeniable and unimpeachable truths of religion, and so forcible are their arguments, that these dangerous books can only influence those who embrace this philsophy, on account of the license it allows their passions, and the freedom it gives them from all moral restraint. Infidelity rejects revelation, ridicules tradition, and calumniates the religion established more than eighteen hundred years ago by Jesus Christ Himself.

SECRET SOCIETIES.
A. D. 1725.

The eighteenth century, so fruitful in errors, also beheld the origin and extension of those secret associations and clandestine assemblies known under the name of Free Masonry. England, which had cast abroad the first seeds of infidelity, was the birthplace of the founder of this dangerous society. An

English lord in 1721 established in Paris the first French lodge, and a few years afterward several existed in the capital and provinces.

In the beginning, these associations did not appear suspicious, and no great importance was attached to the secret of the initiated; but, soon, circumstances aroused the vigilance of the authorities, and very shortly alarming revelations were communicated to the government. It was proved, that among the Free Masons there were men who meditated the ruin of the State and Church; that they were bound by the most frightful oaths; their designs being kept from members whose acquiescence was doubtful. Secret societies were, therefore, proscribed in several countries; Clement XII and Benedict XIV, condemning them under pain of excommunication. These vigorous measures, which seemed sufficient to arrest the incipient evil, only served to spread the contagion, and perhaps impelled it more forcibly toward crime and rebellion; in fact, from this period the most influential and conspicuous characters during the revolution were the warmest advocates of secret societies. Voltaire, Condorcet, Bonneville, Lalande and Volney, the moving spirits of the great political changes; Mirabeau, Chapelier and Fauchet, all belonged to the highest ranks of Free Masonry.

Struck by the wonders it pretended to conceal, and the mysterious trials and absurd ceremonies through which the initiated are obliged to pass, several authors carefully examined this organization, and collected a number of facts, showing its dangerous tendency, and have ascertained by their researches the true spirit and real end of Free Masonry. All the members were not admitted to a knowledge of what transpired in the society, the initiated alone being cognizant of the secret plans and proceedings. Although some of the writers who undertook to unveil the mystery of these assemblies are not altogether reliable, still there are enough undisputed facts extant, to excite distrust and suspicion of Free Masonry. "In short," says an author, "when it is remembered that it was originated by a spirit of irreligion and impiety, and has only extended in proportion as infidelity has increased; that it has never been embraced by any but indifferent and unbelieving persons, and always condemned by sincere Christians, it must be regarded as a dangerous institution, in its nature and consequences."

This opinion is stregthened when the profound secrecy is considered, and the absurd importance attached to its solemn observance. If the end is praiseworthy, what occasion can there be for so much mystery? Why are unlawful and unnecessary oaths imposed on the members? What justifies their theory of knowledge and ignorance, and of what use are their extraordinary trials and ridiculous ceremonies? Has it not been clearly proved that the Masons are the staunch supporters of philosophy, men who by their ideas of liberty and equality excite revolutions, foster a disgust of authority, and engender a spirit of insurbordination?

The entire Catholic world has always manifested its earnest disapproval of these mysterious organizations, which sound governments discountenance as severely as religion condemns them. Pious Catholics are never members of secret societies, and the most lenient judgment which can be passed upon those who frequent such assemblies is, that they are attracted thither, not through religious conviction, but through a desire for liberty of action, and perfect freedom from the wholesome restraints of Christian society.

PROGRESS OF INFIDELITY.
A. D. 1752.

After having shown the origin and principal causes of infidelity, we will proceed to show its rapid progress and disastrous effects. It was toward the middle of the last century that the modern philosophers, until then timid, and only venturing occasionally to utter a few sarcasms against the mysteries of religion, emerged from their obscurity, and proclaimed, without the least shame, the most frightful impieties. For some years, it is true, they had made several attacks upon religion; a few men, without morals or faith, had dared even to attack the pure doctrine and consoling dogmas of Christianity, but were immediately silenced by public opinion; they succeeded only in attracting a few persons of position and wealth, who affected to believe nothing, in order to give free license to their passions. The common people had not yet learned to despise the faith of their fathers, or to trample under foot all that is most sacred and holy in religion.

At the period we have mentioned, however, the

spirit of sophistry had spread through the lowest ranks of society; it extended on every side like a rushing torrent, and promulgated abroad its pernicious doctrines. Voltaire, the leader and chief of the free-thinkers of his time, was the first to throw off all restraint, respecting neither the altar nor the throne, and pouring forth the most shameful sarcasms and dreadful blasphemies. As soon as the signal was given, the new philosophy took possession of the public mind, inundated the capital and the provinces with a perfect deluge of bad books, suited to all ages, sexes, and conditions; corrupt men were bribed to introduce them gratuitously into colleges and country places, and every means were used for a universal diffusion of its poisonous and frightful doctrines. Impiety assumed every hue, and appeared under every imaginable form; was reproduced in a thousand different ways, and attacked Christianity sometimes with ridicule, and again by the most glaring falsehoods. It incited subjects against their kings, and children against their parents and families, and openly inculcated immorality and insubordination.

During this reign of profligacy and impiety, if any defense was undertaken in behalf of religion, immediately violent satires and malicious epigrams assailed the writer with ridicule. If, on the other hand, Christianity was attacked with violence, Voltaire would write a flattering letter to d'Alembert, laud him up to the societies, and a man entirely destitute of genius was suddenly transformed into a great writer. Thus, in a few years, philosophy succeeded in changing the mind and character of a great nation, substituted a frivolous taste in place of a desire for knowledge, fostered egotism in society, destroyed the ties which unite men to each other and to their country, and inspired each individual with an insatiable thirst for gold, thus transforming the most generous and disinterested of nations into a people almost devoid of loyalty. Nevertheless, in the midst of the overthrow of all morality and principle, Christianity has had in every age illustrious defenders, and saints of eminent sanctity and great virtue.

At that period the French court exhibited models of most exemplary piety; the Queen and her children, although surrounded with grandeur and magnificence, imitated the edifying lives of the first Christians, and Madame Louise, her royal daughter, preferred the holy poverty of the cloister to the splendor of a crown. This princess entered the Carmelite convent of St. Denis, where she lived for many years in the practice of the most heroic virtues, submitted to all the requirements of an austere rule, obedient to the voice of a simple Religious, and only distinguished from her companions by a more sublime piety and a more profound humility. While such examples consoled the afflicted hearts of the faithful, the Pope and the French priests showed themselves full of ardor and zeal in repressing the license of the authors, who were enemies to order and morality.

We can mention with honor M. De Beaumont, archbishop of Paris, so justly called the Athanasius of his age; M. De Pompignan, bishop of Puy, who ardently opposed infidelity; and M. Dulau, archbishop of Arles, who deserved to shed his blood for the faith he had so often and so nobly defended. By their side can be placed numbers of priests, who, by the sancity of their lives and their learned writings, avenged religion and silenced her adversaries. Among these was Bergier, the author of "Deism Refuted by Itself," "The Assured Proofs of Christianity," "The Apology of the Christian Religion," etc.; the Abbe Guenee, who, in "Letters of some Portuguese Jews to Voltaire," unites the force of incontestable argument to the most charming wit, and compelled even his opponent to express his admiration of his ability as a writer; Bullet, who may be regarded as one of the ablest apologists of the Catholic faith; Feller, Gerard, Barruel, and a host of others, whose writings are found in almost every library.

But the combined efforts of so many great minds to arrest the progress of infidelity could not recall the people to the pure faith and morality of their forefathers. The evil was too great, the bait too attractive, and error had taken too strong a hold; nothing would save a people who had been taught to disbelieve in the existence of God. It was necessary that in the abyss of misfortune into which they had precipitated themselves they should discover their folly, and acknowledge, that, when separated from God, there can be no true liberty or real happiness for nations or individuals.

THE SUPPRESSION OF THE JESUITS.
A. D. 1773.

The suppression of the Jesuits was the commencement of the long train of disastrous events which for many years fill the pages of history; and philosophy, having deprived the Church of zealous defenders, seemed already to prepare herself for great conquests, and therefore reposed on the ruin she had made. The Jesuits, who were appointed by the government to teach and defend religion, combated with an energy and success worthy of all praise, against heresy and infidelity. Their learned works strengthened the faith of Catholics against the impious productions of modern infidels, and their zeal sustained the faithful when violently attacked by these enemies of Christianity.

Such powerful claims on the gratitude and esteem of mankind excited the implacable hatred of the adversaries of religion, who resolved on their destruction. Corrupt ministers prejudiced the minds of weak and ignorant princes, and the persecution then commenced against the Jesuits. Portugal was the first country to begin the shameful work. At this court there was a wicked wretch who succeeded in gaining the confidence of the king, and was thereby enabled to vent his anger and hatred upon these innocent yet dreaded victims. He commenced by spreading throughout Europe a multitude of libels, charging the Jesuits with the blackest crimes. He accused them of being accomplices to a conspiracy against the king, his master, and petitioned the sovereign Pontiff to suppress the order.

The Pope refusing to comply with this request, the Marquis of Pombal proscribed them throughout Portugal, surrounded their houses with soldiers, who arrested them and cast them into dungeons, from which they were soon dragged to be crowded on board of vessels, which left them, entirely destitute, on the coasts of the Roman states. Spain in a short time followed this example, and France hastened to drive these soldiers of the cross, these companions of the reviled and persecuted Jesus, from her dominions. "Their rules," said the bishop, in a remonstrance addressed to the king in 1772, "had been submitted to parliament, and, after a slight examination, had been condemned." Without listening to their defense or attending to their requests, their rules were declared impious, sacrilegious, opposed to all laws human and divine; and, under the pretext of their having committed crimes, their colleges were closed, their novitiates destroyed, their property confiscated, and their vows annulled. They were deprived of the privileges of their vocation, and driven from the retreats they had chosen.

Proscribed, humiliated, neither citizens nor Religious, without country or possessions, forbidden to exercise the functions of the holy ministry, they were either obliged to become exiles, or sign oaths, which their consciences condemned. These persecutions and insults did not satisfy the enemies of the Jesuits; they desired to obtain their general suppression from the sovereign Pontiff. The Roman Church possessed, in different kingdoms, lands which had been donated by pious kings to the Holy See; these were now confiscated, and the foreign ambassadors, at the Roman court, declared that they would not be restored until there were no more Jesuits; that their entire suppression was the only means of re-establishing union and concord between the Holy See and foreign powers. Clement XIV hesitated, and considered the subject for a long time, and earnestly endeavored to save the persecuted Religious; but, finally, overcome by urgent and pressing misrepresentations, he issued, on the 21st of July, 1773, a brief, which suppressed the Society of Jesus.

Thus was abolished a celebrated institution which had existed for more than two centuries, and which counted nearly twenty thousand Religious, devoted to the arduous duties of teaching, giving missions, and practicing every good work. When an impartial and unprejudiced mind coolly examines the cause of the suppression of the Jesuits, and considers that their enemies were the enemies of the Church and religion; that the crimes imputed to them are destitute of proof, or even the appearance of truth, and when it is proved that these false allegations refer only to a few members, and not to the entire body, whose doctrines and morals were always pure, and finally, when he remembers the services they have rendered the Church, the benefits of education they have procured for many kingdoms, the knowledge and learning they have disseminated, the spirit of piety they have diffused, he must be amazed at the malice that persecuted these admirable men, without a hearing or an examination, and he will be uncertain whether to compassionate those whose glory could not be tarnished by the unjust hatred of so many enemies, or the men who did not perceive that they were condemning virtue and dishonoring merit.

THE TEMPORAL POWER OF THE SOVEREIGN PONTIFF ATTACKED.

The suppression of the Jesuits had been demanded as the only means of re-establishing peace between the Church and the opposing sovereigns, but it became, instead, the signal of discord and revolt against the Holy See. On all sides, pamphlets and libels were launched against the chair of St. Peter; violent and unprincipled men denied its rights, despised its authority, and were not ashamed to repeat the language and revive the errors of Luther and Calvin. In Germany particularly, these dangerous opinions were embraced by many, and several universities imbibed a system of anarchy and revolt against the Church from the perusal of the poisonous works of Febronius. Joseph II, the son and successor of Maria Theresa, countenanced these novelties, and made changes in the discipline of the Church, which nearly terminated in a schism.

Christian schools were superseded by normal schools, and instead of the old chairs of theology, they established general seminaries, independent of the bishops, and appointed, by a special commission, professors infected with all the new errors. A great number of religious houses were suppressed, and others released from their vow of obedience to their superior general. The reform did not stop here; it had been written and published that the bishops were independent of the Pope, and that they could grant dispensations from the general laws of the Church; one of the opposing princes commanded the prelates to confirm this doctrine, and several bishops were weak enough to obey this order. Alarmed at the danger which threatened the afflicted Church, Pius VI addressed several briefs to the bishops and princes, entreating them not to destroy the unity of the Church of God, but his voice was unheeded; he then formed a sudden resolution, and announced to the Emperor his intention of visiting Vienna.

Joseph II received him with respect, and treated him with the consideration due to himself and to his office, and was even induced to modify some of his edicts. Pius VI then left the imperial court, and returned to Rome, distressed at the unsuccessful result of his journey, but consoled by the marks of attachment and respect shown him by the people. Hardly had the sovereign Pontiff returned to his dominions when the schism which for several years had threatened Germany seemed about to break forth. The Emperor, by his new laws, permitted divorces in certain cases, constituted himself a judge in matters of faith, and encroached still more on the rights of the Church. This example was followed by several of the bishops, who desired also to usurp certain essential and inherent privileges of the Holy See.

The three ecclesiastical electors and the Archbishop of Saltzburg united in contesting with the sovereign Pontiff the right of sending nuncios abroad, only reserving for his Holiness the prerogative of dispensations in a few grave and important cases. They convened a congress at Ems, near Coblentz, where four ecclesiastics, who were invested with authority, organized a kind of ecclesiastical constitution, which only left the Vicar of Jesus Christ a vain and empty title of honor, and transformed those who had deputed them into so many Popes.

About the same period an Italian bishop revolted against the Holy See, and embraced the so often condemned errors. Ricci, bishop of Pistoia and of Prato, assembled a synod, and, transforming his friends into judges of the faith, he forced them to frame laws which destroyed the whole hierarchy of the Church, her discipline and her government. In this convention all the changes made by Joseph II and the metropolitan bishops of the German empire were adopted, and Ricci arrogated to himself the power of dispensing even in cases referred to the sovereign Pontiff alone. Thus every thing tended toward a schism, and Catholicity was threatened with a fatal division, when a general outcry arose in Germany, from whence all these troubles had come, against the changes which were being introduced. The archbishop of Malines had the courage to carry his remonstrance to the foot of the throne, to denounce the danger of these innovations, and to predict the disastrous consequences which would ensue to Church and state.

Joseph II, against whom a party of his subjects,

wearied with these continued disturbances, had revolted, finally acknowledged the justness of the archbishop's remonstrance, and the wickedness of the advice he had followed. The evils which had already resulted from the changes he had attempted to introduce throughout his vast dominions struck him with consternation. He accordingly, before his death, which happened shortly after, published an edict revoking and annulling all the previous laws relating to ecclesiastical matters.

The Pope, informed by the Emperor himself of this unexpected step, wrote a most touching brief to the bishops of Germany, in order to put a final stop to the troubles by which their provinces had been disturbed, and thus terminated the strife which had menaced the Church with so sad a disunion. Hardly, however, had she recovered peace on one side, than from a kingdom, which had not taken any part in the dispute she had just succeeded in quieting, arose a frightful tempest which nearly accomplished her destruction. From dreadful trials and continual combats, we see the Church emerge triumphant, manifesting plainly in her endurance and victories the divine hand which sustained her.

PRELUDE AND BEGINNING OF THE FRENCH REVOLUTION.

A. D. 1789.

From the time of the fatal regency of Philip of Orleans, during which immorality and irreligion had made such rapid progress, a spirit of restlessness and universal agitation was felt everywhere. The new doctrines which a weak government had allowed to be spread abroad, advancing principles of a so-called independence and liberty, had enfeebled the respect and love which subjects should entertain toward their sovereigns. On all sides an excessive love for the new order of things was affected, extreme aversion for old institutions, and a public hatred for religion. This condition of affairs brought forth numerous works in favor of liberty, many discourses against ancient laws and customs, and innumerable pamphlets against the faith and the ministers of religion.

Terrified at the approaching storm, which threatened to swallow up every thing, wise and learned men strove to arrest its progress. They warned the king of the danger, and the French clergy, in one of their last assemblies, listened to these remarkable words: "A few more years of silence, and the conflagration will become general — nothing will be left but ruins." In fact, the moment had arrived when unlimited power was given to the spirit of darkness, when impiety should trample upon the saving maxims of religion. Cries of revolt and sedition resounded on every side, with the entire abandonment of all restraint, and incessant demands for perfect liberty of action. These murmurs and demands arose in favor of the pretended reformers; essays on the servitude under which the people groaned were published, and they succeeded in obtaining an entire emancipation from, and revocation of, the edict of Nantes, which banished all the ministers, but not all the Protestants, as has been affirmed.

This joint victory gained, a slight embarrassment in the finances was seized as a pretext for complaining still more loudly of the government. A general assembly was convened, in the hope of relieving the deficiency in the public treasury; but they soon repented of a convention which intelligent men justly dreaded. In fine, hardly had the states-general assembled, when the enemies of order no longer disguised their plans. They demanded, and they obtained that they should not act in a body as in the preceding assemblies, but that the ranks should be destroyed and single votes substituted.

By this proceeding the third estate secured the majority, as it was more numerous than the clergy and nobility united. Thus the first result of the violation of the ancient usages was the triumph of the faction who ruled over the assemblies, and who commenced their exercise of power by issuing the most injurious decrees against the Church and religion. They declared, first, that the ecclesiastical property belonged to the state, and that the monastic vows were provisionally suspended; shortly afterward they put up for sale four hundred million francs' worth of the possessions of the Church, and suppressed all the religious orders. The bishops vainly expostulated against these violent measures, but their voices were unheeded, and their remonstrances of no avail. Anarchy daily increased; blood began to flow, and the factions, proud of their triumphs, promised themselves still greater success.

In the national assembly an ecclesiastical committee had been formed to attend to the affairs of the clergy, but it was almost entirely composed of lawyers not at all in favor of the principles of the Church; this committee drew up a plan of reform, based on the doctrines in which they had been educated. First, they reduced the one hundred and thirty-five bishoprics which existed in France, to eighty, the number of the new departments. They abolished sees, without establishing others; suppressed chapters, abbeys, priories, chapels, and church livings. They decreed that the new bishops should be under the jurisdiction of the metropolitan, or oldest bishop in the province, and not of the Pope, as was the ancient discipline of the Church, being only obliged to write to the Pope in testimony of their communion with the Holy See. They enjoined that the choice of the bishops and priests should be confided to the electoral colleges, and that the vicars should be chosen by the pastors from among the priests ordained or admitted into the diocese, without having recourse to the approbation of the bishop. Finally, they particularly specified that the bishops could not exercise any act of jurisdiction in any thing concerning the government of the diocese, without having conferred with the Episcopal vicars, who thus found themselves invested with a portion of the Episcopal jurisdiction.

Such were the principal articles of the civil constitution of the clergy, which undermined the very foundation of the authority of the Church; deprived her of the right she had always preserved of self-government; regulated her discipline, appointed bishops, and determined the extent of their dioceses.

Scarcely had this constitution been published and sanctioned by the national assembly, when it was universally denounced as contrary to the rights of the Church, her hierarchy and discipline. Submission to its decrees was refused on all sides, and out of one hundred and thirty-five bishops, four only received it, and agreed to abide by its decisions.

Irritated at encountering so much resistance, the assembly proclaimed that all the ecclesiastics who in eight days did not take an oath of fidelity to the civil constitution should be regarded as having renounced the ministry. The Church had the mortification to see some of her ministers, who were carried away by novelty, or beguiled by cunning deceivers, take the oath and submit to the new law; but she was much consoled by the greater number who refused submission, and preferred banishment, persecution, the loss of their parishes, rather than betray their faith. These martyrs were immediately suspended from the ministry, and replaced by those who were willing to take the oath. Thus terminated for a time this deplorable schism, which desolated the Church during those awful days of revolution and terror.

PROGRESS OF THE REVOLUTION—DEATH OF LOUIS XVI.

A. D. 1793.

After destroying the royal authority, causing trouble and division in the Church, suppressing all the religious orders, and depriving the clergy of all their rights, the national or constitutional assembly terminated its sessions, and was replaced by the legislative assembly, whose first deliberations announced the fate reserved for royalty and the Religious. The old decrees against priests who refused to take the oath were renewed; and very soon, these measures appearing insufficient, they were no longer treated with moderation, but condemned to banishment.

The publication of these laws was the signal for a universal persecution throughout France against the priests who remained faithful to the Church. They were driven from their parishes, stoned by the mob, or else ruthlessly massacred; the most severe measures were used to prevent their escaping either exile or death. Four hundred were imprisoned at Laval, and in the large cities, special prisons were built to receive the numerous priests who were arrested; the ruffians dragged the nuns from their convents, and drove the Religious from their cloisters, and the assembly, far from reprimanding these arbitrary acts, prepared to perpetrate still greater crimes. As soon as they felt secure in their power, the assembly adopted the most violent measures, and these succeeded each other with fearful rapidity, and new outrages were but the prelude to horrors which were to reflect irreparable disgrace upon this unhappy country.

Louis XVI was attacked in the Tuilleries, his faithful Swiss Guard massacred before his eyes, and he was obliged to fly, in order to escape the furious brutality of a populace thirsting for blood and plunder. His only resource was to appeal to the assembly, and rely on the mercy of the factions. When the king entered the hall, these savage representatives, instead of compassionating his sorrows, reproached him with the blood which was flowing in all parts of the kingdom, and they deprived him of all his royal privileges. The unfortunate king was immediately arrested, and conducted to a tower in the Temple, accompanied by his wife, children and sister. At the same time the list of proscription was issued, containing the names of those who remained faithful to their religion and their king, and hundreds of victims were thrown into prison. They did not remain long in their loathsome dungeons. On the second of September, the massacre of the condemned commenced, and lasted four entire days; more than fourteen thousand prisoners were put to death during this short period. Over five hundred priests were beheaded at the Carmelite Monastery, at the Abbey and at St. Firmin, and shortly afterward, three bishops and a great number of priests were murdered at Meaux, Versailles, Chalons, Rheims, etc.

During these days of terror, the most frightful scenes of barbarity were enacted; executioners danced and sang around their expiring victims, they even drank the blood which flowed from the gaping wounds their murderous hands had inflicted, and marched about the city in triumph, carrying with them the mangled remains. In the midst of these dreadful outrages, the legislative assembly declared its mission accomplished, and gave place to the convention which terminated the revolution.

The very day of its opening it abolished royalty, proclaimed France a republic, and in a spirit of fury and revenge declared that Louis XVI was guilty and should appear before the deputies of the nation, in order to exculpate himself from the crimes imputed to him. The unfortunate monarch was only allowed a few days to prepare some means of defense; at the appointed time he appeared before the convention, and was treated as the greatest of criminals.

After the expiration of several days, during which his case was debated, the most exemplary of kings listened to the sentence which condemned him to death as a tyrant who had mercilessly oppressed his subjects. Louis XVI was executed on the twenty-first of January, 1793, and his death was the signal for the most horrible massacres. France was inundated with blood; neither rank, age nor sex escaping the dreadful carnage. Whole cities were bombarded, and thousands of citizens perished at the same time.

While the party of the revolutionists spread consternation and death through all parts of the kingdom, the convention abolished the Christian religion, and proclaimed the worship of Reason; they celebrated in the Cathedral of Notre Dame the first feast of this impious devotion. A profligate actress, seated on the altar of the God of chastity, received the homage of the infatuated multitude, calling herself the queen of the gods. The entire kingdom imitated the example of the capital; profane festivals replaced the sacred solemnities of Christianity, and sacrilegious worship was paid to whatever was contrary to virtue. The abominations of paganism were revived by an enlightened people, and the Christian religion, proscribed and banished, was almost without an asylum in the land so richly endowed with favors and blessings from the hand of God.

Every religious exercise was prohibited, the churches desecrated and abandoned to plunder, the consecrated vessels broken and trodden under foot, and the sacred vestments dragged through the streets, These acts of impiety were among the favorite amusements of the populace. The statues and pictures of the saints were destroyed and mutilated; the cross dishonored, and the asylums of charity demolished. The whole kingdom was soon a scene of desolation and ruin. These days of horror produced still greater crimes, and witnessed still more shameful defections. Twenty-seven bishops, appointed by virtue of the famous civil constitution of the clergy of which we have spoken, abjured the faith, and renounced the ministry of the Catholic worship; some even united to their apostacy the most revolting habits, and were not ashamed to disgrace their august office by a sacrilegious marriage.

We will not dwell longer on this sorrowful period, but endeavor to forget the excesses and outrages of this unhappy time, and admire the watchful Providence that has sustained the Church through so many storms, and brought her triumphant through such severe trials. After a violent tempest, He commanded the waters to abate their fury, and peace and serenity was restored.

PIUS VI ARRESTED AND CARRIED TO FRANCE.

France, entirely given up to the horrors of anarchy, had become the prey of a new government, which, under the title of the Directory, was the cause of new troubles, and spread abroad the evils of which she was the victim, and her victorious armies carried with them to the conquered provinces their fatal doctrines. A large part of Italy having been surrendered by its generals, the Directory hastened to change its form of government, to proscribe religion, and to promulgate the destructive principles which, for many years, had occasioned so much evil. Rome, however, was the principal object of the ambitious desires of these wicked enemies of the Christian faith, and it seemed a very great cause of triumph to be able to issue their decrees of banishment and proscription from the very stronghold of Catholicity. The armies of the Republic therefore marched toward Rome, preceded by manifestoes and proclamations, promising the people happiness and liberty, and charging the Pontifical government with outrage and oppression.

Without an army, destitute of assistance, and menaced by a speedy invasion, Pius VI negotiated, through the Spanish ambassador, with the Directory, and obtained, by great sacrifices, an armistice, which was very soon violated. The French troops advanced within the limits of the Papal States, and marched directly to Rome, when General Bonaparte, their commander, hearing that the Austrians were approaching, opened a correspondence with the archbishop of Ferrara, the legate of the Holy See. The Pope, who only asked for peace, agreed to all the conditions proposed. Unfortunately, this treaty was of no longer continuance than the preceding one; the death of a Republican general, assassinated in the midst of an insurrection which he helped to excite, was the pretext for breaking the recently established union. The Papal ambassador was arrested at Paris, and the French troops were ordered to invade the States of the Church.

They advanced without the slightest resistance, proclaimed the Republic and the abolition of the Papal government. General Bonaparte, however, assured the Pope that he should be respected and acknowledged as the bishop of Rome. These promises were soon forgotten, and the night of the nineteenth of February, fifteen days only after the entrance of the French army into the capital of the Christian world, Pius VI was seized and dragged from Rome. A number of cardinals and bishops shared the same fate, and a military government, which exacted heavy contributions from the people, replaced the peaceful sway of the Vicar of Jesus Christ.

The head of the Church, a captive, despoiled of all his rank and dignity, was led from one place of exile to another; the venerable old man, whose virtues and age entitled him to respect, underwent the most barbarous treatment for the remainder of his life; he was separated from all that was dear to him, and exiled to distant countries without the least regard for his age, infirmities, or the inclemency of the season. On arriving in France, Pius

VI was conducted to Grenoble, where he remained for a few days, and where, notwithstanding the hatred of his enemies, he had the consolation of seeing the people hastening in crowds to meet him, and ask for his blessing, which they received with the greatest devotion. On being removed to Valence, he was seized with a sudden faintness and prostration, which terminated in his death. He expired on the twenty-ninth of August, 1799, at the advanced age of eighty-two years, after presiding over the Holy See for more than twenty-four years.

Such was the end of this courageous and holy Pontiff, whose reign was disturbed by so many trials and reverses. His virtues and misfortunes entitled him to the esteem of the Protestants themselves, and Mallet du Pan, a citizen of Geneva, in his journal of the twenty-fifth of May, 1799, thus speaks of his captivity: "Of all the barbarous acts of injustice which compose the history of the French revolution, I do not know if there is one which excites so much indignation as the cold-blooded and systematic conduct of the Directory toward the sovereign Pontiff. His cruel treatment deserves the name of assassination; there would have been less inhumanity in delivering the white head of Pius VI to the axe of the executioner, than to cover it with insults and outrages; drag him from his plundered palace into captivity in a strange land; lead him from prison to prison, allowing him to live, in order to inflict on him still greater indignities and sufferings. And on whom did they practice this horrible violence? on an old man, standing on the threshold of eternity; on a pontiff, whose moderation, meekness, unostentatious and sincere piety, have won the respect of denominations separated from the Church of Rome; on a sovereign without a kingdom, deprived of his rightful power, abandoned by those who should have defended him. Plundered, dethroned, and imprisoned, without having inflicted the slightest wrong on his enemies, what had they to fear from his weakness? What satisfaction or advantage could they derive from such wanton cruelties? How could they injure this dying Pope, whose death or absence would not influence the fate of either Church or State? Was it a hostage they wished to secure, or did the fanaticism of philosophy induce them to add to the number of martyrs whom they had immolated, the chief of a religion they were eager to destroy?"

ELECTION OF A NEW POPE—THE CONCORDAT.

Pius VI was no more, and the princes of the Church, and those whose office it was to elect the Vicar of Jesus Christ, were either scattered abroad or in captivity, and could not meet to give the Church a Pontiff and Rome a King, worthy of them both. When suddenly He who said to the raging waters, "Thus far shalt thou go and no further"— arrested the hand that was inflicting sorrow and distress on nations, stopped the successful career of the French troops, and made the very people who had long since separated themselves from the one, true fold, serve as a triumph to the Church. The French were driven from Rome and Italy, and the Emperor of Germany convened the cardinals for the purpose of electing a successor to Pius VI. They assembled at Venice, formed the conclave, and, after a sufficiently long deliberation, the choice fell on Cardinal Barnabas Chiaramonte, who took the name of Pius VII.

The new Pope commenced his pontifical reign by wise and honorable measures; he hastened to re-establish order in the government of the Roman Church, issued a brief in favor of the Jesuits, whom some princes had allowed to remain in their dominions; and entered at once into a negotiation with the new French government with regard to ecclesiastical affairs. Cardinal Spina repaired to Paris for this purpose, and on the fifteenth of July, 1801, concluded a treaty with the first consul of the Republic. The treaty was not immediately published; it was deemed necessary, at first, to interpose powerful obstacles against its ratification. A part of the legislative body were still strongly opposed to religion, and they relied on the efforts of the constitutional church, which had met in council, to sustain a schism which was springing up on every side.

The first consul, who at that time seemed sincerely anxious to re-establish religion, overcame every difficulty; he convoked a legislative assembly which was favorable to religion and morality, and notified the Constitutionals to disperse. The Concordat was then submitted to the deliberation of the legislative chamber, and adopted as a law of the state. Two papal bulls were published at the same time: the first, explained and ratified the agreement made with the French government; the second, suppressed all the dioceses in France, and created in their stead sixty new ones, divided into ten archbishoprics. Before issuing these bulls, Pius VII had addressed a brief to the French bishops, requesting the resignation of their sees. Out of eighty-one bishops who were still living, forty-five immediately acquiesced, and thirty-six expressed their regret at being unable to follow this example; after a time, however, many of them returned to their allegiance, and submitted to the commands of the Pontiff.

As soon as the Concordat was proclaimed, the exercise of public worship was resumed. The first ceremony took place at Notre Dame, on Easter Sunday; the cardinal legate celebrated the mass; the three consuls, and the legislative body were present. A Te Deum was sung in thanksgiving for the happy change, and for the restoration of Catholicity. Tranquillity, peace and confidence were resumed. The pastors of the churches hastened to leave the strange lands where they had endured a weary exile, and re-appeared among their flocks. France gradually became once more a Christian nation, destroyed the temple of Reason, and abolished the feasts of the Supreme Being.

They re-established the asylums of charity; the teaching of Christian doctrine was resumed, and several of the monasteries were re-opened. The priests traversed the cities and country places instructing the people, and striving to rekindle the nearly extinguished spark of faith in their hearts, and if the Concordat had not been productive of other good results, its opponents would have respected it for this cause alone. But France was not the sovereign Pontiff's only object of solicitude; the churches of Piedmont, Italy and Germany also occupied his attention, and he hastened to provide them with pastors, to re-establish discipline, and to restore the faith which the disastrous events of the late wars had banished and prohibited.

BONAPARTE.

While the Church was engaged in repairing the evils caused by the late disturbances, a man, whose great ambition and wonderful success, at the head of the French troops, had won him honor and distinction, received the title of Emperor. Too happy to escape the terrors of anarchy, France felt as though she had returned to the beautiful days of her ancient glory, and hoped for a time that the warrior whom she had placed at the head of her government would resemble her first sovereigns; but these fond expectations were doomed to disappointment. Europe, exhausted and worn out by long wars, acknowledged the new Emperor, and the sovereign Pontiff was compelled, for the welfare of religion, to obey the command he received, to repair to Paris in order to crown Bonaparte.

Pius VII, on arriving in France, was welcomed by testimonials of the most profound veneration and the liveliest affection; he was amazed at finding so much faith and piety in a people who had been so nearly perverted by the pernicious teachings of wicked men. During his sojourn in Paris, his principal occupation was to provide for the wants of the Church, to interest the government in favor of the clergy, and to obtain a release from the fetters which certain laws imposed on the exercise of the holy ministry.

After remaining some months in France, Pius VII returned to Rome, leaving everywhere the sweet odor of his many virtues; and he left the country for which he had made so many sacrifices, regretting that he had not been able to supply all the wants of her churches. On his arrival at the capital of the Christian world, the Pope, in a secret consistory of cardinals, gave an account of his journey; he spoke of the fruits which religion had produced, and of the reconciliation of Ricci, bishop of Pistoia, to the Roman Church. Thus all seemed to promise peace and concord, when the ambition of a single man destroyed the harmony which was about being restored to the Church. The French Emperor commenced by seizing Ancona, in order, he said, to defend the city from the invasion of the Mahometans and Greeks. This hostility, exercised without the least provocation, betokened a speedy rupture between the two courts. Nevertheless, two or three years elapsed without further demonstration, and during this interval the canonization of several saints was solemnized at Rome, which ceremony had not taken place for the space of fifty years.

The Emperor issued several decrees in favor of the clergy and religion; these were the only good offices he ever rendered them, as he subsequently did every thing to annoy and harass them. Blinded by prosperity, Bonaparte formed the most ambitious plans, and desired the sovereign Pontiff to join a league he had formed against his neighboring monarchs, completely excluding the English. The Pope refused, and showed how opposed such a course would be to his dignity and office if he took part in the wars of Europe. On the reception of this conclusive answer, the French troops were ordered to march toward Rome; they took possession of the city without fighting, disarmed the Pontifical guard, and proceeded to fortify the castle of St. Angelo.

Pius VII protested against these outrages, but his remonstrances were unavailing. The French continued to exasperate his subjects, imprison the most faithful, and treat them as conquered enemies. Already a captive in his own palace, the Pope could only groan over the acts of violence by which they insulted his august person and his loyal subjects, and await with a holy resignation the issue of this revolution; when Bonaparte from Vienna, which city he had entered as victor, decreed the union of the Roman states with the French empire, under the pretext that they had only been granted to the sovereign Pontiffs under the title of fiefs, and to indemnify the Pope for his losses he allowed him two millions of the revenue. Pius VII strenuously opposed this wholesale plunder, and published a bull of excommunication against the authors, abettors, and executioners of the outrages offered the Holy See, without however designating any particular individual.

Enraged at this decisive blow, Napoleon was still more determined to pursue his victim. The Pope was carried off during the night from Rome, conducted to Savona, where he experienced the same shameful treatment endured by his predecessor. Athough guilty of so wicked an attempt, and proving himself to be a persecutor of the Church, Napoleon, nevertheless, published a circular, addressed to the bishops, justifying his seizure of the Church lands. He pretended great zeal for the cause of religion, and, on the Pope's refusing to confirm the nomination of the new bishops, he convoked an assemblage of bishops, in order to devise means for providing for the wants of those churches destitute of pastors. The assembly declared itself incompetent, and proposed to convene a national council, which was opened at Notre Dame on the sixteenth of June, 1814. The result of the deliberations was, that the council could not oppose the papal bulls, which decision so irritated the Emperor, that he dissolved the council, and ordered those bishops who had advised the adoption of this decree, to be taken to the fortress of Vincennes.

A few days afterward, however, the council was recalled, the bishops again met together, and they agreed that the bishoprics could not remain vacant longer than a year; that the Pope should confirm the choice during the six months following the nomination; and that, after these six months had elapsed, the metropolitan bishop could appoint whomsoever he pleased. In consequence of this decision, a deputation of nine prelates was sent to

Savona. The Pope received it, acquiesced in all their demands, and confirmed, by a brief, all of the proposed articles. The brief arrived in Paris, and was submitted to the state council, who, displeased with some of the expressions, refused to receive it. The negotiations were therefore interrupted, and the council dissolved without coming to any final conclusion.

Pius VII, in the mean time, in his banishment at Savona, suffered all the hardships of a long exile, when, without assigning any cause, his persecutors removed him to Fontainbleau. This new prison did not alter his situation, and his captivity received no amelioration. But at length the time had arrived when Providence was to arrest the ambitious career of Napoleon, and restore the successor of St. Peter to the pontifical chair. Innumerable reverses succeeded the triumphs which had hitherto crowned the arms of Napoleon, and the conqueror of so many nations was forced to retreat before his victorious enemies. He arrived in Paris, and a few days afterward repaired to Fontainbleau, in order to commence a new treaty with the Pope. Pius VII made every possible sacrifice, and acceded to all the demands proposed to him, but, perceiving that he was not re-established in his dominions, he retracted all his concessions, and from that time absolutely refused to listen to any proposition or agreement whatever, and replied that he would not discuss these matters until his return to Rome.

It was in consequence of the news he received that Italy was threatened with a speedy conquest, rather than this response, that decided Bonaparte to send the Pope back to Rome. He commanded that a portion of his possessions should be restored to him, and dismissed him from Fontainbleau. Pius VII finally quitted the land of exile, and returned to his dominions on the day that the allied sovereigns entered Paris, and that his persecutor, conquered and forced to abdicate, ended his reign, so disastrous to the peace and happiness of Europe.

RESTORATION OF THE FRENCH MONARCHY.

The yoke of Bonaparte was shaken off, his empire destroyed, and this haughty conqueror of so many crowns was reduced to the sovereignty of the small and uncivilized island of Elba, in the Mediterranean sea. The princes of the house of Bourbon had re-ascended the throne of their ancestors, and their presence seemed to presage future tranquillity. The Pope returned to Rome, obliterated by his paternal goodness the remembrance of the troubles and disturbances caused by his banishment, and the allied sovereigns endeavored to repair, as rapidly as possible, the demoralization of their respective kingdoms. Thus, every thing seemed to betoken the end of the long series of misfortunes and political disasters which, for more than twenty years, had agitated the world, when, suddenly, a fatal conspiracy replaced Napoleon on the throne.

His return from Elba was the signal for new troubles, and new wars. The whole of Europe roused itself against this indomitable enemy, and prepared by their united efforts to overwhelm the faction he had gathered round his standard. One single battle decided the fate of so many nations, whose destinies were to be controlled by the success or discomfiture of the usurper. He was conquered, and his defeat restored Louis XVIII to France, and peace to Europe. The king returned to his capital, which he had been forced to abandon, and was received with the greatest enthusiasm and joy by his subjects, who hastened in crowds to meet him, loading him with blessings and congratulations.

Those who had been most active in the late troubles, gradually returned to their allegiance, and the ancient order of things began once more to prevail. In Rome, the sovereign Pontiff, who had already re-established the Jesuits, entered upon several important negotiations concerning the good of religion. In Bavaria, Sicily and Sardinia, the monarchs loudly proclaimed their sincere conviction of the necessity and importance of religion, and made arrangements with the Holy See for promoting the growth of the faith among their subjects. Spain pursued the same course, happy at having profited by her old sacrifices, and for having been preserved from the evils of the revolution. In France the king declared his earnest desire to see religion honored and reverenced throughout his kingdom; he published decrees in its favor, re-established religious houses, and ordered the final settlement of the treaty commenced with Rome and interrupted by the invasion of Napoleon.

Pius VII did not long enjoy the consolations anticipated from the happy calm which had succeeded so many storms. Death removed from the Church this venerable Pontiff, on the 20th of August, 1823; he was a most exemplary Pope, and he was one whose misfortunes and virtues place him in the ranks of the Pontiffs who have been most generous in their defense of the faith, and in protecting the rights of the Church. Cardinal Della Genga was his successor. Elected Pope on the twenty-eighth of September of the same year, he took the name of Leo XII, and managed the affairs of the Church with a rare prudence. His death, which took place on the tenth of February, 1829, was the occasion of a conclave, which chose, on the following thirty-first of March, a new Pontiff to govern and watch over the flock of Jesus Christ. Cardinal Castiglioni was elected, and took the name of Pius VIII. Cardinal Maurus Cappellari succeeded him on the first of February, 1831, under the name of Gregory XVI, and he in turn was succeeded in 1846, by the venerable and admirable Pius IX, now gloriously reigning. In the year 1830 a new revolution had banished the oldest branch of the Bourbons. The Duke of Orleans, who was placed on the throne under the title of Louis Phillipe, endeavored to calm the passions aroused by the new movement, and the outrages committed by some infuriated men against the temples of the Lord and the clergy were promptly repressed. The revolution of 1830 only served to exalt the virtue and demonstrate the tolerance of the French Church, which enjoys comparative peace and tranquillity at the present day.

REFLECTIONS ON THE SCANDALS.

It is necessary for scandals to appear, our Divine Lord Himself says. It is one of the trials by which He desires to test His servants, in order to render them worthy of their Master. "There shall come a time when charity will become cold, and iniquity abound among mankind." Vice springs from the passions which religion does not destroy; she teaches mankind how to overcome them, but allows the perfect exercise of free will, either to indulge or to avoid them. It is not surprising, therefore, that scandals have appeared in the Church; it is the field in which the tares grow up with the grain, until the time of the great harvest; it is a barn where the straw is mixed with the wheat; a ship in which is found both good and bad fish. All these comparisons which the Gospel employs teach us that abuses and disorders will arise in the Church; but that she neither approves nor tolerates them, but on the contrary, laments, condemns, and abhors them.

So long as the Church exists, scandals will arise among the faithful, and even among the clergy, her ministers. Jesus Christ has promised to the body of pastors, infallibility in their teachings and doctrine, but not sanctity in their conduct. "Go," said Jesus Christ to them, "teach all nations, baptize them, and teach them to observe all that I have commanded you, and I will be with you all days, even to the consummation of time." By virtue of this promise, Jesus Christ is with the clergy, to guard them against all errors, but not to exempt them from sin.

"Although the good example of the pastor is an excellent means of preaching the gospel," says the illustrious Bossuet, "God does not wish to limit the progress of the true faith to the purity of their morals, for those who appear to be saints, may be hypocrites in disguise, but the doctrine which they teach is public, certain, and cannot deceive. He has said, I will be with you in teaching — but He did not say that He would be with them in practicing all that He had commanded. He also adds while speaking to the faithful, 'Follow their teachings, but not their actions.'" Nevertheless their preaching will not be without effect, as the word of God is always fruitful, and as grace never fails to accompany the holy doctrines of religion, the Church will always produce saints, but the saints will sometimes be few in comparison with the wicked. It is certainly miraculous that the multitudes of those who dishonor the Church do not prevent the propagation of religion; that the innumerable disorders and abuses can neither extinguish nor obscure the light of faith, and that the bark of Peter, thus attacked on every side, should still remain uninjured.

Scandals will arise in the kingdom of Jesus Christ, as He predicted that they would, but these scandals will not prevent Him from being with His Church, and her teachings from bearing abundant fruit as her Lord has promised. Thus, during all ages, even the darkest periods, there have always been great and illustrious examples of virtue and sanctity. The precepts of the Gospel have always been practiced by Christians in every condition of life; every century has produced models of sanctity, irreproachable pastors, pure virgins, fervent Religious, laymen faithful to all their religious duties, and true penitents, for it was the sincere desire of repentance, during the eleventh century, when great laxity of morals prevailed, that introduced so many new religious orders. God has raised up extraordinary men, so that they might rekindle piety; the sanctity of the Church consists, therefore, not in the sanctity of all her members, nor only in the sanctity of her doctrines and sacraments, but in there always being saints in her midst, and her including all saints in her fold.

The Church, says the same prelate, is always holy, because she teaches publicly and distinctly the good doctrine of purity of morals, and because her doctrines of piety and virtue will be practiced during all time, even during the most profligate periods. Thus, notwithstanding that the corruption of morals may be great, it cannot be said to be universal, because truth always subsists whole and entire. If there are in the Church wicked and disobedient members, there will always be saints and good men as long as the preaching of the Gospel continues, that is, until the end of time. "We must judge of the Church," says St. Augustine, "not by the bad Christians, but by the good, who will always predominate. The Church tolerates the wicked for a while, and it would be a manifest error to think that the promises of her eternal Author cannot be accomplished even amidst the most shameful abuses and scandals. God has permitted that the heads of the Church should not always be irreproachable men, because the preservation of the Church does not depend on the sanctity of her Pontiffs, but on the word which He has given to be with her until the consummation of ages."

The destinies of earthly empires depend on the conduct of the princes who govern them, but such is not the case with regard to the Church. God Himself has established the Church, and fortified her so strongly that neither men nor time can destroy her. Such is the conclusion to be drawn from certain passages of ecclesiastical history, that refer to the abuses which, at times, pervaded the Church; but far from being scandalized at these disorders, we should remember that they were all predicted, and are the consequence of the present state of the Church. This world is not her place of rest, her country is Heaven; the earth is only a place of probation and trials; a strange land, where she is surrounded with enemies, who vainly strive to deprive her of her most precious treasures — charity and truth.

Although the tempest may be violent, there is no fear of the bark of Peter being submerged. He who commands the sea and winds is the pilot who directs her course, and He will bring her safely to port. Born and educated in the bosom of the Church, instructed in her doctrines, sanctified by her sacraments, inviolably attached to her faith and submissive to her authority, we should be edified by the good work she performs, and lament the evils she cannot prevent, and endeavor carefully to preserve union, through the bonds of peace.

DESTINY OF THE CHURCH.

The prophets had predicted that the Messiah would be a king; that His dominion should extend over the whole universe, and that His reign would be eternal. It is very evident that the empire of Jesus Christ is no other than the Church which He has established. His empire is very different from the kingdoms of the earth; it possesses none of the attributes which elevate earthly kingdoms in the eyes of men, and causes them to flourish and prosper. In the empire of Christ, gold and silver are counted as nothing; the glory of arms is not known to her; she is divested of all these splendors. The Church possesses no other riches than grace, no other strength than virtue. It is an entirely spiritual empire, the reign of truth and virtue; its mission is to enlighten and sanctify mankind. Jesus Christ reigns over the mind by faith, and governs the heart by charity. The only enemies of this empire are error and vice, and the Church is continually engaged in combating them, but she only employs instruction and patience as the means of vanquishing them, and possessed of these weapons, she is secure of victory.

The Christian Church extends among all civilized nations; whatever may be their form of government, she enters and unites herself to it, without changing the political order she finds established, she imparts new strength to them, consecrates their laws and institutions, and becomes the strongest support of the state. The Church is to subsist until the consummation of time; her fate does not depend on the stability of the governments with which she may be allied; the revolutions they experience do not affect her; she exists after nations are destroyed, and survives amidst the ruin of ages. She has seen the decline and fall of the Roman empire, but she remained firm and immovable. She has sustained herself for eighteen hundred years amidst the storms which have arisen on every side, and she will be perpetuated until the end of the world, notwithstanding the tempests which may arise in the future, for it is the destiny of the Church, as long as she is on earth, to be always assailed, but eventually to triumph over all the powers of the world by the assistance of her divine Author. Posterity will find her unchanged, because this perpetual duration has been promised to her, and He who gave this promise is immutable, faithful and omnipotent.

"Read," says St. Augustine, "what has been predicted, behold what has been accomplished, and conclude that the rest will certainly be fulfilled: Prædicta lege, impleta cerne, implenda collige." Yes, the Church will fulfill her glorious destiny; she will continue to advance with a firm step, untouched by human revolutions, until the end of time, in order to unite herself to Jesus Christ, her spouse, in the realms of immortality.

How venerable in the eyes of faith is this Church, the masterpiece of the power of God. Happy those who love and honor her! Attachment to the Church is the characteristic of the children of God; we cannot love God without loving the Church, which is the city in which He reigns, the abode of eternal truth, the sanctuary of divine charity. Happy those who love the Church, who rejoice when she is at peace, who ask this peace of God, and endeavor to procure it by every means in their power. But her true peace will only be found in Heaven; there she will be inundated by the visions of peace of which God Himself is the source. While awaiting this ineffable peace, the Church has combats to sustain on earth; but in the midst of these combats she will have a foretaste of it in the persons of her true children; the peace of God, the peace which surpasses all understanding, and which consists in firmness of faith, in the consolations of hope, and in the union of hearts through charity.

PART THIRD.

CATHOLICITY IN THE UNITED STATES.

We have traced the progress of the Gospel from the time of the Apostles until the present day, in the Old World, and have seen with admiration the divine establishment and miraculous duration of the one true faith. We have mourned over the fall of flourishing kingdoms, the decline of mighty empires, and the destruction of cities and provinces; but amid all this human decay and ruin, we have seen the grand spectacle of the Church of Christ, now hidden in the gloom of the Catacombs, then red with the blood of countless martyrs, persecuted by tyrants, in fine, assailed on every side by the powers of darkness and the passions of men, rise triumphant over all obstacles, and finally plant the emblem of Christianity in the very center of idolatry, pagan Rome. Bright and glorious, the cross, the blessed standard of Christian faith, is found in every part of Catholic Europe; and we now turn to our own country, and see the same sacred symbol raised on high in every town and village of America.

Since the happy moment when the pious Isabella of Spain sent Columbus to discover a new world, and bring a strange people to the knowledge of the one true God, America has been the recipient of

innumerable favors and blessings. When the weary
and dispirited mariners joyfully hailed the welcome
sight of land, after a long and dangerous voyage,
their first action was to sing a hymn of praise,
and the first object which touched the Island of St.
Salvador, was the cross, that precious sign of our
redemption. Thus, claimed as a child of the Church,
in the first moment of her discovery, America has
always been the scene of truly Apostolic labors and
successful missions.

The Franciscans, Dominicans, and Jesuits labored
most assiduously for the conversion of souls, from
the very beginning of the colonial settlements, and
their efforts were amply rewarded by the steady progress of the faith throughout the States. Maine,
New York, Pennsylvania, Maryland, the Valley of
the Mississippi, and the Spanish colonies of New
Mexico, Florida and California, were successively the
theater of missionary zeal, and numerous tribes of
Indians were taught the saving truths of religion,
and became fervent children of the Church. These
admirable works, however, were not accomplished
without many struggles and grievous trials, and several heroic priests won a martyr's crown in the wilds
of the Western continent. Father Padilla, a Fran-
ciscan, and a lay brother fell victims to Indian
cruelty, in New Mexico, in 1542; and Father Rasle,
who lived for thirty-two years among the Penobscots
and Passamaquoddies, was put to death by the English settlers in 1724.

The Jesuit Fathers suffered severely in the State
of New York in their efforts to convert the Iroquois;

CATHOLICITY IN THE UNITED STATES. 539

after succeeding in their labors, the enmity of the English forced the converts to emigrate to Canada, where the nation still exists. In the seventeenth century the Society of Jesus sent missionaries to the West, and we are indebted to Father Marquette, one of the number, for the discovery and exploration of the Mississippi river in 1673, and members of the same society discovered the Falls of Niagara and the almost inexhaustible salt-springs of Salina, in the State of New York. Numerous tribes were converted by these indefatigable priests, but, when the Jesuits were suppressed, the pastors necessarily became fewer, and in some of the settlements the light of faith was for a time obscured. In 1727 an Ursuline convent was founded by the French in New Orleans; the first female religious community organized in the States, and it is still in a flourishing condition. In the year 1570, Jesuits from Florida visited Maryland, with the intention of converting the natives, but were betrayed by their Indian guide and put to death. As this State, however, was destined to become the very center of Catholicity, in the United States, another century had not elapsed before the faith was successfully established within its limits.

About the year 1631, George Calvert, Lord Baltimore, a Catholic nobleman, obtained a charter from Charles I, King of England, for the settlement of Maryland, and a colony of two hundred English families embarked from the Isle of Wight, on the 22d of November, 1633, and reached the shores of the Chesapeake on the the 25th of March, 1634. Father

Andrew White, Father T. Altham and two lay brothers, all Jesuits, accompanied the emigrants, and on the beautiful feast of the Annunciation of the Blessed Virgin, the holy sacrifice of the mass was solemnly celebrated by these fervent exiles, and their new home sanctified by planting the cross on the shores of what was soon to be known as Catholic Maryland. They immediately commenced to build the town of St. Mary's on the river of the same name, and a large Indian hut was used as a chapel. Father White converted several Indian tribes, and in 1639, a priest was stationed on Kent Island, in Chesapeake bay; nearly all the natives of Potopaco (Port Tobacco) were baptized, and the greater part of the Piscataway tribe embraced Christianity. The Jesuit Fathers continued to preach the faith with great success for ten years, some Capuchin friars joining in the good work; but, in 1644, political events suspended their labors. In 1645, a band of lawless soldiers destroyed the colony, banished the governor, and captured the priests. The Maryland Catholics were not, however, destined to enjoy perfect freedom in the practice of the religion for whose sake they had voluntarily left their native land in order to find an asylum in a distant country. The English spirit of Protestantism had crept into the colony, and a persecution was commenced against the Catholics; the provincial government taxed them for the support of the Anglican clergy, abolished their schools, prevented the free practice of religion, and excluded them from public office if they refused to take an oath, which amounted to an abjuration of Catholicity.

A great many remained true to the faith, some returned to the Continent, and others proved false to their God and conscience, by apostatizing.

Notwithstanding this intolerance, divine worship continued to be held in private residences and chapels, and thus the faith was preserved until 1770, when the Catholics were allowed more liberty of conscience. In the early history of Pennsylvania, we also find that missionaries labored for the salvation of souls, and in 1730, Father Greaton, a Jesuit, erected the church of St. Joseph, in Philadelphia, while several towns enjoyed the ministry of Catholic priests. New York, however, at first proved a most unfruitful soil, as the faith was regarded with hatred by the authorities, and the spirit of persecution went so far as to execute a man because he was supposed to be a priest. The oppressive measures of the British government had for some time irritated and incensed the American Colonies, and on the fourth day of July, 1776, an illustrious body of statesmen assembled in the State House in Philadelphia, and by an immortal act declared the colonial States of America free and independent. This may be hailed as the dawn of religious freedom and liberty of conscience in the United States, it being one of the acts of the new constitution, that every individual should be allowed the unrestricted practice of his religion. About this period was felt the necessity of an authorized superior; and in answer to an appeal made by the American clergy, the Holy See invested the Rev. Mr. Carroll with certain episcopal faculties, such as administering confirmation, and appointed him prefect apostolic of America, which position he ably filled for six years, when he was elected bishop of Baltimore, the first bishopric created in the United States.

Bishop Carroll was consecrated at Lulworth Castle, England, by Rt. Rev. Dr. Walmesby, on the 15th of August, A. D. 1790. This distinguished prelate was a member of one of the first Maryland families, an educated gentleman, and a learned theologian. On returning to his diocese he applied himself, with the greatest zeal, to the spiritual advancement of the flock confided to his charge, and convened a diocesan synod, for the purpose of regulating ecclesiastical affairs in the church in America. Accordingly on the 7th of November, 1791, he presided over an assembly of twenty-two clergymen, when many salutary laws for the benefit of religion were adopted. The pastoral letter addressed at this time by the venerated bishop to his extensive diocese is well worthy of perusal; his zealous admonitions and excellent instructions breathing a spirit of Christian charity and love. Before his nomination to the Episcopal dignity, Bishop Carroll had founded a religious academy of learning in Georgetown, D. C., and a Sulpitian Seminary in Baltimore, for the purpose of educating young men for the priesthood.

Numerous European priests visited the United States, eager to lend a helping hand in gathering the abundant harvest which was ripening in every part of this favored country. The bishops assigned each one a particular mission, and, while some labored in the cities and towns, others were sent to convert and evangelize the Indians, enduring cheerfully, the greatest hardships and privations in the service of God and the Church. While fervent priests were thus winning immortal souls to Heaven, pious women were forming themselves into communities for the education of Catholic maidens. In 1790 a Carmelite convent was founded in Charles county, Maryland, and a community of Poor Clares for a time existed in Georgetown, D. C., but were succeeded by the sisters of the Visitation, a cloistered order, living under the rule of St. Francis of Sales, which foundation has proved the mother house of a number of flourishing institutions in different parts of the United States.

The Sisters of Charity were established by Mrs. Seton, first in Baltimore in 1808, and the next year removed to Emmetsburg, Maryland, from which foundation, houses have spread throughout the country; nursing the sick, visiting the prisons, aiding the poor, solacing the orphan, and every other corporal and spiritual work of mercy being the daily occupation of these devoted daughters of charity. The colleges and church of St. Augustine, near Philadelphia, owe their origin to the Hermits of St. Augustine, introduced by Father Carr, in 1790. The Society of Jesus was again re-established in the United States, and several members sent to Georgetown college, which institution, under their learned auspices, has risen to a high rank among the educational schools of the country. The Dominicans also commenced a foundation of their order in 1806 in Washington county, Kentucky, under the superintendence of Rev. Edward Fenwick. It is an interesting fact that the first priest ordained in the United States, the Rev. Stephen L. Badin, was sent to the above mentioned state in 1794, where for many years he exercised the functions of the holy ministry.

In 1793 New Orleans was created an Episcopal See, and Dr. Penalver appointed bishop. For several years, in this diocese, as well as in other parts of the country, the Church was disgraced by many disorders and scandals. But the worthy archbishop Carroll was consoled for these evils and abuses by the creation of four suffragan bishops, and he had the happiness of consecrating Rev. Michael Egan bishop of Philadelphia, Rev. Benedict Flaget, of Bardstown, and Rev. John Cheverus, of Boston, while Rev. Luke Concanen, of the Order of Preachers, was raised to the episcopal dignity in Rome, and consecrated bishop of New York, but died at Naples, when about sailing for America.

We thus see what rapid strides the faith made in the New World, and how successfully apostolic missionaries labored in every part of the United States. These heroic men suffered many and great hardships while cultivating the vineyard of the Lord; the severe frosts of Northern winters, the intense heat of the Southern sun, hunger, thirst, want of proper raiment, the inclemency of the weather, insults and indignities, were cheerfully suffered by these humble followers of the Divine Model, whose command to "Leave all things and follow me!" had been chosen as the rule of their mortified lives. The Sisters of Loretto, Sisters of

Charity of Nazareth, as well as an ecclesiastical seminary, were established by Bishop Flaget, in Kentucky, assisted by Rev. John B. David. An orphan asylum and school were placed under the direction of the Sisters of Charity, in Philadelphia, during the adminstratorship of Rev. Lewis Debarth. But the Catholics of America were now to be deprived, by death, of their zealous and saintly shepherd, the excellent Archbishop of Baltimore, who breathed his last on the 3d of December, 1815, at the advanced age of eighty-one years.

Right Rev. Leonard Neale, his coadjutor, was appointed to fill the Archiepiscopal See. For a quarter of a century this zealous priest had labored for the welfare of the Church, occupying at different periods the positions of pastor in Philadelphia, president of the college, and director of the Visitation Convent, of Georgetown, and eighteen months after his nomination to the episcopal dignity he died in Georgetown, full of years and honor. Rev. Ambrose Marechal, professor at St. Mary's Seminary, in Baltimore, was called to the vacant See, and, immediately after his accession to office, was obliged to exercise his authority, in regard to some matters which were a source of annoyance and scandal to the Church. Rt. Rev. Dr. England, in 1820, was created bishop of Charleston, S. C., and he founded the Sisters of Mercy in his diocese. In 1822 the Marian Theological Faculty was instituted by the sovereign Pontiff, in the university of St. Mary, Baltimore.

In 1818 Rev. Nicholas D. Young erected the first Catholic church in Ohio, and Cincinnati was chosen as the residence of the new bishop, Rev. E. Fenwick, who was placed over a large western diocese. New Orleans was blessed with a most worthy pastor, in the person of Rt. Rev. Dr. Dubourg, who established the Lazarists, viz., priests of the mission, in charge of a college and seminary in Missouri; he also founded a Jesuit college at St. Louis, and a Novitiate of the same order at Florissant. The ladies of the Sacred Heart here began the excellent female seminaries, which have subsequently proved of incalculable benefit throughout the whole country. The magnificent convent of Manhattanville, on the banks of the Hudson, Kenwood, near Albany, Eden Hall, near Philadelphia, the houses in St. Louis, Detroit, and numerous other branches of the same order, are among the finest schools in the United States.

Rt. Rev. Dr. Connolly, a Dominican, about 1815, was appointed to the See of New York, and he and his successor, Rt. Rev. John Dubois, introduced several religious orders in their diocese. Rt. Rev. Drs. Matignon, Cheverus and Benedict L. Fenwick ably administered in succession to the spiritual wants of the growing Catholic population of the See of Boston, and Rt. Rev. Henry Conwell was equally beloved in Philadelphia. His episcopacy was disturbed by the scandalous and unprincipled conduct of Rev. William Hogan, pastor of St. Mary's church, and being summoned to Rome to explain the affair, Rev. William Matthews, of Washington city, D. C., was placed in charge of the diocese during the absence of the bishop.

About this time wonderful miracles strengthened

the faith of American Catholics, the case of Mrs. Ann Mattingly, of Washington city, who was raised suddenly from a dying bed through the prayers of a Novena, offered by direction of Prince Hohenlohe, canon of Olmutz, being one of the most extraordinary; several miraculous events also occurred at the convent of the Visitation, in Georgetown, and St. Joseph, Emmetsburg.

In 1822 the admirable association of the Propagation of the Faith was organized under the auspices of the pious Bishop Marechal, who, six years after, closed his mortal career, on the 29th of January, 1828, and was succeeded by Rev. John Whitfield. On the 14th of October the first provincial council was held in Baltimore, composed of one archbishop, six bishops and twelve clergymen, while several prelates were unable to attend. The second council was called in October, 1833, archbishop Whitfield presiding, assisted by five bishops. The third council took place in Baltimore in April, 1837, Rt. Rev. Samuel Eccleston, the successor of Bishop Whitfield, being at the head of the eight bishops who were present. The fifth council, convened in May, 1843, consisted of sixteen bishops, and the sixth, which met in May, 1846, counted as many as twenty-three bishops. Twenty-five bishops assembled in May, 1849, and in May, 1852, a plenary council met, composed of six archbishops and twenty-six bishops. Councils have also been held in different provinces, but on the 25th of July, 1858, a decree was passed, giving the precedence to the metropolitan See of Baltimore, in virtue of this diocese having been the first erected by the sovereign Pontiff in the United States, hence the archbishop of Baltimore is entitled to the highest rank in every ecclesiastical assembly.

Rt. Rev. Dr. Kendrick, Bishop of Philadelphia, succeeded Archbishop Eccleston, and throughout an episcopacy of over twelve years, was loved and revered for his many virtues, great learning, and his services in the cause of religion. Rt. Rev. Dr. Spalding, the present incumbent, was transferred from the diocese of Louisville to the arch-diocese of Baltimore in 1864, and is regarded as one of the ablest supports of Catholicity in America. On the 7th of October, 1866, the second Plenary Council assembled in Baltimore, at which were present seven archbishops, thirty-seven bishops, two mitred abbots, and nineteen superiors of religious orders, the most Rev. Dr. Spalding presiding as Apostolic delegate.

This brief sketch of the extraordinary progress of the faith in this country, the facts and dates of which are taken from the admirable history of Catholicity in the United States, by the learned and accomplished scholar Dr. C. I. White, D. D., of Washington, D. C., in the appendix to the history of the Church by the Abbe Darras, must excite the wonder and admiration of the faithful in America. Our European brethren are worthy of the most sincere thanks for their zealous co-operation in all the good works commenced and successfully continued in this country, as without the assistance of foreign missionaries the torch of faith could not have illumined so rapidly every portion of the western continent. Placed under the special protection of the

Immaculate Mother of God, by a solemn decree of the council held in 1846, the watchful care and maternal solicitude of the most Holy Virgin over the United States is manifested to-day throughout the whole land. The flourishing state of religion, the great number of churches, the piety, zeal and learning of the clergy, the countless religious orders, both male and female, the success of educational institutions, the many able works daily issuing from the pen of Catholic authors, the excellent weekly and monthly magazines and journals, are brilliant and incontestable proofs of the triumph of the true faith, and presage a glorious future for Catholicity in this country.

The Indian tribes are especially indebted to the members of the Society of Jesus, who for many years have labored so heroically for their spiritual and temporal welfare; and though many have fallen victims to the treacherous savage, these apostolic men have always succeeded in converting numerous tribes to the fold of Christ. We cannot conclude without mentioning the colored portion of our communities, many of whom are pious and devoted Catholics. Always solicitous for each member of her flock, our holy Mother the Church, in establishing schools and affording means of instruction to the negro, has raised the African race from a condition of unbelief and ignorance, and brought them to a knowledge and practice of the saving truths of Christianity. The Rev. H. Joubert, about the year 1828, founded the Oblates, Sisters of Providence, a religious society of colored women in Baltimore, which, with another foundation, has effected great good, in the Christian education of colored children. Let us hope that the Catholic negroes of America will profit by their recent emancipation, and use their freedom as a means for the still more earnest cultivation of piety and religious principles.

PERSECUTION OF THE CHURCH IN PRUSSIA AND SWITZERLAND.

Germany, a soil fruitful in heresy and schism, continued to be the scene of religious disturbance. The bishops of Rhenish Prussia had been strictly forbidden by Pius VII to solemnize mixed marriages, except on certain specified conditions; which prohibition was renewed by his successor, Gregory XVI. Frederick William III, King of Prussia, endeavored to persuade the prelates to disobey the command of the sovereign Pontiff; but the courageous bishops, like true children of the Church, absolutely refused compliance with the royal wishes. Accordingly, on the 20th of November, A. D. 1837, Mgr. Clemens August Count Droste-Vischering, archbishop of Cologne, was arrested and thrown into prison, as was the archbishop of Gnesen-Posen; but instead of weakening the cause, the incarceration of these holy prelates proved of immense service to religion in Prussia, and ultimately saved the Orthodox church in Germany. Switzerland also persecuted the faith, especially directing its attacks against Mgr Marilley, bishop of Lausanne and Geneva.

France was agitated by the struggles concerning

the University monopolies, the freedom of teaching and that of the councils. Mgr. de Quélen died in 1840, mourned by the whole French nation, and was succeeded by Mgr. Affre, who was destined to win a martyr's crown. The strong arm of Providence was still, however, extended over His flock, and the wonderful success of the new confraternities and societies, which were organized about this period, cheered every Catholic heart, and consoled the Church for the persecutions she endured in different countries.

The society of the Propagation of the Faith, and the confraternity of Notre Dame des Victoires, deserves special mention; the former, true to its name, being the means of shedding the light of faith upon heathen nations plunged in the darkness of paganism, and the latter proclaiming the power of the Mother of God, by the numerous miracles and conversions affected through the fervent prayers of its members. France was noted for the piety, zeal and learning of her clergy, such as Mgr. Gousset, archbishop of Rheims and Mgr. Parisis, bishop of Arras; Fathers Ravignan and Lacordaire, models of sacred oratory and eloquence, and Count Montalembert, the illustrious champion of religion and justice; while Thiers and Guizot was forced to record past and present historical events in a more lenient and less anti-catholic spirit.

DEATH OF GREGORY XVI—PIUS IX HIS SUCCESSOR.

A. D. 1846.

On the 1st of June, 1846, the Church wept over the loss of one of her greatest Pontiffs—Gregory XVI—whose wisdom, firmness and constancy in the midst of innumerable trials, have won him imperishable laurels in the annals of history. Fifteen days after his decease, on the 16th of June, 1846, Cardinal Mastai Ferretti, Bishop of Imola, was elected his successor, under the venerated name of Pius IX, and is honored and obeyed throughout the Christian world to-day as the worthy Vicar of Jesus Christ, and the chief pastor of the Church. On his accession to the Pontifical throne, Pius IX evinced a noble and generous spirit, a liberal and enlightened policy, and devoted himself to the spiritual and temporal advancement of his subjects. His laudable conduct at first won deserved applause; but the ungrateful Italians, instigated by such men as Mazzini, Sterbini and Galletti, formed a secret political organization, whose object was the destruction of the Church and State.

Notwithstanding the persuasions of these designing men, the sovereign Pontiff refused to join in the war against Austria, the blame of which was artfully thrown on the Jesuits, whom they represented as friends of Austria and enemies of Italian independence. Popular feeling turned against the worthy and zealous members of the Society of Jesus, and the persecution of the "blacks," as they were called, became so violent they could not appear on the public streets in safety, and were finally driven from Italy. The cardinals were the next object of attack, and every effort was used to deprive the Pope of his most trusty counselors. They were also accused of a secret preference for the Austrian government, with which, it was said, they were in league for the purpose of giving the death-blow to Italian independence; and it was also asserted that they influenced the Pope to such an extent as to prevent him from executing certain measures of reform he wished to institute for the welfare of his subjects.

These plausible calumnies had the desired effect, and the cardinals became the subjects of the hatred and bitter denunciations of the people. At this alarming crisis, Pius IX appointed Count Rossi, in 1848, his prime minister; an able and energetic man, a true patriot, and fully capable of meeting the emergencies of the times. He immediately commenced active measures for the restoration of national peace, and endeavord to quell the growing abuses and disorders which were disgracing the city of Rome. His bold and vigorous acts so enraged the conspirators that they determined to assassinate him, and this excellent man and wise statesman was brutally murdered in the Senate Chamber. Rome was thrown into a state of intense excitement by this frightful event, and during the confusion, Mazzini, Galletti, Sterbini, and others, formed themselves into a committee for the preservation of the public safety, assumed the civil and military command, and marched in procession to the Quirinal, accompanied by crowds of drunken soldiers, and an excited populace.

They refused to listen to any remonstrance of the Pope, or heed his request for time to consider their demands, but behaved in the most violent and shameful manner; they fired the gates of the palace, attempted to scale the walls, and shot Mons. Palma, Latin secretary of the Pope, when he appeared at one of the windows. The infuriated mob kept Pius IX for several days a prisoner in the palace, and learning that the new ministry intended to deprive him of all temporal power, and even threatened his life, his Holiness determined to leave Rome. He accordingly effected his escape with the assistance of the French and Bavarian ambassadors, on the 24th of November, 1848, and fled to Gaeta, in Naples, where he was kindly and hospitably received by the royal family.

The insurgents immediately abolished the Papal government, and declared Italy a republic. During his exile the sovereign Pontiff issued proclamations condemning the acts of the conspirators, and calling on the Catholic countries of Europe for help and protection. Napoleon III was among the first to answer the appeal, and a French army, under the command of General Oudinot, was sent to crush the rebellion, and landed in the papal states in the latter part of April, 1849. Being repulsed in his first attack on the city of Rome, General Oudinot retired to Palo, and waited for reinforcements; in the middle of June hostilities were resumed, and the siege lasted for nearly a fortnight. On the second of July, the French army entered Rome in triumph, and the victorious general dispatched a messenger to the anxious Pontiff, apprising him of the happy intelligence, and of the complete defeat of his enemies. Pius IX remained in Gaeta until the following April, and then returned to his dominions, and quietly resumed the reigns of government. He found the whole kingdom in a state of great disorder and agitation; the people oppressed, commerce suspended, and the whole country suffering from the violent intrigues of the conspirators.

Imitating the forgiving spirit of his Divine Master, this excellent Pontiff pardoned the ungrateful conduct of his unworthy subjects, and applied himself to the correction of all evils and abuses, and the restoration of national peace and happiness. In a short time, the government was more firmly established than ever, public confidence restored, and new vitality infused throughout the Papal dominions. Thus, by calmness, prudence, wisdom, and moderation, Pius IX won the reluctant admiration of his enemies, and endeared himself still more to his faithful and loyal children. While the machinations of wicked men were thus striving to destroy the power and glory of the Holy See, and subjecting the Vicar of Jesus Christ to insults and indignities, God was preparing a new consolation for His suffering spouse.

From the earliest ages, the Church had taught that Mary, the mother of God, had never been sullied for one moment by the stain of original sin, but it was not until the nineteenth century that this belief was declared an article of faith. After his restoration to the Pontifical throne, Pius IX, on the 8th of December, 1854, solemnly declared the Immaculate Conception of the Blessed Virgin Mary a dogma of the Church, and commanded it to be received as such, by all the faithful. This glorious testimony to the sinlessness and purity of the Queen of Heaven, was hailed with joy and gratitude by the whole Church, and the eighth of December is annually celebrated as a day of triumph and thanksgiving throughout the Catholic world.

In 1862, Pius IX canonized a number of martyrs who suffered for the faith in Japan, and on the 29th of June, 1867, the splendid church of St. Peter's in Rome was the scene of a most gorgeous and impressive ceremony. Five hundred bishops from all parts of the globe, and 25,000 ecclesiastics of all ranks, on this day assembled by invitation of the Sovereign Pontiff, to assist in the celebration of the eighteen hundreth anniversary of SS. Peter and Paul, and the canonization of several new saints and martyrs. No effort was spared to render this great event the most magnificent pageant of modern times, and five hundred prelates, representing every portion of the Catholic world, testified the love and devotion of all the faithful to the illustrious successor of St. Peter, our saintly and beloved Pius IX.

PROGRESS OF CATHOLICITY IN ENGLAND AND SCOTLAND.

Within the last few years the number of conversions to the Catholic Church have been very numerous, both in England and Scotland. Many clergymen belonging to the Anglican communion, have resigned valuable livings and entered the one true fold of Christ. Some among them were distinguished for their literary attainments, and since their admittance into the Church they have labored unceasingly to promulgate the doctrines of the ancient and universal faith—the names of Faber, Newman, Manning and Wilberforce, are sufficient proof of the truth of our assertion. In 1848 the hierarchy was re-established in England by Pius IX, who appointed Dr. Nicholas Wiseman, Cardinal Archbishop of Westminster. He was a man of varied accomplishments, a great linguist, and a most admirable writer and controversialist; he was succeeded in the See of Westminster by Dr. Henry Edward Manning, the present occupant, who is a convert from Anglicanism. A vast number of conversions have taken place among the highest nobility of England and Scotland, and daily accessions are being made to the ranks of the faithful. Churches are being built and chapels dedicated in places where a few years ago it was a penal offense to offer up the holy sacrifice of the mass. The Catholics of Great Britain have every reason to thank Almighty God for the signal favors He has bestowed upon them. The prejudice of ages is gradually disappearing, and, to quote the language of a cotemporary — "The day has arrived in England when the Protestant premier and the Catholic primate shake hands, not merely as private friends, but also as representative men; and when they were seen not long ago in familiar intercourse at the foot of the steps of the throne in the House of Lords, they were for the moment living signs and symbols of that vast and happy change which has come over the relations between the English government and its Catholic subjects."

IRELAND.

Up to the reign of Edward I of England, Ireland was comparatively tranquil; but at that time the Irish, led by Edward Bruce, brother of the famous Robert Bruce of Scotland, made another desperate struggle to overcome the English. After various successes, however, they were defeated, and Bruce slain. During the civil wars between the houses of York and Lancaster, in England, between the years 1453-1485 the Irish people were warm adherents of the house of York, and by their fidelity to that house brought down upon themselves many severe and cruel trials. The measure of their misfortunes was filled in the reign of Elizabeth, who, actuated by a vindictive spirit of religious bigotry, created laws for the purpose of extirpating the Catholic religion from Ireland. The horrid details of the persecutions under which the Irish people labored in consequence of these fiendish enactments, during three centuries, make the heart sick. Notwithstanding this cruel and inhuman policy, the object was never gained. On the contrary, Ireland clung with even greater tenacity to the Catholic religion, and has remained to this day, through all her trials, unswerving and uncompromising in her devoted attachment to the faith which she received from the sacred mission of St. Patrick.

During the reign of the Stuarts, Ireland suffered great misery, but after the execution of Charles I, and the accession of Oliver Cromwell to power, the unfortunate country passed through an ordeal of remorseless cruelty unparalleled in the annals of any nation. From that period to the time of James II the unhappy people of Ireland, stripped of their rights, despoiled of their possessions, governed by strangers toward whom they entertained the strong hate which centuries of cruel wrong had engendered in their hearts, and compelled to contribute toward the support of a religion they despised, made no active resistance to the power of England. At that time, however, James II, having been forced to abandon the throne on the approach of William, Prince of Orange, found in the Irish people his warmest and most devoted friends. The result of their generous struggle is known; the battles of Boyne and Aughrim blasted the hopes of James, and entailed upon Ireland additional miseries, although by the terms of the treaty of Limerick, which was grossly violated by the British government, the people of Ireland imagined that they had secured themselves from further persecution.

The heinous oppression and injustice of the British

government toward the people of Ireland continued without restraint up to the period of the American revolution, when, the coasts of Ireland being exposed to the attack of American privateers, and the British government being unable to guard against them, a large portion of the Irish people armed in their own defense, and enrolled themselves under the name of Irish Volunteers. This noble band, with arms in their hands, afterward extorted from the peers of Britain much that repeated appeals to her justice had failed to obtain; the power of the British Parliament to bind Ireland was renounced in the year 1782.

But this concession proved an inadequate relief, and when the French revolution of 1789, and the events growing out of it, were agitating Europe, the Irish people made a gallant but ineffectual effort to obtain that complete independence, to which, as a nation, they aspired. This struggle took place in the year 1798, and is called the rebellion of that year. It was speedily crushed by British bayonets, and two years after, 1800, through the influence of fraud, bribery, corruption, and intimidation, the infamous act of union passed the Irish Parliament, at once annihilating the independent nationality of Ireland, reducing her to the degrading position of a province, and exposing the noblest rights of her people to the arbitrary control of a foreign government, and an unfeeling and despotic ministry.

Since that period, Ireland has languished through years of misery and degradation, and though the passage of the emancipation act, in 1829, removing many of the disabilities which oppressed the Catholic population, gave some hope that she might yet regain, by peaceful efforts, her sacred rights, she still remains a province; and the noble efforts of Daniel O'Connell, after his triumph in the cause of Catholic emancipation, in the year 1829, have yet produced no satisfactory results. The cry for justice, which, from the impoverished and starving millions of Ireland, has constantly risen to the British throne, has been cruelly disregarded, and famine and pestilence, with all their attendant horrors, which have stalked through the devoted island—the terrible fruits of British cruelty and injustice—have failed to soften the stony heart, or awaken a feeling of sympathy in the bosom of that remorseless government. An attempt was made, in 1848, by certain members of what was known as the "Young Ireland Party," entirely to throw off the British yoke; but from various, yet obvious causes, like all former attempts, it proved a failure, and only added to the misery it was intended to relieve.

Since then, however, the horizon of the Catholic Church in Europe has become dark and gloomy in some parts, but bright in others. For the first time since the Reformation we see Ireland freed from the most unjust and cruel burden of supporting the English Church and its ministers; we see her people for the first time in many centuries breathing the pure and invigorating air of religious toleration, proclaimed by the liberal majority of England, which fact was accomplished by the persistent efforts of the premier, the Hon. Mr. Gladstone. Fenianism undoubtedly made an impression upon the leaders in the English Parliament, and it is owing to the terror its organization inspired, that the English government felt impelled to make concessions, which, it is to be hoped, will be followed by many others, so that Ireland, relieved from English tyranny and oppression, and her children from being forced to seek shelter in other countries, may yet enjoy the happiness of remaining in their own dear and beautiful Emerald Isle.

Without intending any invidious comparison to other nationalities who have rendered such great services to the cause of Catholicity in America, we may be allowed to ask the question: If Ireland had not been persecuted, what would have been the state of religion in the United States, as well as in other parts of the world? The liberality of the Irish when called upon to assist in the erection of churches, their never failing co-operation in all good works, and their unbounded respect for the clergy, entitles them to the gratitude of whatever people they live among. Let us then admire the inscrutable ways of God, who causes good to come out of evil.

PRESENT STATE OF THE CHURCH IN EUROPE.

While we see the star of liberty rising over Ireland, we see, on the other hand, Russia, Austria, Bavaria and Spain trying to extinguish the light of the Catholic faith in their respective countries. Russia, pretending, as she does, to be one of the most enlightened powers in the world, is in reality most cruel and tyrannical as regards her Catholic subjects, especially the

Catholic bishops and priests of the empire. The Emperor, who claims to be the head of the Church in Russia, will not permit the Catholic bishops to communicate with the Pope of Rome; and woe to the faithful servant of God who chooses to obey God rather than the Emperor—a living martyrdom or exile to Siberia will surely be his portion! It can be truly said of Russia, that she is the most intolerant country in Europe, and that China, Japan and other pagan nations excel her in real civilization and humanity. The day will come, however, when the Lord shall take revenge upon her for the innumerable cruelties practiced by her upon Catholics.

Although Russian intolerance and persecution should serve as a warning to all other princes and countries, we find on the contrary, that civil liberty, which beyond all doubt is making great progress in Europe, has become a subject of contention among Catholic rulers. Austria, a Catholic country, has endeavored to deprive her schools of Catholic influence, by taking the control of them from ecclesiastics, and placing the same in the hands of certain officials of her weak and wicked government. The concordat between Rome and Austria has been thus annulled by the latter; Monseigneur Rudiger, bishop of Linz, however, remained faithful to the concordat, and as he opposed the infamous scheme, he was arrested for disobedience, and sentenced to two weeks' confinement, but the punishment was remitted by the Emperor. It is to be hoped that the courageous conduct of the bishop of Linz will act as a check upon the government in its endeavor to make infidels of the Catholic youth of Austria. If these men were real statesmen, they would readily understand that to alienate Catholics from their religion, is equivalent to making them unfaithful citizens.

In Bavaria, also, a severe conflict is going on between the government and the Church, on account of the former wishing to deprive the latter of the control of the education of Catholic children. If a Catholic government openly attacks the Church and her ministers, how can it be expected that the Catholic clergy will be honored by the great mass of the people, who as in the times of Luther confound political with religious liberty, and who, after having removed religion from the schools, and the altars from the churches, will not hesitate to undermine the already unstable government of Bavaria.

In Baden the spirit of darkness still prevails. As of late in Austria and Bavaria, so also in Baden, the subject of discussion, the education of youth, has not as yet been settled, although the late most venerable Archbishop Herman, of Freiburg, strove earnestly to maintain the rights of his Catholic children.

Sad as are the prospects in the above named states, they are as nothing in comparison to the changes that are now going on in Spain; for, since the expulsion of Queen Isabella, that country has been in a state of political and religious confusion. The first act of the provisional government was to expel the Jesuits and suppress other religious orders, and many atrocities were committed in churches and upon priests and nuns.

If we turn our eyes towards Prussia, we find there the Catholic Church as free as in America, and her school system even superior to that of the United States, the land of religious liberty. Although the government is Protestant, the Catholic clergy has the entire control of the Catholic schools, which are supported by the government; and, while Protestants and Jews enjoy the same privileges, there is more harmony and charity among different denominations, than here in America, where, in regard to public schools, the same injustice is practiced as formerly in Ireland in regard to the established Church; for the Catholics of the United States are taxed to support schools in which their faith is held up to ridicule, and at the same time are obliged in conscience to support their own private schools, although they are entitled by right to the same privileges and support from the government that Protestants enjoy. It would be well, therefore, for America to imitate Prussia, not only in regard to the school system, but also in the administration of justice to Catholics.

The Holy Father, Pius IX, the indefatigable and ever watchful pastor of the flock of Christ, has assembled all the Catholic prelates of the world in Ecumenical Council, which was opened on the 8th of December, 1869, seven hundred and seventy-nine (779) bishops being present. It is the first council held since that of Trent; and it is a remarkable fact, that, whereas, at the council of Trent, there were but three English speaking bishops, of whom two were Irish and one English, there were in the Council of the Vatican, in 1870, no less than one hundred and sixty English speaking bishops, the great majority of whom were Irish by birth or descent.

All eyes are fixed upon Rome; for great benefits are expected to result from the council. May the Holy Ghost enlighten the bishops now gathered together, so that at the termination of their labors the whole world may exclaim as with one voice: "*GLORIA IN EXCELSIS DEO, ET IN TERRA PAX HOMINIBUS BONÆ VOLUNTATIS.*"

CHRONOLOGICAL TABLE.

CHRONOLOGICAL TABLE.

EMPERORS, WITH THE DATES OF THEIR ACCESSION.	POPES, WITH THE DATES OF THEIR DEATH.	PRINCIPAL EVENTS. THE DATES MARK THE BEGINNING OF EVENTS, AND THE DEATH OF PERSONS.		SAINTS, WITH THE DATES OF THEIR DEATH.	
A.D.	A.D.	A.D.		A.D.	
14 Tiberius.		33	Conversion of St. Paul.	33	St. Stephen.
		34	Gospel of St. Matthew.		
37 Caligula.		38		44	St. James the Greater.
41 Claudius.		51	First Œcumenical Council of Jerusalem.		
54 Nero.	68 St. Peter.	64	First Persecution.	69	St. James the Less.
68 Galba, Otho, Vitellius.					
69 Vespasian.		70	Destruct'n of Jerusalem.		
81 Domitian.	87 St. Linus.				
	91 St. Anacletus.	95	Second Persecution.		
96 Nerva.		97	Gospel of St. John.	107	St. Ignatius.
98 Trajan.	101 St. Clement.	106	Third Persecution.	107	St. Simeon.
	109 St. Evaristus.				
117 Hadrian.	119 St. Alexander I.				
	127 St. Sixtus I.				
	139 St. Telesphorus.				
138 Antoninus.	142 St. Hyginus.	150	Apology of St. Justin.		
	157 St. Pius I.				
161 Marcus Aurelius.	168 St. Anicetus.	166	Fourth Persecution.	166	St. Polycarp.
	177 St. Soter.	171	Montanists.	167	St. Justin.
		174	Thundering Legion.	177	St. Pothinus.
				179	St. Symphorian.
180 Commodus.		180	Mission to India.		
193 Pertinax.	192 St. Eleutherius.			203	St. Irenæus.
193 Septimus Severus.	202 St. Victor I.	202	Fifth Persecution.	205	St. Perpetua.

CHRONOLOGICAL TABLE.

Year	Emperor/Ruler	Year	Pope/Saint	Year	Event	Year	Saint
211	Caracala and Geta.						
218	Macrinus.						
218	Heliogabalus.	219	St. Zephyrinus.			229	St. Hilarion.
222	Alexander Severus.	222	St. Callistus I.	220	Clement of Alexandria.	231	St. Gregory Thaumaturgus.
		230	St. Urban I.				
235	Maximin.	235	St. Pontian.	235	*Sixth Persecution.*		
		236	St. Antcrus.				
				245	Mission to Gaul.		
238	Gordian.	250	St. Fabian.	245	Tertullian.		
244	Philip.	252	St. Cornelius.	249	*Seventh Persecution.*		
				251	Schism of Novatus.		
250	Decius.	253	St. Lucius.	253	Origen.		
251	Gallus.	257	St. Stephen I.				
253	Valerian.	259	St. Sixtus II.	257	*Eighth Persecution.*	258	St. Cyprian.
260	Gallienus.						
268	Claudius II.	269	St. Dionysius.	275	*Ninth Persecution.*		
270	Aurelian.	274	St. Felix I.	277	Manichæans.		
275	Tacitus.						
276	Probus.						
282	Carus, Carinus, and Numerian.	283	St. Eutychian.				
284	Diocletian and Maximian.	296	St. Caius.	303	*Tenth Persecution.*	291	St. Sebastian.
		304	St. Marcellinus.	304	Theban Legion.	304	St. Vincent.
						305	St. Alban.
305	Constantius Chlorus and Galerius.	310	St. Marcellus.	313	Conver'n of Constantine.		
		310	St. Eusebius.	314	Donatists.		
312	Constantine.	314	St. Melchiades.	319	Arians.		
				325	Second Ecumenical Council at Nicæa.		
		335	St. Sylvester I.	326	Conver'n of Æthiopians.		
337	Constantinus & bro's.	336	St. Mark.	330	Invention of the Holy Cross.		
				337	Arian persecution.		

CHRONOLOGICAL TABLE (A. D. 340 to 683)—Continued.

EMPERORS, WITH THE DATES OF THEIR ACCESSION.		POPES, WITH THE DATES OF THEIR DEATH.		PRINCIPAL EVENTS. THE DATES MARK THE BEGINNING OF EVENTS, AND THE DEATH OF PERSONS.		SAINTS, WITH THE DATES OF THEIR DEATH.	
A.D.		A.D.		A.D.		A.D.	
361	Julian the Apostate.	352	St. Julius I.	340	Sapor.	341	St. Paul the Hermit.
363	Jovian.	365	St. Felix II, adm'r	357	Hosius.	356	St. Antony.
364	Valentinian & Valens.			360	Macedonians.		
375	{ Gratian and Valentinian II.	366	Liberius.			375	St. Athanasius.
379	Theodosius.					379	St. Basil.
				381	{ Third Ecumenical Council at Constantinople.	389	{ St. Gregory of Nazianz.
		384	St. Damasus.	383	Vulgate translation.		
		399	St. Syricius.	385	Theodosius.	393	St. Ambrose.
395	Arcadius & Honorius.	401	St. Anastasius I.	399	Mission to the Scythians.	400	St. Martin.
		417	St. Innocent I.	412	Pelagians.	407	St. Chrysostom.
		418	St. Zosimus.	420	Nestorians.	420	St. Jerome.
		422	St. Boniface.				
425	{ Valentinian III, in the west.	432	St. Celestine.	431	{ Fourth Ecumenical Council at Ephesus.	430	St. Augustine.
		440	St. Sixtus III.	448	Eutychians.	444	{ St. Cyril of Alexandria.
		461	St. Leo I.	451	{ Fifth Ecumenical Council at Chalcedon.		
		468	St. Hilary.	457	{ Vandal persecution in Africa.	461	St. Simeon Stylites.
475	Romulus Augustulus. *Fall of the Western Empire.*	483	St. Simplicius.				

CHRONOLOGICAL TABLE.

	Emperors of the East.		Popes		Events		Saints
474	Zeno.						
491	Anastasius I.	492	St. Felix III.				
		496	St. Gelasius I.				
		498	St. Anastasius II.	496	Conversion of Clovis.	500	St. Asaph.
		514	Symmachus.			511	St. Genevieve.
		523	Hormisdas.	511	Rogation instituted.		
518	Justin I.	526	St. John I.	525	Foundation of Monte Cassino.		
		530	Felix IV.	529	Council of Orange.		
527	Justinian.	532	Boniface II.			530	St. Benedict.
		535	John II.			530	St. Remigius, or Remy.
		538	Agapetus.				
		540	Sylverius.			545	St. Clotilda.
		555	Vigilius.	553	Sixth Ecumenical Council.	565	Gildas.
		560	Pelagius.	558	Conversion of Visigoths.		
565	Justin II.	574	John III.				
578	Tiberius II.	578	Benedict I.				
582	Phocas.	590	Pelagius II.			595	Gregory of Tours.
		604	St. Gregory I the Great.	596	Conversion of England.		
		606	Sabinian.			607	St. Augustine of Canterbury.
		607	Boniface III.			615	St. Columban.
610	Heraclius.	614	Boniface IV.	622	Hegira of Mahomet.		
		618	Deusdedit.	628	Exaltation of the Cross.		
		625	Boniface V.	630	Monothelites.		
		638	Honorius I.	648	Mission to the Low Countries.	650	St. Gertrude.
641	Constantine III.	640	Severinus.			662	St. Maximus.
641	Constans II.	642	John IV.	651	Aidan, bishop of Lindisfarne.	658	St. Eligius, or Eloi.
		649	Theodoro I.				
		655	St. Martin I.				
		657	St. Eugenius I.				
668	Constantine IV, Pogonatus.	672	Vitalian.				
		676	Deusdedit II (or Adeodatus).	680	Seventh Ecumenical Council.		
		678	Domnus I.				
		682	Agatho.				
		683	St. Leo II.				

CHRONOLOGICAL TABLE (A. D. 685 to 961) — Continued.

EMPERORS, WITH THE DATES OF THEIR ACCESSION.		POPES, WITH THE DATES OF THEIR DEATH.		PRINCIPAL EVENTS. THE DATES MARK THE BEGINNING OF EVENTS, AND THE DEATH OF PERSONS.		SAINTS, WITH THE DATES OF THEIR DEATH.	
A. D.		A. D.		A. D.		A. D.	
685	Justinian II.	685	St. Benedict II.				
		686	John V.				
		687	Conon.	690	Mission to Friesland.	690	St. Benedict Biscop.
		701	St. Sergius I.			703	Adamnan of Iona.
		705	John VI.				
		707	John VII.			709	Aldhelm, abbot of Malmesbury.
		708	Sisinnius.	711	Moors in Spain.	712	St. John of Beverly.
711	Leo III, the Isaurian.	715	Constantine.	723	Conversion of Germans.	735	Venerable Bede.
		731	Gregory II.	737	Iconoclasts.	738	St. Wilbrord of Ripon, b'p of Utrecht
741	Constantine V. Copronymus.	741	Gregory III.			755	St. Boniface.
		752	St. Zachary.	755	Patrimony of St. Peter.		
		752	Stephen II (died before his consecration).				
		757	Stephen III.	767	Persec'n of Iconoclasts.	766	Egbert of York.
		768	Paul I.	778	Conversion of Saxons.		
775	Leo IV.	772	Stephen IV.	787	Eighth Ecumenical Council.		
780	Irene.	795	Adrian I.	800	Charlemagne crowned.		
800	Charlemagne.						
802	Nicephorus.	816	St. Leo III.			804	Alcuin of York, tutor to Charlemagne
811	Stauracius.	817	Stephen V.				
820	Michael II.	824	St. Pascal I.	826	Conversion of Danes.		

CHRONOLOGICAL TABLE. 573

829	Theophilus.	827	Eugenius II.			
842	Michael III.	827	Valentinus.			
		844	Gregory IV.	830	Conversion of Sweden.	835	St. Ansgar.
		847	Sergius II.	844	Conversion of Russia.		
		853	Leo IV.	850	Mouri-h pers'n in Spain.		
867	Basil.	858	Benedict III	855	Conversion of Bulgaria.		
		867	Nicolas I.	856	Rabanus Maurus.		
		872	Adrian II.	869	Ninth Ecumenical Council of Constantinople.	877	St. Ignatius, patr'h of Constantinople.
		882	John VIII.	877	John Scotus Erigena.	877	St. Neot, abbot of Glastonbury.
		884	Marin I.	880	Conversion of Hohemia.		
886	Leo VI.	885	Adrian III.	882	Hincmar of Rheims.		
		891	Stephen VI.	891	Photius.		
		896	Formosus.				
		896	Boniface VI.				
		897	Stephen VII.				
		897	Romanus.				
		898	Theodore II.				
		900	John IX.	910	Asser, B'p of Sherborne.	910	St. Berno.
		903	Benedict IV.	910	Order of Cluny founded.		
		903	Leo V. Christophorus.	910	Conversion of Normans.		
912	Constantine VII, Porphyrogenitus.	911	Sergius III.				
		913	Anastasius III.				
		913	Lando.				
		928	John X.				
		928	Leo VI.				
		931	Stephen VIII.				
		936	John XI.				
		939	Leo VII.				
		942	Stephen IX.				949	St. Odo of Cluny.
		946	Marin II.	950	Persecution by Moors in Spain.		
959	Romanus.	955	Agapetus II.			961	St. Bruno.
						961	St. Odo of Canterb'y

CHRONOLOGICAL TABLE.

EMPERORS, WITH THE DATES OF THEIR ACCESSION.	POPES, WITH THE DATES OF THEIR DEATH.	PRINCIPAL EVENTS. THE DATES MARK THE BEGINNING OF EVENTS, AND THE DEATH OF PERSONS.	SAINTS, WITH THE DATES OF THEIR DEATH.
A.D.	A.D.	A.D.	A.D.
14 Tiberius.		34 Conversion of St. Paul.	33 St. Stephen.
		38 Gospel of St. Matthew.	
37 Caligula.		51 First Ecumenical Council of Jerusalem.	44 St. James the Greater.
41 Claudius.			
54 Nero.		64 *First Persecution.*	68 St. James the Less.
68 Galba, Otho, Vitellius.	68 St. Peter.		
69 Vespasian.		70 Destruct'n of Jerusalem.	
81 Domitian.	87 St. Linus.		
	91 St. Anacletus.	95 *Second Persecution.*	
96 Nerva.		97 Gospel of St. John.	
98 Trajan.	101 St. Clement.	106 *Third Persecution.*	107 St. Ignatius.
	109 St. Evaristus.		107 St. Simeon.
117 Hadrian.	119 St. Alexander I.		
	127 St. Sixtus I.		
138 Antoninus.	139 St. Telesphorus.		
	142 St. Hyginus.	150 Apology of St. Justin.	
	157 St. Pius I.		
161 Marcus Aurelius.	168 St. Anicetus.	160 *Fourth Persecution.*	166 St. Polycarp.
	177 St. Soter.	171 Montanists.	167 St. Justin.
		174 Thundering Legion.	177 St. Pothinus.
			179 St. Symphorian.
180 Commodus.		180 Mission to India.	
193 Pertinax.	192 St. Eleutherius.		202 St. Irenæus.
193 Septimus Severus.	202 St. Victor I.	202 *Fifth Persecution.*	203 St. Perpetua.

CHRONOLOGICAL TABLE.

211	Caracala and Geta.	219	St. Zephyrinus.	220	Clement of Alexandria.		
218	Macrinus.	222	St. Callistus I.				
218	Heliogabalus.	230	St. Urban I.				
222	Alexander Severus.	235	St. Pontian.				
235	Maximin.	236	St. Anterus.	235	*Sixth Persecution.*	229	St. Hilarion.
						231	St. Gregory Thaumaturgus.
238	Gordian.			245	Mission to Gaul.		
244	Philip.			245	Tertullian.		
				249	*Seventh Persecution.*		
250	Decius.	250	St. Fabian.	251	Schism of Novatus.		
		252	St. Cornelius.	253	Origen.		
		253	St. Lucius.				
251	Gallus.	257	St. Stephen I.	257	*Eighth Persecution.*	258	St. Cyprian.
253	Valerian.	259	St. Sixtus II.				
260	Gallienus.	269	St. Dionysius.	275	*Ninth Persecution.*		
268	Claudius II.	274	St. Felix I.	277	Manicheans.		
270	Aurelian.						
275	Tacitus.						
276	Probus.						
282	{ Carus, Carinus, and Numerian.	283	St. Eutychian.	303	*Tenth Persecution.*	291	St. Sebastian.
284	{ Diocleslan and Maximian.			304	Theban Legion.	304	St. Vincent.
		296	St. Caius.			305	St. Alban.
		304	St. Marcellinus.				
306	{ Constantius Chlorus and Galerius.	310	St. Marcellus.	313	Conver'n of Constantine.		
		310	St. Eusebius.	314	Donatists.		
312	Constantine.	314	St. Melchiades.	319	Arians.		
				325	{ Second Ecumenical Council at Nicæa.		
		335	St. Sylvester I.	326	Conver'n of Æthiopians.		
		336	St. Mark.	330	{ Invention of the Holy Cross.		
337	Constantinus & bro's.			337	Arian persecution.		

CHRONOLOGICAL TABLE (A. D. 340 to 683)—*Continued.*

EMPERORS, WITH THE DATES OF THEIR ACCESSION.		POPES, WITH THE DATES OF THEIR DEATH.		PRINCIPAL EVENTS. THE DATES MARK THE BEGINNING OF EVENTS, AND THE DEATH OF PERSONS.		SAINTS, WITH THE DATES OF THEIR DEATH.	
A.D.		A.D.		A.D.		A.D.	
361	Julian the Apostate.	352	St. Julius I.	340	Sapor.	341	St. Paul the Hermit.
363	Jovian.	365	St. Felix II, adm'r	357	Hosius.	356	St. Antony.
364	Valentinian & Valens.			360	Macedonians.		
375	Gratian and Valentinian II.	366	Liberius.			373	St. Athanasius.
379	Theodosius.					379	St. Basil.
				381	Third Ecumenical Council at Constantinople.	389	St. Gregory of Nazianz.
		384	St. Damasus.	385	Vulgate translation.	397	St. Ambrose.
395	Arcadius & Honorius.	399	St. Syricius.	385	Theodosius.	400	St. Martin.
		401	St. Anastasius I.	399	Mission to the Scythians.	407	St. Chrysostom.
		417	St. Innocent I.	412	Pelagians.	420	St. Jerome.
		418	St. Zosimus.	430	Nestorians.		
425	Valentinian III, in the west.	422	St. Boniface.	431	Fourth Ecumenical Council at Ephesus.	430	St. Augustine.
		432	St. Celestine.				
		440	St. Sixtus III.	448	Eutychians.	444	St. Cyril of Alexandria.
		461	St. Leo I.	451	Fifth Ecumenical Council at Chalcedon.		
		468	St. Hilary.	457	Vandal persecution in Africa.		
475	Romulus Augustulus. *Fall of the Western Empire.*	483	St. Simplicius.			461	St. Simeon Stylites.

CHRONOLOGICAL TABLE.

	Emperors of the East.						
474	Zeno.	492	St. Felix III.	496	Conversion of Clovis.	500	St. Asaph.
491	Anastasius I.	496	St. Gelasius I.			511	St. Genevieve.
		498	St. Anastasius II.	511	Rogation instituted.		
		514	Symmachus.	525	Foundation of Monte Casrino.		
518	Justin I.	523	Hormisdae.	529	Council of Orange.	530	St. Benedict.
		526	St. John I.			590	{ St. Remiglus, or Remy.
527	Justinian.	530	Felix IV.				
		532	Boniface II.			545	St. Clotilda.
		535	John II.	553	Sixth Ecumenical Council.	565	Gildas.
		536	Agapetus.	558	Conversion of Visigoths.		
		540	Sylverius.				
		555	Vigilius.				
565	Justin II.	560	Pelagius.				
578	Tiberius II.	574	John III.				
582	Phocas.	578	Benedict I.				
		590	Pelagius II.	596	Conversion of England.	595	Gregory of Tours.
		604	{ St. Gregory I the Great.				
		606	Sabinian.			607	{ St. Augustine of Canterbury.
		607	Boniface III.			615	St. Columban.
610	Heraclius.	614	Boniface IV.				
		618	Deusdedit.	622	Hegira of Mahomet.		
		625	Boniface V.	628	Exaltation of the Cross.		
		638	Honorius I.	630	Monothelites.		
		640	Severinus.	648	Mission to the Low Countries.	650	St. Gertrude.
641	Constantine III.	642	John IV.	651	{ Aidan, bishop of Lindisfarne.	662	St. Maximus.
641	Constans II.	649	Theodoro I.			665	St. Eligius, or Eloi.
		655	St. Martin I.				
		657	St. Eugenius I.				
668	{ Constantine IV, Pogonatus.	672	Vitalian.				
		676	{ Deusdedit II (or Adeodatus).				
		678	Domnus I.				
		682	Agatho.	680	{ Seventh Ecumenical Council.		
		683	St. Leo II.				

572 HISTORY OF THE CHURCH.

CHRONOLOGICAL TABLE (A. D. 685 to 861) — *Continued.*

EMPERORS, WITH THE DATES OF THEIR ACCESSION.		POPES, WITH THE DATES OF THEIR DEATH.		PRINCIPAL EVENTS. THE DATES MARK THE BEGINNING OF EVENTS, AND THE DEATH OF PERSONS.		SAINTS, WITH THE DATES OF THEIR DEATH.	
A. D.		A. D.		A. D.		A. D.	
685	Justinian II.	685	St. Benedict II.	690	Mission to Friesland.	690	St. Benedict Biscop.
		686	John V.			703	Adamnan of Iona.
		687	Conon.				
		701	St. Sergius I.			709	{ Aldhelm, abbot of Malmesbury.
		705	John VI.				
		707	John VII.	711	Moors in Spain.	712	St. John of Beverly.
		708	Sisinnius.	723	Conversion of Germans.	735	Venerable Bede.
711	Leo III, the Isaurian.	715	Constantine.				
		731	Gregory II.	737	Iconoclasts.	738	{ St. Wilbrord of Ripon, b'p of Utrecht
741	{ Constantine V, Copronymus.	741	Gregory III.	755	Patrimony of St. Peter.	755	St. Boniface.
		752	St. Zachary.				
		752	{ Stephen II (died before his consecration).	767	Persec'n of Iconoclasts.	766	Egbert of York.
		757	Stephen III.	778	Conversion of Saxons.		
775	Leo IV.	768	Paul I.	787	{ Eighth Ecumenical Council.		
780	Irene.	772	Stephen IV.	800	Charlemagne crowned.		
800	Charlemagne.	795	Adrian I.				
802	Nicephorus.					804	{ Alcuin of York, tutor to Charlemagne
811	Stauracius.	816	St. Leo III.				
		817	Stephen V.				
820	Michael II.	824	St. Pascal I.	826	Conversion of Danes.		

CHRONOLOGICAL TABLE.

829	Theophilus.	827	Eugenius II.			
842	Michael III.	827	Valentinus.	830	Conversion of Sweden.	835	St. Ansgar.
		844	Gregory IV.	844	Conversion of Russia.		
		847	Sergius II.	850	Moorish pers'n in Spain.		
		853	Leo IV.	855	Conversion of Bulgaria.		
867	Basil.	858	Benedict III	856	Rabanus Maurus.		
		867	Nicolas I.	860	Ninth Ecumenical Council of Constantinople.	877	St. Ignatius, patr'h of Constantinople.
		872	Adrian II.				
		882	John VIII.	877	John Scotus Erigena.	877	St. Neot, abbot of Glastonbury.
		884	Marin I.	880	Conversion of Bohemia.		
		885	Adrian III.	882	Hincmar of Rheims.		
886	Leo VI.	891	Stephen VI.	891	Photius.		
		896	Formosus.				
		896	Boniface VI.				
		897	Stephen VII.				
		897	Romanus.				
		898	Theodore II.				
		900	John IX.				
		903	Benedict IV.	910	Asser, B'p of Sherborne.	910	St. Berno.
		903	Leo V, Christophorus.	910	Order of Cluny founded.		
912	Constantine VII, Porphyrogenitus.	911	Sergius III.	910	Conversion of Normans.		
		913	Anastasius III.				
		913	Lando.				
		928	John X.				
		928	Leo VI.				
		931	Stephen VIII.				
		936	John XI.				
		939	Leo VII.				
		942	Stephen IX.	950	Persecution by Moors in Spain.	943	St. Odo of Cluny.
959	Romanus.	946	Marin II.			961	St. Bruno.
		955	Agapetus II.			961	St. Odo of Canterb'y

HISTORY OF THE CHURCH.

CHRONOLOGICAL TABLE (A.D. 963 to 1204).—Continued.

EMPERORS, WITH THE DATES OF THEIR ACCESSION.		POPES, WITH THE DATES OF THEIR DEATHS.		PRINCIPAL EVENTS. THE DATES MARK THE BEGINNING OF EVENTS, AND THE DEATH OF PERSONS.		SAINTS, WITH THE DATES OF THEIR DEATH.	
A.D.		A.D.		A.D.		A.D.	
963	Nicephorus Phocas.	964	John XII.	964	Conversion of Poland.		
		965	Leo VIII.	965	Hoduard.		
969	John Zimisces.	965	Benedict V.				
		972	John XIII.			988	St. Dunstan, arch-b'p of Canterbury.
975	Basil II. and Constantine.	974	Benedict VI.			992	Oswald, archb'p of York.
		974	Boniface VII.				
		983	Benedict VII.				
		984	John XIV.				
		985	John XV.				
		996	John XVI.				
		999	Gregory V.	1001	Conversion of Hungary.		
		1003	Sylvester II.				
		1003	John XVII.	1005	Invention of the gamut, by Guido d'Arezzo.		
		1005	John XVIII.				
		1009	John XIX.	1005	Ælfric, the grammarian, archb'p of Canterbury.		
		1012	Sergius IV.				
		1024	Benedict VIII.				
1025	Constantine.	1033	John XX.	1041	Truce of God established.	1038	St. Stephen of Hungary.
1028	Romanus III.						
1034	Constantine Monomachus.	1044	Benedict IX, abd.	1050	Heresy of Berengarius.		
1042	Theodora.	1046	Gregory VI.	1054	Election of Popes reserved to Cardinals.		
		1047	Clement II.				
		1048	Benedict IX rest.				
		1048	Damasus II.	1055	Schism of the Greeks.		
		1054	St. Leo IX.				

CHRONOLOGICAL TABLE. 575

1056	Michael VI.					
1057	Isaac Comnenus.	1057	Victor II.		1063	St. Peter Damian.
1059	Constantine XI.	1058	Stephen X.			
1067	Michael VII.	1061	Nicolas II.		1069	Lanfranc, archb'p of Canterbury.
1078	Nicephorus.	1073	Alexander II.		1095	Wulstan, bishop of Worcester.
				1079	Abelard.	1099	Osmund, bishop of Sarum.
1081	Alexis Comnenus.	1085	St. Gregory VII.	1142	Carthusian order.	1101	St. Bruno.
		1087	Victor III.	1084	Council of Clermont for the first Crusade.	1109	Ingulphus, abbot of Croyland.
		1099	Urban II.	1095			
				1098	Cistercian order.		
				1100	Godfrey of Bouillon.		
				1103	Order of Fontevrault.		
				1105	Peter the Hermit.		
1118	John Comnenus.	1118	Pascal II.	1118	Order of the Templars.		
		1118	Gelasius II.	1125	Tenth Ecumen. Council. (First of the Lateran).	1134	St. Norbert.
		1124	Calixtus II.				
		1130	Honorius II.	1139	Eleventh Ecumenical Council.		
		1143	Innocent II.	1143	William of Malmesbury.		
1143	Manuel Comnenus.	1143	Celestine II.			1153	St. Bernard.
		1145	Lucius II.			1164	Peter Lombard.
		1153	Eugenius III.			1170	St. Thomas of Canterbury.
		1154	Anastasius IV.	1160	Vaudois.		
		1159	Adrian IV.	1179	Twelfth Ecumenical Council.		
1180	Alexis Comnenus.	1181	Alexander III.	1190	Teutonic order.	1197	Longchamp, bishop of Ely.
		1185	Lucius III.	1190	Third crusade.		
		1187	Urban III.	1200	Universities.		
		1187	Gregory VIII.	1202	Fourth crusade.		
		1191	Clement III.				
		1198	Celestine III.				
1203	Alexis IV.						
1204	Alexis V.						

CHRONOLOGICAL TABLE (A. D. 1204 to 1521)—*Continued.*

EMPERORS, WITH THE DATES OF THEIR ACCESSION.		POPES, WITH THE DATES OF THEIR DEATH.		PRINCIPAL EVENTS. THE DATES MARK THE BEGINNING OF EVENTS, AND THE DEATH OF PERSONS.		SAINTS, WITH THE DATES OF THEIR DEATH.	
A. D.		A. D.		A. D.		A. D.	
1204	*Latin Emperors at Constantinople.* Baldwin I.			1205	Thirteenth Ecumenical Council (Fourth Lateran).		
1206	Peter Courtenay.			1209	Carmelites.		
				1210	Friars minor.		
				1212	Clares.		
1216	Robert Courtenay.	1216	Innocent III.	1216	Dominicans.		
				1217	Fifth Crusade.		
				1224	Mission to Prussia.	1221	St. Dominic.
1228	Baldwin II.	1227	Honorius III.	1245	Fourteenth Ecumenical Council.	1226	St. Francis of Assisi.
		1241	Gregory IX.			1228	Langton. Abp. of Canterbury.
		1241	Celestine IV.	1248	Seventh Crusade.	1230	St. Clare.
		1254	Innocent IV.	1256	Augustinians.	1231	St. Anthony of Padua
				1256	Sorbonne.	1245	Alexander of Hales.
1261	*Greek Empire.* Michael Palæologus.	1261	Alexander IV.	1264	Corpus Christi.	1253	Robert Grosseête, bishop of Lincoln.
		1264	Urban IV.	1270	Eighth Crusade.		
		1268	Clement IV.	1274	Fifteenth Ecumenical Council.	1270	St. Louis.
		1276	Gregory X.			1274	St. Thomas Aquinas
		1276	Innocent V.	1274	Reunion of the Greeks.	1274	St. Bonaventura.
		1276	Adrian V.				
		1277	John XXI.				
		1280	Nicolas III.				
1282	Andronicus II.	1285	Martin IV.	1288	The Greeks relapse into schism.	1286	Hugh de Balsham, bishop of Ely.
		1287	Honorius IV.	1299	Institut'n of the Jubilee.		
		1292	Nicolas IV.	1309	Popes at Avignon.		

CHRONOLOGICAL TABLE.

1328	Andronicus III.	1294	St. Celestine V.	1311	Sixteenth Ecumenical Council.	1308	John Duns Scotus.
1341	John V & John VI.	1303	Boniface VIII.	1312	Suppres'n of Templars.		
		1304	St. Benedict XI.	1320	Trinity Sunday.		
		1314	Clement V.	1327	The Angelus.		
		1334	John XXII.	1340	Saturday abstinence.		
		1342	Benedict XII.				
		1352	Clement VI.	1370	Missions of Tartary.	1373	St. Bridget.
		1362	Innocent VI.	1376	Return of the Pope to Rome.		
		1370	Urban V.	1378	Great schism of the West	1380	{ St. Catherine of Sienna.
		1378	Gregory XI.	1388	Feast of the Visitation.		
1391	Manuel II, Palæologus	1389	Urban VI.				
		1404	Boniface IX.				
		1406	Innocent VII.	1414	{ Seventeenth Ecumen. Council at Constance.		
		1409	Gregory XII, *abd.*				
		1409	Alexander V.				
1425	John VIII, Palæologus Constantine VII.	1413	John XXIII, *abd.*	1439	{ Eighteenth Ecumenical Council at Florence.	1428	} William of Wyckham.
		1431	Martin V.	1439	Reunion of Greeks.		
				1440	Return to their schism.		
Emperors of Germany.		1447	Eugenius IV.	1449	End of the Western schism.		
1440	Frederick III.			1453	{ Constantinople taken by the Turks.		
				1454	Order of the Minims.		
		1455	Nicolas V.				
		1458	Calixtus III.	1476	Feast of the Conception.	1471	Kemple.
		1464	Pius II.	1492	{ End of Moorish dominion in Spain.	1486	} William of Waynflete.
		1471	Paul II.	1492	America discovered.		
1493	Maximilian I.	1484	Sixtne IV.	1504	Mission to Congo.	1507	St. Francis de Paula.
		1492	Innocent VIII.				
		1503	Alexander VI.				
		1503	Pius III.	1517	Lutherans.		
1519	Charles V.	1513	Julius II.				
		1521	Leo X.				

CHRONOLOGICAL TABLE (A.D. 1523 to 1814).—*Continued.*

EMPERORS, WITH THE DATES OF THEIR ACCESSION.	POPES, WITH THE DATES OF THEIR DEATH.	PRINCIPAL EVENTS. THE DATES MARK THE BEGINNING OF EVENTS, AND THE DEATH OF PERSONS.	SAINTS, WITH THE DATES OF THEIR DEATH.
A.D.	A.D. 1523 Adrian VI.	A.D. 1524 Mission to Mexico. 1525 Capuchins. 1530 Confession of Augsburg. 1532 The Recollets. 1533 Calvinists.	A.D.
	1534 Clement VII.	1534 Schism of England. 1540 Company of Jesus. 1541 Missions to India. 1545 Nineteenth Ecumenical Council at Trent.	1535 Sir Thomas More. Fisher, bishop of Rochester. 1535
	1549 Paul III.	1549 Socinians. 1549 Missions of Japan. 1554 Missions of Ethiopia. 1554 Missions of Brazil.	1552 St. Francis Xavier.
1556 Ferdinand I.	1555 Julius III. 1555 Marcellus II. 1559 Paul IV.	1562 Carmelites. 1563 Council of Trent closed. 1563 Seminaries instituted. 1568 Barefooted Carmelites.	1556 St. Ignatius. 1568 St. Philip Neri.
1564 Maximilian II. 1576 Rudolph II.	1565 Pius IV. 1572 St. Pius V.	1572 Massacre of St. Bartholomew. 1580 Missions of China. 1582 Reform of the Calendar by Gregory XIII.	1582 St. Teresa. 1584 St. Charles Borromeo.
	1585 Gregory XIII. 1590 Sixtus V. 1590 Urban VII. 1591 Gregory XIV. 1591 Innocent IX.	1591 Order of Ursulines. 1591 Abjuration of Henry IV.	1591 St. John of the Cross. 1591 St. Louis of Gonzaga.

CHRONOLOGICAL TABLE. 579

1611	Matthias.	1605	Clement VIII.	1595	Persecution of Japan.		
		1605	Leo XI.	1602	Mission to Paraguay.		
				1610	Order of the Visitation.		
				1611	Missions of Canada.		
1619	Ferdinand II.	1621	Paul V.	1613	French Oratorians.		
		1623	Gregory XV.	1621	Bellarmine.	1622	St. Francis of Sales.
1637	Ferdinand III.	1644	Urban VIII.	1625	Lazarists.	1640	St. Francis Regis.
		1655	Innocent X.	1646	Sulpicians.	1641	St. Jane Chantal.
1657	Leopold I.	1667	Alexander VII.			1660	St. Vincent de Paul.
		1669	Clement IX.	1679	Christian Brothers.		
		1676	Clement X.	1684	Revocation of the Edict of Nantes.		
		1689	Innocent XI.				
		1691	Alexander VIII.	1704	Bossuet.		
1705	Joseph I.	1700	Innocent XII.				
1711	Charles VI.	1721	Clement XI.	1713	Bull *Unigenitus* against Jansenists.		
		1724	Innocent XIII.	1714	Bourdaloue.		
		1730	Benedict XIII.	1715	Fénelon.	1719	B. De la Salle.
1740	Charles VII.	1740	Clement XII.	1742	Massillon.		
1743	Maria Theresa.	1758	Benedict XIV.				
1765	Francis I.	1769	Clement XIII.				
	Joseph II.	1774	Clement XIV.	1774	Suppression of Jesuits.	1783	B. Benedict Labre.
						1787	St. Liguori.
1790	Leopold II.	1799	Pius VI.	1801	Concordat with Napoleon	1802	B. Maria Clotilde.
1792	Francis II.						
1806	*Emperors of Austria.* Francis I.			1809	Captivity of Pius VII.		
				1814	His deliverance.		

CHRONOLOGICAL TABLE (A. D. 1814 to 1869)—*Continued.*

EMPERORS, WITH THE DATES OF THEIR ACCESSION.		POPES, WITH THE DATE OF THEIR DEATH.		PRINCIPAL EVENTS. THE DATES MARK THE BEGINNING OF EVENTS, AND THE DEATH OF PERSONS.		SAINTS, WITH THE DATES OF THEIR DEATH.
A. D.		A. D.		A. D.		A. D.
1835	Ferdinand.	1823	Pius VII.	1814	Jesuits restored.	
1848	Francis Joseph I.	1829	Leo XII.	1829	Cath. Emancipat'n Act.	
		1830	Pius VIII.	1848	Pius IX, at Gaeta.	
		1846	Gregory XVI.	1848	Death of the Archbp. of Paris.	
			Pius IX.	1850	Re-establishment of the Hierarchy in England.	
				1854	The Immaculate Concept'n decreed, Dec. 8.	
				1869	Twentieth Ecumenical Council (First of the Vatican), assembled Dec. 8th.	

INDEX.

	PAGE.
Preface,	3
Introduction,	5

PART I.

Preaching of the Apostles,	13
Wonderful progress of the Gospel,	17
Virtues of the first Christians,	20
Council of Jerusalem,	23
Death of St. James the Lesser,	27
First persecution under the Emperor Nero,	30
Terrible prophecy against the city of Jerusalem,	32
Destruction of Jerusalem,	35
Second persecution under Domitian,	39
Last actions of St. John,	40
Division in the Church of Corinth,	43
Third persecution under Trajan,	46
Trajan interrogates and condemns St. Ignatius to death,	48
Letter of St. Ignatius to the faithful at Rome,	51
Martyrdom of St. Ignatius,	53
Apology of St. Justin,	56
Fourth persecution under Marcus Aurelius,	59
St. Polycarp, bishop of Smyrna, is arrested and carried before the proconsul,	61
Martyrdom of Polycarp,	64
The thundering Legion,	66
Persecution in Gaul,	69
Torments endured by the Holy Martyrs,	71
Humility of the Holy Martyrs,	74

INDEX.

	PAGE.
Last combat of the Holy Martyrs,	76
Martyrdom of St. Epipodius and St. Alexander,	79
Matyrdom of St. Symphorian,	81
Apology of Tertullian,	84
Continuation of the Apology of Tertullian,	87
Fifth persecution under the Emperor Severus,	89
Martyrdom of St. Ireneus, bishop of Lyons,	91
Martyrdom of St. Perpetua and St. Felicitas,	94
Examination and condemnation of the Holy Martyrs,	96
Execution of the Martyrs,	99
Beautiful qualities of Origen,	102
Works of Origen,	104
Continuation of the Apology of Origen,	107
Sixth persecution under the Emperor Maximin,	110
Seventh persecution under the Emperor Decius,	112
Martyrdom of St. Pionius,	114
Eighth persecution under the Emperor Valerian,	117
St. Cyprian is arrested and banished,	119
Martyrdom of St. Cyprian,	122
Continuation of the persecution in Africa,	125
Admirable constancy of a child,	127
Punishment of the persecutors—charity of the Christians,	130
Ninth persecution under the Emperor Aurelian,	132
Tenth and last persecution under Dioclesian,	134
Martyrdom of St. Quintin,	137
Martyrdom of the Theban Legion,	139
Martyrdom of St. Victor of Marseilles,	142
Martyrdom of St. Vincent of Saragossa,	145
Reflections on the persecutions,	148
Constantius Chlorus favors the Christians,	153
Conversion of Constantine,	155
Triumph of Christianity,	158
Finding of the True Cross,	160
Origin of the Hermits. St. Anthony,	163

INDEX. 583

	PAGE
St. Hilarion establishes monasteries in Palestine,	166
Life of the Hermits,	169
The Arian Heresy,	171
Council of Nice,	174
The Emperor is deceived and exiles St. Athanasius,	176
Frightful death of Arius,	179
Recall and justification of St. Athanasius,	181
Violence practiced by the Schismatics,	183
The Emperor Constantius causes trouble in the Church,	186
Zeal of St. Hilary of Poitiers for the Nicene Creed,	189
St. Martin, bishop of Tours,	191
The Emperor Julian wishes to re-establish Paganism,	194
Julian undertakes to rebuild the temple of Jerusalem. His death,	197
The Emperor Jovian protects the Catholic faith,	199
Valens renews the troubles of Arianism,	202
Fearlessness of St. Basil, bishop of Cesarea,	204
Admirable courage of a Christian woman,	206
Valens reprimanded by St. Basil,	208
Virtues of St. Gregory of Nazianzer,	210
The Macedonian heresy,	213
Ecumenical council of Constantinople,	215
Clemency of Theodosius,	218
Fall and repentance of Theodosius,	220
Schism of the Donatists,	223
Celebrated Conference at Carthage. Termination of the Schism,	225
The Pelagian heresy,	227
Intrigues and obstinacy of the Pelagians,	229
Errors of the Semi-Pelagians,	231
St. Jerome,	234
Virtues and sufferings of St. John Chrysostom,	236
The Nestorian heresy,	238
General council of Ephesus,	241
Eutychian heresy,	243

	PAGE
General council of Chalcedon,	245
Great qualities of St. Leo,	248
Conversion of Scotland and Ireland,	250
Conversion of the French,	253
Baptism of Clovis,	255
Virtues of St. Genevieve,	257
Origin of St. Benedict,	259
Foundation of the Monastery of Monte Cassino,	261
Fifth General council. The Three Chapters,	263
Conversion of England,	266
St. Augustine consecrated bishop of Canterbury,	268
Mahomet appears as a prophet,	270
Taking of Jerusalem by Chosroes, King of Persia,	272
The Holy Cross discovered and returned to Jerusalem,	275
Heresy of the Monotholites,	277
The sixth general council,	279
Conversion of Germany,	281
Martyrdom of St. Boniface,	283
Heresy of the Iconoclasts or Image breakers,	285
Violence of the Iconoclasts,	288
Seventh general council and second council of Nice,	290
Beautiful characteristics and holy zeal of Charlemagne,	292
Charlemagne revives literature,	294

PART II.

Charlemagne is crowned Emperor of the West,	297
Conversion of the Danes and Swedes,	299
Conversion of the Sclavonians and Russians,	301
Conversion of the Bulgarians,	303
Photius usurps the See of Constantinople,	305
Infamous deceptions of Photius,	308
Re-establishment of St. Ignatius. Eighth general council,	309
Reflections on the Heresies,	312
Invasion of the Barbarians. Scandals. Tenth Century,	315

	PAGE
Re-establishment of discipline in England,	317
Restoration of discipline in Germany,	320
Re-establishment of monastic discipline in France,	322
The work of reformation continued by the successors of St. Bernon,	324
Reformation of the Clergy,	326
Conversion of the Normans,	329
Conversion of the Hungarians,	330
Heresy of Berengarius,	334
Schism of Michael Cerularius, patriarch of Constantinople,	337
Troubles in Europe on the subject of investitures,	339
Foundation of the Carthusian Order,	340
First Crusade,	342
Expedition of the Crusaders,	345
Establishment of the Military Orders,	347
Institution of the Premonstrants,	349
St. Norbert is created bishop of Magdeburg,	351
Foundation of the order of Cistercians,	353
St. Bernard is made abbot of Clairvaux,	356
Celebrity of St. Bernard,	358
St. Bernard preaches the second Crusade. His death,.	360
Foundation of the order of the Trinitarians,	362
Martyrdom of St. Thomas, of Canterbury,	365
The third Crusade,	367
The fourth Crusade,	369
The establishment of the Minor Brothers,	371
The order of St. Francis confirmed. His Apostolic labors,	374
Congregation of the Preaching Friars,	376
St. Dominic obtains the confirmation of his order,	379
Birth and education of St. Louis, King of France,	381
St. Louis obtains the Crown of Thorns for France,	384
First Crusade of St. Louis,	386
Captivity of St. Louis,	388

INDEX.

	PAGE.
Journey of St. Louis to Palestine,	390
Second Crusade. St. Louis. His death,	393
Virtues of St. Thomas, of Acquin,	395
Virtues of St. Bonaventura,	397
First re-union of the Greeks. Second Council of Lyons,	400
Western Schism. Council of Constance,	402
Condemnation of Wickliff and John Huss,	404
A new inducement for the re-union of the Greeks. Council of Florence,	407
Capture of Constantinople by Mahomet II,	409
Establishment of the order of Minims,	411
The heresy of Luther,	414
Calvin adds to the errors of Luther,	416
Violence of the Protestants,	419
Variations of the Protestant Churches,	421
Schism in England,	424
Conversion of the Indies,	426
Continuation of the Apostolical labors of St. Francis Xavier,	430
Opening of the Council of Trent,	432
Doctrine of the Council on original sin,	435
Doctrine of the Council on the justification of the sinner,	437
Doctrine of the Council concerning the Sacraments,	439
Doctrine of the Council on the Sacrifice of the Mass,	441
Doctrine of the Council on penance,	444
Doctrine of the Council on confession,	446
Doctrine of the Council on satisfaction,	448
Doctrine of the Council on Extreme Unction,	450
Doctrine of the Council on Purgatory, indulgences, reverence of the Saints, etc.,	452
Conclusion of the Council of Trent. St. Charles Borromeo,	454
St. Theresa. Reformation of the Order of Mount Carmel,	461
Errors of Baius. Renewed violence of the heretics,	465

	PAGE
St. Francis of Sales,	469
State of religion in Japan,	473
Origin of Jansenism,	478
St. Vincent of Paul,	482
Progress of the faith in China and other countries of the earth,	487
The causes of Infidelity,	491
Secret societies,	494
Progress of Infidelity,	497
The suppression of the Jesuits,	501
The temporal power of the Sovereign Pontiff attacked,	504
Prelude and beginning of the French Revolution,	507
Progress of the revolution. Death of Louis XVI,	511
Pius VI arrested and carried to France,	516
Election of a new Pope. Concordat,	519
Bonaparte,	522
Restoration of the French Monarchy,	527
Reflections on the Scandals,	530
Destiny of the Church,	534

PART III.

Catholicity in the United States,	537
Persecution of the Church in Prussia and Switzerland,	550
Death of Gregory XVI — Pius IX his successor,	552
Progress of Catholicity in England and Scotland,	557
Ireland,	558
Present state of the Church in Europe, and the Ecumenical Council of the Vatican,	562
Chronological Table,	567

www.ingramcontent.com/pod-product-compliance
Lightning Source LLC
Chambersburg PA
CBHW031932290426
44108CB00011B/529